Prof. Dr. med. Walter van Laack

To Perceive The World With Logic

Author
Prof. Dr. med. Walter van Laack
Specialist for Orthopaedics, Specialized Orthopaedic Surgery,
Physical Therapy, Sport Medicine, Chirotherapy, Chinese. Acupuncture

Cover
Designed by my son Martin

Pictures
All pictures designed by my two sons Alexander and Martin

Translation
Translated by Anneliese Wolstenholme, Roetgen/Aachen/Germany
from the German original "Mit Logik die Welt begreifen",
1. Edition published on September 24th, 2005.
Once more I thank her very much for her kind and patient cooperation.

For all my beloved ones

First Edition
Published on 24th September 2007

© 2007 by Prof. Dr. Walter van Laack,
van Laack Book-Publishers, Aachen (Germany)

All rights reserved. This book may not be translated, reproduced or transmitted in whole or in part in any form or by any means, electronic or mechanical, including photocopying and recording or by any information storage and retrieval system including the internet and all existing and future media without the prior written permission of the author.

Printed by
BoD GmbH, Gutenbergring 53, 22484 Norderstedt/Germany

Softcover/Paperback
ISBN 978-3-936624-08-3

Contents

Foreword
Klaus Müller, Captain of the PSV "Royal Clipper", Scotland ... 5

Part 1: Introductory Remarks
1.1) What we believe, what we know ... 7
1.2) Timeless arrogance ... 10
1.3) The Problem of the Horizon ... 17
1.4) Why Logic in particular? ... 19

Part 2: The Basic Principles of New Thinking
2.1) About Numbers and Counting ... 25
2.2) The Philosophy of Numbers ... 32
2.3) Universal Background ... 45
2.4) From (finite) Singularity to Multiplicity ... 50
2.5) Absolute Perfection: the Golden Section ... 65
2.6) The Limits of Feasibility ... 71
2.7) Form and Number determine Structure and Function ... 75
2.8) The Three Musketeers in Action ... 81
2.9) A Truly Smart Genetic Code ... 89
2.10) A Divine Metaphor ... 94
2.11) Six Rules Define the World ... 101
2.12) Everything is Ordered in Measurement and Number ... 103
2.13) Every Being Goes its Eternal Way ... 107
2.14) The World is Full of Interfaces ... 111
2.15) Straightforward and Cyclical ... 120
2.16) What Pythagoras Obviously Already Knew ... 130

Part 3: Our Cosmos
3.1) Pure Materialism ... 139
3.2) The Universe Today ... 141
3.3) Critical Questions – Plausible Alternatives ... 144
3.4) The Cosmic Onion ... 156
3.5) Light and Space ... 159
3.6) The Big Bang is buried ... 163
3.7) Shedding a new Light on Creation ... 168
3.8) The Polar Symmetry of Time and Space ... 169
3.9) Where is the Antimatter? ... 185

3.10) Symmetrical Differences betwen Spirit and Matter 187
3.11) Electricity and Magnetism and the
Standardisation of the Four Elementary Forces 192
3.12) Physical Oddballs: the Double Slit Experiment
and the Aspect Experiment 196
3.13) Why Pierre de Fermat was Right 203
3.14) Epilogue 205

Part 4: Life and Spirit
4.1) Numbers Play a Role Again 207
4.2) Mutations are Not the Only Explanation 213
4.3) Evolution by natural selection 218
4.4) Evolution and Theodizee – a philosophical approach 222
4.5) Curiosities of Evolution 225
4.6) Spiritual Fields in the Service of Heredity? 229
4.7) Convergences: Strange and Unexplored 232
4.8) Apes and humans: Who is Descended from Whom? 235
4.9) Life, Spirit and their Hardware 243
4.10) There is Light in our Cells 252
4.11) The Nervous System and the Brain 254
4.12) Brain and Spirit 262
4.13) Evolution from a Different Viewpoint 277
4.14) Human Individuality is Unique 281
4.15) Numbers Help in the Evolution of Life and Spirit 288
4.16) Final Remarks 292

Part 5: The World is an Integrated Whole
5.1) My Alternative World Model 295
5.2) Final Remarks 322
5.3) Excursion: Death is an Interface of Life 330

References 333

Books from the Author in English and German 340

Foreword

The only way to truth, be it matter or spirit, is to perceive the world with logic.
Walter van Laack has already dedicated five German books in eight years to this topic – after 25 years of intensive study.
Faith, developed freely and logically, endows us humans with meaning, joy and love. In this new volume his platform of ideas is presented in a clear and understandable way. Science and faith do not confront one another but rather constitute a unit. Walter van Laack has taken a path which can be followed with joy and hope.
This book – as the previous ones – propagates the notion of eternal existence and not the mere belief in it. Of course, it must be acquired by clear thinking.
We are all scientists and believers. Walter van Laack has succeeded in describing the world exactly as we experience it.
His aim is to show that materialists cannot fill science and reason with wisdom, and devout fundamentalists are unable to experience truth with reason.
Here, however, demands are made on reason and emotion and both benefit from it. This is the objective of this book.
No, Walter van Laack does not wish to be a teacher, but he wants to guide us with reason and emotion to develop our own thoughts and convictions.
We will experience God during our studies and we shall be able to confirm and learn afresh knowledge already within us. Reason retains the joy within us and death is plausibly integrated into a broader pattern of life.
Beneath our sky-high sails reaching up to the clouds and over many years we have more than once philosophised on board, looking out over the sea. We have been continually discussing and disputing by word and by soul, enriching our lives.
It is clear that wind and waves convey knowledge and faith. Our time together on board and here in Scotland remains unforgettable for me – his thoughts and my own have created an exciting picture of the world within me. I hope that the reader of this book may feel and experience the same.
In Part 2, about the new thinking, and Part 4, Life and Spirit, we find the foundation for Walter van Laack's new platform of ideas. It invites us to discuss the matter with ourselves and to ponder over it. It is not a new religion that is started here, but rather that logic marks an interface between spirit and matter. Only these acting together provide the unity in which we live and in which all things exist. Science and spirit form a single entity within a perfectly organised world.

No, this book does not promise to provide the ultimate order and the perfect world formula. Yet God and faith are transported to a higher level. Science terminates in faith as does religion.

Logic and love are essential in acquiring the right faith.

Plato called them the three elements of existence: reason, emotion and desire, and "To Perceive the World with Logic" provides here the necessary balance. Such balance is certainly not easy to achieve but it is indeed essential in order to live in freedom and serenity with love and hope.

I am thankful to Walter van Laack for this book. Read, think and recognise; it will be good for your soul.

Klaus Müller
Skipper PSV "Royal Clipper"
Inveraray in Argyll (Scotland), 4th May 2005

Part 1

Introductory Remarks

1.1) What we believe, what we know

According to our present school of thought a gigantic primeval explosion took place about 15 billion years ago, give or take a few, practically from nothing. It followed that, by pure chance, our world emerged in all its almost unbelievable complexity which we can only fathom today.
And just after the Earth had found its "fixed place in orbiting around the central star of our solar system, the sun", about four to five billion years ago, another gigantic event, known as evolution, was set into motion, which led to the development of the human race – at the time being at least the endpoint of the process. Some people rashly characterise us therefore as "creation's crowning glory". The term "creation" is, however, used by habit and is borrowed rather thoughtlessly from various religious perceptions, since for a growing number of people the term creation no longer has a place in serious consideration of the overall cosmic development. In this modern view of the world it is pure chance alone which was and still is the main engine behind any kind of evolution.
In line with this perception a further indescribably complex cosmos, namely the human brain, started to develop over a relatively short period of a few hundred thousand or, at the most, a few million years; what caused this has still not been clarified. This absolutely fantastic organ now leads us to believe in our ego, our self-awareness and our own personality and that we possess our own free will. Not only is coincidence consider as being the central engine for practically all cosmic development, unlimited dominance is granted to matter as being the product of this coincidence: somehow created in the Big Bang at some time, matter creates new matter and everything is composed of matter even our spirit!

If we ask leading scientists in our world today, an internationally renowned cosmologist, for example, or a physicist, an evolutionary biologist or a respected brain scientist, these fundamental attitudes are beyond dispute.

People with different opinions are ridiculed, regarded with suspicion, mocked in scientific circles and, in the worst case, attacked by powerful media as being dangerous for our society.

Of course, everyone is prepared to admit that there are still many unsettled details which need further explanation. Far too often, however, people truly believe today that we will finally find the missing jigsaw pieces within a few years or decades.

Dear readers, humans seem to be on the home run – let us congratulate ourselves!

During the 70s and 80s of the last century I began to have growing doubts as to whether this view of the world could be right. More often than once I had been very near to death myself and in the course of time I had to watch many people die, among them quite a few who were very close to me and whom I loved dearly. This is why I began to ask whether the death of a person really is his or her irrevocable end. And while at the beginning I still believed in the finality of death, I have a fundamentally different opinion today. Meanwhile, for a long time now already, I am absolutely convinced that humans die only physically and that what we call "death" is by no means the personal end.

This change of mind stands in blatant opposition to the generally accepted and vehemently defended public world view.

A practising medical specialist and professor it might be better advised to keep such ideas private. For the pursuit of a career in a renowned scientific institute this would certainly be good advice. I know of cases where such convictions have ruined the further scientific career of their protagonists.

However, I am an economically independent free spirit and when my beloved father died far too early in 1996 I decided to start writing books defining my convictions which had already grown right away and not to wait until I retired as I had originally planned. In five of the seven books which have already been published in German – of which this is the sixth to be also published in English – I deal with the question as to whether death is the irrevocable end. My gradually matured fundamental conviction that death is not really the end of a person necessitated a new view of the world since the currently accepted notions render death irrefutably as being final.

Therefore, I searched for new explanations, plausible interpretations for accepted observations and perceptions. After several years I arrived at a completely new, an alternative view of the world, into which the notion of the survival of physical death could easily be integrated. My new view of the

world, which in many respects stands in contrast to the spirit of our times, demands, of course, extensive explanation. Therefore, I have discussed in all my books the two crucial natural scientific aspects of our world, the universe and life.
I highlighted both of these complex issues from slightly different perspectives than usual. I tried to draw parallels between the inanimate universe and life on earth necessitating completely new explanations if they are not to remain ignored as mere coincidental coexistences. Such new explanations, however, allow for an alternative view about origin and development of all matter and creatures. This is what I call looking "over the rim of the bowl".
In my search for this new explanation mathematics took on a major role.
Don't let this scare you; all we need here are simple geometric forms, numbers and numerical proportions. It seems that they are especially suited to help to describe and explain many processes and events in our world in a better and more understandable way. We keep meeting them amazingly often on all the main highways and byways of the universe and not least also within ourselves.
Of course, I will take great care to fully integrate all really confirmed facts of our current knowledge into my notions.
Therefore, it is essential to separate strictly authentic facts from mere interpretations. Much of what is considered to be certified knowledge today is in fact only the interpretation of various measurements which may be open for completely different explanations.
With this seventh volume I will define finally my perceptions of an alternative view of the world in a way which is understandable for everybody and which is simple and clear and simultaneously logical and comprehensible. Then, bit by bit, the understanding will grow that nobody should be afraid to die since death as we suppose it does not exist. This perception will be of comfort for many.
While I am writing these lines one of the most awful natural disasters since time immemorial has hit many countries bordering on the Indian Ocean. A seaquake near Sumatra caused a huge Tsunami wave which claimed more that 270,000 human lives. Millions of relatives needed real comfort from one second to the next. Therefore, I believe I am able to say from the bottom of my heart that some day in full consciousness they will all meet again their loved ones, which they have lost in such a tragic way!
With this book I want to meet every single reader on his or her personal level of knowledge and understanding. This will, of course, make frequent repetition unavoidable. However, no one should fear that the world is only understandable for people with special knowledge. I am convinced that it is basically very simple.

Complexities and complications generate themselves slowly from the very simple which is not complicated in itself.

My alternative view of the world is able to accommodate without difficulty all the central basic beliefs of the world religions and surely also the essence of many a myth and the ideas of great thinkers and philosophers of all times.

In addition, it seems to me to be even the essential pre-condition for a fundamental improvement of our human society: it disproves both the notorious disbelievers and the fundamentalists among the believers regardless of the religious inclinations to which they adhere. And every one who learns to perceive the world as I believe it really is will in future do everything to change it into something better – and everyone is invited to do so!

An alternative view of the world seems to be overdue.

And when would have been a better time to have started than the Einstein-year 2005, the 50th anniversary of his death and the 100th anniversary of his most famour theories?

Aachen, January 2005 (German Original) and May 2007 (English Translation)
Prof. Dr. med. Walter van Laack

1.2) Timeless Arrogance

Upon matriculating from high school in 1874 Max Planck, just 16 years old, turned to the then famous Munich professor of physics Philipp von Jolly and asked whether he would recommend studying physics. Today von Jolly's answer seems grotesque when he said that everything worth being researched had already been researched and that only a few gaps in our knowledge remained. Only a few decades later the ideas of Max Planck and Albert Einstein revolutionised physics more than anything before.

Times change but the arrogance of humans does not.

We might presuppose today could assume now that mankind has indeed undergone such a turbulent development over the last 100 years, especially in the field of natural sciences, that such gross miscalculations are unlikely to happen again.

But far from it! Nearly every day new perceptions materialise. Often enough they stand in complete contrast to existing tenets which are then decreed as being wrong. In most cases these are only small pieces in the jigsaw of today's knowledge. Unfortunately we are deceived into thinking that these great trend-setting theories are confirmed and consistent. We should, however, remember that many small pieces will eventually inevitably change the overall picture of the jigsaw. Here are some examples:

Only a few years ago it was believed that a construction plan must be recognisable in the human genome for everything that makes up a human being. It was assumed that not only our physical construction, our appearance and the functions of our organs, but also our behaviour, our intelligence, our character, i.e. all important characteristics of our personality, were encoded in it. Meanwhile the human genome has been decoded to a large extent. Now we know that there are only 25,000 genes, each of which is comparable to one single chapter of our complete construction and operation manual. This means that we possess far fewer genes than some weeds and certainly inconceivably less than anyone had formerly expected.

It defies belief that such a small number of genes might really explain a human being in all his or her diversity, especially since approximately 99% of this meagre number of genes is identical to those of chimpanzees and 99.9% to those of every other human being on earth[1]. A jester who wants to make jokes about this …

It seems much more realistic and logical to assume that "lower" forms of life, and I by that I mean those which possess less "spirit" than humans – like weeds for example – simply need more information fixed *physically* into their genes. Does this mean that forms of life with *more* "spirit" need fewer genes?

Such a perception presumes, of course, that spirit is not merely a product of the physical brain – a mere epiphenomenon. Rather it suggests that the spirit must rise above the brain level which is inherent in every individual and must be able to communicate on a "higher" level, i.e. on a purely spiritual level. That is exactly what many renowned brain researchers so vehemently contest today with much media attention. This, what we call "spirit", is for them only such an epiphenomenon, a product of our brain. I will demonstrate that this is *not* so!

We can imagine that weeds can only communicate on a very limited scale since their "spiritual" development has not progressed very far. Therefore, clear, written instructions, so to speak, are essential which necessitate a bigger genome.

Communication becomes more flexible, simpler and much more comprehensive if it gets rid of the paper. We have all experienced this. Since computers and the internet have taken firm hold in very many households and practically all professional and institutional levels, the cultural development for large groups of mankind has been accelerated even more. The invention of alphabets, later the use of paper as a simple means of distribution, much later

---

[1] Human Genome Project, USA, 2004

the art of printing, and the invention of telephones and telegraphy in the 19th century are the real quantum leaps in our cultural evolution. Technology points the path along which evolution has probably progressed since time immemorial: it is consistently replacing the original physical basis by a purely electronic and more immaterial information transfer and storage. A binary number code is the immaterial or virtual information medium of modern technology and the computer provides the physical storage which is still necessary today.

We also know our own physical data storage system: it is our brain. Whereas only a few years ago we still assumed that everything was somehow physically stored *within* the brain, we know today that that is not the case. We have progressed and assume today that information is stored as something immaterial. This still does not go far enough for me: our brain works in the same or in a very similar way as a computer operator (from the outside) who exchanges information with other users via the internet and not automatically. This, however, is (still) disputed by the majority of scientists today. If this were the case, we should expect that many a weed possesses more genes than a human being. The relative volume of "written records" of increasing complexity laid down in genes has been reduced in the course of evolution. We find here similarities to our modern offices: in the past we needed immense storage space with endless shelves for meters and meters of folders filled to the brim with closely written pages. Today, even more information is stored on small computer chips, or directly in the internet, already a virtual data network.

Would it not be rational to assume that life in general also uses a form of virtual information storage? Let us ponder upon this assumption and from now on let us name this very flexible and immensely capacious immaterial storage "spirit".

The following might give us a very interesting indication as to what this non-physical spirit is:

In 1966 an American couple, Mr and Mrs Reimer, took their twin boys of seven months to hospital for a minor operation – a circumcision.

Unfortunately serious complications occurred: during an electrical haemostasis: Bruce's penis was severely burned. Psychologists advised the parents to remove his male genitals, to fashion female sexual ones and to educate the boy as a girl.

It was thought that, during his puberty, it would be possible to turn him into a perfect woman by administering the appropriate hormones. The only flaw would be that it would be impossible for him to have children. This was all done and Bruce became Brenda. Finally it was decided never to tell her the truth. Soon this case became famous and it was taken up especially gratefully by the movement for women's rights – since it was believed that this case could finally prove that the conventional patterns of male and female behaviour can indeed be altered by education alone. But again, far from it! From a very early age, although educated demonstratively as a female, Brenda resisted all efforts to turn her into a girl. She vehemently refused to wear dresses; she fought like a boy and tried to urinate while standing upright. During puberty, Brenda disliked her body so much that she attempted suicide at least once. Nevertheless, she agreed to keep taking the female hormones, probably hoping that everything would turn out right in the end.

As time went by, however, she needed increasingly constant psychiatric care and she continued to reject her femininity. When Brenda was 14 years old her father could not stand it any longer and he told her the true story. Brenda decided to have another operation to convert her back to a fully functional man again as soon as possible. And the former Bruce, then Brenda finally became David.

When he was 23 years old, he married but was later divorced. In 2000 David gave his story to the media. Meanwhile his brother, Brian, who suffered from schizophrenia, had committed suicide. David, who could never accept his brother's suicide nor his own life story, also committed suicide later.

This tragic case demonstrates two things: firstly, with how much chutzpah and arrogance do scientists stick to dogmas even when it is already recognisable that reality seems to be completely different. Secondly, the case of Bruce-Brenda-David Reimer in the USA demonstrates that neither genes nor education *alone* determine the personality of a human being.

Behind the scenes of what we know about this case there simply must be something more: and that cannot be something purely physical – this also seems to be evident. Therefore, as a working hypothesis, we should assume that our personality has a kind of non-physical, spiritual existence which operates independently of any physical environment.

Yet, there is not much support among scientists for this hypothesis and especially not among renowned brain researchers. So what?

If we scrutinise the rather contradictory positions of renowned brain researchers it becomes apparent that it is usually those representing a strongly materialistic perception (therefore I term them – ambiguously – "spiritless") who are publicly asked for their opinion in the Western opinion-forming media machinery. It follows that it is purposefully single-sided, filtered information which is served up to us as modern knowledge. It is only on rare occasions that we recognise that contradicting perceptions exist even among renowned scientists. It seems very simple today to consider such perceptions, which match the spirit of our opinion maker, as (seemingly) confirmed knowledge. There will be more about this later, of course.

Here are some more examples of modern misapprehensions:

Up until the mid 1980s people with gastric ulcers had large parts of their stomachs removed. This approach mostly ignored completely the cause of the disease. Surgeons did not know any better and were sure they were doing the right thing. Professional opinion was convinced that an excessive production of acid in the stomach caused ulcers. Later, the pharmaceutical industry finally stopped these operation-orgies by developing effective anti-acid pills. During the 1990s the market was saturated with these new pills. However, the pills still did not treat the real cause of the condition. Only a few years ago it was established that in most cases the reason for ulcers is an infection with helicobacter bacteria. People are now treated with a special antibiotic and their stomachs remain intact.

Speaking of bacteria and other small critters and parasites:

The belief that lingering and chronic inflammations, which remain in the body for many years or even decades, are one of the main reasons for many serious diseases is gaining more and more ground. Even heart attacks, Alzheimer's disease and some types of cancer are at least aggravated if not entirely caused by them. And many of these chronic inflammations are started off by infections with all kinds of micro-organisms which we take in every day, often without even noticing. Myriads of parasites are constantly living in our bodies. The latest discovery is the existence of so-called nano-bacteria which are a 30 millionth millimetre in size. In fact, they should not really exist since, according to expert opinions, they are too small to contain all the substances and structures which are essential for maintaining a cell metabolism. However, especially such chronic-lingering inflammations seem to weaken the immune system considerably in the long run and make way for much worse diseases.

They also manipulate the human body's resistance in such a way that the inflammation process progresses even if the perpetrating bacteria are no longer found in the body. All things considered, it seems that our present "world picture" regarding the development of serious diseases must be revaluated. In medical circles such fundamental change of opinion is accepted with much more grace since medical scientists are used to it.

The omniscience, which "strict" natural scientists often like to display, is not so much present among medical scientists. Many things are seen in a more "relative" way. The reason for this is that the "turnover times" of knowledge differ. The "turnover time" defines the time elapsing before new knowledge makes old knowledge obsolete and replaces it or, at least, changes its foundations.

Since the beginning of mankind this "turnover time" of technological-natural scientific knowledge has accelerated slowly until it gained tremendous speed over the last few centuries and especially over the last few decades. Nevertheless, in medical science, development has been even faster for a fairly long time. Changes which overturn existing knowledge and turn it into its direct opposite are happening now more on a daily basis in medical science. I have seen so many medications come and sometimes go after only a short time. Comprehensive tests had shown that they all were extremely effective, absolutely safe, etc.... However, the patients did not react as the remedy intended...

Misconceived dogmas unfortunately often have even fatal consequences. Especially tragic in this context is, for example, the "blunder" of Australian genetic researchers. A few years ago the British scientific magazine "New Scientist"[2] wrote that they wanted to create a virus by means of genetic engineering which would reduce the propagation rate of mice. However, unfortunately, they created a virus which was absolutely fatal for the entire mice population and which was related to the virus causing smallpox. In the end this virus even killed animals which had been inoculated against it.

Such an example documents yet again the hubris of many researchers at all times. Prior to this experiment it was not only generally assumed that genetic engineering would render viruses less dangerous, no, it was also assumed, as a survey among genetic scientists carried out by the magazine "New Scientist" five years previously had shown, that the creation of new dangerous viruses would be very difficult to say the least, if not entirely impossible.

Please do not get me wrong. With this example I am not expressing any disapproval for genetic engineering. On the contrary, in general I think it is very important and even essential in the long run and probably very useful. Nevertheless, we have to understand that our knowledge is at all times just as perishable as our bodies. Therefore, it is especially important today to try and retain the overview and not loose the perspective.

During the Middle Ages people still firmly believed in the geocentric perspective of the world, a perception introduced by the Greek nature philosophers *Aristotle (384-322 B.C.)* and *Ptolemy (100-170 A.D.)*. According to this view the earth is a disc and lies in the centre of the universe. However, *Aristarchos of Samos (310-230 B.C.)* already established shortly after Aristotle that the earth was a sphere which revolved round the sun (heliocentric

---

[2] New Scientist, No. 2273

perspective). All he needed for gaining this insight was a bit of mathematics. Simple geometric forms such as rectangular triangles, projected between earth, moon and sun, showed him the right direction. However, it took more than another one and a half thousand years before *Nicolaus Krebs,* known as *Nicolaus of Kues (1401-1464),* and later *Nicolaus Copernicus (1473-1543)* took up the perception of Aristarchos again. While Kues died too early to gain attention in his lifetime, Copernicus succeeded a few years before he died and overturned the world view completely. Up until then, however, he had to hide his ideas for decades because he was afraid of being ridiculed and chastised. His ideas were too revolutionary and the lobby guarding the existing system was too strong. While in those days it was mainly the representatives of the omnipotent Catholic Church entrenched in the government and the clergy who did not tolerate even justified doubts to the existing world view, it is the scientific lobby today which is hardly less influential. The reason may be that this lobby seems to be linked commercially to the gigantic and very influential media machinery. Millions of people today like to be constantly presented with new and cleverly marketed books or showy computer-animated films promoting succinct terms such as "Big Bang". Critics of these ideas are often ridiculed, or at best ignored as esoteric misfits.

Of course, the question arises as to whether alternative perceptions are at all necessary, since generally recognised models exclude all possibility of doubt. However, I think we have to admit it was never any different.

And today we know how often such perceptions were only the expression of human hubris and arrogance and which have been smiled at long after. There have always been observations which were incompatible with the world view of the time or which could not be explained in a plausible way. Respectable objections have been and still are assiduously and willingly ignored. And people have at all times tried to adjust perceptions dear to them by means of artful manipulations to the latest knowledge so as not to conflict with the assumed coherence. I will discuss some of these artful manipulations of science later in this book.

To conclude this chapter I would like to state again that my criticism of some modern natural scientific perceptions concerning our world should not be misunderstood.

Much of what we know today has helped us to progress with regard to epistemology. Much of what we know today has also helped mankind to progress. However, there are two sides to everything in this world and where there is light there is also shadow.

I see a long shadow in the fact that we are increasingly unable to see the wood for the trees. Far too often we tend to ignore daily experiences, human emotions and also historic, mystic and religious traditions, examples or wisdoms. This, however, throws us all back. Many a natural scientific perception is a mere interpretation based on various motifs. These could be a real love for truth and the search for truth but also the spirit of the age, personal attitudes, the ambition of individuals or the commercial hunt for quotas.

Truth can easily be pushed to the sidelines. And that leads to a modern form of human suppression. Humans are robbed of their perspectives and forget how to be of service to themselves and their brethren because they no longer love either themselves or their neighbours. Altruism begins, however, as the Bible points out so impressively, with the love of God. But what becomes of the love of God if science no longer has space for God? The foundation of human (co-)existence collapses. This is why my criticism is so important.

Let us hope it is not too late!

1.3) The Problem of the Horizon

As already mentioned, I believe that the big problem of our time, not only with the natural sciences but also of governments and societies, is the growing complexity in almost all areas and on all levels. The main reason for this is the growing ramification in all scientific fields and the increasing necessity for specialisation linked with it. Our knowledge of the world expands dramatically in ever shorter periods and branches out like the branches of a huge treetop into more and more directions.

Towards the end of the Middle Ages the title "Doctor universalis", the universal scholar, still existed, a title which was bestowed upon *Albertus Magnus (1193-1280)* and *Thomas Aquinas (1225-1274)*. Today, however, most scientists put their personal focus on a more and more specialised narrow field and they are working and doing research at best as a member of a team. Hardly anybody glances at the activities of scientists working in adjacent areas. I watch this development and it fills me with sorrow. On the one hand it is inevitable that scientists tend to lose the overview since it is almost impossible to compare the results of one research with those obtained in other fields of science. However, only by comparing results might it be possible in good time to revise conclusions which may have been made too hastily. In addition, there is the danger that some observations may not be assessed properly since, due to a distorted perspective, their importance may not have been recognised.

A beautiful parable told by the English author *Godfrey Saxe (1816-1887)* based on a Hindu tale may make this point clear.

Saxe describes six blind men who try to visualize an elephant. They all feel the animal with their hands and are absolutely convinced that they know everything there is to know about its nature and appearance. However, they fail to notice that they had each perceived only a small part of the animal, in a similar way to that of a mathematician who perceives only mathematics, or a chemist who perceives only chemistry, etc., as is often the case. The first blind man thought there was a wall in front of him. The second, who only touched the tusk, thought it was a spear. The third touched the trunk and thought it was a big snake and the fourth thought it was a tree because he touched a sturdy leg. The fifth touched the ear and thought it was a fan and the sixth only touched the tail and thought it was a rope. In the end they quarrelled with one another as to which of them was right.

Today, we experience the same problem, I think. When we consider the sciences separately and only look at the numerous independent results we may arrive at differing independent interpretations which, in themselves, seem perfectly justified. However, when taking all results into consideration, we are confronted with more doubt than certainty and the question arises as to whether a bolder and more comprehensive interpretation would not be more appropriate.

The critical issue is not the observations, the numerous measurements or the results of single experiments. The problem lies solely in the interpretations and the inadequate integration into the whole. Interpretations, however, will always result in different evaluations depending on whether only single results are evaluated or various observations are considered within a broader context and then compared with each other. Only if results are contemplated within a broader context going beyond our own horizon can the correctness of the evaluation be critically checked. Interpretations are too often influenced by social attitudes, political-ideological and religious-fundamentalist dogmas – in short, by the prevailing spirit of the time. A lack of insight ensures the promotion of incorrect interpretations of correct observations thereby concealing their real meaning.

Something else seems very important to me in this context. Up until now, experience has always shown us that, most notably, the final scientific truth can be easily integrated and possesses simplicity and beauty to a large extent. Many very important scientists have pointed this out expressly mostly at the end of their creative periods, for example the renowned English mathematician and astro-physicist *Sir Arthur Eddington (1882-1944)* or the two German physicists *Albert Einstein (1879-1955)* and *Erwin Schrödinger (1887-1961)*.

In my opinion "Simplex sigillum veri (est)", which translated means "simplicity is the hallmark of truth", is a very important requirement for explanations dealing with the world in which we live. The simpler and more beautiful a theory, the better its chances of bordering on truth. Simple, beautiful and going beyond our own limited horizon – that must be our motto. Should, however, simplicity be one of the fundamental principles of scientific truth, then it should in fact be possible to depict it in a simple way, understandable for everybody.

1.4) Why Logic in particular?

The word logic derives from the Greek word "logos" which means primarily "word", but also "reason". Logic is the doctrine of rational thought and actions. If reason is involved we would also include today such terms as "pragmatism" and "common sense". In other words, logic means reasoning with a clear head, without prejudice and without being influenced by external factors, and acting with a sense for usefulness and reality.

Logic dominates the reasoning of the old Greek philosophers, and *Aristotle (384-322 B.C.)* deals with it even systematically. He saw it as an instrument of thinking which helps to use the knowledge of the time properly for establishing the truth.

Knowledge and truth are not at all synonymous. Rational thinking is essential for knowledge to be able to contribute to truth. In other words: knowledge may also cause us to leave the path leading to truth – especially when truth is only illusory because it has not been plausibly and judiciously controlled by logical thoughts and actions.

This seems to have happened many times in the course of history: over many centuries the earthly representatives of Christianity have determined the path to truth according to their own rules. Other perceptions which were not word-for-word congruent with the written records or with later interpretations of the Old and the New Testament were fought mercilessly. Countless thinkers and researchers were killed, many were at least muzzled. As their representative I would mention here only the famous Italian astronomers *Giordano Bruno (1548-1600)* and *Galileo Galilei (1564-1642)*. Bruno's life was ended at the stakes and Galilei only survived because he was exceptionally well respected and because he was forced to renounce his observations in the end by the massive pressure from the inquisition.

Our modern times are characterised by an especially stormy development of natural scientific knowledge. Many a core conviction propagated by the Catholic Church has been exposed as being untenable whereby the power of the Catholic Church has been gradually curtailed. Natural science revolutionised reasoning and empiricism developed. Sensory experience and not religion was supposed now to lead to the truth. Everything that could not be seen, heard, felt or measured, i.e. that which could not be observed, was of no substance in the search for truth. Representatives of this epoch were the British philosophers *John Locke (1632-1704)* and *David Hume (1711-1776)*.

Immanuel Kant (1724-1804) entered into the controversy between religious and purely rational and natural scientific perceptions with his two most important works "Critique of pure reason" (1781 and 1787) and "Critique of practical reason" (1789). Originally Kant was convinced that cognition could be attained by means of "pure reason" while for him religious perceptions remained speculation and, therefore, were *a priori* hardly suitable for establishing the truth.

As an avid admirer of David Hume, however, he tended more and more to the notion that natural scientific knowledge could only be obtained by means of sensory observations. Finally, however, he discovered that this was too biased and he looked for a compromise, the proverbial third path between reason and observation. Kant established that the observation, something passive, must always be the starting point. That which has been observed, however, must then be subjected to reason, an active operation. Kant noticed that both are essential and that neither of the two abilities is superior. Without sensuousness we could not sense an object, without reason we could not think about one. Thought without contents is "empty", concepts without sensory perceptions are "blind". The mind, according to Kant, cannot look at things and the senses are unable to think. Only the combination of both enables cognition to emerge. Humans must use their intellect to understand the perceptions gained from sensuous experiences, i.e. with the aid of natural science. This is the only way to develop ideas or thoughts which put cognition into a context which includes all sensuous experience. Everything beyond perception, e.g. the entirety and the necessary, the soul, the world and the mischievous, remain unrecognised by science.

Kant recognises the independent existence of reason as the expression of the spirit. He postulates the co-existence of two worlds, the spiritual world, which is only accessible by the intellect, and the physical world, which can only be experienced by sensuous perception. Kant says: *"Due to reason we are already*

aware now that we exist in an intelligible realm, after our death we will look at it and recognise it and then we are already in a completely different world, which is, however, only different in is appearance, where we will perceive the things as they really are in themselves!"
(Kant's Lectures about Metaphysics, 1782/83)

In addition to the intellect as the more theoretical aspect of reason, Kant sees another practical aspect as being the freedom of human action. This is assigned to us as a postulate of the unconditional, the absolutely necessary within ourselves.

This means: every human being must adjust his/her actions according to moral principles in such a way that they are as coherent in themselves as are events in nature the necessity of whose occurrence we constantly recognise. This leads to the "Must", which became famous as "Kant's Categorical Imperative" and which is the exact opposite of arbitrariness, the mere compulsive will and desire.

Immanuel Kant appeals to all humans to use their own freedom, to be noble and good and to gain cognition by applying science and reason by means of our own thinking.

Even today we can only clearly underline Kant's notions in this form.

As so often in history, Kant's notions were partly misunderstood and partly misinterpreted after his death. The individual human character which Kant especially emphasises was degraded to an unreal mere apparition by the German philosopher *Arthur Schopenhauer (1788-1860)*.

And Kant's notion of the thinking and human reason as the antipode to a sensuous experience was transformed to the real existence of "common-sense" by the German philosophers *Johann Gottfried Fichte (1762-1814)*, *Georg Wilhelm Friedrich Hegel (1770-1831)* and *Friedrich Wilhelm Joseph von Schelling (1775-1854)*. Only something which is rational is real and that which is real is also rational; this is the new truth. This truth later became the basis of a new, worldly religion: today we talk of ideology or of political conviction. Kant, however, vehemently rejected the opinion that everything which is thinkable must really exist and everything which cannot really exist must prove itself as a contradiction in thinking. I allow myself the objection that something could perfectly well exist if it is thinkable, this does not, however, include necessarily everything thinkable.

The philosophers of the late 18th and early 19th century assigned an independent state of existence to the "new rationale of reason ". At the same time the human individual, the source of all reason and everything reasonable, became quite irrelevant. Thus an individual historical developmental process was assigned to "reason" itself, thereby making it independent of the individual human being's freedom always to act reasonably.

The individual human being was no longer important in the act of being reasonable. It existed without him and in the new rationale it became in itself the centre of its own historic developmental process.

No matter how long and stony the path to reason may be, it will be followed, since reason exists as its own ideal and is not dependent on anyone to be reasonable. Since the individual human being had been made irrelevant, the question of whether the human individual in Kant's sense also acted and thought with reason became just as unimportant. For Hegel it was every bit as wrong to enforce freedom because freedom must unfold on its own.

Since everything in this world has two sides, as I will demonstrate later in this book, both contrary notions, that of Kant and those of his philosophical successors, must be considered together.

I believe that reason indeed exists as an independent ideal, just as justice and love exist. However, it cannot develop without life which carries its development.

Without humans neither reason nor freedom, neither love nor justice make sense. Without humans the ideal would never find itself. Even if such ideals were really to exist as a goal, it would be humans who remain at the centre and be the catalysts of their sensible development.

However, considering human individuals as being only second rate prepared the ground for the inhuman regimes of the 20th century.

An important milestone for this development was provided by *Karl Marx (1818-1883)*. He emphasised solely the collectiveness of a society and completely disregarded the actual value of every single individual.

This completely obliterated Kant's notion of individual human freedom towards good, balanced thought based on reason. Thus, due to a philosophical misinterpretation of freedom and reason, Marxism was born as the basis of socialism and communism.

At the same time natural science passed through an extremely rapid development during the 19th and 20th centuries. Unfortunately, even today, the human spirit seems unable to cope with this development as the numerous terrible excesses of human aberration have repeatedly shown ever since.

Human wisdom has been unable to keep pace. Therefore, it is not surprising that, in the course of time, more and more major difficulties have appeared which render it necessary to get the increasingly multitudinous results of scientific observations under control with the aid of reason-based human thinking. It follows that primarily those appropriate comprehensive theories are presently missing which could reconcile this enormous amount of knowledge.

Furthermore, it is only the purely natural scientific method which is generally accepted as being of avail to assist cognition. All other possibilities are thus practically replaced or at least strongly challenged.
In many countries, especially those of the Western world, religious notions ceased to play an important role.
In Europe this process seems to be progressing even faster than in the USA which apparently does not seem to be generally recognised. The turning away from all kinds of religiousness surely explains why life on earth has become significantly less safe over the last few years and why —especially in Islamic, but also in other religious oriented societies today — more and more radical-fundamental groups have emerged. Exaggerated religious notions today interrupt the pendulum of cognition just as natural scientific arrogance does both of which renounce the spirit and the divine without offering convincing evidence. Both are wrong in my opinion and neither helps to develop the world! The term "divine" should stand here as a general concept which includes all societies, no matter whether they mean God, Allah, Brahman or Manitou or a general spiritual entity, something superior, beyond our comprehension, but nevertheless some personality, etc.
This is exactly what the Bible means when we read in the Ten Commandments that we should not make an image of God for ourselves. This commandment is most certainly not meant as a prohibition but rather an indication that it will not be possible for us humans to create an image and, therefore, we should not even attempt to do so. Many religions unfortunately do not adhere to this commandment – not even those of Christian denomination – and the many competing images of God and the Divine are the ultimate reason for so many superfluous disputes between believers.
It would be better by far if humans returned to Kant's perceptions. At the same time humans should learn not to ignore religious convictions and traditions which have been part of the human culture for thousands of years. Humans should accept religion as an important third orientation in addition to science and to their own free reason. Religions are the collected experience of earlier generations and cultures and as such they are a priceless treasure in human history.
Within this cultural order, logic, as the expression of free and reasonable human thinking, gains a new significance. As the source of deliberate and balanced human decision making it advances to become the proper key to cognition. And in my opinion this is right.
In this context my book is meant to be an important if not even a crucial contribution for a better understanding of our world.

Science and religion provide the multifaceted raw material and the human intellect weighs it carefully. This means also that our interpretation should not be biased and partial.

Part 2

The Basic Principles of New Thinking

2.1) About Numbers and Counting

My very first arithmetic book at the beginning of the 1960s was entitled "The World of Numbers". In those days I could not yet imagine the dynamite that such a school book title could contain.
Numbers are still considered to be just a useful invention of humans. For many dealing with numbers – unless it is for necessary mathematical operations or in mathematical science – belongs to the realm of mysticism and numerology. Mathematical games may be quite entertaining now and then, but the general opinion is that this is not a "serious science". People who think that numbers have symbolic powers or even a real existence are usually shrugged off and relegated to the realm of occultism and esoteric.
This has not always been the case. There were times when no one thought it objectionable to believe in the real existence of numbers and geometrical forms. Understand me correctly: the real existence of a geometrical form says that e.g. a circle, a triangle or a square really IS as real as e.g. a tree or your car.
In this context the Greek philosopher and natural scientist *Plato (427-347 BC)* talked about a really existent idea of such forms. This basic assumption means nothing else but that the real existence of spiritual values or of spirituality is plainly recognised. However, if a geometric structure exists which can be described explicitly by numbers then we can indirectly assume that numbers also exist in reality.
For many people today it is difficult to follow this train of thought which sounds quite absurd. However, it should be much easier for us in these modern times to deal with such ideas. After all, we live in the era of electronic data processing (EDP) and computers; we have even made ourselves

increasingly familiar with virtual storage and the internet. Our ancestors, on the other hand, undoubtedly believed less in the real existence of numbers and forms. We, however, who handle virtual pictures in our daily routine – this is what we do when we surf the Internet – we have difficulties with these ideas. Who would dispute today that these pictures are real, even if we cannot grab hold of them like an object. Once something is published on the Internet it is accessible everywhere as long as the server allows it to be. And what if the "server" of the world is God?

It will not be much longer before we can store our entire knowledge on minuscule data storage devices. For "spiritual" information the dimension of space is irrelevant. We will come back to this statement later. There will even come a point in time when the physical storage of data will become obsolete: we will by then have created a stable information network in space without computers, servers or other physical components, all based on pure energy.

About 30 years ago we still photographed our environment by means of analogous cameras, which stored each single picture on film; today digital cameras are increasingly used which, compared with pictures of the past, store images with an ever decreasing loss of detail. Any print made later could be the original. Digital information details will in future far exceed those stored analogously. In other words: the quality will continue to increase. Some time or other it will correspond to reality.

Any digitally stored information however complex it may be, such as a piece of music, a picture or a long movie, which is recalled later somewhere in the world will really exist albeit not physically touchable. It is merely a digital formation.

Furthermore, it is always and everywhere simultaneously accessible: arry your satellite television set around in your house from room to room, into the garden or into the garage. Switch it on wherever you find a socket: you can watch the same programmes everywhere.

The real existence of digitally stored information, i.e. numbers, should be easy for us to understand. In my opinion this metaphor gives us a very important key for understanding our world as it really is.

I must disappoint those of us who insist that there must be something physical because they believe that matter is the true and only reality of our universe and that everything depends on it and is based on it. In reality matter is, nothing but "frozen energy" as the famous German physicist *Albert Einstein (1879-1955)* said so aptly, and, therefore, it only seems to be touchable:

All matter in the universe, every stone, every planet and, of course, also every living creature – including you and me – are made of countless atoms which are connected with one another in more or less complex compounds.

However, in reality every one of these so seemingly compact atoms is a mere whiff of nothing.
At the centre of all atoms is the atomic nucleus. This too is composed of even smaller particles. I will come back to the real nature of these particles later in this book. For the moment it is sufficient to realise that all chemical elements – or in simpler words: all matter in this world – are based on the smallest element, hydrogen. Its atomic nucleus has only one particle, the proton, which, as we say, has a positive electrical charge. A much smaller particle, the electron, which has a negative electrical charge orbits the proton at a tremendously high speed. Due to the opposite charges of the two atomic particles, the atom itself appears electrically uncharged.
The hydrogen atom is the building block for all matter in the world.
For better understanding let us imagine that the atomic nucleus of hydrogen is the size of a cherry stone with a diameter of about one centimetre. In this case the diameter of the electron would measure only a fraction of a millimetre and would orbit this nucleus at a comparatively immense distance of approximately one kilometre.[3].
Between these two objects there is absolutely nothing, just a complete void!
Solid matter is really just an illusion. It is created by the conduct and the charge of all particles combined within an atom. The immense speed with which the electron orbits the nucleus creates the impression of a sphere, similar to a single bucket which is swung fast in a high arch and creates the optical illusion of a closed circle. The same illusion is created by a wheel with only one spoke: if we spin the wheel really fast we gain the impression of looking at a solid disc.
The opposing electrical charges of the particles together with their own rotation give the whole system stability.
Of course, humans are composed of the same atoms.
Therefore, viewed objectively, this pure illusion appears to us as a "solid" reality. A lock can only be opened by the key that fits. However, there could be other locks with their individual keys existing side by side.
However, they would not "know" about one another because none can "recognise" the others.
As I will explain later, even these few small components of an atom are in the last instance just pure information.

---

[3] The atomic nucleus of hydrogen has really a diameter of approximately a ten-trillionth centimetre (10^{13} cm). The entire hydrogen atom has a size of approximately a hundred-millionth centimetre (10^8 cm).

These "cling" together in such a way that the objective illusion of solid matter is created. Everything that consists of the same "illusion of matter" – and this also includes humans – must inevitably perceive itself as "solid matter".

However, since information is something spiritual, a spirit must exist in reality, otherwise there would be no matter. Something else follows as well: it is spirit which creates matter, and not the other way round!

In the end, nothing remains of our long-standing perception of "solid matter". In reality, matter as a whole shrivels down to a mere conglomerate, to a kind of tangled knot, containing something purely virtual and yet really existing, i.e. information.

Imagine you are sitting in front of a computer screen playing a game: purely virtual people contact one another. Sadly, in most of these games usually everybody is shooting everybody else which is bad enough[4]. Imagine now that these virtual creatures have become so complex that they are able to register their contact with other virtual creatures and that thereby they develop a kind of virtual sympathy for others. Computer scientists are already working on such programs – it is really only a question of sufficient computer power.

Such a virtual creature would, however, only be able to establish contact with and to "experience" other creatures based on the same program code. It would also be possible to play other games of a similar kind on the same and on other computers. Imagine now all these games were mixed and all played simultaneously on the internet. All this would be possible without the virtual creatures of one game becoming aware of those of various other games, would it not?

Today we already store information digitally and, therefore, practically without loss. To store something digitally means nothing more than to store it by means of numbers. In the world of modern computers we only use two numbers: 0 and 1. This is known as the binary code. The figure "0" means "no information" or just nothing and "1" means "information". With just these two numbers "0" and "1", or in fact even simpler with just one single number, "1", which is either there or not (in which case "0" is a mere place holder) we are enabled to describe everything we want on the computer, today and in future. We could also express this a little more philosophically:

"1" means "TO BE". There is only "TO BE" or "NOT TO BE".

Thus the circle is complete, by way of the simplest of geometrical forms: numbers seem to be predestined as an effective and simple store for all the information in our world, and thereby also those bits of information which make up all the details of our bodies. Basically we only need the number "1".

---

[4] Meanwhile, fortunately not so in the very new virtual world: "Second Life"

With this number all other numbers can be produced, and even complicated calculations can be accomplished at random just by counting.

How is "4" produced? Of course it is nothing more than $1+1+1+1$. What is 3×2? It is just $(1+1) + (1+1) + (1+1)$. Subtractions and divisions, and also exponentials and roots are principally produced in a similar way. We simply add together. In the procedure we realize that there are positive and negative numbers, since otherwise subtractions or divisions would be impossible.

These simple examples show that our world is a world of symmetry and polarity: +1 and -1 are symmetrical and also polar, in opposition to one another. Everything in this world is based on this principle. We have already recognised this in positive and negative electrical charges. We also see it in men and women or in anatomical features such as the right and left hand. All these examples show the omnipresence of polar symmetry detectable in our world.

In the same way as "1" can produce all numbers and facilitates all arithmetic operations, hydrogen is the building block for all other chemical elements, the basic substances of our universe. All elements contain a whole-numbered multiple of hydrogen protons.

Hydrogen possesses only one proton, the positively charged particle, and, in addition to balance that, it has a negatively charged small electron. The next element is helium with 2 protons and accordingly 2 electrons, then follows lithium with 3/3, beryllium with 4/4, etc.

All other elements of the universe follow this pattern according to the number of their protons along the complete sequence of ordinal numbers; there is no element missing with, for example, 17 or 36 protons. They are all there.

It is especially interesting that there are exactly 81 elements which exist naturally in a stable form, i.e. they do not disintegrate radioactively. I will come back later to the specific importance of this number.

In the past many people have always suspected and also recognised that these numbers, especially the sequence of integral numbers or whole numbers (1, 2, 3, 4, etc.), and, also, as I will explain in detail later, the sequence of prime numbers, must play a very important role everywhere in the cosmos.

What happens, for example, when we listen to beautiful music? The famous Greek mathematician and nature philosopher *Pythagoras (approx. 580-496 B.C.)* established that harmonic musical intervals are based on integral ratios (e.g. 3:5, 2:3).

It follows that music is a combination of numbers which seem to appear wherever something is to be regulated – in this case the vibration of air. Critics may argue now that physical matter is needed for the creation of music since without air there would be no music but only the abstract rules on which music may be based.

Superficially this may be right. In fact, there is sufficient air on earth and the entire universe is composed of ample matter for which there is certainly a reason. However, although the universe is made of matter it seems not to be made of matter alone; the number ratios on which music is based seem to have nothing to do with matter: they merely determine the harmony of music. My example shows that even if there were no matter – in this example air – which could vibrate in such a way that we hear beautiful music, the rules also apply without air.

In 1977 the satellite Voyager-1 was sent into space to travel through our solar system and at some time or other to reach an adjacent solar system. In the hope that it might meet some alien intelligence at some point it carried a golden sound recording disc with a diameter of 31 cm containing the sounds of Earth.

Various data were engraved on it which were supposed to give alien creatures details of our existence and culture. Compositions by Wolfgang Amadeus Mozart and Johann Sebastian Bach were among them. I ask myself whether one day it might be possible to store such information without using the physical data media known to us today. I suggest that it will indeed be possible one day and that we will be able to master the necessary technology.

From all this it follows that information – and that includes especially numbers or, in general, something intangibly spiritual – already existed before what we call matter appeared.

Once again it becomes clear: the spiritual created the physical, in the same way that music as integral vacillation ratios existed long before Beethoven composed his symphonies.

In nature we see more amazing examples:

On the large surfaces of the upper leaves of the Venus Fly Trap there are three single hairs. Insects are attracted by the red color as well as by the nectar and they crawl around on the surface of the leaves. This they may do without being harmed at all just as long as they do not touch one of the three single hairs. Even if they touch them once nothing will happen, but if there is a second contact within twenty seconds the trap shuts:

The leaves close and, unless the insect is really tiny, it cannot escape and is soon digested. As the British producer of animal-films, *David Attenborough*, wrote it seems that by "counting to 2" single leaves were prevented from being trapped accidentally.

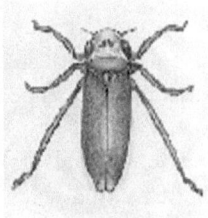

Another example: two species of cicadas inhabit the same area in North America. They differ only in their cycles of reproduction. The larvae of one species stay in the ground for 17 years, and those of the other only for 13 years. During this time they live on the juices of tree and bush roots. They must really be able to count, which has in the meantime been proved by experimental studies.

When their stage as a larva ends they come to the surface for some time as adult insects, capable of reproduction. They then reproduce rapidly before dying. The only plausible explanation for the existence of the two clearly distinguishable larva stages of 17 and 13 years is that the adult insects are prevented from cross-breeding thereby ensuring that *both* species remain independent. Here I would like to draw your attention to the gestation period of 13 and 17 years. Both are prime numbers which can only be divided by the number 1 or by themselves. They also seem to play an important role in the divine rules and regulations of the world.

Another accidental example is that of a small thread-worm known as C. elegans[5] which is barely one millimeter long. It is not just any animal, it is the one which evolutionary biologists have researched most in the entire world. Although it is indeed very small, this worm is extremely complex and is well equipped with everything which bigger animals have too, such as sexual organs, for example, muscles, skin, intestines and even a primitive kind of brain.

All this is constructed from only very few cells – and, even more interesting, there are exactly 959 cells in a male and 1031 cells in a female animal. That is a fact, but few seem to have noticed that both numbers are prime numbers.

Humans do not have to learn what 2 and 3 mean after they are born; they already know as recent results of neuropsychological research show. Up until a short time ago it was believed that only experience teaches humans to interpret the world. However, by means of sophisticated experiments astonished researchers had to acknowledge that small infants are already able to determine between various colours and forms, to recognise the distinctive sound of their native tongue, that they have a remarkably good memory and

---

[5] Caenorhabditis elegans

that they are fascinated by numbers! Even the smallest infants are able to count: if an infant watches two dolls disappearing behind a screen and sees only one reappearing it is expecting the other doll to be still behind the screen. If the screen is taken away and the infant sees another two dolls it reacts with surprise and watches the scene for some time with amazement.

Numbers and counting seems to be inherent in nature since primeval times. Humans seem to be the first creatures, at least on earth, to consciously recognise them, discover them for their own purposes and use them, since only they are able to abstract and to think in symbols.

Numbers and counting become the basis of mathematics which with all its complexities, equations and interconnections, created by humans, can always be traced back to simple counting.

Our computers work in exactly the same way: they merely add together numbers, positive and negative ones, nothing else!

2.2) The Philosophy of Numbers

More than 2,500 years ago the famous Greek philosopher and mathematician *Pythagoras (approx. 580-496 B.C.)* became convinced that numbers are of outstanding importance in the world. As already mentioned he recognised, for example, that musical harmonies are based on a whole-number relationship of oscillations. He also established that all triangles whose three sides have a whole-number ratio of 3 : 4 : 5 or a multiple thereof are right-angled. At school we all had to learn the Pythagorean theorem $a^2+b^2 = c^2$. The Babylonians had already used these three "Pythagorean numbers" to determine hours, minutes and seconds. One hour has 60 minutes, which is the product of 3 x 4 x 5, one minute has 3 x 4 x 5 seconds and one hour 3^2 x 4^2 x 5^2. These time units have been in use for more than 3,000 years already. This suggests that the calculation system of the Babylonians was based on 60.

The number sequence 3-4-5 is not a coincidental. It is the result if we subtract two obviously universal core values, the "Golden Section" and the "Limit of Feasibility", from one another.

In the Chapters 2.5, 2.6 and especially in Chapter 2.16 I will explain these interconnections in detail.

The Pythagoreans were of the opinion that everything in the world was determined and organized by numbers. For them a number itself was already something divine and a mediator between the divine and the profane. I believe that the Pythagoreans were much nearer to the truth in many ways than many a renowned astrophysicist today.

Plato (427-347 B.C.), without doubt the most famous student of *Socrates (469-399 B.C.)*, established the so-called "Theory of Ideas". According to that physical objects in the world are based on something immaterial – an "idea" which is purely spiritual. These ideas alone are the real, true beings according to Plato. This includes, of course, numbers and also geometric forms. Although circles and spheres exist in various sizes, the principle of "circle" or "sphere" and the idea behind each remains the same and is existing in reality. Our thoughts alone enable us to gain access to this world of really existing ideas.

Plato told us, and I agreed with him in my argumentation in the preceding chapter as I also did with Kant's perceptions, that, although we may perceive the world with our senses we will never really be able to fathom its true nature. This can only be achieved by conceptual thinking which is less a matter of experience than rather a kind of recollection (anamnesis).

Solomon's Book of Wisdom (III, 11.20) in the Bible tells us: *"You have set all things in order by measure and number and weight"* and the Latin father of the church *Aurelius Augustinus (354-430 A.D.)* thought that numbers are *"a form of God's wisdom present in the world and recognizable by humans"*. In principle I can only underline this statement. We must admit that numbers and certain basic geometric forms are not a human invention but we should consider them as being a rather useful discovery.

In nature, i.e. in the physical world, we never find circles or spheres in their ideal form.

The Danish author *Peter Höeg (*1957)* wrote in his thriller "Miss Smilla's Feeling for Snow": *"Geometry. Deep inside we have a kind of geometry. My teachers at university used to ask repeatedly what the reality of geometrical terms was. Where is, they asked, a perfect circle, a real symmetry, an absolute parallelism if we cannot construct it in this imperfect world? I gave no reply because they would not have understood the self-evidence of the answer and its incalculable consequences. Geometry is an innate phenomenon in our consciousness. The outside world will never produce a perfect snow crystal. Yet the glittering and immaculate knowledge of perfect ice is embodied in our consciousness."*

If there are no exact realisations of circles, spheres or triangles and other geometrical forms anywhere in nature, where do they come from? How do we know of them?

It seems they exist as exact guidelines or blueprints which in their manifested reality never reach perfection.

However, in the same way as an ice crystal or a snowflake is only almost as perfect as the basic geometrical pattern, so are all great cosmic phenomena such as the so-called background radiation of the universe or the velocity of light.

More on this later in Part 3.

Furthermore, if the really existing perfectionism, e.g. a perfect circle or a right-angled triangle, is only found in the spiritual world, then it must be as difficult for us humans as it is for nature to produce these forms in the same perfection by the physical means of our world. This is indeed the case as the old Greeks realized with perplexity: with our possibilities to describe, for example, a circle with numbers – we call this mathematics – we cannot achieve the same perfection of the spiritual archetype or the idea as Plato puts it.

For the circumference of the circle or its area there are no "even" values. We are always impeded by the infinite or irrational number π. The same applies to the surface area or the volume of a sphere or to the famous right-angled triangle. Here, the longest side, the hypotenuse, is always infinitely irrational when both other sides are of even lengths – unless they relate to one another in accordance with the Pythagorean numbers 3, 4 and 5.

Therefore, in the course of human history numbers and some basic geometrical patterns were often attributed symbolic powers since they have been repeatedly discovered in nature.

Countless generations of humans re-identified them as important pillars in world affairs. Over time they became interwoven in numerous legends and anecdotes and became thus imbued with a mystical background. This explains again why their significance as being the possible pillars of our earth is categorically rejected today and banished to the world of esoteric.

Of course, it is as problematic today as it has always been if in our search for understanding complex world structures we rely entirely on a mysticism which has gradually formed based on stories and in which numbers and basic geometrical forms are of paramount importance.

But is such a perspective so basically wrong just because it has its drawbacks? Or should it not rather be considered as a great challenge? Might this even offer an important orientation guide facilitating a new and integrated and, therefore, possibly accurate approach to the whole question?

Should we decide to take this approach then we must separate the wheat from the chaff.

In order to do this we need our sound common sense, i.e. a logic which explicitly demands such an unimpeded approach to the subject matter.

Since our human cultural history has so often attached such importance to numbers and simple geometrical forms and as so many humorous anecdotes exist bout it I will go into more detail in this chapter.

The Old Testament of the Bible was written in Hebrew script, a script which consists entirely of consonants. This makes it rather difficult to read and to

understand. I will illustrate this with an example concerning a famous misunderstanding. This is, by the way, one of the reasons why many people today refuse to explore in all seriousness biblical matters – unfortunately.
You all know the following story in the Old Testament[6]:
".... *And the Lord God said: It is not good that the man should be alone; I will make him a help suited for him.* ...*And the Lord God caused a deep sleep to fall upon Adam, and he slept; and he took one of his ribs and closed up the flesh instead thereof. And the rib, which the Lord God had taken from man, made he a woman and brought her unto the man.*"
Based on the comments given by the Bible-researcher *Paul Hengge* I would like to explain the true sense of this text and to show how big the influence of the current spirit of time is: today we would replace the word "help" by "partner". In the original Hebrew script we do not find anything about a "deep sleep". The exact word is "thardema" which means rather a "state of epistemic ability". The ancient Greek called this condition "extasis" which is the origin of our word ecstasy which is, however, the exact opposite of deep sleep. This state of epistemic ability afflicted the "human" and not only the "man" as it is often interpreted. At this point in time man *and* woman must have already existed. This is evident since in the history of creation "Genesis", the first chapter in the Bible, it says:
"*And God created man in his own image, in the image of God he created them, male and female he created them.*"
As to Adam's "famous rib", since the Hebrew script only consists of consonants it is necessary to add vowels in order to understand the words and connections. Here the interpretation begins already. The word "rib" is chosen by most of the earlier Bible translators for the Hebrew world "zl". These two consonants, however, mean nothing but "bent" or "arc" and were in those days often used as a synonym for the male phallus; in those days as still today the genitals were often only mentioned indirectly or they were paraphrased. If we choose the translation "penis", then the next two terms "instead" and "flesh" make sense in the metaphor of the alleged creation of Eva out of Adams rib: the Hebrew word "bssr" (in the sense of bassar) could be flesh, but means also "the lower"; and in Psalm 139 this becomes apparent when we read *"you have knitted me together in my mother's womb"*.
If we read the biblical text as it was really written and replace it with modern words, we could formulate it as follows:
"And the creative power let the human being fall into a state of epistemic ability and took its member and sealed it in the female (lower) flesh." This describes the important moment of incarnation. Humans realize what

---

[6] Holy Bible, Old Testament, Genesis 2.18 and 2.21.

propagation means. Animals are not aware of it. Animals reproduce instinctively, without recognizing the action and its consequences.

This is not the first and only time that the Bible seems to tell the truth. However, it is written in a language which people were able to understand at a certain time. At other times, like today, it is difficult to understand due to differing circumstances and influences – in principle this is unjustified. In the same way – unjustified – it causes some uncontrolled interpretation since some people take such inadequate translations strictly verbatim and accept it as the wrong "truth". This applies to some ecclesiastical institutions as well as a number of Christian sects or sectarian movements such as the above mentioned groups of creationists mainly in Australia and the USA.

The Bible is full of vivid images, i.e. metaphors, which made it easier for people at various times to understand the content. In order to understand such metaphors properly today we have to explore in detail the relevant cultural-historical background of the time. A typical example is the famous demand Jesus makes over which many people today only shake their heads: *"If someone strikes you on the right cheek, turn to him the other also."* In this case not the translation prevents us to understand this properly but the fact that we do not know sufficient of the old Jewish moral concepts. Therefore, we ought to understand this sentence in a completely different way than with the complete lack of understanding we have today. At the time when Jesus lived most people, as today, were right-handed. If somebody wanted to punish or to humiliate somebody else especially badly he would give his opponent a hard blow on his right cheek with the back of his right hand. Such a humiliation could only be counteracted by hitting the aggressor slightly with the palm of the hand on the *left* cheek. So, this sentence of Jesus should be interpreted in such a way that if somebody has made a mistake he should have the opportunity of making up for his mistake by offering him the left cheek. Who would want to contradict this?

The Hebrew script is also a number and picture script: each letter is associated with a number and a picture. The sequence, quantity and combination of numbers make up the complete meaning of statement.

We can justifiably say that the old biblical testament in the Hebrew language is written in a real symbolic script. Many of its statements are probably still misinterpreted today.

If we only consider the text as such, errors and misunderstandings are inevitable in addition to those which are caused by mistranslations.

It is understandable that many people today consider this fantastic cultural heritage, the bible, to be nothing but a gigantic albeit obsolete book of fairy

tales unless they devote some attention to the meaning of numbers and their innumerable combinations. The value and usefulness of the Bible correlate especially with our knowledge about the meaning of numbers.
Numerologists distinguish between numbers imbued with positive and negative meanings.
Although most people today deny believing in numerology because they think they are so extremely modern, informed and non-mystic, we all fall at times under the spell of certain numbers.
Have you ever tried to sit in row no. 13 in an aeroplane? Maybe you did not do it because you are unconsciously afraid of the number 13? Or you feel just uncomfortable because the number 13, at least in our cultural circles, is considered to be unlucky? However, even if you are "courageous", you will probably look in vain for row no. 13; in many aeroplanes there is no such row. Many hotels do not have a 13th floor and no room with that number. Numerologists assume that the uneasiness with number 13 is based on the fundamental fear humans have when a new era starts, in this case with the number 13. The number 12 stands for a completed perfection: Jesus had 12 disciples and he himself, being the 13th, disappeared. The way of the Cross had 12 stations. Day and night have 12 hours each and the year has 12 months. For many people the number 12, the product of two key numbers of our world (which I will explain in detail later), the numbers 3 and 4, seems to stand for something perfect. It is overpowered by number 13, which, therefore, for many seems sinister. Yet number 13 also possesses positive elements. In Greek mythology Odysseus is the sole survivor of his adventurous journey being forced to leave his 12 companions to their deadly fate. Completely different is the story of the pirate Klaus Störtebeker: when, after a long and previously unsuccessful chase, he was finally taken prisoner by Hamburg's authorities in 1401 he was sentenced to death and was to be beheaded. His entire pirate gang was lined up beside the scaffold. Störtebeker then asked the executioner to let those members of his gang go free whom he managed to pass whilst running headless. According to the legend he managed to pass 12 of his men, who were allowed to leave the scene as free men, before he finally collapsed. The 13th was then duly executed together with all the others remaining. Many numbers are traditionally of great importance. *Endres* and *Schimmel*, for example, describe the number "3" as the number of "comprehensive synthesis", the number "4" as "physical ordinal number" and the number "5" as the "number of the animated"
The two world religions Christianity and Hinduism both know the trinity as the central principle. Obviously this is the reason for the assumption of a "comprehensive synthesis" which is represented by the number "3". It is

known on the one hand in the trinity of God Father, Son and Holy Ghost, on the other hand in the highest God Brahman, together with Vishnu, the preserver and the God of love and Shiva the destroyer and regenerator.

Three points form a triangle and three lines close it – this is how Plato pondered about the number 2 two and a half thousand years ago, and he saw the world constructed out of triangles.

In fact, three points of information clearly define the simplest geometrical figure, the circle. Three coordinates of its circular arc are the optimal information and logically the simplest. If one point on its arc is chosen in addition to its central point one further point of information is needed to see what is meant. Regardless of how we approach this, in any case it is sufficient to obtain a maximum of three points of non-finite, pure information.

Each small finite point, be it as small as it may, is in itself again an even smaller circle. At some point there must be a finite point, the smallest finite point or circle. In theory this game may be continued in infinity. Eventually the smallest points which still define a finite circle must be nothing but pure information.

There is then the interface between spirit and matter, between immaterial information and finite point, the circle.

The information points are coordinates; they are no longer finite and possess no space at all. We can consider them to be infinitely small. In the same way as numbers do not end, we can consider them to be innumerable. Information points are something purely spiritual. However, they are still as real as the smallest finite circle which they describe.

This example shows that there must be infiniteness as well as finiteness and that there must be an interface between the two. Infiniteness and finiteness are the two flipsides of one coin. The existence of the coin proves the existence of its two sides.

In the same way as at some time a finite circle is so small that only (infinite) information points are clearly defining it, any kind of finiteness has its infinite opposite side and vice versa. Everything has a polar symmetrical counterpart. Interface in this context does not mean that the natural laws of the two symmetrical but opposed "worlds" can be simply mixed. Finite objects can only exist in a finite number and they are only finitely small or big. Infinitely many or infinitely small finite objects do not exist. This is the reason why two world-famous paradoxes are easily explainable. The first tells the story of Achilles and a tortoise. This story is quoted by Aristotle and goes back to the Greek philosopher *Zenon of Elea (approx. 460 B.C.)*:

Achilles and the tortoise start a race. The animal is granted a slight start. According to Zenon Achilles would never be able to overtake the tortoise although it is much slower. Each time Achilles has covered a stretch, the tortoise has also moved a bit further.

Of course, our common sense tells us that Achilles could easily overtake the tortoise after only a short distance, just as we can overtake any car on the motorway, even if it is far in front of us, if we only increase our speed and move faster. The reasoning error in this paradox lies in the fact that distance and time are finite, even if theoretically they can be dissected into infinitely many sections. The sum of infinitely many time intervals is not infinite but finite. This can easily be explained using the reciprocal value of all whole numbers as an example: i.e. $1/1, 1/2, 1/3, 1/4 \ldots 1/\infty$. The sum of 1 and all following reciprocal values of ordinal numbers, i.e. of $1/1 + 1/2 + 1/3 + 1/4 + \ldots + 1/\infty$, tends to 2, and that is a finite value.

If we consider this sequence of reciprocal values in itself, it follows: regardless of the magnitude of the denominator the fraction will never be zero. Infinitely many numbers can be arranged between zero and 1, i.e. in a finite interval. The constant division, a theoretically ("spiritually") infinitely repeatable action, is carried out here within a limited, i.e. finite space, between zero and one, where zero, nothing, is never reached as opposed to the number 1.

The same applies to our smallest finite reality, the finite point. Regardless of how often we divide it further, we will never reach the value zero. In practice ("physically") there is a smallest value for it. In theory ("spiritually"), of course, it could be divided further and further.

The zero which is never reached means in my book always nothing, as the Latin origin, nulla figura, tells us.

I will explain this in more detail later.

The second paradox was established by the Bremen physician and hobby astronomer *Wilhelm Olbers (1758-1840)*. In his lifetime it was assumed that our universe was infinitely large. Olbers claimed that in an infinitely large universe there must be an infinite number of bright stars. In that case, however, the universe ought to be as light as daylight night and day since an infinite amount of light would shine from an infinite number of directions. As we know it is not always as bright as daylight because, even in an infinite space, there cannot be and is not an infinite but only a finite number of stars. Based on the above explanation we may infer that an infinite space cannot be defined as a physical space since something physical is always finite. That is my view as well.

However, from a purely logical point of view the opposite conclusion must also be possible, and this is what scientists have done up until today: they assume that the universe simply cannot be infinite since they consider it as being something physical. They conclude that the universe must have an outer boundary. I believe that this conclusion is wrong. Should the universe, however, have an infinite extension, as I believe and which I will explain in detail later, then it cannot be of physical nature. This means, it must be something spiritual. If we consider our cosmos to be primarily space containing pure information then it can indeed be infinite. Within this space there is a finite amount of matter. In accordance with this perception we could be tempted to assume that matter must be created *within* this (prepared and already existing) space and did not create it. This is the general assumption today, however, I think this too is wrong. I believe that spirit, i.e. pure information, creates matter, as the example of the composition of the smallest finite point shows. Matter then creates the space of information, something spiritual. This means that spirit creates matter and matter creates spirit. It is similar to the Chinese Yin and Yang (see Chapter 2.10).

We can easily follow this train of thought if we look at ourselves: we living beings are created by spirit, the fact that we live should prove it; because life itself is something spiritual (see Part 4).

With our physical body we exist in this physical world and we create a new spirit by further and further differentiating, personally and in general, the existing spiritual potential which is available to us (see Parts 4 and 5).

If the smallest finite circle is created by pure information why should the universe and its (finite amount of) matter not also be created by pure information and even be constantly regenerated?

The Gospel according to St. John starts as with the following words (New Testament, 1.1-1.3): *"In the beginning was the Word, and the Word was with God, and the Word was God. The same was in the beginning with God. All things were made by him and without him was not any thing made that was made."*

If we replace the term "word" with the modern term "information" this concept fits exactly.

Infinity does indeed exist. Should you still have difficulties in imagining this then you should do the following: place yourself between two mirrors which are exactly opposite one another and you will observe that you are reflected an infinite number of times.

Since everything in this world seems to have a finite and an infinite aspect we run the risk of mixing them up. However, we have two categorically separate worlds. They stand in opposition to one another (they are polar) and each is the mirror image of the other. Both exist side by side but are simultaneously completely separate from each other. Someone existing in one world has difficulties perceiving the other. The following little analogy may help: imagine you are a creature which can only crawl along a straight line. You are one-dimensional. Another, polar-opposite dimension stands perpendicular to this line on which you are living. It forms a right angle to your world and, of course, for you this perpendicular would not be recognizable as a line. If you notice it at all you would see it as a small point. Nevertheless, between these two "worlds made of lines" there is a connection: it is your interface.

Numbers are pure information.
If the smallest, no longer divisible finite circle is finally defined solely by information this would mean:
Information creates matter.
If pieces of information keep reappearing at key positions in the universe, e.g. in the form of certain numerical values, it can only mean that they are of vital importance.
This being so, we may assume that there is a mathematical construction plan and we may try to simulate it. Then the "spiritual principles" of such a construction plan, i.e. the numbers and forms on which it is based, must themselves be just as real existing as the matter created by them. Or was *Eugene Paul Wigner (1902-1995)*, born in Hungary and awarded the Nobel Prize for physics in 1963, correct with his hypothesis that numbers are "groundless effective"? I am of a completely different opinion. Mathematicians themselves, by the way, observe that it seems much easier to practise mathematics than to philosophize about it. The American mathematician *Reuben Hersch* (Albuquerque, New Mexico) comments on this, very aptly in my opinion: *"It is like salmon: they know how to swim upstream, but they do not know why!"*

At first this sounds amazing, yet it is true: one and the same number may stand for completely different pieces of information – it depends on the calculation system in which it is used.
In a calculation system different from the decimal system (DS), for example the hexadecimal system (HDS), a system based on the number 16, the sum of 9+9 would be the HDS-number 12, while in the decimal system with which we are familiar the result is 18, of course.
Numbers are suitable for transferring information only to a limited extent. They must always be seen in the context of their common framework, in their own calculation system.
It is always universally valid and, therefore, far more realistic to define the required information clearly in geometrical terms: geometrical forms and ratios provide this clear information.
Moreover, the following reverse conclusion must also be permitted:

If everything in the universe is encoded in the same way by a certain calculation system, then we ought to expect that somewhere along the way intelligent beings developing within this system will automatically use this key for the sole reason that their observations of nature will practically force it upon them.

When humans have ten toes and ten fingers, it is certainly convenient to choose the decimal system as a calculation system.

Humans being part of the whole universe must submit to the same natural laws as everything else. If we think that there is a calculation system laid down in the universe as a kind of code key then we should also be able to find it in humans. Hence it can at least be assumed that the decimal system which, initially for purely practical reasons, is based on the human anatomy can also, following logical considerations, be the relevant key for universal laws and rules – as a working hypothesis, so to speak.

That it was the decimal system which was selected was probably more of a discovery than a new invention. Based on their daily experiences with each other and with the conditions in this world humans were encouraged to calculate with a system based on the number 10.

An imaginable really existing mathematical construction plan for our world could indeed be based on the decimal system because from a logical point of view this would be rational. Due to their daily contact with this system humans then started to utilize it. Basically such a construction plan would, however, also function with any other calculation system. The calculation system is really of secondary importance.

I will show that such a construction plan really does exist.

I also believe that it is based on the decimal system. For this reason, the cosmic and terrestrial interconnections become especially transparent for us from this point of view. Other calculation systems allow us to draw the same conclusions, but make it more difficult to recognise them. The construction plan remains the same.

To end this chapter I would like to entertain you with some more numerology.

While in Germany the number 13 is generally considered to be an unlucky number, in other countries it is different: in Italy the number 17 is an unlucky number and in China the numbers 4 and 7 are rather unpopular because they stand for death and the grave. On the other hand, the number 9 is a holy number in China. For the Chinese the number 3 represents the smallest complete cycle. This reminds us of the smallest finite unit I mentioned earlier, the circle, which, regardless of how small it is, remains a circle.

By means of three pieces of information, e.g. the coordinates of the circular arc, it can clearly be defined. Three times 3 is 9. In so doing, we generate a new, even bigger and also complete cycle made of three smaller complete cycles which brings it to a perfect closure.

The number 9 is followed by number 10, which represents, according to Stelzner *"perfection on a higher level of being"*.

In the Bible we read, for example, that there were 9 generations before the Flood nearly destroyed the world and in the 10th generation Noah headed for a new beginning with his ark – and Jesus died in the 9th hour on the cross.

The adventurous wanderings of Odysseus lasted 9 years and after 9 years under siege Troy was conquered. Similar examples exist in abundance, and there are also plenty of examples for other numbers to which special importance is attributed by mysticism, esoteric, numerology, religion or philosophy.

For others the number 12 is the first great perfection since it is composed of 4 cycles of 3. This makes sense since the number 4 symbolizes infinity. We can, for example, divide time into past, present, future and eternity. The cross, the symbol of the dying Jesus and holy in Christianity, has 4 parts. Even physicists believe in a four-dimensional space-time, as Einstein presented it – which I will modify, however.

As to the "perfection" of the number 12, there are plenty of examples full of symbolism: Jesus had 12 disciples, his way with the cross had 12 stations – and, last but not least, our year has 12 months.

We find a lot of mysticism and symbolism attached to almost every ordinal number up to the symmetrical presentation of the number 12, i.e. up to the number 24. The number 24, the product of the first four ordinal numbers (1x2x3x4=24) appears especially in the biblical description of the end of the world, the Apocalypse, when it basically says: there are 24 thrones with the 24 Eldest positioned around God's throne in the middle.

The number 8 is for many people an example of perfect symmetry since it is formed of a double, or more precise, symmetrically symmetrical symmetry: the first symmetry is the 2, the double symmetry is the 4 and this is then crowned by the 8. The octagon shows this harmonious and beautiful symmetry which gives it special importance in architecture. The central octagon of the magnificent cathedral in Aachen is world famous and it is one of the numerous UNESCO World Heritage Sites. In China a lot of money is paid for car number plates with the numbers 8 or 9, while nobody wants to have a 4 or a 7. As I already mentioned, in China the number 4 stands for "death" and the number 7 for "grave".

According to the story of creation (Genesis) in the Bible God created the world in 6 days and he rested on the seventh. The number 6 became a divine and the number 7 a holy number. In Psalm 90 we read with reference to the lifespan of humans: *"Seventy years is the span of our life"*. The number 7 also turns up in the Apocalypse: 7 torches burn in front of the divine throne representing the 7 spirits of God. In the Islamic religion 7 is a very important number because the sum of the numbers on opposite sides of a dice is always 7 (3+4; 2+5; 1+6).

According to the Greek physician *Hippocrates (460-377B.C.)* it is always the 7th day of a disease and all subsequent days divisible by 7 that are critical. We all know the saying: a cold lasts for seven days if we consult a doctor and it lasts for a week without a doctor.

Furthermore, a medical rule of thumb says that it takes seven years for all the cells in the human body to be regenerated. This is different in Chinese medicine where a differentiation is made between the male and the female cycles: the female lasts 7 years and the male 8 years.

As you can see there are many games to be played with numbers. However, it is also very tempting to attribute numbers with mystical meanings. It is a matter of course that numbers are the beginning of any kind of mathematics; however, nobody can say what they really are. As I will show later, numbers can be found everywhere in the universe and, surprisingly, often the same numbers are found in important key positions.

It is a matter of course that any kind of mathematics starts with numbers; however, nobody can explain what they really are. As I will show later, numbers are found everywhere in the universe and surprisingly often the same numbers are found in important key positions.

Although there is a plethora of numbers connected with superstition and mysticism, we must ask ourselves whether this is reason enough to relegate the search for a possible real existence and to banish the impact of numbers in the world to the realm of esotericism and deem it unscientific.

Superstition and mysticism play only a secondary and mainly entertaining role in this book. Such examples are meant to remind us particularly that humans at all times and in all cultures have paid humble and reverent tribute to numbers. They also urge us not to consider them as being mere curiosities on our path to becoming "scientific beings" in our day and time.

It is about time that science, mysticism, religions and philosophy were reconciled in harmony with each other.

We show indescribable arrogance if we focus on only one aspect, thereby even shrouding our view of the whole picture. In the past this applied mainly to religions – especially to the Catholic Church. Today various religious groups are again starting out on this misguided path. Unfortunately scientists are also treading the same path today, albeit with a different premise. Instead of demanding the unconditional acceptance of certain, allegedly divine commands and prohibitions and the unquestioning belief in a rather obscure but vividly described heaven, hell, the hereafter and other things, they claim the exact opposite: no God, no spirit, no ego, no free will and, of course, no personal survival of the physical death. Is this any better?

Therefore, they should not be surprised when doubts about their doctrines increase and more and more humans, even entire societies, neither understand nor accept them.

Of course, the result is no less problematic; since natural scientific cognition is without doubt still the most important basis for our further development – but it is not the only one.

Natural scientists today must put up with the fact that their interpretations are viewed critically and are corrected when reason, logic, common sense and our everyday experience tell us something different. Furthermore, in our modern times, they must face up to the challenge posed by religions and myths. An arrogant disregard for these will prove absolutely fatal and will in the end make the pendulum of acceptance swing in the opposite direction which is also the wrong approach.

Are numbers and basic geometrical forms a really existing part of nature or are they merely invented by humans?

For Albert Einstein numbers were *"an invention of the human spirit, a self-made tool"*. For Plato numbers and geometry stood for the idea behind everything and all matter in this world.

The German-Polish mathematician *Leopold Kronecker (1823-1891)*, a genius of mathematical logic, said simply: *"Numbers are made by God!"* And the Italian astronomer *Galileo Galilee (1584-1642)* said: *"Mathematics is the alphabet which God used to create the universe."*

2.3) Universal Background

As in most cultures on earth in the past and today, we base our calculations on the decimal system, a calculation system based on the number 10. The fact that we use this system goes back to ancient India. The English mathematician, physicist and cosmologist *John Barrow* described the decimal system as the *"most successful intellectual invention ever made on our planet"*.

The number 10 is the sum of the first four ordinal numbers, i.e. 1, 2, 3 and 4.

Most researchers are of the opinion that the decimal system was chosen by humans due to their anatomy – we have 10 fingers, 5 on each hand. On earth all living beings, with the exceptions of insects and arachnids, show this paired arrangement of 10, although this is not always obvious. Horses, for example, have hooves, cows have cloven hoofs, and birds only have 3 claws – however, these are all regressions of the original composition. Provided we accept that there is a universal and mathematical plan then it seems reasonable to assume that nature "invented" this grouping of 10 in the form of 2x5 because it was part of the plan. Pairing and symmetry represented by the number 2 is the central basic foundation of all existence. The ordinal number 5 is the first "real" prime number not only because it is only divisible by 1 and by itself but also because it follows the same equation as all following prime numbers "$6n\pm1$" (see Chapter 2.5).

It is the last of only five numbers which suffice to make up the basic construction plan of the entire universe. This is the first almost mystical speculation. Humans, who are part of this cosmic order and who are also equipped with a pairing arrangement of five, discovered the decimal system as being a reasonable way of organizing their everyday lives.

Based on this, there is another speculation: everything applicable to us on earth is also applicable in a similar way to everything everywhere in the universe. Should we eventually find other life in the universe – and I am convinced that the universe is teeming with life – then it will be subject to the same construction principles as everything we already know on our beautiful earth.

My next hypothesis, which seems to be completely consistent with other daily experiences, is the consequential result of the arrangement of 10 in the form of 2x5.

Everything in the universe happens according to plan.

All structures are created on the basis of certain basic geometrical forms and follow the ordinal numbers. Everything is created in a polar-symmetrical configuration, i.e. it is symmetrical and simultaneously in opposition to one another. Herewith we come across a number of striking conformities.

Only a few basic geometrical forms, if connected with one another in a plausible way, provide all important key parameters of our universe. They are the core of the plan. We humans are used to calculating everything and to applying numbers to it. We keep looking for data describing areas, circumferences, volumes, etc. Everything is expressed in numbers. Although by using numbers we utilize spiritual guidelines, the arithmetical operations are human inventions. The results depend on the calculation system used. The geometrical plan, however, is not changed by it.

Take a circle as an example. Regardless of whether it is large or small, or whether its radius is measured in centimetres or inches – any kind of calculation system may be used – the circle remains the same. Its measurements do not matter at all; a circle will always be a circle.

Let's take a closer look at the circle: it seems trivial – but it always has a limited, therefore, finite circumference and a limited, therefore, finite area. If we measure its circumference and its area we will surprisingly never arrive at an "even" result – no matter which calculation system we use. A rational number which describes the circumference or the area of a circle does not exist. The result will always be a number with an infinite number of places after the decimal point, the irrational number π.

This simple example gives us an understanding of infinity. The circle obviously has a finite and an infinite aspect which allows us to recognise the universal polar symmetry of this world which is present even in the simplest of geometry. The example of the arithmetical description of an arbitrary circle by means of numbers shows us: wherever finiteness exists, infiniteness exists also.

Everything in the world has two symmetrical and simultaneously opposite aspects. For mathematical calculations we need to decide on one calculation system. This is not necessary for the purely geometrical description of coherences.

If we describe our observations in physics, cosmology, chemistry and biology by means of a decimal calculation system, which, as I already mentioned, seems reasonable, a great number of coherences in nature become transparent in a comprehensive and rather simple way. I will go into this in detail in the next chapters. In this way it becomes easier for us to broaden our view beyond our own noses which is absolutely essential.

Scientists agree today that we – and all other life on earth – only exist because life is facilitated by a multitude of closely defined and miraculously suitable, extremely beneficial environmental conditions.

The Swiss professor for astronomy, *Andreas Tamann,* said (2004): *"The universe is so incredibly favourable that it seems to have been planned!"*

If the conditions had only been slightly different we would never have had a chance to exist. Indeed, our entire universe would be unthinkable without the continuous strict adherence to narrow limits.

However, the consequential conclusion of most scientists is by no means that our world could in fact be the result of a regulating and "strong hand", however it may be natured. Since they refuse a priori practically any discussion in this direction declaring it unscientific, in the long run they embolden those radical groups propagating the biblical creation story, the so-called creationists which are steadily growing mainly in Australia and the USA. They maintain that all life on earth began only 10,000 years ago and they feel supported by alleged findings of Noah's Ark on Mount Ararat, for example, in today's Turkey.

They even ignore serious doubts in their view of the world when modern research methods present a completely different picture. They understand biblical stories in a strictly literal sense and for them the Bible is really a history book.

As the two typical examples I mentioned above demonstrate, the Bible rarely tells us really authentic facts.

It is rather a conglomeration of documents from a wide variety of origins and of various levels of importance. Interpretations of actual historical events constitute only a very small part of the Bible, which does not make it in any way less important.

Creationists are Christian fundamentalists who do not really differ from radical followers of other religions, except for their (as yet) peaceful behaviour. They all tend to accept dogmas which to me seem far from any reality.

However, are modern natural scientists with their perceptions really so much better if in the end so many of their central theories raise more questions than they answer and if a multitude of verifiable daily experiences of many people remain unexplainable and must even be ignored?

More than ever scientists today are convinced that both the beginning of the universe and all later evolution were determined by coincidence alone. Of course, coincidence is also considered to be the most important power for the creation and development of all life on our earth over unfathomable long periods of time. Coincidence here means mutation. Survival chooses the best mutations in the daily battle for existence. This is known as selection. Later on, coincidence is surely somewhat watered down by a further factor which is generally acknowledged: cooperation resulting from communication. However, its central role remains unchallenged.

This, I believe, is too little or even fundamentally wrong. I think I am in a position to show in a plausible way that the further evolution proceeds the less important the role of mutation becomes and with it the role of coincidence for further development. Evolution even seems to grow increasingly afraid of coincidence.

If there had not been such an unbelievable number of extremely fortunate chains of coincidences, as the majority of scientists assumes, we would not be here to think about all this in retrospect. After all, nature needed billions of years to complete this arduous path – and, therefore, it seems that it has had sufficient time.

We would have to thank this unbelievable luck as the exclusive cause of our rather accidental existence. We could now ponder rather "aimlessly" about the reason of all these processes and whether they are due to more than accidental circumstances.

There are, however, a number of serious critics.

They claim that, if considered in an unemotional and realistic way, even the assumed long periods of time, which seem so immeasurably long to us, must have been far too short to have brought about everything by pure chance. To explain the evolution of life by pure chance can be compared to constructing a jumbo jet or an ocean liner by means of a tornado, which gyrates long enough over a few scrap yards.

This does not prevent the majority of modern scientists from publishing their materialistic perspective in such a dogmatic, media-effective way, ideally suited to our social-political Zeitgeist, so that nobody dares to believe in anything different. Anyway, the ordinary man in the street is hardly able to follow the discussion.

The world seems to be far too complicated and complex for him to join the debate. Today, it is no longer possible to become a "universal genius" as they were known in the middle ages given that the multitude of scientific details to be followed up ramify like the branches of a huge tree. However, even the greatest of treetops has a central trunk. Today this is often ignored.

Even very religious people become exasperated by their faith today and scientists throw oil on the fire with their recent claim to have found a "religion-gene". This is indeed ludicrous; but normal people are unable to counter such arguments. Basically religious people turn into quiet sceptics, since it asks for extraordinary strength to stick to one's intuitive conviction in our allegedly so omniscient and enlightened times. To be looked upon with pity as belonging (for evermore) to the past is sometimes the best inoffensive attitude we may experience.

However, as I have asked before, are all these assumptions and theories, which are being continually presented to us as long confirmed knowledge, indeed correct?

Certainly not! On the contrary: in my opinion, formed over decades, quite a number of them are not even worth the paper they are written on (although I do not doubt here that a scientist or two will say the same about my perceptions).

However: many lateral thinkers in the past went through the same experiences, and at all times the old leading generation had to die out before new knowledge could take root. To me it seems to be much the same today.

There seem to be two main simple geometrical relationships which are of great importance in the cosmos. Let us call them the perfect ideas of the Spirit. If we "pull them down from heaven", i.e. if we try to calculate them, they result in infinite or irrational number sequences.

The same applies to the real perfection of the "blueprint" which can be found nowhere in the real world, as Peter Höeg wrote.

There are always small deviations from the ideal as calculations and observations show. Yet, one thing seems certain: the two simple geometries to which I refer here appear with great regularity at all significant positions in our world.

In the next chapter I will disclose their secrets.

Finally, I will show that, by consequential "creation", these and some other, similarly simple geometric forms may be derived from a very small given initial state after only a few steps. Together with the ordinal numbers and their reciprocal values they are the most important basic principles and they control everything of significance in the universe. There are only a few basic conditions essential for the construction plan of our world.

The famous German mathematician and astronomer *Johannes Kepler (1571-1630)* said: *"Geometry existed already before the world was created. It is as eternal as the spirit of God."* The great German philosopher *Immanuel Kant (1724-1804)* determined: *"The entire nature is actually nothing else but a combination of events in accordance with rules."*

2.4) From (finite) Singularity to Multiplicity

Allow me to introduce a little intellectual game. Please imagine you are the "Creator". Please do not think that I am being presumptuous or blasphemous. There are computer games on the market now in which your children do something similar even if in a different form. My experiment only needs some simple geometry. A few construction steps are quite sufficient – in accordance with my favourite motto: *"Simplex sigillum veri (est)"*, which translated from Latin means: "Simplicity is the hallmark of truth."

Our everyday experience seems to tell us that the world is finite. All objects known to us have a finite space, they are three-dimensional. Therefore, we probably assume that something similar applies to the entire universe. It is only over the last few years that even renowned, albeit materialistically orientated cosmologists and physicists started to doubt this. Nevertheless, a spatial infinity is hardly imaginable for us.

If we now look for the smallest existence then it is without doubt the finite point (see previous chapter). It is a fact: no matter how small we draw it, as long as it can be drawn, i.e. as long as it remains a part of our (material) world, it still remains, as small as it may be, a small circle. The circle is thus the smallest *finite singularity* we know. With three information points of the circular arc we are able to determine it clearly in any coordinate system.[7].

Our creation game starts with the smallest possible finiteness, the finite point which is a circle and for which we need exactly three non-finite coordinates, i.e. three pieces of information, in order to depict it. For us humans these pieces of information are something virtual, i.e. something we cannot really touch. However, this also means: for at least as long as there are humans who are "really existing creatures" and who store pieces of information, these pieces of information are in good hands – and thus they themselves are also real.

Now we go a step further and carry this idea forward to a higher level, the level which we usually consider as being superior to us and which many (including me) identify as divine or as being God.

We assume that there is indeed such a level. An increasing number of people unfortunately have their doubts; therefore I choose my words carefully while I develop my working hypothesis.

If this is correct, then all information which is deemed "divine" or "being with God" must also be regarded as real as long as the divine or God exists. In accordance with our notion this means eternally.

In the same manner as we carry pieces of information and ideas around with us throughout our life, which remain real as long as we live, since we may turn them into a *finite* creation at any time, the "divine" pieces of information and ideas are real, as long as God exists. For example: I have carried the thoughts for this and my previous books around with me for many years, almost 30 years now, and in the latter years of the last century I started to put pen to paper. By writing them down they become a *finite* reality. My thoughts, however, existed long before that and they were, therefore, just as real since *I* am real. The same applies, of course, with imperative logic consequence also to God and his thoughts, ideas or, in general, his treasury of information. The Gospel according to St. John puts it aptly: *In the beginning was the word and the word was with God and the word was God."*

---

[7] See explanations in Chapter 2.2

Three non-finite pieces of information thus determine our first finite creation, the finite point which still remains the smallest of circles. This simple logic explains a perception which can be found in many religions but which an increasing number of people today can no longer understand: the religious tradition of the trinity of deities, or of God. In Christianity God is "triune" and consists of God Father, Son and Holy Ghost. In Hinduism God Brahman is simultaneously also Vishnu und Shiva. The divinity which is perceptible to humans in every finite creation, i.e. in any kind of object in our world, is in reality also a trinity just as the finite circle consists of three units of information – its coordinates.

I would like to add yet another thought with reference to the depiction or the more detailed description of a circle. First, we can always draw a circle. But we can also calculate its circumference and its area. For this we need mathematics, a conglomeration of useful methods, created by humans and based on something spiritual, i.e. numbers.
While mathematics and its rules have been developed by humans, numbers existed long before we learned how to handle them. In past centuries mathematicians were almost euphoric about calculating the smallest finite point, the circle; since an evidently finite circle cannot be described in finite values by means of the calculation skills of finite creatures such as we.
In other words: any calculation of circumference and area of any arbitrary circle leads to infinity. For this purpose the infinite circle constant π, which we also term "irrational" because it cannot be exactly defined, was introduced two thousand years ago. The ancient Egyptians already calculated with a rough approximation of π.
The value we usually use today goes back to the Greek mathematician *Archimedes of Syracuse (287-212)*.
Any finite creation is thus based on non-finite information. They are both inseparably interconnected. They belong together in the same way as finiteness and infiniteness are the flip sides of one and the same coin. The infinity of time is known as eternity. Finite and infinite spaces must exist in the same manner as finite and eternal times. We notice that everything in this world has its own finiteness and infiniteness, although we are not (do not want to be) always immediately aware of it.

We now proceed with our intellectual experiment with the act of creation starting with the smallest finiteness, the circle.

Based on this first creation we will create some further realities. For this purpose we only need a few basic rules, since otherwise floodgates would be opened to uncontrolled growth.

For each new creation we introduce two guidelines. On the one hand the finite point, the smallest circle, should grow, i.e. increase in size, and also propagate itself, i.e. increase in number, in free adaptation of the biblical motto: *"Be fruitful and multiply."*

On the other hand every new introduction should be unequivocally retraceable to already existing information whereby every new invention must simultaneously strive for perfection. So far so good.

First of all, based on the pieces of information from the first circle a new, second circle of equal size is created which is the exact mirror image of the first one. With this duplication symmetry and polarity appear now on the scene.

The two illustrations below show these first two steps:

Step 1, the beginning:

Any, even the smallest but finite point is a circle. It is clearly defined by 3 coordinates or more, generally by 3 points of information. I will call the circle of our first creation K1. Its radius is arbitrary and, to simplify matters, I will call it 1 ($r=1$, basic circle). Its central point is called M1.

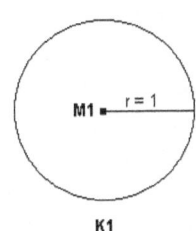

Step 2, the polar-symmetrical duplication:

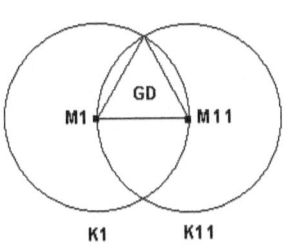
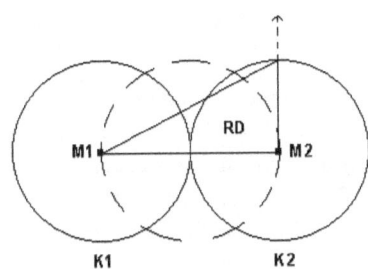

Our first new creation should now proliferate. Since uncontrolled growth is not allowed, everything must follow a logical construction plan. Therefore, in the drawing on the left, an auxiliary circle M11 is created. On the right hand side it is only drawn in a broken line. It is determined by the radius of the circle. Thus equilateral triangles are created in the circle (GD). They structure the circle internally – there are six in each one. Their outer lines form a hexagon (see page 58).

The first real new creation is the new circle K2 which is a mirror image of circle K1, i.e. it is polar-symmetrical and of equal size. The connecting line between the central points of both circles (M1 and M2) distinguishes the first dimension or the first level. Since the smallest finite point is a circle, the second level is created at the same time and thus the further development is defined. Inevitably it is directed to the perpendicular on M2 (broken vertical line with arrow). Thus a rectangular triangle is created (RD).

The original instruction in our little intellectual experiment was, in free adaptation of the divine request in the Bible: "Grow and multiply", whereby this development must proceed in logical steps based on one another. Beyond that, only perfection as far as possible is required whenever something new is developed.

Step 3, the ideal division, the Golden Section:

Starting point fort his step is the previous illustration: Two mirror-image circles and the second level are created. The rectangular triangle which was created here (RD) cuts the second circle K2 on its circular arch. Thus a new point of information is created

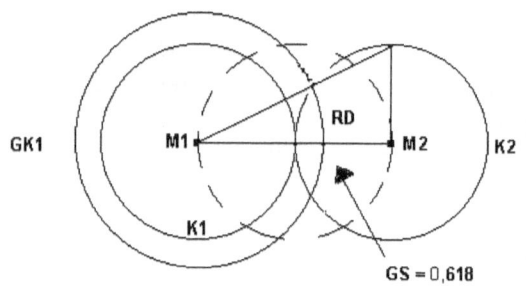

which now facilitates the creation of the first larger circle (GK1).

The new larger circle cuts the rectangular triangle (RD) on a cathetus, the connecting line between the central points of our first two circles K1 and K2. This intersection point constitutes the "Golden Section" (GS). This term was coined by the German physicist *Georg Simon Ohm (1789-1854)*, whose name is still used for the unit of electrical resistance.

If we now ask for the assistance of mathematics again and calculate the distances to both sides of this intersection point GS, which separates the connecting line between the two circular points into two sections of unequal length, then the ratio between them is 1,618.... to 0,618....

The number sequence 6-1-8 is, just like the circular constant π, also infinite or irrational.

The "Golden Section" is simultaneously the result of a "division into extreme and mean ratio". This means: any arbitrary distance can be divided into two sections in such a way that the total distance has the same ratio to the longer section as the longer section has to the shorter section.

We can proceed from here as we like, it will always result in a ratio of 1,618 : 1 or, the reverse division, of 0,618 : 1. This means that the longer distance amounts to 61,8% of the total distance.

The illustration below, drawn by my son Martin, illustrates this:

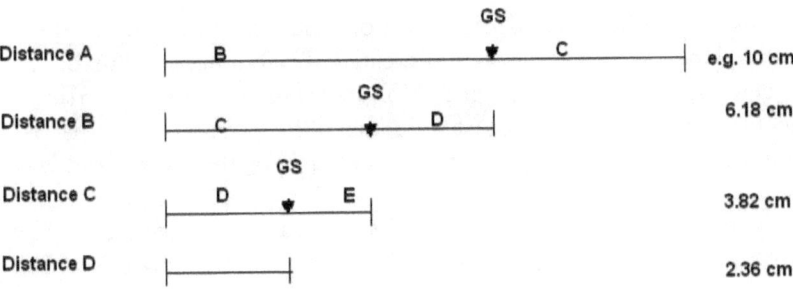

Once again we have to realize that, although it seems easily possible to determine the Golden Section (GS) exactly, and thus in a "finite" way, by drawing it, it is impossible to calculate it accordingly. Various geometric forms can only be described inadequately by our methods. Finiteness and infiniteness are both also polar-symmetrical parts of the Golden Section. We will come across the number sequence 6-1-8, our arithmetical interpretation of a geometrical interrelation, frequently and everywhere in our world. Geometrical rules seem to serve as spiritual information in the background in this world.

Step 4, the first perfection in multiplicity – the square:

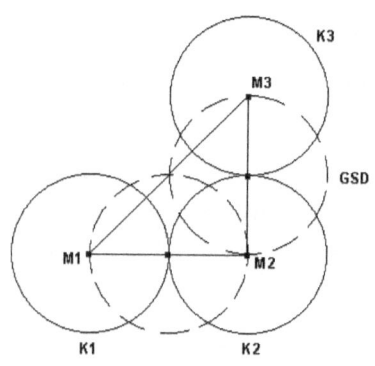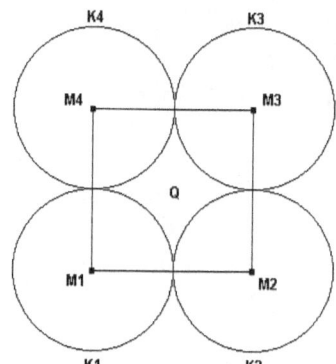

By means of another intermediate step our creation proceeds to the second level, the plane. A third circle (K3) is created. The connecting line between the three central points M1, M2 and M3 describes an isosceles triangle. The completion of the initial smallest unit, the finite point or the smallest circle into multiplicity is demonstrated by the creation of the fourth and last circle (K4).

Thereby a square is created (Q) which is a new geometrical form in multiplicity, developed from a first finite creation. The square is at the same time a qualitatively new unit.

While the first unit, the finite point or smallest circle, is still clearly defined by three "virtual points" or purely spiritual information points, the new unit in multiplicity, the square, is clearly defined by four finite points, the four circles.

After only a few steps our intellectual experiment creates something physical out of pure information. In a sense we could say: matter is generated by spirit. We could also say: infiniteness creates something finite. These few steps also show how after only a short reflection all important geometrical forms[8] can be fully developed from only one initial circle following the "divine" command to grow and to multiply.

---

[8] Meant here are the equilateral triangle, the rectangular triangle, the isosceles triangle and lastly the square as well as the first two important geometrical interrelations, the regular internal hexagon and the Golden Section.

Step 5, the highlight:

Over the preceding four steps the square was created as the first new perfection in multiplicity.
It surrounds the basic circle as shown in the drawing to the right.

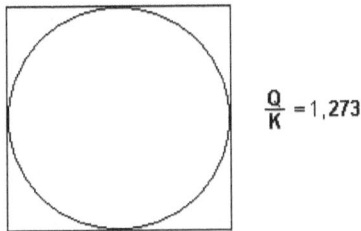

$\frac{Q}{K} = 1,273$

The finite geometrical ratio between square and circle, its quotient, can again be determined arithmetically rather imperfectly only by an infinite, i.e. irrational number. It is the number sequence 2-7-3 which is explained in detail in later chapters.

The two number sequences 6-1-8 und 2-7-3 are, of course, the results of calculations in the decimal system. In any other calculation system the result would be different. The calculations would, however, be based on the same geometrical relations of arbitrary dimensions. The calculation system used is of no importance, since it does not influence the relation between the two forms circle and square.

Nevertheless, I would like to refer to the earlier explanations given in the last few chapters. Subsequently, I am convinced, based on a great number of plausible cues, which are entailed by common sense and daily experiences, that the decimal system is favoured in our world.

The generation of the square as the first perfect unit in the physical, i.e. materialistic, multiplicity out of the initial, non-physical unit of the circle defined by purely spiritual information, is closely connected with the first four ordinal numbers, i.e. 1, 2, 3 and 4.

The next two numbers, 5 and 6, are, as I will explain later, connected with this evolutionary history in a geometrically plausible manner, the number 7, however, is not.

Let us begin with the number 6 which is reflected in the regular hexagon. In the first step in my intellectual experiment we duplicate the first circle by which an equilateral triangle is generated GD (see page 53).

Six equilateral triangles fit into a circle. If their intersection points with the circle are connected, a regular hexagon is created:

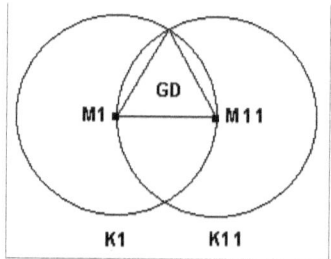 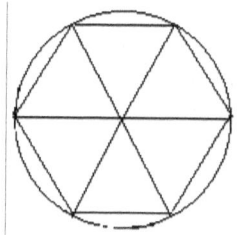

All geometrical forms up to the regular hexagon divide the circle from which they are generated into *finite* angular degrees. A heptagon, on the other hand, is the first geometrical form with irrational angles and can thus no longer be described in exact values.
The number 7 represents a definite cut.
The pentacle represents the number 5. A regular pentagon can be drawn around it. Translated from the Greek the term pentacle only means "five lines".

That is why the term pentagram is often used as a synonym for both regular pentacles and pentagons. The pentagon divides the circular arc into 5 sections with 72° each. The number 72 is the product of 3 x 24, two important values to which I will come back later.

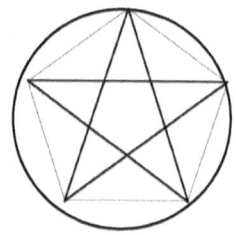

The cross, among other things the symbol of Christianity, has in its middle the cross point, i.e. in addition to its four endpoints it has a central fifth point which connects all the others. Maybe this is the reason why in many religions and myths the number 5 is described as the divine number and the number of love; since love has a connecting function just like this fifth point, the central point of the cross.
The number 5 is also considered to be the number of all living things. In nature we often find the number 5, e.g. the five petals of a rose. Not least, humans are a perfect example for the "superior" pentade. They possess two paired lower and upper extremities (symmetrical and polar four) but only one (asymmetrical and un-polar) head which is simultaneously the topmost centre.

At all times regular pentagons and pentacles have been very popular symbols for various secret societies, of philosophical and religious associations and fraternities. Today pentacles still adorn the flags of the USA and China, in the past also that of the Soviet Union.

For thousands of years Chinese acupuncture has provided a classical example with their traditional teachings of the 5 elements. They are always connected in the direction of mutual "creation" to a regular pentagon. Within this pentagon a pentacle can be drawn when the mutually "restraining" or "despising" elements are connected with each other.

For the Babylonians the goddess Ishtar was the symbol for sexual love, but also for perfection and beauty. The pentacle was her attribute. For the ancient Greeks she became Venus, the goddess of love. The ancient astronomers already observed that in the course of eight years the second nearest planet to the sun draws a perfect pentacle into the night sky against the background of the zodiac. Therefore the ancient Greeks named this planet after their goddess Venus. However the number 5 has been the symbol for love not only since Pythagoras's time.

Based on this special astronomical constellation the Olympic Games took place every eight years and their symbol was the pentacle. Today the cycle for the games has been halved and the pentacle has turned into the five Olympic rings. The reason was to put more emphasis on the modern spirit of the games and to their taking place in harmonic partnership.

A fundamental reason for the traditional mystification of the pentacle and the pentagon may be the fact that they exhibit an almost divine-mystical geometry as the famous German mathematician and astronomer Johannes Kepler (1571-1630) showed later.

Into each pentagon we can draw an infinite sequence of ever smaller pentagons which alternate with ever smaller pentacles up to the upper most un-polar centre S. All these in theory infinitely alternating figures are generated by the division into extreme and mean ratio, the Golden Section.

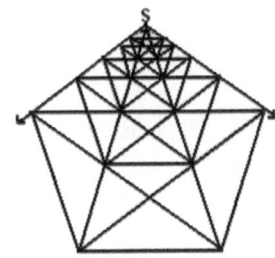

The most obvious key points of all existence – circle, square, golden section and pentacle, represented by a naked man with outstretched arms and legs – we see in the famous drawing made by Leonardo da Vinci in 1509.

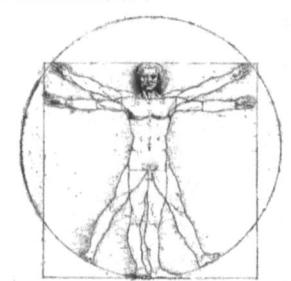

The idea for this sketch goes back, however, to about 30 B.C. to the Roman architect *Marcus Vitruvius Pollio (about 55 B.C. – 14 A.D.)*, called *Vitruv*, and the only book still preserved which he wrote about the architecture in ancient times (De architectura libri decem).

Step 6: The order of 24 as the highest perfection:

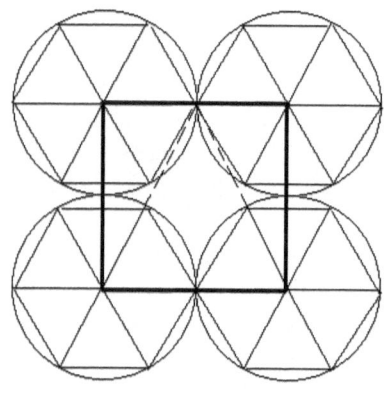

The square was generated from the circle as a completely new form. The newly developed outward two-dimensionality is initially completed by four circles. Each of these circles is structured inwardly. Each circle contains six triangles which together make a regular hexagon. Over the 4 circles of the new multiplicity a total of 24 equilateral triangles are thus produced.

This seems to be another conclusive, geometrically sound indication that any form of finite existence is structured outwardly in a cyclic **24**-rhythm but inwardly always in a 6-rhythm.

It is possible that the ancient Babylonians two and a half thousand years ago already realized this fact and therefore decided to adopt this obviously very useful time unit which has been valid ever since.

Out of three non-finite and thus non-physical, i.e. purely spiritual information points the first physical existence is created – let us call it the physical unit – the finite point, a circle.
Following the biblical motto, "Grow and multiply" a new finite unit, the square, is soon generated within the physical multiplicity by means of plausibly comprehensible, simple and clear rules.
The initial circle, simultaneously the interface between the purely spiritual information and its physical finite manifestation, exposes two firm principles of order: one pointing inwards, the order of 6 and another pointing outwards, the order of 24. Due to the arc of the circle being the smallest finite manifestation, the external and the internal structure are not linear but cyclic.

From a single finite point, the smallest conceivable circle, as the starting point and thus from a *finite singularity* we generate the square, the first new object in *multiplicity* which encompasses and surmounts this finite singularity.
Up until then the expansion of the first circle to the square was purely laminar, i.e. **two**-dimensional. After the new perfection is reached in the multiplicity the next step must be a new quality leap.
This is found by opening up the space, a further now spatial dimension, i.e. the expansion into **three**-dimensionality.
A possibility how to do this would be the following:

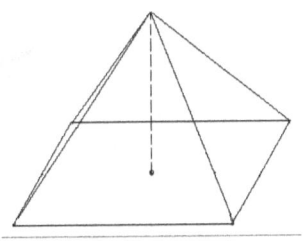

With the aid of a fifth circle which is erected perpendicular to the working face, we gain a regular pyramid with a square base, the tetrahedron.
The ancient Egyptians constructed the burial chambers for their God-kings in the same way.

To open up space in this manner is, in my opinion, a self-evident logical conclusion for us humans since only this method corresponds with our natural conception of space as something **three**-dimensional.

I believe, however, that a different alternative perception is better.
We will find it easily if we reconsider the important steps of my intellectual model in an objective and also strictly logical manner.

The development of the **two**-dimensionality, i.e. the plane, by an outward expansion is only achieved by means of the third circle, which is generated vertically or perpendicularly, i.e. at a right angle to the starting *line* of the first two circles (see Step 4).

The elevation over the **two**-dimensionality and thus the development of the **three**-dimensional space as a new qualitative orientation, must, therefore, also be carried out in a vertical, i.e. rectangular position to the starting *geometry*, since only this would be *unequivocally* defined by the preceding process.

However, the starting *geometry* itself is a plane and no longer a line. This means the space can only be developed by means of a second plane which is perpendicular to the first. The space is thus initially developed by means of a completely different x^2y^2-geometry, which is **not three**-dimensional **but four**-dimensional as is shown in the illustration below.

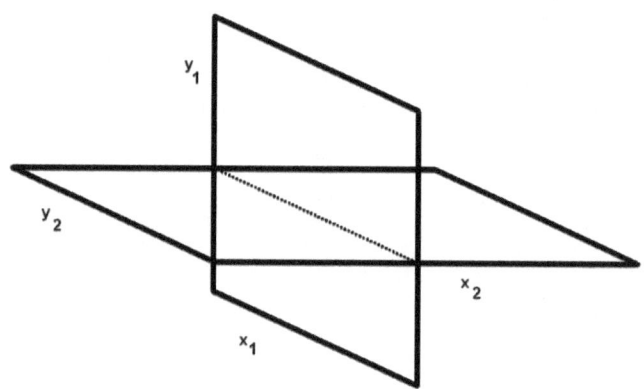

Let us conclude my intellectual experiment of this chapter by applying its results to our world, the universe and all life.

Let us assume that two planes which transect each other at right angles are defined by numbers and that they are cyclically structured in accordance to the order of 24. The numbers extend from 1 to infinity.

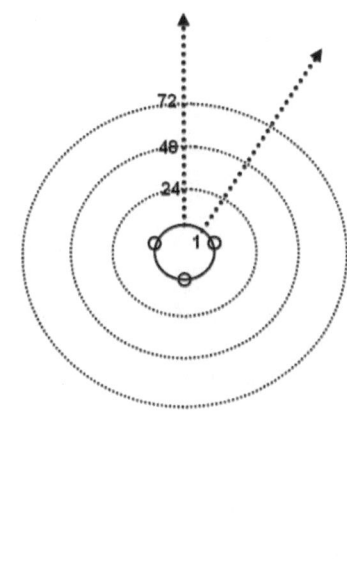

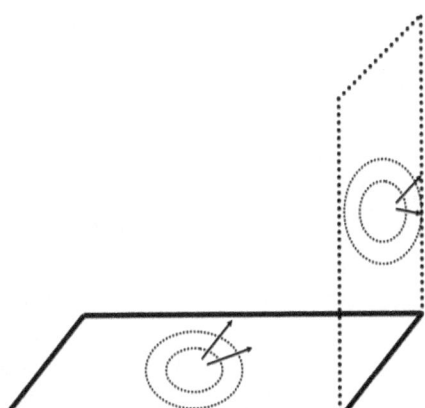

Then we would have two planes which infinitely transect each other at right angles and, due to the infinite number structure, a real spatial and infinite **four**-dimensionality.

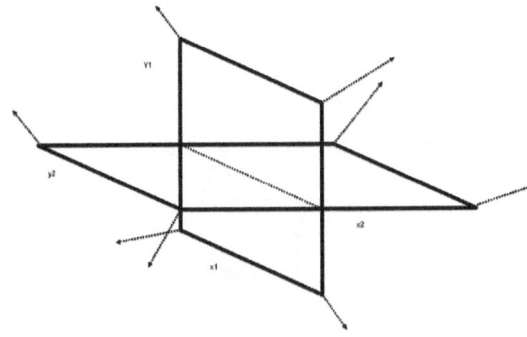

Albert Einstein was right when he recognised that our universe must be four-dimensional. However, he knew of only three spatial dimensions. In spite of his genius it was a mistake not to define a fourth, real spatial dimension! Instead he constructed the four-dimensional space-time model which is still recognised today but is in my opinion fundamentally wrong.

Cosmic space, the universe, is primarily a purely spiritual construct. It adheres to simple geometrical specifications and is infinitely structured by numbers. In the first instance, however, its expansion requires the generation of physical existences. Later on, all additional objects manifest themselves there and they participate in its expansion. Space is thus inevitably the result of any kind of finite BEING in the same way as the "spirit" follows on from a brain. As little as the spirit is the *product* of the brain – the spirit being merely a differentiated field of information (see Part 4 and 5) for which the brain is essential – as little is space a real product of matter; because its expansion is based solely on spiritual rules – its intrinsic geometrical information units. Only these instigate its infinite expansion by means of the infinite sequence of all ordinal numbers. Since space and time are inseparably connected with each other – although not as the four-dimensional space-time construct propagated by Einstein – the universe will exist infinitely according to our best human judgement.

Space itself is infinite and four-dimensional. Finite and three-dimensional objects are first generated and developed within it – which then generate and develop again space. Since space itself is infinite there is no higher dimension which encompasses it.

Symmetry and polarity are universal laws which are inherent in everything and everybody like the two sides of a coin.

Three- and four-dimensionality are just as inseparably connected with each other in this manner just as spirit and matter, cyclic structures and linear number sequences, finiteness and infiniteness or eternity.

Space and time also follow this law – and finally also life and death. I will come back to all these existentially evocative subjects later.

I am convinced that simple geometrical forms and their plausibly consecutive connections or courses constitute the divine framework according to which everything in this universe is generated and developed.

This framework is the irrevocable basis which also leaves enough freedom for all kinds of developments. In the course of time some further small rules have been added which are obviously meant to keep all development on a clearly defined course; a course towards the self-conscious spiritualization of the entire world in highest perfection and in the largest possible multiplicity.

My first chapter finishes with a number of hypotheses. The following chapters must now show that my thoughts are plausible and, therefore, presumably fundamental.

In the end a completely new, alternative view of the world will emerge which comprehensively integrates all our observations.

It is urgently needed in order to save the human beings from their own home-made destruction! The currently acknowledged perception cannot do this since the most important factor is missing: the conviction that there exists a superior, infinitely loving, divine dimension, whatever we may call it, God, Brahman, Allah, Manitou or something else, and to which we owe everything which brought forth the entire universe and thus also us humans. We all are part of a gigantic development. Every single one of us is important, since every single one is also a spiritual personality which never gets lost.

2.5) Absolute Perfection: the Golden Section

"In the beginning was the Word, and the Word was with God, and the Word was God." These are the words with which the St. John's Gospel starts. A word is already a form of complex information, and God's word is, from our perspective today, a synonym for information which determines our world. Numbers are also information units as are geometrical forms. Together they constitute the divine code.
The first "physical" creation is the finite point, i.e. the smallest circle, and the first six ordinal numbers generate it in the narrower sense, since they subdivide this circle rationally (see previous chapter).
Each one of these first six numbers conveys a certain meaning:
The number 1 stands for the divine, God or the unity of the spirit. It stands for the initial state of everything that has been and is created and thus it is the first divine number. It stands for every kind of beginning and for any ever so small unit of information. It stands as a symbol for any unit which functions as an interface between the "worlds" (see Chapter 2.14).
The number 2 stands for the polar symmetry, the formation of something symmetrically opposite to the initial state and thus also for the creation of matter out of the spiritual background.
The number 3 stands for finite space, i.e. for all three-dimensional objects. It is the basic number of any kind of physical existence and determines the material structure. In mathematical calculations involving powers it functions as the basis number (see Chapter 2.7).
The number 4 stands for infiniteness, spatial four-dimensionality and determines the function of structures. In a mathematical power it has the function of the exponent (see Chapter 2.7).
I will call the number 5 the second divine number, since it is the first "real" prime number. The number 5 is the starting point of an infinite sequence of prime numbers which are divisible only by themselves or by 1 and which

follow the general formula "6n±1" (n = consecutive whole numbers). The first three numbers, which usually also rank among prime numbers since they are only divisible by themselves or by 1, I exclude here deliberately which is plausibly explainable (see Chapter 2.3).

The frequency of prime number twins, i.e. cases in which the lower as well as the higher number in the formula "6n±1" is a prime number, decreases with higher ordinal numbers (n), slowly at first, but later rapidly (it follows the Euler number, see Chapter 3.4).

Prime numbers obviously control a number of effects in cosmic space such as light and gravitation (see Part 3), for example.

The number 6 structures closed, i.e. three-dimensional spaces, inwardly. It has the highest packing density. Honeycombs are structured by hexagons, for example.

The number 7 is no longer deducible by a simple geometrical development (see previous chapter). The heptagon is no longer regular and it is the first polygon which does not subdivide the circle, the initial geometry of this "creational model", into rational angular degrees. Therefore, this number is a turning-point.

Some readers may presume that this is pure esoteric, but I will demonstrate that this is not so.

Perhaps some of you may wait for the number 0, the "twin of infiniteness" as Charles Seife names it in a book title.

In our calculation system the zero is a placeholder and in this function sensible and useful. The zero stands for non-existence, the "nothing". The zero is polar-symmetrical to the BEING (see previous chapter). This stands in opposition to the assumption of most of our temporary scientists. However, my answer to this is: he who wants to get to the source must be able to swim against the current!

The natural progression of a small number of geometrical developmental steps gives reason to assume that six numbers and two geometrical relations are the determining factors for the prevailing conditions in our world. The Golden Section is one of them. The ratio between the area of the square, as the new unit in multiplicity, and the circle, as the initial geometry initiating it, can be calculated (see previous chapter). In both cases it is irrelevant which calculation system is used. The only precondition is that the chosen system must be used throughout for all calculations. We in our society have chosen the decimal system as the most sensible and useful one as most cultures before us.

Although it only plays a secondary role here, I think that humans in fact orientate themselves to the "standard of the World". I will explain this several times in detail.

In the decimal system the result of the "Golden Section" is the number sequence 6-1-8.

With this division into extreme and mean ratio (see previous chapter) it is completely irrelevant whether the longer distance is divided by the shorter one or vice versa. In the first case the result is 1.618, in the second it is 0.618.

Of course, the number sequence 6-1-8 is not conclusive. In fact it is an irrational number and, therefore, infinite. With our calculation methods it is not possible to define "divine geometry" precisely. All measurements and calculations revolve around an ideal, its proper value. We are unable, however, to calculate this ideal spiritual model exactly. This already fascinated the ancient Greeks hundreds of years before Christ. This is a fact we keep discovering regularly in our world. One of many examples is the velocity of light which is obviously orientated to the number 3 but never actually meets this value exactly.

The Italian mathematician *Leonardo Fibonacci von Pisa (ca. 1180- ca.1250)* among others discovered the number sequence 6-1-8 by means of an amazingly simple intellectual experiment reflecting the propagation of rabbits. What would happen, asked Fibonacci, when one pair of rabbits produced a pair of baby rabbits every month? At the same time every new generation of rabbits would reach sexual maturity after 2 months and would also start to produce baby rabbits. In the first month one pair of rabbits would produce *one* new pair. In the second month there would be *two* pairs (the parents and the young pair). However, since the young ones do not reproduce before they are two months old, there would be another young pair reproduced by the first parents. In the third month the first parents would reproduce again and – for the first time – also the first young pair, etc.

The statistics would look as follows:

Month:	1	2	3	4	5	6	7	8	9	10	11	12	13	14	15
Number of pairs:	1	1	2	3	5	8	13	21	34	55	89	144	233	377	610

The second line is a regular number sequence, since from the third number onwards, which refers to the moment when an additional pair of rabbits also starts to have a litter regularly every month, the following number equals the sum of the two preceding numbers. These numbers have been known as "Fibonacci Numbers" ever since.

If two consecutive Fibonacci numbers are divided by one another the result is as follows:

1:1 = 1; 2:1 = 2; 3:2 = 1.5; 5:3 = 1.667; 8:5 = 1.6; 13:8 = 1.625; 21: 13 = 1.615; 34:21 = 1.619; 55:34 = 1.618.

On the other hand, if the lower number is divided by the higher one the result is 0.618. In both cases the number sequence is identical 6-1-8.
The term "Golden Section" is obviously excellently appropriate.
Psychologists claim to have found out by means of various tests what it is that makes the female body so especially attractive in the eyes of the majority of males. The result seems very simple. The waistline must be a bit less than 70% of the hip measurement. I would bet that an accurate calculation comes up with a value of approximately 0,618 (=61,8%).

In fact, now it is interesting that this Golden Section can be found everywhere in nature. We could almost say that nature strives, wherever possible, to reach the Golden Section.
From an abundance of examples in botany I will quote but a few here. Spectacular is the spiral or overlapping arrangement of petals in many plants, such as sunflowers, daisies, thistles, agaves, many palm trees, even cabbages and roses. Sometimes two consecutive petals divide an imaginary circle around themselves in the angle of the Golden Section, sometimes flowers, leaves or scales are arranged in spirals which are turned in both directions in the ratio of the Golden Section, as we can see in fir cones or pineapples. In the same manner the growth of the spirals of a snail-shell are identical to a spiral nebula, i.e. a galaxy in the vast cosmos or the spirals of a hurricane. The distances between their spiral lines always increase in the ratio of the Golden Section. The distances between the nine planets of our solar system *(Titus-Bode-Rule)* and their revolutionary periods and those of their moons follow the Golden Section.
Or something completely different: if we stretch our arms out horizontally to our sides then the ratio of the length of each arm to the shoulder length is that of the Golden Section. The same applies to the ratio of the upper arm to the lower arm or the upper leg to the lower leg. The distance between the soles of our feet to our navel and from there to our head also follows the Golden Section. The same applies to the ratio between the distance from our shoulders to our fingertips and the distance from our elbow to our fingers and the ratio in our legs is similar (see the sketch by Leonardo da Vinci according to Vitruv, page 60).

When we consider the phalanxes of our fingers and toes and the relevant metacarpal bones in our hands and feet then we realize that the ratio between each of two adjacent phalanxes is the same as major and minor, i.e. they also relate to the Golden Section. The same can be found in various proportions of the face.

Countless examples can be found in the proportions of human anatomy, which for artists is, of course, a well-known orientation. The Golden Section is a universal phenomenon and it stands for perfection and something optimal. The same applies to animal anatomy.

Take a horse, for example: the distance from its hooves to its underbelly compared to the circumference of its rump bears the same ratio as the Golden Section. Other proportions follow the same pattern.

Geometrical relationships can be defined by numbers. The Golden Section can only be defined by irrational numbers.

Conclusion: a geometrical relationship which stands for perfection has an exact equivalence in nature but can only be defined inadequately by numbers and human calculations.

Mathematically the Golden Section can simply be derived from the development of so-called "binomial formulae".

An abstract mathematical number development thus reflects a variety of natural processes.

Now a few beats of music. One octave has, as we all know, eight notes and seven intervals. The oscillation ratio of the first note to itself is, of course, 1:1 or 1.0. The ratio between the first note and the first note of the next higher octave, e.g. c and c' is 2:1 or 2.0. The consecutive notes, whose intervals swing around the number of the extreme and mean division like a pendulum which gets nearer to the point with each swing, show the following sequence of intervals:

	c	c'	g	a	as	as+
	1/1	2/1	3/2	5/3	8/5	13/8
or	1.0	2.0	1.5	1.667	1.6	1.625

Here too, we can see clearly how the successive relations follow those of Fibonacci's number sequence. The remaining difference to the number 1.618 is very small. This means that there should be an optimal interval between notes which is slightly wider than the perfect quint and which corresponds exactly to the Golden Section resulting from the extreme and mean division of the octave.

This was already recognised by *Johannes Kepler (1571-1630)*. For him it followed that the Golden Section was the result of a "divine division"*(Latin: proportio divina)*. The interval we are looking for here would then be the "purest" or "most perfect" quint. The (normal) quint is derived from the number 5 and it is the largest interval (e.g. between c and g upwards, i.e. three whole tone steps and one semitone step) within one octave, which is regarded as being completely consonant in music.

Together with the succeeding quart (between g and c') the octave is now harmonically divided into two sections of different size.

Both are milestones on the path to a real extreme and mean division. This fact indicates also that the number 5 itself, the first real prime number after 1, must be of special importance. The famous Italian violin maker *Antonio Stradivari (ca. 1644-1737)* utilized the Golden Section for determining the exact position of the hole for the f in his ingenious instruments, so that a perfect quint could be played on them.

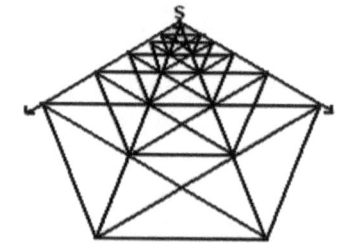

At this point I would like to recall the illustration in the previous chapter. The original was designed by Kepler, who drew a (theoretically) infinite sequence of regular pentagons which were interleaved, grew smaller and smaller and led to a collective peak (S). Thus a figure is generated in which pentagons alternate with pentacles.

Within them we find automatically regular arrangements alternating between acute angled and obtuse angled equilateral triangles.

We can also say that the basic elements of a large variety of geometrical forms are collected here. The uncountable triangles divide their sides towards the peak of the figure (S) (i.e. towards "infinity") again in the extreme and mean ratio of 1: 1.618 or 1: 0.618.

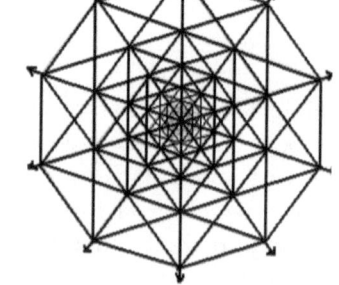

Kepler, however, saw in this figure only a small part of real perfection since the pentagrams can be joined together graphically to an absolutely perfect "decagon" this again being orientate to the decimal system. According to *Ernst Bindel* this figure resembles a perfect diamond.

In nature there seems to be a real, fixed optimal number sequence for divisions.

The Golden Section thus stands for an "optimal division". The Golden Section is pure perfection.

In nature the Golden Section is found so regularly that we cannot avoid the impression that nature is actually striving for it. Many architects of past times integrated it in their construction plans for large buildings. We can, for example, detect it in the main proportions of the Parthenon in the Acropolis at Athens as well as in the cathedrals of Milan and Cologne and in the Egyptian pyramids. All these buildings have resisted the adversities of nature, modern pollution and the worst chaos of wars. The cathedral at Cologne even survived numerous bomb attacks during World War II without collapsing.

Obviously the decision to base the construction of colossal buildings on the Golden Section was very wise. Some modern buildings cannot keep up with this. What did Leonardo da Vinci say about the Golden Section? *"The proportion is not only found in numbers and measures but also in notes, in landscapes, in times and places in every existing power."*

Although the term "Golden Section" was coined only about 200 years ago the phenomenon of the division in extreme and mean ratio (optimal) was well known a few thousand years ago in ancient high cultures such as in Egypt, Babylon and Greece. Nevertheless, some historians ascribe its discovery to the Greek mathematician *Euklid (about 300 B.C.)* because he published a textbook about the entire mathematics known at the time.

2.6) The Limits of Feasibility

Apart from the Golden Section there is another geometrical relationship which is obviously reflected everywhere in the universe.

Towards the end of my little creational game of a growing and multiplying finite point, the smallest circle, the expansion of the two-dimensionality culminates in the square – the new perfect unit in multiplicity.

If we divide the area of the square by the area of the circle we arrive at another geometrical relationship which, in the decimal system is also described by an infinite, i.e. irrational number with the sequence 2-7-3.

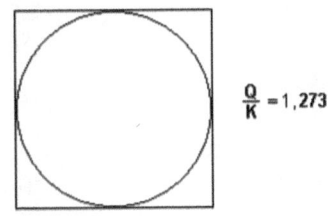

$\frac{Q}{K} = 1{,}273$

It is found mainly in key positions in our universe.

It seems that the sequence 2-7-3 characterizes the limits of feasibility. It stands for the optimal on the brink of the possible. Since this number sequence can also be calculated in the decimal system on the base of a purely geometrical interrelation it is legitimate to compare it with similarly established values in our universe.

When we measure temperatures in Germany we usually use the decimal scale named after the Swedish astronomer *Anders Celsius ((1701-1744)*. The essential for life on our planet earth and presumably for all creatures in the universe is water (H_2O). All the elements and, therefore, all of their chemical compounds exist in three different phases or states of aggregation: solid, liquid and gaseous. All forms of life need liquid water, which is probably the most important substance and which, according to the latest findings, is to be found in abundance everywhere in the universe. Celsius divided the liquid state of the water into 100 decimal degrees between its melting point and its boiling point. The Swedish scientist *Carl von Linné (1707-1778)* then defined the melting point with 0°C and the boiling point with 100°C. However, zero centigrade is not the lowest possible degree of cold, as we know. The boiling point of nitrogen, for example, is about -195°C, i.e. below that nitrogen remains liquid for another 15 degrees below that. There is, however a lower temperature limit which *can* never be exceeded anywhere in the universe. This is known as the *"absolute zero"*. This lies at about -273°C. However, it is found nowhere in the universe due to one simple reason; temperature (heat) is generated by the movement of particles and at -273°C nothing can move anymore – anywhere. The universe would be motionless and rigid.

Scientists long ago discovered that, regardless where we look, we will find the same temperature everywhere in the universe, one which is slightly higher than the absolute zero and which deviates by exactly 2.73°C upwards. This is known as the background radiation (BGR).

The famous British physicist, *Sir William Thomson*, called *Lord Kelvin (of Largs, 1824-1907)*, introduced a decimal temperature scale (the Kelvin scale, K) which starts at the absolute zero (-273°C). According to this the melting point of water is, of course, +273 K.

The background radiation (BGR), which is extremely uniform (isotropic) in all directions of the universe and forms a sort of basic temperature of the cosmos, is fairly precisely 2.73 K (see Part 3).

Cosmologists will object at this point and remind us that the COBE-Satellite[9] has meanwhile enabled us to establish that the BGR is in fact not really all that steady and that it does fluctuate. However, these fluctuations are very small and amount to less than one three millionth of a degree. And please keep in

---

[9] COBE= **C**osmic **B**ackground **E**xplorer; on an orbit around the earth since 1989

mind that the number sequence 2-7-3 is not a rational, i.e. an "exact" value but the arithmetical result of a geometrical relationship.

If we recognise a spiritual framework for our cosmos in geometry then everything manifested in this world must show a small and "irrational" deviation from these ideal values! Modern cosmologists consider this "heat" as being some kind of afterglow following the Big Bang, which is supposed to have brought forth the universe some 13-15 billion years ago.

They ignore the probably correct relevance of this exact temperature value since they cannot recognise it without using geometry.

Therefore, in some scientific books and articles the BGR is specified by the completely inadequate approximation of 3 K (instead of 2.73 K).

Here are some more examples to illustrate the fundamental importance of the number sequence 2-7-3 which I will only mention briefly.

According to *Gay–Lussac's* well-known law of physics, all material in our cosmos contracts by exactly 1/**273** of its volume if the temperature is lowered by 1 degree whilst under constant pressure and it also expands by the same amount if the temperature is raised again by 1 degree.

Another example: The radius of the moon is exactly 0.**273** times the radius of the earth and the rate of acceleration of the moon on its orbit around the earth is 0.**273** cm/s^2. A *sidereal* month, i.e. a real lunar month, is **27.3** days as is also the *synodical* rotation of the sun. Scientists today discuss that our moon is a real twin planet of the earth and that it had to adopt this order of magnitude to enable it to stabilize our earth in the solar system in a favourable and lasting manner.

The gravitational acceleration on the sun is **273** m/s^2.

The earth revolves around the sun in one year or exactly 365.25 days (a year according to the Gregorian calendar, introduced in 1582 has 365 days and every leap year 366 days). The reciprocal value of this number is the decimal sequence **2-7-3**.

At university, students of medicine learn that a human pregnancy lasts an average of **273** days which is **10** lunar months; the length of pregnancy, therefore, equals the reciprocal value of the number of days in a year.

Our air is, as we all know, a mixture of various gases. Yet only small changes in the ratio of its composition would probably have tragic consequences for our survival. With an optimal quota of 21% oxygen and 77% nitrogen, the ratio of oxygen to nitrogen is 0,**273** or **27,3**%.

Of course, critics will now argue that it is incorrect and arbitrary to use humans and their partly "artificial" environment as a plausible indication or even proof for the existence of universal benchmarks. I disagree.

Let us consider the historical course of human evolution backwards. I chose us humans since we represent today the preliminary peak of spiritual development on earth at least. For us, and thus for the accomplishment of this extraordinary spiritual state of development, an optimal composition of the gaseous mixture of our air, as we find it here on earth, is absolutely essential.

The smallest fluctuation would have made any kiond of life impossible. In order to generate this atmosphere it was absolutely essential that the sun was situated at an exactly defined distance and that both earth and moon maintained a stable orbital system. The sun is a fixed star in a universe with a rather stable temperature throughout, the weak background radiation. Each one of these interdependent constellations is closely connected with the number 273.

In my earlier book "Key to Eternity" this observation persuaded me to state that there are sufficient reasons to assume for certain that very important developments in our universe always strive in a straight line to achieve the optimal number sequence. The world is not "satisfied" before these values are actually reached.

Meanwhile I can even go a step further, since I have demonstrated that the two number sequences 6-1-8 and 2-7-3 are only the arithmetical (decimal) representation of a natural development.

They are generated as the natural result of *propagation and growth* of the simplest geometrical form, the finite point. From this we can logically conclude that the construction of our whole world is generally based on a simple mathematical order.

It is imperative that this exists in reality and it must have done so since time immemorial. Geometrical forms and numbers are something purely immaterial, and their existence must be seen as being completely independent of energetic condition in the conventional sense.

The principle of the conservation of energy according to the indisputable laws of thermodynamic physics is not primarily decisive wherever simple geometrical forms and ordinal numbers influence the world and organize its structures and processes themselves.

It is numbers and forms which almost force all matter into certain channels or conditions. The current almost hectic but completely unsuccessful search for various substances which supposedly exert profound effects on matter, such as gravitons for gravitation and gluons for the cohesion within atomic structures, would become completely superfluous.

However, geometrical forms and ordinal numbers are only *one* factor of a superior spiritual world. If numbers and forms could now already be suggested to be really existing spiritual qualities, then even the greatest sceptics would stop bellyaching over the acceptance of further and more differentiated spiritual qualities.

2.7) Form and Number determine Structure and Function

After only a few steps my simple intellectual experiment, which considered the propagation and the growth of the simplest geometrical form, the finite point and thus the smallest circle, created all the important basic geometrical forms which we know today. Based on these all further forms can be developed.
At the same time two especially succinct interrelations emerged. Those of the Golden Section and the quotient of the new unit in multiplicity, the square, and the initial circle (see Chapter 2.4).
Neither of these are new, independent forms, rather only special measurements. They are inevitably generated by this initially purely theoretical creation on the drawing board.
The first measure, the Golden Section, was generated with the changeover from mere propagation to additional growth. The second measure was the result of the direct comparison between the optimal new creation (square) and its optimal initial value (circle).
I think it is worthwhile to give some thought to these interrelations which seem at first to be so trivial.
If we look upon the small and the big things in this world then we will notice that we keep finding exactly the same interrelations wherever we look.
In the previous two chapters I already mentioned a number of examples. It is interesting to note that the Golden Section with its number sequence 6-1-8 is always to be found wherever a process of reproduction and growth takes place. The quotient 2-7-3 stand for the square and the circle as the representatives of new creation and initial conditions and they can be found everywhere at the borders to new creations. For example, the absolute zero point and the background radiation (BGR) in our universe are typical boundary values which I term here "new creation": the physical world in which we live (see Part 3 and 5). On the other hand, the growth of the spiral arms of all galaxies or the distances between the planets in our solar system, all follow the Golden Section along an imaginary spiral, in the same manner as do petals and fir cones, which are in different ways adjusted in analogy to this pattern.

There can be no doubt that the relationships to growth and propagation here are just as close as those of the famous "rabbit breeding" established by Fibonacci of Pisa.

The decimal numbers 6-1-8 and 2-7-3 derived from geometrical relationships seem to be measures for important functions in this world.

Similar to the whiplash with which a lion tamer controls his animals they ensure that certain configurations, adjustments or behaviours are maintained.

The geometrical forms, on which my intellectual experiment is based, control all manifestations and specifications.

This explains why planets and stars are always spheres and why it is that their orbits around their central star are primarily circular. Elliptic orbits result from various influences, i.e. other forces. I will come back to this later.

They are based on the circle which inevitably becomes a three-dimensional sphere in an infinite four-dimensional real space.

Each new physical reality is generated from spheres and only later may it develop into other forms because it is based on the idea of a circle. In the same manner every human being develops from a spherical fertilized ovum.

The basic principle of structure and function, controlled by forms and numbers, is found everywhere in the world.

We can even go a step further with this duality.

In the initially two-dimensional external multiplicity a finite point, the "smallest" circle, accomplishes its first comprehensive perfection in the form of a square.

Each initial circle is exactly defined by 3 points – or, generally, by three points of information. They are not finite. As pure points of information they are spiritual points, coordinates or specific positions.

Of course, they exist in reality; because, just as ideas "in" our brain exist at least as long as our brain functions, "God's" ideas exist as long as "God" exists.

From our perspective this means eternally.

In my intellectual experiment the square was generated from four circles. For an unambiguous definition each point must be defined by the information of the circle to which it belongs. For Circle 1, the initial circle, we could term the points of information P11, P12 and P13. A second symmetrical circle which emerges from Circle 1 as a mirrored image is also clearly defined by three non-finite, immaterial spiritual points. They already carry the information that they belong to the second circle, e.g. P21, P22 and P23. For a circle we can specify three positions, for two circles, however, there are already 9 positions if we consider them together as a new "unit" or *one* structure. If we look for all possible positions of those information units which clearly define them – initially for the first two circles together – we obtain the coordinates P11/P21, P11/P22, P11/P23, P12/P21, P12/P22, P12/P23, P13/P21, P13/P22, P13/P23, a total of nine coordinates.

If there are three circles there will be 27 coordinates. The number of possible positions is, therefore, a function on the basis 3 – there being 3 information points for each circle – and the exponent gives the number of circles involved. The number of building blocks necessary for the clear definition of our circles – of their "structure" – is arithmetically the basis number. It is, of course, the constant "3".

The "function" is the number of circles involved and is allotted the role of the exponent. Thus we have a number 3^n, where "n" means the number of circles. Put simply it follows: exponents give the orders to the basis numbers which obey them accordingly – as can be seen in the following illustration by my son Martin:

The helmsman sits at the top like the exponent on the basis number. This comparison should remind us of the famous pictures of St. Christopher who carries the child Jesus as the helmsman on his shoulders through the water. Is it possible that this Christian imagery is a symbol for the exponent and the basis number? (Illustration by Martin, 1999).

When in my creational game with the growth and propagation of the finite point, the smallest circle, the process has arrived at the first perfection in multiplicity, the square, by means of the four circles required, it has already automatically utilized both number sequences 2-7-3 and 6-1-8 which are so important in our universe and also – via the number of equilateral triangles and internal division – the number 24.

In order to define clearly all four circles – with which the square as the first unity in multiplicity is newly created – 3^4 (= 81) specific positions are necessary.

With the number 81 we are confronted with yet another extremely important number. It too can be found everywhere in the universe and it stands for a clear limitation of any physical expansion. There are, as I will explain in detail later, exactly 81 chemical elements existing naturally and which do not disintegrate spontaneously, i.e. which are stable. There are exactly 81 code positions in the genotype of all life and not, as biologists mistakenly believe today, only 64 (= 4^3) combinations of code components, known as nucleotides.

A relatively simple, concise and self-contained intellectual model is sufficient and we have all we need to explain the basic structures and conditions of the entire universe.

Four finite points, the smallest circles, soon form a first new perfection, the square. Within its own limits each circle contains the possibility of dividing or structuring itself internally. This is made clear by the fact that its area can be defined solely by means of an infinite, irrational number. The square of four circles forms the first extensive perfection in a still **two**-dimensional external multiplicity. The process of growth and propagation gives us all the important geometrical forms and relationships which apparently control the entire universe. This also includes the indication that our universe must be four-dimensional and infinite whilst we humans consider it to be *three*-dimensional.

Albert Einstein was the first to recognise the necessity of four-dimensionality. But he drew the wrong conclusion from that and constructed a four-dimensional space-time continuum. Although, as I will explain in Part 3, space and time do in fact become an inseparable continuum due to the development of the physical world, each one of these aspects maintains its own four dimensions.

The first four ordinal numbers are especially important.

If we add them up the result is the perfect number of the Pythagoreans, the number "10". This is a little more evidence that in the cosmic reality the decimal system is the favoured counting and calculation system of this world. Once more it seems that we humans discovered the decimal system as being especially useful for us because nature opted for it long since.

In principle, of course, all other calculation systems are imaginable – however, the decision against them seems to have been made on a different level. Since my creational game with the four circles and the square brings forth the first perfect new creation reflecting a complete *inherent* order of symmetry and polarity, we find that the number "10" is realized in our world mainly as 2 packs of 5 as, for example, our 2 sets of 5 fingers and toes, etc.

From the outset we are all moulded by evolution – it is very easy for us to *grasp* an amount of 5 objects. Quantities exceeding this amount we must *count*. You may test this using the illustration on the right: My son Martin has drawn a nice example to demonstrate this.

You see seven sections with different objects. We immediately register objects up to a total amount of 5 without having to count them.

Our simple initial experiment of growing and propagating finite points, the smallest circles, has created a real number family in its "act of creation". The history of our world can indeed be explained in an alternative – if not better – way by the first four ordinal numbers alone, the zero denoting "nothing" as the opposite of BEING, which means in this case existence, in addition to the numbers 10, 24, and 81 and the number sequences 2-7-3 and 6-1-8. A better way in this instance means that it is probably closer to reality.

A this point I would like to emphasize again that this number family and all the important geometrical forms are generated in their entirety by means of **two**-dimensions. **Three**-dimensional space, the only we humans recognise, does not play a role, since **three**-dimensional space emerges from a **four**-dimensionality on which it is based in reality which itself is an (infinite) **two**-plane geometry in the form of x^2y^2.

Based on these rather simple interrelations we obtain some further important information.

The number 1 stands at the beginning for something new and the beginning of a further development of our finite point. The number 5 also describes something new. It is the first point of a new spatial three-dimensionality. This is probably why the ancient Egyptians chose pyramids as tombs for their pharaohs.

The fifth point – the summit of the pyramid – stands perpendicularly above the square. The chosen distances SA and MA are divided in accordance with the Golden Section. First and foremost, however, the summit of the pyramid represents human nature since humans access the three-dimensional space by means of the number 5.

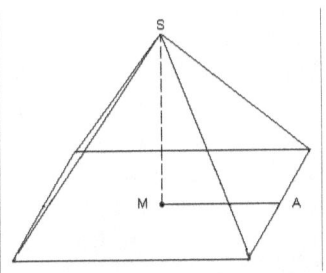

Humans only perceive this kind of space since infinity is incomprehensible for them whilst the three-dimensional space is finite. However, the space of our universe is, in fact, infinite: it is four-dimensional. Even so, the number 5 becomes the symbol of the spirit.

If we take another look at our initial circle we notice that we have a structure of equilateral triangles which can theoretically be continued into infinity towards the inside, starting with 6 triangles which are generated automatically and which indicate the division cycle (illustration by Martin).

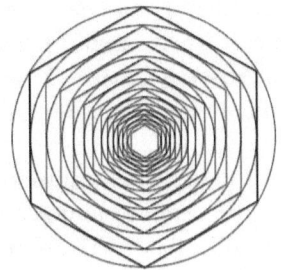

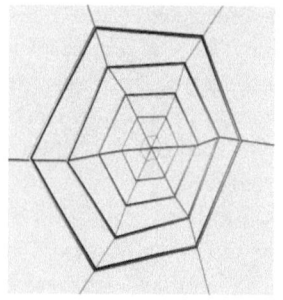

This internal division in the form of regular triangles looks very much like a spider's web. How does the spider know that it should work in this manner? It cannot help doing so because it always works to a plan (Illustration by Martin).

A seventh triangle cannot be depicted in a rational manner, i.e. with an "even" angle specification. Each angle is irrational, infinite.

The number 7 also offers something completely new; the key to transcendence.

In mathematics the numbers 5 and 7 are prime numbers as are the numbers 1, 2 and 3. All successive prime numbers follow the formula $6n\pm1$ where n could be replaced by all whole numbers until infinity. The numbers -1 and +1 can also be defined by this formula with n=0. The numbers -1 and +1 are the polar-symmetrical starting points for both infinite sequences of ordinal numbers.

They represent the development of all existence and, therefore, they hold an exceptional position, to which I will return later.

The numbers 2 and 3 do not really fit into the pattern of prime numbers, since they do not follow the general formula $6n\pm1$. Therefore, they should no longer be considered as real prime numbers.

The sequence of infinite "real" prime numbers starts with the number 5. "Prime" means something like the "first", the "new". Prime numbers obviously have a very important function in our world, as I will explain later.

They also have another outstanding feature: around the formula $6n\pm1$ we always find at first prime number twins, such as 5 and 7 for n=1, 11 and 13 for n=2, and 17 and 19 for n=3. With the increasing value of "n" the number of prime numbers decreases and thus also the number of prime number twins. Here is an example: if we replace "n" by the number 4 then the resulting numbers are 23 and 25 according to the formula $6n\pm1$. The number 23 is a prime number; however, the number 25 is the first one which does not follow the pattern.

If we assume that numbers have a controlling function in our world then it must be of great importance that the occurrence of prime numbers and their twins decreases with an increasing distance from zero (see Part 3).

2.8) The Three Musketeers in Action

In the thrilling novel by the French author *Alexandre Dumas* with the title *"The Three Musketeers"* three heroes join forces to fight for law and order. A small comparison illustrates again the resemblance to the order in our universe: here it is the three numbers 10, 24 and 81, which function as "musketeers".
We can find them everywhere in the universe in a variety of locations.
For example, all chemical elements in our universe, i.e. all the building blocks of our physical world, exist either as so-called pure substances or in a maximum of 10 small deviations as *isotopes*. As already mentioned, the number 10 characterizes the decimal system with which the majority of humans and cultures have calculated so successfully for thousands of years without feeling the need to look for something better.
Usually this choice is credited to the fact that humans count by using their ten fingers. It is hardly assumed possible today that there might be a real or even universal basis for this. However, it is legitimate to ask whether the number of fingers and toes we have, in a system of 10 ordered in 2x5, is not a strong indication of the real existence of the decimal system in our world.[10]
In the previous chapters I already answered in the affirmative for myself and provided evidence by means of intellectual experiments. It seems that any kind of physical existence can only be rationally imagined as the expansion of an initial finite singularity into a polar – opposite – and symmetrical duality. This duality as the proverbial flip side of the coin can be found always and everywhere in the world. It is the basis. Thus the representation of 10 fingers and toes in an inverse form of 2x5 seems immediately plausible and self-evident. The addition of all numbers from 1 to 10 results in the number 55. This number also features the number 5 twice and its cross total is also 10. The English mathematician *Barrow*, who certainly did not intend to integrate mysticism into the world of numbers, nevertheless states in his beautiful book *"Pi in the Sky"* that the number 10 is simply optimal. If the number were too small the calculation system would not be efficient enough and if the number were too large too many single digits and numerals would be needed. Furthermore, due to its *"pleasant symmetry"* the decimal system is very simple.
It is interesting to note that, when comparing the calculation systems which were used in 20 of the most important civilizations over the last few thousand years from the ancient Egyptians till modern times, 15 of them – or 75% – used the decimal system. Three of the civilizations used 20 as the basis and two used the basis of 60. These two numbers are merely a multiple of 10,

---

[10] This is the genetic configuration of all creatures on this earth and in view of the assumed universality also of all possible creatures in our universe.

though. Not one culture used "uneven" values although from an objective mathematical point of view in principle any kind of basis is suitable. Solely our computers today use the binary code with the basis 2 which must be seen, however, under completely different aspects. It makes a difference only between "being" and "not being", i.e. the information "1" and the information "0".

This is, however, nothing else but the absolute base and not a real calculation system. The binary code was also copied from nature, as I will show later.

Already the Babylonians, as well as the Mayas and the Chinese used denominational number systems in which the position of each digit defined its value. That corresponds with our number system which originated in India and was passed via the Arabian countries[11] to our western civilization.

The Hebrew alphabet, in which the original Christian Bible was written, starts with the letter "Alef" (א).

It consists of the letter Jota mirrored on a diagonal axis. Each Hebrew letter is related to a number and a symbol. The Jota corresponds to the number **10** and to the symbol of a hand with 5 fingers. The letter Alef is related to the number **1** and to the symbol of a bull. Since the Hebrew language consists only of consonants, the letter (A)l(e)f cannot really be pronounced which is why this first letter in the Hebrew alphabet is called the unpronounceable.

This kind of analysis entices us to play the whole range of numerological and religious symbols. The First (God) is unpronounceable (indescribable as it is meant in the biblical commandment when it says that people should not make pictures of God). It symbolizes strength, the power to act, the symbol of the bull. It includes all the symmetry and polarity which becomes evident in subsequent actions, i.e. in the manifestation of the idea in our world. Each of these symmetrical and polar manifestations contain the number **10** as the criterion of (complete) perfection on a (system-) level. Via this level the next one can be perceived.

The **10** corresponds with unity again but on the next higher level since it is a merely transported and, therefore, heightened version of **1**. The two hands ("the Jota in the Alef") simultaneously manifest the universal duality, expressed here in 2x5 fingers.

The basic order in our world is thus already included in the original, or divine, unity.

Strikingly, all this is expressed by one single Hebrew letter. I do not intend to go into further details here about the historical, mystical or religious references concerning the peculiarities of the number **10**. I already made some comments on this in Chapter 3. I would just like to emphasize again at this

---

[11] This is still noticeable since Arabs write numbers from left to right and letters from right to left.

point that the number **10** always symbolizes a typical new start on a new and simultaneously higher level, or in a completely different dimension. The parallels to the decimal system are apparent.

I think there lies at least a grain of truth in every mystical and religious primeval experience. Then this should certainly be understood as a clear indication that the decimal system is the favoured number system embodied in reality in our world.

This presupposes, of course, that numbers themselves are embodied in reality in our world, i.e. that they exist in reality. There are abundant further indications for this as the analysis of the number **24** will demonstrate.

In the previous chapter I pointed out the important group of prime numbers. They also seem to perform important controlling functions which I will explain later. Apart from the numbers 2 and 3, which probably have a special status due to certain circumstances, all prime numbers follow the formula $6n\pm1$ (see previous chapter).

Up until n=3 we always obtain prime number twins (5 and 7, 11 and 13 and 17 and 19). *Below* the number **24** (for n=4) we find the real prime number 23, *above* the number 24, however, there is no prime number. 25 is the *first prime number square*, i.e. 25 equals 5^2. from a purely mathematical point of view this means that the number **24** characterizes the first break, it being connected again with the 4th ordinal number (since the break occurs at n=4).

The alphabets of two important historic civilizations, i.e. the new Hebrew and the Greek alphabet, each possesses **24** letters. Other alphabets, like ours, for example, have more than one letter for similar or even the same sounds[12].

The writing in ancient Egypt also consists of **24** single-layered hieroglyphs. *Stelzner* wrote in his book that in mythology the number **24** always appears "when something single merges into something great".

In the New Testament of the Christian Bible we find the Book of Revelations of St. John. St. John describes his prophetic vision of the apocalypse: **24** thrones are arranged in a circle (!) with **24** elders sitting on them who will sit in final judgement over the world. Every year on the **24**th of December we celebrate Christmas Eve, the day when the light, personified by Jesus, the Son of God, came into the world and started a new era. And, of course, I would like to remind you again that our day has a cycle of **24** hours, which has been recognised in all civilizations since the time of the Babylonians but is still considered to be a mere human invention. Pythagoras was probably the first

---

[12] V and f, and c and z are pronounced in the same way in the German alphabet so that also only 24 different sounds remain.

to recognise that all pure (consonant) musical intervals together form integral relationships.

All this leads us to the assumption that humans too are "organized" according to integers; how else can we explain our ability to pick out immediately a dissonant chord, i.e. a chord not based on a whole-number relationship, as wrong or disharmonious and unsatisfying? If we sought to describe all musical intervals, i.e. octaves, quints and quarts, which are all in principle natural intervals of an octave, in continuous integers then we could only do so in a rhythm of **24**.

The biblical example of the revelation of St. John with its **24** thrones demonstrates as well the special arrangement of the **24** in the form of a circle or cyclically. Let us suppose that the religious-mystical contains a grain of truth, as in the adage "in dubio pro reo"[13], and let us assume that the number **24** may possess a real significance in our world. Then we are bound to conclude that in principle the number **24** arranges everything in the form of a circle.

This apparent cyclicity of the number 24 in our world can be supported by an every day observation: if with a high-speed camera we photograph a drop of water or milk falling on to the surface of the liquid we will notice that always, without exception 24 small droplets splash out in the form of a circle. My son Martin drew the sketch shown below. *Stelzner*, who also referred to this example, wrote: "*We can approach this phenomenon with physical and mathematical theories as often and as exactly as we wish: the 24 and their context remain*".

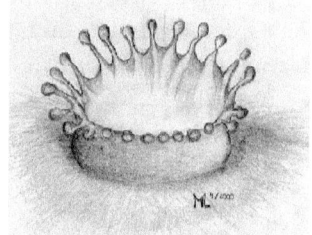

When a drop of water or milk falls on to the surface of the liquid, without exception exactly 24 small droplets splash out. This example also shows the cyclical interconnection between the partial and the entirity in our world.

We already know that the **10** as well as the **24** have a common mathematical background based on the first four ordinal numbers:

As is: $1 + 2 + 3 + 4 = 10$
So also is: $1 \times 2 \times 3 \times 4 = 24$

The first four ordinal numbers lead us to the first two "musketeers", the numbers 10 and 24, one by addition and one by multiplication.

The first four ordinal numbers can also be combined whereby the next higher type of arithmetical operation is introduced.

---

[13] Latin: in doubt for the defendant

For the third "musketeer" it follows: $\quad\quad\quad\quad\quad\quad\quad\quad\quad\quad 1^2 \times 3^4 = 81$

If we work with powers alone then we arrive at the starting number 1 again, because it is: $\quad\quad\quad\quad\quad\quad\quad\quad\quad\quad 1^{2 \times 3 \times 4} = 1$

In Chapter 2.4 I already explained how a perfect multiple, represented by the number **4**, can be generated from an initial first finite singularity, the circle, represented mathematically by the number **1**.

The square is the new unit in a recognizably higher dimension.

Of course, this "expansion" bypasses the numbers 2 and 3. All this seems very trivial at first. But, although it might sound so unbelievably simple, these four numbers nevertheless contain the central mathematical idea of the entire universe.

The use of all three possible (positive) arithmetical operations, i.e. addition, multiplication and powers (the three opposite negative operations follow on inevitably according to the laws of symmetry and polarity) enable the numbers 10, 24 and 81 – as well as the way back to the unity 1 – to be calculated from the first four ordinal numbers. For Pythagoreans the number 10 was the most perfect number of all. It is the characteristic and eponymous number of our decimal system which is, in my opinion, the favoured number system on which mathematics is based in our world.

The number 24 seems to be the characteristic number for all natural and cyclical processes in the universe.

Let me give you now some more comments concerning the number 81 which can also be naturally calculated from the first *four* ordinal numbers by the next higher type of arithmetical operation.

In chemistry lessons at school we learned about the periodical system of chemical elements. We were taught that there are **83** elements in our universe which are stable and natural. *Plichta* pointed out that actually there are only **81** natural and stable elements. Two in this series, the elements technicum (no. 43) and promethium (no. 61) are unstable and can only be produced artificially[14]. Of the remaining **81** elements the smallest element, hydrogen, with the atomic number **1** takes an outstanding position: it is the most abundant and most important element in the entire universe. All other elements are based on it.

It is almost like the star of a series of elements in which each element has exactly one proton[15] more than the preceding one. All elements in the world are arranged neatly in a harmonic order, and it is certainly no mere accident that this corresponds to the order of our ordinal numbers.

---

[14] Technetium was artificially produced for the first time in 1937 and Promethium in 1945.
[15] A proton is a positively charged particle of the atomic nucleus.

If we accept that the decimal system is the favoured and real numerical system embodied in our world then we may also divide the number 1 in a different denominational position, e.g. the 100, by 81.

This produces the result 1,234567(8)(9)(10)(11)(12)....(∞)[16], which means that the reciprocal value of 81 shows all ordinal numbers up to infinity. The inverse value is polar-symmetrical to the initial value.

This also means that our numbers are an inversion of the real embodied, natural maximum expansion of all matter which is controlled by the number 81. Here again the number 1 holds a prominent position.

This is why the genetic code of all life should also be controlled by the number 81 and this seems to apply to the entire universe. Modern biologists, however, see this in a completely different way. Often and, in my opinion, too hastily and carelessly, this code is even described as "degenerate".

In the genetic code four possible organic molecules, so-called bases, are arranged in groups of three, known as triplets. Each one of these 4 molecules represents, in a manner of speaking, one letter of the genetic alphabet.

Each genetic "word" consists of three letters and one word then determines which amino acid (AA), the smallest building block, is fitted into a protein, the building material of all life.

There are 20 different amino acids. Depending on the code they can be combined at random to form long molecular chains, i.e. proteins. Proteins are not only the essential material for all forms of life but are also the builders and their tools needed for working *within* an organism, i.e. the enzymes.

If, then, four different bases, arranged in groups of three, are responsible for the linking of 20 possible amino acids together to form long protein molecules, then we discover that there are $4^3 = 64$ possible combinations for the encoding of amino acids. It follows that several of these base triplets must be responsible for one and the same amino acid. Biologists consider this to be an extravagance of nature and describe the genetic code, therefore, as degenerate.

But this is by no means the case! On the contrary, this code is extremely "cunning" in that – and I already explained this in my previous books – it effectively eliminates the risk of accidental changes, i.e. mutations, which in most cases cause more damage then benefit. I will explain this in detail in the next chapter. At this point I highlight the most important perception: up to now, nobody has recognised that, although the calculation $4^3 = 64$ is

---

[16] This arithmetical operation for representing the periodical fraction with infinite positions along all ordinal numbers (also beyond the number 10) is simple but shall not be explained in detail here. For further reference I recommend to have a look in mathematical textbooks.

arithmetically correct, it is by no means important for the number of possible encodings.
The proposition was utterly wrong.
A thorough analysis of the possible base combinations enabled me to prove for the first time that the number of possible *triplets* is of no importance whatsoever. It is more the evaluation (or the position) of the bases *within* the triplet which decides the type of amino acid to be encoded. In the last instance there is always only one single base *position* which decides the combination of a protein. If we transform the genetic code into such a positional system then exactly 84 possible base *positions* can be observed. Three of these base *positions*, however, generate so-called nonsense-triplets. As the term already indicates they are unable to transport one single amino acid. Indeed, when they appear, all further protein production is terminated. In the end this leaves 81 ($=3^4$) effective base positions by which amino acids can be combined to proteins.
Among the chemical elements hydrogen takes a prominent position, as we have seen, since it is the starting point for all further elements. The genetic code also has *one* triplet, defined by *one single* base position, which sets off the whole range of protein production. It is known as the start codon.
To our amazement it seems that everything from chemistry and biology – and this includes all the elements and the entire genotype – is defined by one and the same number, 81, in the form of 80 + 1. As I have already demonstrated, the number 81 can be derived from the numbers 1 to 4.
The question now arises, of course, as to the meaning of the factor 1^2 or why I chose *all* the first four ordinal numbers to calculate the number 81, whereas a calculation with only the numbers 3 and 4 as in 3^4 may seem quite sufficient. This appears correct only at first glance; the incorporation of 1^2 is absolutely essential and points us in the right direction!
Only one calculation is needed for each of the "musketeers" 10 and 24, in one case an addition and in the other a multiplication. If I calculate the number 81 in "my very own way", i.e. with all the first four ordinal numbers $1^2 \times 3^4$, I now use *two* different arithmetical operations.
And here we have yet another important key – subtly hidden – for enabling us to understand our world:
The numbers 10 and 24, in exactly that order, describe the purely spiritual and immaterial basis of our universe: The number 10 defines the numerical system to which all things relate. All numerical systems are in principle equal in worth but one is favoured and this preference is explainable. With the number 10 the first decision is made. On this lowest level it is decided on which basis the

numbers are to work and control. Mathematically the smallest "musketeer" can also be derived from the simplest arithmetical operation, the addition.

When it has been clarified just *how* mathematics is to work in our world, then it must be decided on the next level *how* the world is to expand. This involves the question of the space *within and with which* our physical universe will later exist. A decision must be made at this point as to *how* everything should be arranged in number and form and how it should all expand.

The most obvious result of this decision is the "circle" which is defined and controlled by the number 24. From a mathematical point of view it results from the next higher arithmetical operation, the multiplication of the first four integers. This arithmetical operation is also still "homogenous", i.e. only one calculation method is used since the result is still something purely immaterial which is encoded: the number 24 is the spiritual information for order and expansion of all processes and events.

But the third number, the 81, is the first having anything to do directly with matter. It defines the maximum quantitative expansion, i.e. the number and distribution of the most important goods *within* space.

Now, at this point, something of utmost importance happens: although 81 can also be derived from the first four numbers, now, for the first time, it is reached by *two different* arithmetical operations. The number 3^4, which itself results in 81, stands for the maximum expansion of all purely physical matter. But, in consequence, the factor 1^2 is now a sign that all matter is in actual fact a combination of two completely different parts, one of which can be and is easily overlooked since it possesses nothing physical. The factor 1^2 proves in a purely mathematical-logical way that every kind of matter simultaneously possesses something that "adheres" to it, which seems to be "invisible" but nevertheless belongs to it imperatively: it is the pure *information* "to be" – or, in other words, the *information* of its own existence!

Every kind of matter informs us of its existence by way of the "BEING" which is inseparably connected with it. Any kind of physical existence be it ever so small is also composed of information, any kind of complex existence of an appropriately complex information. Any kind of information, and thus also that of the "BEING", is something immaterial, something spiritual. It follows that spirit is an inseparable part of matter.

Any kind of matter carries something spiritual. Both are the two sides of one and the same coin. It is mathematics which suggests this perception logically and unambiguously.

Mathematics provides the *proof* that there is a universal, very subtle dualism between the spiritual information of all existence and its physical part. And since the omission of the arithmetical operation 1^2 is perfectly possible from the mathematical point of view when calculating the number 81, it proves that the connection between spirit and matter is not bound to obey the thermodynamic conservation laws.

By means of my "divine analogy" in Chapter 2.10 I will explain this in more detail. Here at this point, I would just like to state that all kinds of matter in this world actually possess an informational (spiritual) *and* a physical BEING simultaneously. And it now becomes clear that any expansion, any formation and any construction of physical BEING inevitably possesses a spiritual quality at the same time. And, of course, due to this spiritual quality, all matter, since it is also based on spiritual and not merely on physical principles, also possesses an eternal aspect.

2.9) A Truly Smart Genetic Code

Genetics deals with hereditary changes from generation to generation. In 600 B.C. already the Greek poet *Theognis of Megara (540-470 B.C.)* criticized the marriage habits of his fellow citizens in that they preferred to choose their partners for commercial reasons. He claimed that a choice based on character had resulted in the best of breeding successes in animals.

In his book *"The Republic"* Plato *(427-347 B.C.)* ponders over the possibilities of achieving an *"Enhancement of Mankind"* by appropriate selective breeding. *Aristotle (384-322 B.C.)* already assumed that sperm was the carrier of hereditary transmission. I already discussed in my previous books the revolutionary discoveries of the famous English natural scientist *Charles Darwin (1809-1882)* and our modern evolutionary theories based on his ideas. I will come back to this in Part 4.

A number of other scientists searched for a comprehensive theory which could describe the mechanisms of inheritance – however, many attempts remained unsuccessful. The first approach, which is still valid today, was developed by pure luck by the Augustinian abbot *Gregor Mendel (1822-1884)* in 1859. By choosing the garden pea Mendel focussed on very suitable research material since peas are self-pollinating and contamination by external pollen can be prevented. In addition, he was very lucky insofar as the characteristics which he observed and counted in successive generations were positioned on different chromosomes. Chromosomes were unknown in Mendel's day.

Today we can compare them in a simple way to single volumes of an extensive encyclopaedia. Although Mendel's results were published in 1865 in the Journal of the *Natural History Society* of *Brno* – today in the Czech Republic – they remained unnoticed for almost 40 years. In about 1900 Mendel's work was rediscovered by three botanists, the Dutchman *Hugo de Vries (1890-1964)*, the German *Carl Correns (1864-1933)* and the Austrian *Erich Edler von Tschermak-Seysenegg (1871-1962)* and it soon became very popular.

Mendel's Laws clearly proved that certain phenomena are inherited over all generations according to certain rules.

The cell-biologists *James Watson (*1928)* and *Francis Crick (1916-2004)*, who used a molecular-biological decoding method to decode the bio-chemically inherited substance DNA[17] in 1953, made it possible to examine and prove in a plausible and experimental manner the "how" of inheritance on the molecular level. According to this, our genetic material, the genome, consists of two chains of organic chemical constituents entwined around each other, which is generally known as the double helix. Yet, "organic-chemical" by no means signifies "life". Such material is merely a necessary preliminary stage in accommodating, or better perhaps, in enveloping "life" in this physical universe. However, these extremely complex molecules can by no means be considered as life itself.

At a certain phase during the division of a cell *(mitosis)* this "double helix chaos", comparable to a ball of wool, presents itself as separate threads, known as chromosomes.

They are composed biochemically of long chains of nucleic acids which are, therefore, collectively known as *DNA* or *RNA*, depending on their function and structure. Each of these nucleic acids consists of a large number of smaller units known as nucleotides.

One helix spiral is complete after every 10 nucleotides, entwined in an anti-clockwise (left) direction. Each nucleotide possesses 3 components, one phosphoric acid molecule, one sugar molecule with five carbon atoms per molecule (pentose), and one base. The base alone is the decisive factor since it determines the genetic code of each nucleotide.

In other words only the bases represent the letters of the genetic alphabet. There are 4 different bases in the DNA, adenin (A), guanine (G), cytosine (C) and thymine (T) and in the RNA thymine is replaced by uracil (U). Due to various processes, which I will not explain in detail here, these 4 letters of the genetic code are used to combine so-called α-amino acids (α-AA), the building blocks of all life, to proteins.

Now, nature always combines 3 bases together to form a triplet. We can compare the triplet to a word and say that each word of the genetic code consists of exactly 3 letters. And a triplet always carries one amino acid. Bases which are arranged in a different way in a triplet probably encode a different amino acid.

---

[17] DNS = Deoxyribonucleic acid, chain molecule of the genome.

There are exactly 20 different amino acids. Today another 2 are usually added. However they are only variants of the recognised 20 α-AAs.
In such cases a nonsense-triplet, which normally contributes nothing to the protein synthesis (see below), is used incorrectly.[18]
The arrangement of the bases to triplets is essential for logical reasons. Only by using 4 x 4 x 4 (= 4^3 = 64) bases can the known 20 (basic- or α-) amino acids be encoded. If there were only two bases combined in "duplets" to encode one AA, then only a maximum of 16 (=4 x 4), i.e. four amino acids less than necessary, could be encoded.
However, as there are theoretically far more possibilities with 4^3 = 64 to encode the available 20 amino acids there is usually more than one triplet available for the transport of each AA. This is of great importance. It seems to be one of the reasons for the random influences on the genotype, such as *mutations,* remaining much less pronounced, i.e. less noticeable than genetic scientists usually assume.
Furthermore, I believe nature actually protects the genotype rather effectively against mutations because in fact a greater number of possible codes renders the protein synthesis less prone to interference.
However, modern biologists describe the genetic code as being "degenerate" because of the great number of possibilities. I call this ridiculous. They seem to think that nature is extravagant and wasteful just because fewer codes would be sufficient. The word "degenerate" is used here in a rather negative sense. I do not believe it is like that at all. With 4^3, or 64, theoretical possibilities of combination, we see superficially indeed an inversion of the elementary 3^4-law which we know and which led us to the third musketeer, the number 81.
However, the number 4^3 is by no means decisive. In fact, the number 81, i.e. 3^4, is far more important for protein synthesis.
I was the first to demonstrate this in detail already in 1999. For understanding universal laws this perception is of fundamental importance.
The following illustration of a code sun, drawn by my son Alexander, makes this clear. The base names of the t-RNA are abbreviated by their initials (A-U-G-C).

---

[18] Selenocystein, discovered in 1996, "misused" the triplet UGA, frequently found, and pyrrolysin, discovered in 2004, "misused" the triplet UAG, found in so-called archaebacteria.

By means of *four* bases, which are always arranged in groups of *three*, known as nucleotide-triplets, all 20 amino acids (α-AAs), which are combined in biological bodies to proteins, can be encoded by the genetic code. In so doing several triplets may determine one and the same AA. For example, 9 AAs are linked by 2 triplets each.

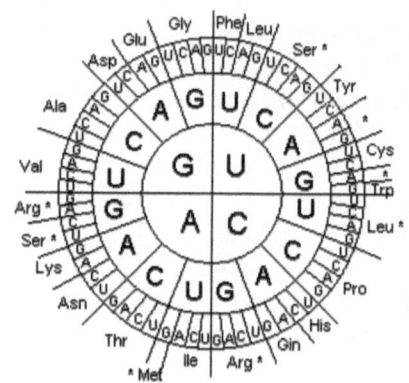

In total 84 code *positions* can be created. Three of them, however, encode so-called nonsense-triplets, i.e. there is no AA available for them and they always terminate a synthesizing process. Thus exactly 81 – or 3^4 – exact code *positions* remain. One of these codes always operates as the start-codon (AUG).
In the same way as the table of elements lists 81 natural and stable chemical elements in the whole of the universe, the genotype of all life in this universe is also based on 81 "contractually effective" code positions. They clearly determine the position of each genetic letter, the nucleotide with its free bases. If one of these letters is altered by mutation or if it is altogether deleted so that the configuration of the triplets is relocated, it would not render the entire text unreadable. By marking a fixed position in the compound the body "knows" immediately where the problem lies and is able to eliminate it before it causes major modifications in the total construction.
Like hydrogen, which adopts a special position in the classification of chemical elements, the start-codon characterizes a similarly unique position in the genetic code. In both cases nature works with the number 81 in the form of "80+1".
In the same way as 20 so-called *pure* forms of elements exist among these 80 chemical elements, exactly 20 *alpha*-amino acids are encoded by 80 possible combinations.
If we assume, as I suggested, that the genetic code works by means of 81 exact and contractually effective position specifications, then single mutations cannot bring so much "misreading" into the process which induces the production of proteins (protein bio-synthesis). Incorrect base positions occurring during protein synthesis would attract attention and the repairing powers in the body would straighten everything out. This would confirm common observations that, although mutations occur frequently and often cause great damage (e.g. cancer), in most cases the organism seems able to

cope with them. It recognises them, as I assume, because they simply carry a "wrong" number. With the advancing age of an organism the ability to recognise this error and to eliminate it decreases, and that is why cancer occurs more often.

However, for the understanding of evolution, my theory has tremendous consequences. Mutations as the engines of evolution are gradually degraded (not, however, eliminated). At the beginning of the evolution of all life mutations may have played an important role, however, the further evolution *mechanisms* progressed the more other and increasingly more target-orientated instruments were developed which started to influence and control the entire evolution.

Here it is again clearly demonstrated that a strict order is recognisable through the number 81 alone. It is valid for all stable and natural elements of our universe as well as for our genome, the genetic code. This seems to me to be rather conclusive proof that neither the genetic code nor the number of elements in our universe is based on accidental events.

The number 81 can be derived from the numbers 3 and 4 written as 3^4.
This value also results if the famous equation of *Albert Einstein* $E = mc^2$ is squared and we write $E^2 = m^2 c^4$, whereby c is the velocity of light with the factor 3 (x a power of 10).
It follows: $E^2 = m^2 \times 3^4$
As already demonstrated in the previous chapter, in the decimal system the factor 3^4 (=81) equals the reciprocal value of all ordinal numbers from "1" to infinity.
There are 20 α-amino acids and 20 pure elements – elements without variants (pure isotopes) – in the universe. They all occur in the form of "19+1". For example one AA has only one single carbon atom, all the remaining 19 have at least two. They are optically active. 19 out of 20 pure isotopes carry an uneven number of protons and only 1 element has an even number of protons.
There must be reasons why nature works in this manner. If we add 19 to 81 the result is 100, which, from a decimal point of view, is simply a further digit. No other arbitrary calculation system could demonstrate this in the same manner.
In the previous chapter I explained why the number 81 should not be described merely by 3^4, but rather in the form of $1^2 \times 3^4$, i.e. by using all the first four ordinal numbers.
Similarly the numbers 24 and 10 were derived from the first four ordinal numbers by addition or multiplication.

Thus it becomes recognizable that our entire physical universe is based on the columns of the number 1 to 4. Simplex sigillum veri (est).[19]

2.10) A Divine Metaphor

"There are innumerable definitions of God. However, I worship God solely as the Truth". This quotation goes back to *Mahatma Gandhi*, the great Indian statesman and it certifies his deep religiousness. In this chapter I will attempt to demonstrate the divine origin of our world in a small but very appropriate metaphor.
Again mathematics will help, especially since meanwhile the fundamental importance it seems to have in the entire universe will have become rather clear.
Let us examine the value "1" in more detail; mathematically it represents the first (whole number) reality.
The number 1 stands for the initial circle, the first finite point in my intellectual experiment in Chapter 2.4. Herewith growth and propagation can be constructed by following simple geometrical rules. Step by step the decisive numbers of our universe are thereby generated.
Therefore, we may ask now, where does the number 1 come from? – How is it generated?
Of course, the "1" as number must be also spiritually determined just like the smallest finite point (circle), which geometrically represents the number 1.
This circle is defined by 3 just as real but non-finite information points. Initially this gives us a somewhat abstract analogy for the principle the knowledge of which is essential if we want to understand the true development of our world.
In later chapters I will imbue this statement plentifully with "practical life". My perception, which I find myself repeating, is mostly consistent with the mainstream perceptions of almost all religions, myths and early philosophers.
Mathematically we can extract the square root of 1^2 the result of which is 1. Since 1^2 represents the same value as simply 1 and since the root of 1 can also be -1, we may establish the following simple series:
$(-1)^2 = +1$ and $(+1)^2 = 1^2 = 1$ or $1^2 = (-1)^4$.
If we can take the square root of +1 then, logically, it must also be possible to take the square root of -1. Everybody knows, however, that there is no mathematically deducible rational number which when multiplied by itself, i.e. when squared, results in −1. "Human" mathematics reaches its limits here, limits unknown to logic, of course. The Italian mathematician *Rafaello Bombelli*

---

[19] Latin: "Simplicity is the hallmark of truth" – one of my favourite quotations.

(1526-1572) was the first to introduce the so-called imaginary number "i" to account for this.

It represents the number which irrefutably must exist in reality, but which we humans with the means at our disposal obviously cannot describe. Therefore, it is described as imaginary, but – it has to be emphasized again – there is no doubt at all that it must exist.

We can only describe it as a picture or maybe as a letter. Mathematics – here reduced to a system of numerical logic – *proves* to us in quite a different way, i.e. by the very necessity of introducing the imaginary number "i", the existence and the influence of a completely different and yet just as real dimensionality.

It follows: $i^2 = -1$ und $(-1)^2 = +1$ und $(+1)^2 = 1^2$ $[= 1 = (-1)^4]$.

I will apply this simple relationship now to my theories. Then we can assume that every kind of physical existence, e.g. in the simplest case the geometrically depictable finite point, the "smallest" circle, must inevitably be generated from something which surely exists but which we cannot describe or express any further with elements of the same system.

This demonstrates that we humans can *neither* explain with the system properties known to us, *nor* perceive with our senses the cause and the beginning of our own existence or that of the universe which we inhabit.

Yet, if we accept the comparison mathematics offers us then it follows that no first finite reality, whatever its properties, can be generated from *nothing*.

And the nothing is mathematically symbolized in our western civilization by *zero* thanks to *Leonardo Fibonacci of Pisa*.

We can then establish that in addition to the zero as a "number" representing nothing, there are obviously *two* symmetrical integral real existences, *one on each* side, i.e. **-1** and **+1**.

Mathematics not only illustrates the geometrical development of points and circles, as already employed in my intellectual game about a geometrically controlled logic point and circle development, but it also provides us with another beautiful analogy for the creation of our entire world.

This can also be applied to all further evolutionary developments.

Everything in the world began as a creation from an entity which we cannot further describe or even imagine. This creation was certainly not a unique act but a long process and it is impossible to obtain detailed information about its beginning and its progress. This unimaginable on which this creation is based, is known as "God" in all religions. The irrational value "**i**" invented by mathematical manipulation can in this metaphor be considered as being the smallest unit of God – a gross over-simplification, of course.

It is from the "i", and not from *zero* or *nothing*, that two real, yet separate, symmetrical and polar levels of existence are generated one after the other.

One of them is our physical world: this is the *later* level of existence and can clearly be described in its manifestation and expansion with the positive integers and their squares, starting with 1^2. The other, the earlier reality, which is hidden and largely invisible from the physical world, must then logically be in form and content symmetrical and polar to the first, i.e. it must be on a purely spiritual level.

In the beginning an incomplete, not yet differentiated, spiritual reality is generated and in the course of eons differentiated by an indescribable and unimaginable higher spiritual entity, which we call God. Step by step by means of and together with this spiritual entity the physical world is created and simultaneously further developed in harmony with the spiritual entity. Finally, both worlds are inseparably interconnected.

This, which I deduce with logic but which I must painstakingly explain step by step to convince the spirit of our time to rejuvenate the belief in God and our spirit, was more easily understood by people of past times. I believe, they had the better deal. To explain these relationships in the Bible it says in plain and simple words, Genesis, 1.1: *"In the beginning God created the heavens and the earth."*

Our ancestors surely knew that "heaven" meant the spiritual world and that "earth" stood for the physical world. Today we are naive enough to believe that God is *in* the (cosmic) sky and that dead souls are on "cloud seven". The same almost infantile naivety is revealed by the reply the French astronomer *Pierre Laplace (1749-1827)* gave to *Napoleon's* question as to God's whereabouts in his *Mécanique céleste*[20]: *"Sire je n'avais pas besoin de cette hypothèse"*[21]. Russian cosmonauts expressed similar opinions in the 1960s.

Are you thinking that my perception is merely a nice theory? Not at all!

There is no doubt that the Golden Section, imperfectly described by the ratio with the number sequence 618, i.e. 1.618..., has a central significance in our world. It is not for nothing that it is also known as the "divine division" and not for nothing that we are fascinated by the fact that somehow real perfection is always connected with it. The number sequence 2-7-3 also keeps recurring. It shows that we have come up against the limits of feasibility. In its form 1.273... in my little model of creation it is the result of the division of the square as the first new perfection in multiplicity by the initial circle (see

---

[20] French: mechanics of heaven
[21] French: "Sire, this hypothesis was never required."

Chapter 2.4). The limit of feasibility in my world model also signifies an interface between the physical and the spiritual world which creates and precedes it.

According to my metaphor the ratio 1,273... equals "-1" and the "Golden Section", i.e. 1.618..., "+1". In the same manner as the "-1" is the square root of "+1", so is the transcendental number 1.273... the square root of 1.618... - with a deviation of only 3,7%.

Interesting is also the other end of the scale. My figurative comparison of the development of this world out of "i" (= indescribable, divine origin) via "-1" (= spiritual reality) to +1 (= physical manifestation) up to $(+1)^2$ (= growth and propagation of physical manifestation) leads us to another logical conclusion.
Between zero and ±1 there is a limited (*finite*) distance which can accommodate *infinitely* many numbers, i.e. all reciprocal values of 1 (= 1/1) via 1/2, 1/3, 1/4, to 1/∞.
On the other side the distance for the infinite number of possible integers, the ordinal numbers over zero, is not restricted. *Infinitely* many numbers on an *infinitely* long distance.

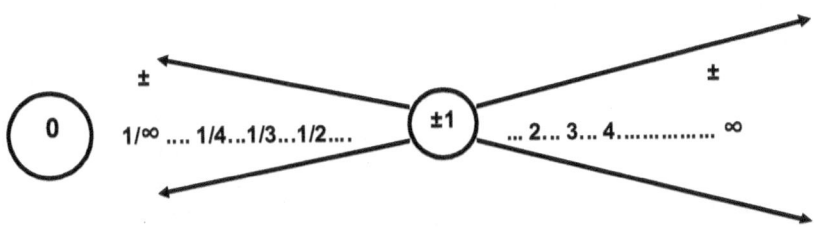

All matter follows a growth and a disintegration process. Both progress according to a universal pattern and are described by a mathematical function on the basis of the transcendental number "e". This goes back to the Swiss mathematician *Leonhard Euler (1707-1783)*.[22] Growth and disintegration are opposites, whereby growth is (theoretically) infinite and simultaneously unlimited, whilst any kind of disintegration can also be (theoretically) infinite, yet simultaneously it must be limited by its original state and its quantity.
If we transfer this thought to my metaphor from "i" via "-1" to "+1" and finally to $(+1)^2$, then Euler's number "e" must be represented by $(+1)^2$. As I have explained, the number "+1" as the "metaphoric interface signifies the

---

[22] Euler's number e = 2,718281828459...; the equation is: $f(x) = f_0 e^x$

Golden Section. If we square 1.618... the result is 2.618... The difference of this product to the irrational Euler number is again only 3.7%.

If we now transfer my "divine metaphor" to a product of the physical world which has irrefutably gone through a long period of spiritual evolution, to simplify matters let us choose mankind, then it follows: we humans must partly be *limited* and yet simultaneously we must have an *infinite* part within this finiteness (limitation). There must also be an *unlimited* and *infinite* part. The only plausible explanation which accommodates both these requirements is that humans possess a limited body with a limited brain, but an unlimited spirit. They both exist independently of one another and yet together like two sides of a coin. The same applies to life as the inevitable limit of the limited part: every human being must die. However, death affects only the physical part of humans and their spirit. The lifetime of the body is limited, but the spirit cannot be considered as being limited. Death is the interface beyond which the spirit develops further in eternity, i.e. temporally unlimited.

In the same way as in my analogy "-1" is polar and symmetrical to "+1" and surely absolutely real, so are the spiritual and the physical world two realities which are polar and symmetrical to one another in a uniform whole world.

Both realities are as real as you and I, both of us being in fact only externally physical creatures. Maybe we should say that the spiritual part of the world is some kind of "parallel universe", although this term is usually used in science fiction and means something completely different in that context.

The *spiritual* part of this one world is the starting point and precursor for the development of the *physical* part of the world, i.e. for something *we* perceive as our universe. The spirit also provides the central ideas and thus the principally spiritual basis for all the physical beings generated later. The spirit is the world of immaterial information for any kind of being. It is the other side of the same coin.

In our modern language the spiritual world can best be compared to an immeasurably gigantic internet. It is "God's internet".

In contrast to *Plato's (approx. 427-347 B.C.)* theories and those of his many spiritual disciples up to the present day, the spiritual world does not, in my opinion, provide us with anything approaching all the ideas for everything which is already finished in this physical world.

"God's Internet" is more or less empty and undifferentiated at the beginning except for some basic and rather simple rules and parameters.

It represents, therefore, only an enormous potential which must be discovered and differentiated, i.e. it must be filled in. Here I would like to refer to the ancient Chinese philosopher *Lao Tzu (approx. 7th century B.C).* and his *"Tao-Te-*

King", which roughly translated means *"The Book of the Way and its Virtue"* or the book of the spiritual rules of this world.

Lao Tzu talks of a more profound secret within the secret, the *"Wu Gi"* in which all differences are still inseparate and indiscriminate and which is usually depicted by a simple circle! Within this circle the mere possibility of being is found, in a manner of speaking this is chaos.

As the French mathematician and astronomer *Pierre Laplace (1749-1827)* was able to show about 200 years ago, our world would have had no chance whatsoever of creatively producing anything new, i.e. what we call emergence, if there had been ready-made models for everything.

The "continuous creation of new forms and systems on the basis of already existing ones" is, however, surely a very important characteristic of our world.

But I can neither agree with the many modern scientists, such as some decades ago the Austrian philosopher *Karl Popper 1902-1994)*, who claim an accidental emergence as being the *sole* engine for *any* kind of development in the world. My position is *between* Plato and Popper and I believe that any emergence is subject to certain parameters to which it adheres.

This is why I can give no credence to the suggestion that some amazing physical natural laws and extremely limited natural constants occurred suddenly and by accident and the rest was "perpetually" left to its own devices in a purely physical world. I rather believe that a continuous interaction took place between two worlds existing in reality, the spiritual world and the material world, the latter of which is usually the only one we recognise and accept.

They are probably two sides of one and the same coin which continuously but very subtly influence one another as the ancient Chinese symbol of Yin and Yang suggests. The spiritual reality is the one which influences the physical part of this world initially with the aid of certain universally applicable principles of order. Among these are the principles of simple geometrical forms and ordinal numbers. Over extremely long periods of time the initially scarcely differentiated spiritual background can and must change continuously due to the constant feedback it receives from the slowly developing physical world until it is finally perfected.

Highest perfection with a maximum of variety is the cosmic maxim.

This is in some respects characterised by that which the French theologian and anthropologist *Teilhard de Chardin (1881-1955)* described as the Omega Point. According to this we are all in one sense God – a God in emergence.

It seems possible to be able to draw on metaphors based on simple mathematical relationships in order to construct a plausible explanatory model for the world. This is so *because* we can see that such a model inevitably – and regardless of the calculation system on which it is based – produces certain numbers which inherently impose themselves on us at especially significant points in our physical world. Therefore, we can move a step further and be even more precise:

From the real – but for us imaginary - "i", being the smallest comparable unit of "divine transcendence", emerges the divine *idea* of a world *"in his own image"*. Divine thoughts or, in the words of the Bible, *"God's Word"*, correspond to i^2, which is the same as -1, the analogy for the spirit.

It follows that the manifestation of this idea as a spiritual world is $(-1)^2$. This is simultaneously +1, which already indicates the coming physical transformation or the interface, since the "1" (here: +1) stands for the initial circle which has not yet achieved a spatial dimension. The square of +1, i.e. $(+1)^2$, represents the smallest "real physical" existence. There are two number sequences originating from +1, the first of which being the sequence of all ordinal numbers from 1 to infinity. This represents the spatial four-dimensional expansion.

The second is the sequence of their inverted values, i.e. 1/1, 1/2, 1/3, 1/4 etc. to 1/infinite. This is also an infinite number sequence. However, in contrast to the first it is spatially limited, since it its limited by 1 and zero. It represents all physical existence, i.e. all three-dimensional objects in our world. Universal space is infinite; all objects contained in it, however, are limited – i.e. they are three-dimensional.

Since we usually write $(+1)^2 = 1^2$ as just 1 it is especially easy not to notice that it is also $(-1)^4$. Therefore, in the analogy I chose, we tend to overlook the actual spiritual background and the spiritual origin of all physical existence.

In every smallest physical existence, i.e. in every randomly chosen *finite* point, the (purely spiritual) information of its *existence* is inherent. Each and every existence also possesses a purely spiritual side, the information of its BEING.

This theory could already be deduced from the necessity of describing the number 81, this being the measuring unit for physical expansion, not simply as 3^4 but, rationally, as $1^2 \times 3^4$ (see Chapter 2.8).

Every single atom, therefore, is *not just* a mere physical, finite, small point in our cosmos. It simultaneously also provides the information that this atom

exists. In the same manner every single human being – constructed of zillions of atoms in extreme complexity – is thereby an immense immaterial field of information which is an absolutely perfect three-dimensional "informal" mirror image of each and every one of us. Since this mirror image is already inherent in a physically manifested human being, it of course remains intact even if its physical environment collapses, or if the human being dies.
Every single existence in this universe, be it animate or inanimate, is – according to my analogy – a coin with two sides which are symmetrical and polar to each other.
Each existence has one side for its physical identity and the other for its immaterial information of its BEING – however complex this may be. It is extremely exciting for me to work out the consequences of this for our perception of the animate and inanimate world and for such important existential matters as infinity, eternity or immortality.
The great German philosopher and naturalist *Gottfried Wilhelm Leibniz (1646-1716)* wrote 300 years ago: *"Imaginary numbers are a fine and wonderful refuge for the divine spirit, almost an amphibian between to be and not to be."*[23]

2.11) Six Rules Define the World

From the previous 10 chapters we can draw the following conclusions:

1) **Nothing comes from nothing:** Zero, nothing, is the opposite of being, but nothing can be generated there from. In Cologne, my beautiful birthplace, this has always been common knowledge.

2) **No BEING stands alone:** Everything has a polar mirror image. In the same way as "+1" there is also "-1". Matter is mirrored in spirit.
Everything is ordered according to symmetry and polarity, i.e. in diametrical opposition.

3) **All being emerges from BEING:** We are unable, however, to describe the last BEING in detail and we are incapable of imagining it.
Just as we can extract the square root of "+1", which is "-1", so must there also be a square root of "-1". Although it is impossible to quantify it, it must nevertheless exist. We simply cannot imagine it. This root is known by mathematicians as "i". And "i" is thus the smallest *symbol* for the real existence of God.

---

[23] Quoted from Simon Singh, "Fermat's last Theorem", see List of References.

4) **All BEING is interdependent:** In the same way as "i" produces "-1" and "-1" produces "+1" so all spiritual matter emanates from God and all physical matter emanates from spiritual matter. The Bible tells us simply and aptly: *"In the beginning God created the heavens and the earth."* In this analogy spirit becomes the heaven and matter earth.

5) **Every BEING develops itself consistently forward:** If something is generated, i.e. it IS – regardless whether it is "-1" (metaphorically: spirit) or "+1" (metaphorically: matter) – then it develops itself further in eternity (without temporal limit):
"-1" becomes "-2", then "-3" until "infinitely minus", "+1" becomes "+2", etc. until "infinitely plus".

6. **Only physical matter is finite and limited, while spiritual matter is infinite and eternal:** Physical matter is always developed from something spiritual. Therefore (spiritual) information of BEING, i.e. something purely spiritual, adheres to all physical matter. It is merely the other side of the coin. Whilst everything physical is subject to decay and is thus temporally limited, this does not apply to its other side, the (spiritual) information of its BEING. The information of its BEING is infinite and will remain in existence even if the physical matter no longer exists in its original form: the side of information is eternal. It follows, as I already explained in the previous chapter, that there will never be an end to a personality which has once been generated since it is something purely spiritual.

And, unlike the strange procession in Echternach (Luxembourg) in which people take two steps forward and one step back, each single personality will continue its forward develop forevermore.

The objective of this world is to achieve its spiritualization in maximum variety and highest perfection. The spirit returns to itself.

Maximum variety also means, however, that nature prefers the individual when the spirit becomes aware of it.

This is the case with humans. One of the greatest thinkers of the Middle Ages, the Scotsman *John Duns Scotus (1265-1308)*, already emphasized the importance of human individuality and remarked that the individual is the *"true aim of nature"*.[24]

---

[24] By the way, during the last two years of his life Duns Scotus taught at the university in my hometown, Cologne, and he was buried there after he died.

Every single personality keeps on developing itself forever and in so doing contributes to the perfection of the world.

We in our mundane lives already notice that our perception of time becomes increasingly subjective and blurred with advancing age, and time seems to run faster each year; the pure spirit, however, no longer feels time at all, since time is non-existent for it. Eternity is not boring. I will explain this in more detail later.

2.12) Everything is Ordered in Measurement and Number

We know **three**-dimensional, closed spaces and bodies, and I believe that a spatial **four**-dimensionality of an infinite space exists in reality. The starting point of all this is the finite singularity of the circle which expands and creates the **second** which is polar-symmetrical to the finite singularity. The first four ordinal numbers are reflected in my little "history of creation".

The addition of the first **four** ordinal numbers leads to the number **10**. It seems no mere coincidence that in this world we prefer the **decimal** system for calculations.

If the first **four** ordinal numbers are multiplied by one another we arrive at the number **24**, and, as I suggested, by a *rational* combination of these four numbers, multiplied and written in the power mode, we arrive at the number **81**.

They all are important key numbers in our universe. By means of a simple geometrical growth and propagation process and by way of two transcendental geometrical ratios (1.618... and 1.273...) we arrive at the very important number sequences **2-7-3** and **6-1-8**.

Both are irrational numbers and thus an expression of the imperfect implementation of the spirit in the physical world. The number **273** seems to be the constant for the maximum expansion within the bounds of feasibility, whilst the number **618** seems to stand for optimal realizations, i.e. for perfection.

If the most important so-called natural constants are considered from this point of view, amazing things become apparent:

All natural constants are rigid physical quantities which can be measured experimentally and which describe those special key parameters found in science for the existence of all matter in the physical universe as we know it. One of the declared aims of dedicated scientists is, of course, to connect these numbers in a rational way, i.e. to develop a common universal theory.

But, they have not yet succeeded in doing so. At first glance my ideas in this direction also seem rather farfetched. Nonetheless, I believe this is a legitimate and also plausible attempt to lend support to my hypothesis of combination which is consistently based on simple mathematical logical considerations.

Each of these natural constants fluctuates only very slightly around the measured value – at the very most by a few percentage points. Were they not as stable as they obviously are – and that is undisputed among all scientists involved – then our universe could not exist, nor could atoms or solid matter, nor could galaxies or planetary systems and planets, and, of course, the existence of life would be impossible.

1) A very important natural constant is the **velocity of light c**.

It is thanks to Albert Einstein that this is recognised as being the absolute limit for speed. Its measured value is 2.99792458×10^8 m/s, i.e. nearly 300,000 kilometres per hour. In all probability the ordinal number **3** actually stands behind this measured value and is thus the actual decisive, orientating "spiritual" value[25].

In the decimal system the upper limit of the actual measured value of c is reached by multiplying the number **3** with an arbitrary multiple of the number 10 (i.e. 10^n, where n is any whole integer) according to the decimal unit of measurement chosen (i.e. m/s or km/h).

We recognise again that the actual measured values in our physical world always fluctuate slightly around their "spiritual orientations" and they are never really absolutely exact. Although, from an optical point of view, the circle is round and finite, its area and circumference can only be defined inadequately by means of an irrational number value.

At this point I spontaneously recall that so beautiful and fitting dialogue in Peter Höeg's thriller *"Miss Smilla's Feeling for Snow"* in which he suggests that there must be an ideal in our world which exists unrecognised in the background and which serves as an orientation but is never quite realized in its physical manifestation (see Chapter 2.6).

The speed of light is a constant which also attains the "ideal" on which it is obviously based as close as makes no difference, this being the decimal multiple of the ordinal number **3**. This ideal renders it a constant. The divergence of the actual measured value from the number **3** is a mere **0.069%**. Light is not created by the interaction of two bodies.

It is rather related to the expansion of space in the universe which is expressed by the product $\mathbf{3 \times 10^n}$. I will come back to this in detail later. In

---

[25] This was firstly established by *Plichta* and I took up the point gratefully in my previous books and explained it in detail.

contrast the effects between interdependent spatial bodies are expressed by the reciprocal value of this product.
Instead of 3×10^n these are expressed by the reciprocal, i.e. the factor: $1 : (3 \times 10^n)$ or $1/3 \times 10^{-n}$.

2) **Gravitation** is such a force. It is always in force between at least **two** (**three**-dimensional) bodies. It follows that we can form a product by multiplying the number **2** by the reciprocal value mentioned above under 1), i.e.: $2 \times (1/3 \times 10^{-n})$ or $2/3 \times 10^{-n}$ which equals $6.6666... \times 10^{-n}$.
After the velocity of light the most important constant in our universe is the **gravitation constant**.
It has the value $G = 6.67259 \times 10^{-19}$ (Nm^2/kg^2) which shows a deviation of only **0.088%** from its calculated value.

3) **Planck's elementary quantum of action**, also known as **Planck's constant (h)** is similar. It expresses the constant measure of *the smallest effect* between two bodies in our universe.
Again the same factor $(1/3 \times 10^{-n})$ must play a role since it is the reciprocal value of the constant of spatial expansion and the velocity of light and stands for all effects working inwards. Since it is a force between two bodies it must again be multiplied by 2 (i.e. $2/3 \times 10^{-n}$).
In fact its measured value is $h = 6.626075 \cdot 10^{-34}$ (J/s).[26]
The deviation here is only **0.61%**.

4) The **two** most important nuclear particles, the "proton" and the "electron" may be considered as being polar to each other. The proton carries a positive and the electron a negative charge. The hydrogen atom, which is by far the most important and most common atom in the entire universe, contains only these two. And they are in fact two extreme opposites – not only with regard to their opposing charges but also especially with regard to the difference in their sizes. This is also expressed in the proportions of their masses to one another. This is known as the **mass quotient**.
It is also a natural constant and amounts to **1,836.152701**.
Is it not astonishing that the factor $2/3 \times 10^n$ (where n=1) which I mentioned above, multiplied by the parameter for maximum expansion, the feasibility, i.e. **273**, gives very nearly the same result again?
It is: $2/3 \times 10^1 \times 273 = 1,820.9$.
Rounded up, the deviation is only **0.84%**.

5) The **elementary charge** is also an important natural constant.

---

[26] J = Joule is also a decimal unit for energy. It is 1J = 1 Nm (New tonmeter) = 10 kgm^2/s^2

It was certainly meant to be an *optimal* value. To demonstrate this, the mathematical construction plan for our world, as I have defined it, provides us with the "Golden Section", that is with the number sequence **618** i.e. the ratio **1.618** to 1.

The actually measured value for the elementary charge is **1.60217733 · 10⁻¹⁹** (C) /[27]. The deviation amounts to a mere **0.99%**.

6) And finally we arrive at the so-called **fine structure constant** α, which determines the limit for distances between each **two** smallest physical building blocks.

If its value were not **1 : 137.0359895** (± a bit!) then atoms could not combine to molecules as they do. Instead of water, metal, stone and sand, for example, we would have nothing but a hotchpotch of atoms.

Thus, it also seems to have something to do with the number sequence for the limits of expansion, the feasibility, which is the number **273**. This again has something to do with the force between **2** bodies so that, analogous to the other constants, the factor **2 : 273** must logically be used.

After a simple reduction of this value we arrive at **1 : 136.5**, which shows a mere **0.39%** deviation from the actual measured value.

7) In the strict sense the numbers **273** and **618** are not natural constants; nonetheless they are the constants for perfection and the limit of feasibility and are often misjudged. In previous chapters I acknowledged their importance and I was the first to demonstrate their derivation by very simple geometrical considerations in several of my earlier books.

I also formulated the apt metaphor for the creation of spirit and matter out of an indescribable divinity: via "i" at first "-1" is created, then "+1" and finally $(+1)^2$ by simple squaring (see Chapter 2.10).

Modern scientists ascribed a real existence only to physical perceptions. If we regard the world within these parameters a multitude of observations indicate that the number sequence **273** always marks the limits while **618** always proves to be the value for perfection and optimum.

Everything physical is subject to regular growth and disintegration which can be described by **Euler's number (e = 2.72...)**. This means there are two limits of physical existence, one "upper" and one "lower" limit.

The number sequence 273 is derived from the geometrical ratio between the new square and the initial circle (=1.**273**...), in my simple intellectual experiment concerning the development of the world.

---

[27] C = Coulomb = As = Ampère second, which is a decimal measure of the quantity of electricity.

The Golden Section is thereby also created with 1.**618**...
Transcribed to my metaphor mentioned above it follows:
$(1.273...)^2 \approx 1.618$ and $(1.618)^2 \approx e$ (see Chapter 2.10).

To summarize:
In all the important natural constants mentioned above, the first three ordinal numbers, **1, 2** and **3** and also the next number, **4**, the decimal factor, **10**, which is the sum of these numbers and finally the standard values for maximum and optimum, i.e. the number sequences **273** and **618**, all seem to be key players.

2.13) Every Being Goes its Eternal Way

In an intellectual game everything physical in this world can be reduced more or less to a gigantic complex of smallest units. From a two-dimensional point of view this is the finite point.
Regardless of how small it is it is always a small circle. However, if it is not finite, then it is information, a coordinate. Every smallest circle can be clearly defined by a maximum of three such coordinates. I described these connections in detail in Chapter 2.4. It follows that every ever so small entity has two sides:
These are its physical BEING and the information which defines it. It is of no importance whether we speak of a circle, an atom, a stone, a living cell or a human being. With increasing complexity the number of smallest physical units on which the object or creature is based also increases and thus its information content. Of course, the information content is constantly changing. As we travel through the world, we constantly leave new information traces at many places in the course of time. What happens with the first part, the finite matter, in the example represented by the finite point, the smallest circle, and what happens to the second part, the information which is extremely exact and clearly defines everything?
Well, it is generally well known what happens to the individual physical units, the stones, galaxies and living creatures. We observe it every day. At some point in time everything wears down and living creatures die. However, the physical building blocks themselves do not disappear.
They merely change their appearance: other building blocks are generated which are then available for other objects and creatures. As it says: Ashes to ashes and dust to dust.
Physics, with its laws of thermodynamics, proves that physical matter cannot simply disappear.

Matter, as Einstein impressively demonstrated with his famous equation $E=mc^2$, is a kind of frozen energy that is for ever indestructible – somehow. But what is energy? It is probably some kind of information. Therefore, it is far more interesting for us thinking human beings to experience what happens to information which is inseparably connected with everything.

The answer is very logical and simple if we take into account what was mentioned above.

If something has been created as a smallest unit, as the finite point, the information of its existence, its BEING, remains intact eternally because this is predetermined by the ordinal numbers which are the information scaffold for all BEING.

Each unit expands along all ordinal numbers into multiplicity.

Numbers are pure information and they determine the expansion into infinity. In the same manner the information content of any kind of existence can be structured infinitely inwards, i.e. within a limited space. The reciprocal values of all ordinal numbers are responsible for this.

Any finite, i.e. **three**-dimensionally existing, *closed* body is inseparably connected with the infinite sequence of all really existing numbers which is so to speak its immaterial flip side.

Inwardly, the structuring of information is infinite as is that pointing outwards. However, while that pointing inwards is limited by three-dimensional space, that pointing outwards has no limits. In other words: if a finite point is created, this being the smallest conceivable circle, then an information matrix of numbers is immediately generated around it which infinitely structures its internal, i.e. its limited, space. The number π – the expression for infinity – already fascinated the ancient Greek philosophers.

Another information matrix of numbers is generated by expanding outwards. This is not only infinite but also unlimited since the expansion of information around even the smallest of objects, or as I call it philosophically, around the smallest of BEINGs, follows the infiniteness of real four-dimensional space.

The finite point, i.e. the smallest conceivable circle, cannot be clearly defined by even three non-finite, pure information points. This smallest finite unit is also generated from something. This is, however, something non-finite. The smallest finite unit is then generated from a multiplicity which is non-finite and informational.

These facts are probably symbolized by the biblical and Hindu trinity, i.e. the Holy Trinity of God the Father, Son and Holy Ghost, or Brahman, Vishnu and Shiva.

The fact that we cannot give a detailed explanation of the imaginary origin "**i**" of ordinal numbers as being the "smallest part of God" complies with biblical tradition. Therefore, the first commandment demands that we should not make images of God. Of course, this does *not* mean that we humans are not allowed to do so, rather that we *cannot* do so.

The number **1** being the smallest unit of information and the immaterial information of BEING, its very *existence,* which automatically adheres even to the smallest bit of matter (analogy to the finite point) we find the evidence already mentioned, for a basic truth in many biblical tales. The term "information" in the sense of modern data processing was unknown to the authors of the Bible, of course. Furthermore, abstract terms such as "i" and "1" sound far too prosaic and could not really fascinate as yet scientifically ignorant people. It was far better to use words like God and "the word". Therefore, the Gospel according to St. John starts with the words: *"In the beginning was the word and the word was with God and the word was God. All things were made by him and without him was not any thing made that was made."*[28]

In our world we realised long ago that all physical building blocks tend to form increasingly complex structures over the course of immense periods of time.

Our solar system, our life-giving earth and, of course, all living creatures are evidence for this. Whilst the smallest physical building components are practically indestructible this does not apply to complex physical structures with which they are combined.

On the other hand, the total *information* adhering to all and however complex entities, is immaterial. Therefore, it is indestructible no matter how complex it may be. It remains intact even if the physical environment to which it is closely connected not longer exists in all its own complexity. If my attempt at an explanation is accepted, an amazing theory of the English private scholar *Julian Barbour (*1937)* becomes almost imaginable:

He claims that there is a universe without time. For him, what we understand by time is a pure illusion. All imaginable worlds, therefore, exist at the same time. Temporal events are frozen as mere pictures in so-called time capsules. Thus all movement and past events are a perfect illusion.

In line with my explanations, I suggest that everything that ever existed or took place remains in existence eternally side by side as part of an immeasurably gigantic data network (see Parts 3 and 5).

In practice this means that everything can be accessed at any time and that we can continue to relive everything. Time and space are polar-symmetrical in exactly the same way as are value and reciprocal value. Still, it is impossible to access and influence historical events retroactively. A violation of causality is absolutely inadmissible. All events at all times remain within their own

---

[28] The Bible, New Testimony, St. John, 01.01.-01.03.

dynamic for all eternity. I will explain and unravel these seemingly complicated relationships in detail later.

My creational game around the growth and propagation of a finite point, i.e. the generation of a square as the symbol of multiplicity arising from the finite singularity of the smallest of circles, demonstrates that there are two consequences:

On the one hand I have shown that an internal order is generated insofar as each ever so small finite item structures itself inwardly. Its inseparable connection with the infinite sequence of all ordinal numbers and their reciprocal values drives is progression into infinity. Yet, this internal structure will never reach the value zero.

I already mentioned this in Chapter 2.10. The initial circle is comparable to the limited distance between zero and 1.

On this stretch we can find any number of fractions or, expressed in mathematical terms, the reciprocal values of all ordinal numbers from 1 to infinity ($1/2, 1/3, 1/4, ..., 1/\infty$). The result is an infinite number sequence on a limited section of the number ray.

Growth and propagation can be expressed mathematically by the infinite quantity of ordinal numbers.

In my intellectual experiment a square is generated in the newly created multiplicity from the finite point, the smallest conceivable circle. This is at first a purely laminar expansion following the principle of polar-symmetrical growth and propagation.

In consequence and quite logically the space now extends itself to the next higher dimensionality in the geometry of two planes interconnected perpendicularly to one another. It has the mathematical formula x^2y^2 and, since it is also structured by all ordinal numbers, it is, of course, infinite. It is in fact a real four-dimensional space which replaces Einstein's four-dimensional space-time model. It is based on a number structure defined by the *squares* of all ordinal number, i.e. $1^2, 2^2, 3^2, 4^2 ... \infty$.

In contrast to the inward-pointing infinite number sequence of the reciprocal values, limited between zero and 1 (the plane of the finite point), the outward-pointing number sequence – once it is "set into motion" – runs infinitely and is absolutely unlimited.

It is limited neither temporally nor spatially because there is simply no numerical limit to it.

This is a very important indication that the universe is indeed *infinite* and *eternal*, deriving directly from the creation of a single finite point.

Growth and propagation are basically orientated to the infinite sequence of numbers and, when based on the four-dimensional (world) space, to that of their squares.
Any internal structuring which occurs within the three-dimensional physical object is also infinite, but in this case it is spatially *limited*. Externally, however, everything can continue to develop *infinitely* and *unlimited*.

Two infinite number sequences emanate from the real existence "+1", the inward pointing sequence of reciprocal values being *infinite*, but simultaneously *limited*, and the outward pointing being *infinite* but simultaneously *unlimited*; the same applies, of course, to the polar-symmetrical real existence "-1".
It becomes obvious that *two* worlds must exist. On the one hand they are *separated* from each other; on the other hand both of them *together* constitute our *one* world.
They both derive from the indescribable and inexpressible, simultaneously personified entity, which/whom we know as "God", and they are both the direct result of a "divine creation". Once created, they both keep developing, in two opposite directions without limits and eternally.

2.14) The World is Full of Interfaces

One smallest finite singularity, the finite point, or the smallest thinkable circle expands into multiplicity thereby creating a new unit, the square. Finite singularity and multiplicity are two sides of one and the same coin and mutually dependent on each other like Yin and Yang. Each new unit which is generated by a multiplicity and expands itself to a new multiplicity, stands on a higher level. The finite point, our initial circle, is, for example, still one-dimensional, the square composed of four finite points is two-dimensional.
Of course, we find this phenomenon everywhere in nature. The Russian-Belgian physicist and chemist *Ilya Prigogine (1917-2003)* was able to prove that organic components (multiplicity) in an initially disordered state transform to a previously unknown higher and ordered state (new unit) if sufficient energy (information!) is constantly supplied. He was awarded the Nobel Prize for Chemistry in 1977 for the discovery of these so-called "dissipative structures".
Every unit is derived from multiplicity which then proceeds to become a unity on a higher level. A quality jump follows, whereby the new unit becomes something completely new. It is now the interface between the preceding and the succeeding new multiplicity. As such it always possesses aspects of both areas of existence. They are the two sides of one coin.

Everything, every structure or form, every development and, therefore, also every temporal process, has two sides which are symmetrical and polar to one another. There is always such an interface between them.

From a mathematical point of view this unit is simply described as **1**.

From the viewpoint of **1** the subjacent multiplicity is represented by the infinite sequence of the reciprocal values of all ordinal numbers (division), the new multiplicity which starts here is represented by the infinite sequence of the ordinal numbers themselves. Each physical unit has an interior which can, theoretically at least, be divided infinitely often, albeit in a limited space. The external space is not limited, it is controlled by an infinite and unlimited vastness.

In the same manner every temporal process has – again from the viewpoint of such a unit – a limited "before" and – again in theory – an unlimited "after". The latter is known as eternity, which contains infinitely many possibilities.

The perception of infinity has always been difficult to understand for us humans. The reason is that we are usually accustomed to consider everything from a purely physical point of view. From this physical point of view infinite amounts do not exist. All (physical) amounts are finite. I already pointed this out; every total amount of theoretically infinitely many partial amounts is in fact a finite amount. Therefore, Achilles was able to overtake the turtle and Olbers's Paradox (see Chapter 2.2) was not really paradoxical at all, since even in an infinite universe there cannot be an infinite number of stars – because the infinite universe is and can in reality not be a physical space but a spiritual or, less mystical, a space of information. I will explain this later.

The theoretically infinite number of partial amounts mentioned above contained in a limited space corresponds to the reciprocal values of all ordinal numbers. If we add them all up and determine the limiting value as they become smaller and smaller and approach infinity, their sum still remains finite.

Infinity remains an abstract term. It possesses, however, a reality which can in fact be experienced in a purely spiritual dimension.

In our physical world we are allowed to use it because after all infinity is somehow part of our everyday life. If we place ourselves between two mirrors we will be reflected infinitely often. Nevertheless, we will only recognise a finite number of reflections. The sum of the smaller and smaller reflections is finite, although in theory there is an infinite number of them.

The development of a unit by means of a multiplicity and the polar-symmetrical continuation due to the development of a new multiplicity is a *unique* process in the relevant system because the new multiplicity is infinite and unlimited. Theoretically it should be possible for a new unit to be generated. However, this could only happen, if the initial system of the infinite and simultaneously the unlimited development in the multiplicity is not fundamentally disrupted. This would mean, however, that any further (higher) unit would have to contain or encompass the untouched multiplicity on which it is based with its very own development. It must be impossible to terminate the process in which a non-finite unit is striving towards a new multiplicity. The eternal cycle of processes is a typical characteristic *within* every system in this world and it may be that the non-finite total system is also subject to cyclical processes. However, every single process must remain untouched in itself with its already existing, very own and infinite development.

It is essential to understand this fundamental perception in order to answer such central questions as, for example, that concerning the personal survival of physical death and the possibility of reincarnation. In my books dealing specifically with "death" I have repeatedly covered this subject matter in detail since 1999.

I mentioned at the beginning of this chapter that *Ilya Prigogine* discovered the spontaneous development of new and higher system levels. He called it the phenomenon of *"dissipative structures"*. According to this, an increase in the supply of energy can suddenly cause organic compounds to be reorganized to a higher and ordered state. A new coordinated unity is generated from a multiplicity. If the supply of energy is cut off, they return to their previous chaotic, lower and uncoordinate state.

If we apply this important biochemical discovery to a temporal process whilst incorporating the basic principle of the two symmetrical and polar infinite number sequences of all ordinal numbers and their reciprocal values we obtain the following results:

From a theoretical or purely spiritual standpoint, a new and higher unity emerges "over the course of a limited period of time" from an infinite *potential* of subordinate structures, i.e. a multiplicity. From the standpoint of this new unity all steps which led to it can be described and compared with the inverse values (fractions) of all integers between 1 and infinity.

Considered as a finite, i.e. physical, mass they will attain their highest value shortly before they become a new unity as is shown in the following illustration by my son Martin:

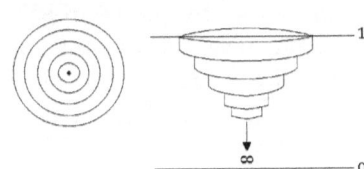

Once this new unity has been attained,

a potentially infinite but simultaneously unlimited and thus, for our understanding, eternal development commences as the next illustration by Martin demonstrates quite clearly:

If we take a closer look we find this principle demonstrated repeatedly in our world. Please note that in the interest of a better understanding I chose a linear representation here. In reality processes in our world are cyclical (e.g. the seasons).

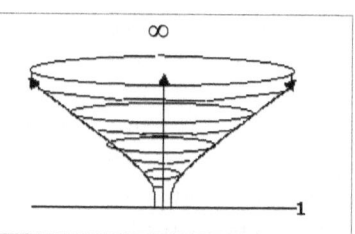

Therefore, it would be reasonable to assume that every development of an encompassing new unit from a multiplicity and further to an infinite and simultaneously unlimited multiplicity is a cyclical process which is omnipresent in the world.

Here, two characteristic universal processes are inseparably connected by an interface, mathematically the "1".
The world is full of such interfaces which especially connect the spiritual world with the physical world. I will explain some of them in detail in later chapters.
The number sequence 2-7-3 results from dividing the area of the square and the area of the initial circle by one another in the simple intellectual experiment. Observations show that exactly this value is repeatedly found in key positions in our world. It always represents a limit – or, as I call it, the limit of feasibility. The 273 is such an interface in this world.
The photon, i.e. the smallest unit of electromagnetic radiation or, in simpler words, a single, so-called particle of light, is also an interface. It is simultaneously the quantized information of the spiritual world and the massless energy quantum in the physical world.
The physical world is in the last instance the finite part of the whole. It structures the infinite sequence of the squares of the reciprocal values of all ordinal numbers (see Chapter 2.13). It follows that light must loose intensity, in the same way as any other electromagnetic radiation does in the vastness of the cosmos, which is primarily non-physical (see Part 3).
In the same manner gravitational forces, i.e. simply gravitation, must decrease when facing outwards and it must increase when facing towards a physical body. Electromagnetic radiation (e.g. light) and gravitation are natural *effects* of matter in cosmic space.

Isaac Newton (1643-1727) already described the effect of gravitation in his inverse-square law. The search for so-called gravitons as physical mediators of gravitation is thus superfluous. Gravitation is an effect in space and, therefore, follows mathematical laws on which this primarily spiritual space is based and by which it is infinitely structured (see Part 3).

It follows that light as an interface has a spiritual side. Every particle of light, i.e. every quantum, is the smallest information unit and corresponds mathematically to the number "1".

This information value of light expands along the squares of all ordinal numbers infinitely into the universe and exists eternally. In mathematical terms this means: the number "1" is multiplied by the square of each ordinal number. Thereby its value is not changed. The "spiritual framework" of space remains unchanged (see Part 3).

Whilst the physical side of light, i.e. its effect and thus its strength or intensity, decreases more and more through the inverse values of all ordinal numbers its informational value of BEING remains constant for ever.

The atomic nucleus is another such interface with a physical and a spiritual-informational side. From a physical viewpoint it is the end of a theoretically *infinite* number of nuclear particles, quarks, which are again imaginable along the inverse squares of all ordinal numbers. Of course, in practice, there can only be a *finite* number of physical nuclear particles.

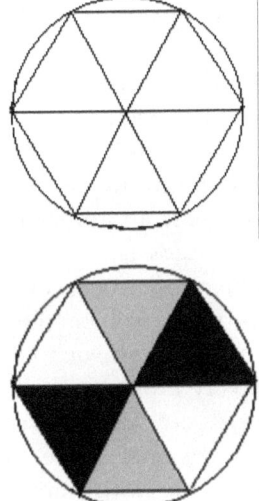

If we consider again my simple intellectual experiment of the outwards-developing finite point, the circle, we find an internal structure in the form of six equilateral triangles which form a regular hexagon

Taking a closer look at the triangles we can observe that always two of them are polar-symmetrical to each other (here: marked in white, grey and black). We observe a typical structure of six triangles into three pairs.

Let us go back to the atomic nuclei, the quarks.

It is interesting to notice that there are also six of them, structured into three polar-symmetrical pairs. These three pairs of quarks form a triplet and accumulate in such a way that they form the coordinates, i.e. the three dimensions, of finite bodies. Such a body formed of three pairs of quarks is then called proton.

Towards the outside the atom expands around the atomic nucleus, from a physical as well as a spiritual point of view; because any ever so small physical something possesses also the (spiritual) information of its own BEING and both of which are the flip sides of the same coin.

The physical side of the atom is, of course, as all matter, always finite. If we consider the whole atom as being one unit then it follows:

It is limited towards the inside and structured as my intellectual experiment of the growing and propagating finite point, the smallest circle, indicates. The circle is optimally structured towards the inside by the regular hexagon of three polar-symmetrical pairs of triangles. In contrast, a regular heptagon cannot be defined rationally. A heptagon has irrational (infinite) angles.

In fact there are only up to six atom shells round an atom which are completely occupied with electrons. The electrons strive to form pairs with opposite directions of spin. This is inevitable because the atom is a three-dimensional body of two infinite planes which penetrate one another at right angles (see Chapter 2.4)

Although there are atoms with seven shells they either do not exist naturally, i.e. they must be produced artificially, or they are not stable. Furthermore, the seventh shell, the so-called Q-shell, is always incomplete. More atomic shells do not exist.

Further theoretical deliberations show that the number 7 represents a definite break. I will come back to this later.

If we consider the "spiritual side" of the atom, i.e. the information part, then the following becomes obvious: along the reciprocal values of all ordinal numbers an infinite division pointing inwards, i.e. within the nucleus, must be *conceivable*. It is indeed possible that on a lower level, i.e. analogue to the new and smaller hexagon within the internally structured circle, other sub-nucleus particles will be discovered which then build up numerically in the same manner analogue to quarks.

Every atom expands outwards with the information of its BEING, i.e. its existence, along the squares of all ordinal numbers into the infinite, true four-dimensional space. It follows that the pure information of its existence continues into eternity. From a mathematical point of view the information of a finite body's existence. i.e. the 1 or 1^2, is multiplied by the squares of all ordinal numbers. In a similar manner – by combining the first four ordinal numbers in a rational way — we arrive at the number 81, the limiting number for the maximum physical expansion (see Chapter 2.8, number of positions in the genetic code and number of stable and natural elements in the entire universe). It follows: $1^2 \times 3^4 = 81$.

If we now take a look at something completely different, the evolutionary history of our earth, then we detect something similar.
Over the long period of several hundred million years — immeasurable for us but still finite — the diversity of species increases slowly at first, later it gathers speed and in the end the number of varieties almost explodes. Due to natural catastrophes, whole species were exterminated, a pattern which was probably repeated several times. From a mathematical point of view the ratio of any physical perfection or the "Golden Section", i.e. the sequence 1.**618**, is squared and results in Euler's number **e** (see Chapter 2.12).
At the end of this development only a few million years ago, humans arrived on the stage of life. With them a new higher unit emerged and evolution, as I see it, switched horses.
The development of this immense number of species slowly drew to an end. However, this did not mean the end of diversity. On the contrary, it started to grow even more dramatically, but in a completely different way, i.e. on a completely different and higher level. At first, the diversity of life was generated by ever new collectives, species or classes. Within these, single individuals were for a long time more or less interchangeable. Only when mammals and especially the primates appeared on the scene did this pattern slowly change. The total number of species is, of course, a finite quantity, it is limited. When humans appeared the development of new species ended rather suddenly, but not the variety. The variety even increased, but from then onwards only within one single species, that of humans. The development of single individuals entailed a completely new, potentially infinite and also unlimited diversity, because the new diversity was to be really characterized by the spiritual factor alone. Humans thus became the interface "1" in the evolution of life on our earth, between the collective and individual development on the one hand and the pursuit of physical and spiritual perfection on the other.
The scene was no longer dominated by potentially infinite but rather by numerically limited numbers of *different species* with mainly physical differentiations and extensively uniform characters and comparable physiognomies. Evolution's new direction crystallised according to which only one new species is further developed: human beings. And they started to dominate bit by bit everything else on earth. And humans are indeed of

infinite *individual* diversity, because this diversity is based on something spiritual, emotional and cultural. Something spiritual, however, is not countable and is thus infinite and unlimited. However, since for humans death limits the infinite development of the *individual spiritual* factor, there is a contradiction. Therefore, this limit cannot exist.

If we consider the development of spiritual diversity alone and its physical representation within the framework of evolution we see a similar picture.

Over several hundred millions of years neuronal structures and their interconnections, i.e. nerves and colonies of nerve cells slowly developed and began to communicate with each other.

Later, over only a few tens of millions of years, this development accelerated considerably. However, over a few hundred thousand years, probably even over a shorter period of time, an incomparable, almost explosive, multiplication of these nerves, their colonies and interconnections was set into motion. The end of this gigantic process has so far been marked by mankind: humans possess a fully developed und immensely complex interconnected brain.

It is especially amazing now, that this kind of brain has remained practically unchanged over the few hundred thousand years since humans in their present form "homo sapiens (sapiens)" started to live on this earth. Its present complexity did not develop over the last hundred or thousand years but was already developed in humans at times when some people still compare them to especially well-developed apes. What happened?

Evolution had switched horses again. Although the immense diversity of specific matter, i.e. the neuronal anatomical structures and their interconnections, had reached a relative maximum and the development had slowly drawn to an end, this does not indicate by any means that the development of spiritual diversity had also been terminated.

On the contrary: a development process had started, almost identical to that applied to the development of the total number of neuronal structures, without further adequate anatomical adjustments or the further expansion of brain matter or brain structures. Slowly at first, then faster, and finally almost like an explosion the spiritual diversity increased with its tremendous *individual* differences based on one and the same type of brain with almost identical layouts.

Over a long period of time the diversity of life and thus also the spiritual diversity was spread over all species, whereby every grouping of species represented one individual unit and as such developed itself to perfection. Now, however, the diversity of life and spiritual diversity are something purely *individual* and they strive towards perfection within only one species, human beings.

The basis of spiritual diversity, so to speak the necessary hardware in our physical world, is the brain which is practically identical in all individuals. It has remained almost unchanged over many thousand years.

By means of the human brain as a further and simultaneously the newest interface "between the worlds", the (immaterial) spirit expands quantitatively and qualitatively into infinity, because spiritual and emotional diversity are immeasurable, quite the contrary, they are infinite and unlimited.

Before humans appeared on the scene the spirit was represented by zillions of various animal brains. Within one and the same species specific spiritual differences did not exist. The spiritual development occurred in consonance with the development of new and higher species, i.e. of *collectives*, and the overall spiritual development of the species was largely proportional to the development of more complex brains.

The human brain, determined by the "quantum leap" of its complex cerebrum, has apparently reached the character of an anatomically "final stage" which nonetheless and entirely without further physical new inventions or differentiations proceeds to conquer new horizons. Spiritual development has by no means reached its end. On the contrary – its evolution really starts now and proceeds, since it is something immaterial, even unlimited, analogue to the infinite sequence of all ordinal numbers

Spiritual abilities grow further even – and often then especially appropriately – if the underlying basis, the hardware "brain" is already fully grown. This applies especially to all spiritual qualities and emotions which have no direct physical counterpart.

In other words: of course, language is also something spiritual, however, it is inseparably connected to the whole machinery of language-relaying structures of the body (e.g. tongue, mouth, lips, larynx, etc.).

Any form of thought (later also the thinking of language) as well as all really *deep and differentiated* emotions, such as love, mourning, sense of justice, etc. are in principle independent of any physical structure. And especially these develop comparatively more strongly in the adult brain – i.e. without the adequate physical correlative. Not only are the immense, but limited quantities of brain cells and their interconnections the essential basis of an almost infinite spiritual diversity, they do not even have any adequate counterpart. This is why spiritual diversity is indeed something unlimited, which can be found in every single individual of one and the same species, human beings.

It is quite obvious that for the further development of the "entire spirit" *individuality* is of far more importance than the collective spirit. The "Cologne"

Scotsman *Duns Scotus* already indicated this during the Middle Ages, as I already mentioned (see page 102). Only the individually and differently developing spirit in every single one of us leads to far faster and bigger growth with comparatively more diversity.

Humans and their brains in their entirety are thus not merely the latest but also some kind of "special interface" of evolution. However, not only humans exist on both sides of this world, the spiritual and the physical side. Many animals, mammals and even birds, also seem to possess a far higher spiritual development level than commonly accepted today.

Yet humans alone are the only beings on this earth which are able to become really aware of this situation and its uniqueness.

The apparent discrepancy between the human personality, which matures only with age, and the human body, which deteriorates increasingly at the same time, should be of utmost importance. From this point of view it is utterly absurd to assume that the physical death of a human being should simultaneously be the personal end.

A spiritual and emotional process of growth which incessantly progresses into old age without creating adequate new formations of brain matter and interconnections – on the contrary, the physical body deteriorates simultaneously – will and must naturally and for logical reasons survive the physical death.

Death is, therefore, only the end of an important stage in every human life but it is not the end of the dying person him/herself.

Death itself thus becomes an important interface in the eternal spiritual development process in every one of us. From this perspective it is absolutely essential in order to set this process into motion in a manner which is recognizable for us today.

2.15) Straightforward and Cyclical

In my opinion there exists an independent, completely real spiritual level. It derives from something indescribable: we call it God, others call it something else, yet in principle they all mean the same.

Allow me to continue to name it God, but only in lieu if all the other generally similar or equal perceptions and convictions.

The physical world emerges via an independent spiritual world from a divine origin. In the beginning they are both to a large extent as undifferentiated as an empty book still waiting to be written. Some things are determined, of course. They are the basic parameters for the history of a gigantic evolution which encompasses and includes everything – the spiritual as well as the physical world and the decisive regulations which are to accompany this fantastic evolution. The formative scope is nevertheless huge. This enables us to talk justifiably of emergence, i.e. the creative generation of each level of being out of the preceding level, and also of indeterminism, i.e. the indefiniteness of development processes. Of course, right from the beginning they are both not really completely free, due to clear-cut "spiritual" basic conditions.

One of these "spiritual natural laws", for example, determines the special processes necessary for the development of matter and space.

Everything must happen in a simple, safe and correct manner. This is facilitated by strictly logical consistency on the one hand and a framework based on the infinite sequence of all ordinal numbers on the other.

Based on this the decisive geometrical ideals are quickly generated which in the background then, as Plato already postulated, represent the spiritual ideas of all BEING, according to which this world is constructed. These geometrical ideals transform spiritual infinity into physical finiteness. At the same time the relationship between them determines the important limits and key parameters for perfection and feasibility.

The transformation of spiritual infinity into physical finiteness generates an all-including dualism in the sense of a polar, i.e. opposite, symmetry. Thus are created time and space, animate and inanimate matter, life and death (see part 3, 4 and 5).

Life is also a spiritual concept. The creation of life by means of inanimate, organic matter indicates new and very important additional basic parameters in our world: life signalizes that the spirit is on the move to itself.

The aims and objectives are to differentiate a spiritual field, which is initially completely undifferentiated and is lying idle and blank, by constant interactive further development thereby achieving maximum perfection with the largest possible diversity at the "end of all time".

The second law of thermodynamic, which is an important basis in the physics of our universe, now really begins to make sense:

According to this, the whole world approaches ever more disorder, ever more chaos in the course of time. An antique cup which falls from a table and is smashed cannot be restored to its original state without additional energy input (e.g. restaurateur, manual work, glue, colours, etc.). It remains broken and time cannot be turned back.

However, everything in this world has two sides. This seems to be a natural law which is supported by various observations. If one side is missing we should not doubt the law, but we must search for the other side. Of course, this thermodynamic law which states that – due to irreversible time all matter approaches increasing chaos – also has an appropriate counterpart.

I call this second side of the universal coin simply "the spiritual principle". Just as all matter approaches disorder and time is irreversible whilst space is constantly expanding, so the spirit strives towards ever higher perfection in constantly growing diversity. Time and space are the flip sides of one coin, an important aspect which I have already explained in detail in my previous books and to which I will come back later.

One of my favourite philosophers is certainly the French all-round scientist and theologian *Pierre Teilhard de Chardin (1881-1955)*.

Teilhard talks of the *"immaterial energy of things"* which is expressed in *"life"*. In a continuing evolutionary process life progresses to individualization and leads finally to an individual consciousness. Furthermore, he maintains that only *"love"* can set in motion the increasing integration of all matter in this universe and simultaneously act as a tireless engine and keep everything running at all times. Although love is a *"universal principle"* humans put up a strong resistance to it. Humans are presently representing the highest level of evolution, but they are by no means the final result of a convergent development of the universe which is inexorably progressing ever further. Evolution has by no means come to an end. *"We all are God, so to speak"*, as Teilhard de Chardin said, *"- God in emergence!"* This cannot be expressed in any better way. And I can only agree wholeheartedly.

Let us go back to the generation and development of the physical components of our world.

In spite of an enormous amount of creative freedom (emergence and a "moderate" indeterminism) it is self-evident that certain rules must exist which are entirely of spiritual, i.e. immaterial nature. This supportive corset is formed from the infinite sequence of all ordinal numbers, some simple geometrical forms, and the logical interaction between them.

It is a common characteristic of numbers that they can progress into infinity in, theoretically both, possible directions of existence, which are in symmetrical positions towards zero, i.e. nothing, whereby every single unit of information is transported into infinity.

In principle they do not need a geometrical structure which is why we imagine them in general as being linear, i.e. like a number ray pointing in two opposite directions.

Three (immaterial) bits of information, i.e. something spiritual, form the first (physical) space, the smallest finite point, which still is, as I explained in Chapter 2.4, always an infinitesimally small circle.

Four such circles lead to the first new perfection in multiplicity, the square, generated by connecting the central points of all four circles. The initial circle is simultaneously the internal circle of the square. The ratio between these two geometries, initial point and first complete new creation is 1.273....
The number sequence 2-7-3 is obviously the value for the limit of physical feasibility (see Chapter 2.6).

Around the square we can draw another circle, its circumcircle, by means of its four corner points, i.e. four (physically represented) bits of information, the newly created finiteness. This circumcircle can again propagate to four new circles and form a new and bigger square, in which this circle again becomes the internal circle. Around the new bigger square another circumcircle can be drawn and so forth (see drawing by Martin).

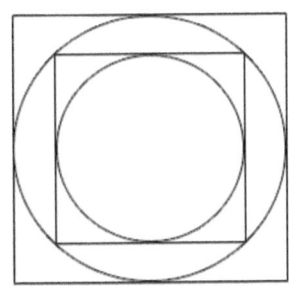

As I already explained in Chapter 2.4, the forming of the square over the four circles is connected with the number 24 since each initial circle is internally structured by six equilateral triangles.
A continual spatial expansion can be constructed by concentric circles which increase in size outwards.
In other words: the first circle expands in layers similar to onion skins. Simultaneously it is inseparably connected with the ordinal numbers and outwardly structured in sections by the number 24.
If we assume that all matter in this world has a spiritual basis and is created by information, then the finite point as an infinitesimally small circle is the real origin of all physical development and thus that of the entire universe.
Every single circle starts its own onion-skin structured infinite spiritual expansion over the infinite sequence of all ordinal numbers with which it is inseparably connected.
Around each circle an infinite area of information, something purely spiritual, is generated by means of integer numbers.
The model of two intersecting planes perpendicular to each other and which are infinite because they are encoded by ordinal numbers, leads regressively to a three-dimensional sphere as the spatial manifestation of the circle in four-dimensionality. Furthermore, it explains the infinite information space quite plausibly. This space is, of course, empty since it is immaterial spiritual; it is, as already mentioned, a pure information space. It is structured by numbers, or

more exactly, by integers which form shells around each new smallest sphere in a 24-rhythm and which expand into infinity, i.e. eternity. Matter is generated by spirit and by means of matter something newly spiritual is generated, initially the infinite space which in its turn accommodates new matter again.

The universe is practically empty as we know from the experiments conducted by *Edward Morley (1838-1923)* and *Albert Michelson (1852-1931)*.

There is no "ether". We believe that it is a space which is limited by light which has hurried ahead ever since the unimaginable Big Bang some 13-15 million years ago.

I think that this is wrong! Not only that, as I will explain later in detail, there never was a Big Bang in the known sense, it is also not true that light inevitably determines spatial limits.

As Einstein correctly recognised, light expands into space with a constant speed and becomes weaker the further away it moves. The expansion of light equals the expansion of space since they are both encoded by numbers alone. Cosmic space itself, our universe, is, however, something completely different. It is something purely spiritual; it is an expanding information space which is encoded alone by ordinal numbers and forms onion-like shells around each smallest unit of matter. In the same manner as numbers are not limited so is the universe unlimited.

Every piece of matter is thus the creator of its own infinite information space and is also a cosmic central point.

Let us take a look at the origin of the world's evolution. Integers play a decisive role, as do geometrical ideals which automatically arise from the smallest unit, the finite point, the smallest circle. The ordinal numbers can be regarded as being something linear: their origin is zero whence they expand into infinity in two directions. The first physical unit, the circle, and its expansion into multiplicity, the square, which then facilitates a new unit, the circumcircle, and which subsequently serves as a basis for the continuation into another new higher multiplicity (larger square, etc. see illustration page 123, forces the numbers into a cyclical expansion into infinity.

The linear and the cyclical factor are two additional sides of one and the same coin, whereby the linear factor represents infinity on the spiritual side and the enforced cyclical factor represents the physical side.

Due to time, which we *perceive* as being linear, we humans sense this spiritual and, in fact, continuous linearity. In our physical world, however, neither time nor continuousness exist. Everything in the universe can be traced back without exception to purely consecutive events of the smallest quantum processes. We all know that matter cannot be divided infinitely. It is of no importance whether the atom as a whole or the atomic nucleus or its nuclear particles is the latest model for the smallest unit. It might still go on for a long time as my model of the internal structuring of the smallest circle in the rhythm of 6 allows us to assume.

Many scientists will still be earning their merits with this in the future; however, they will not really be advancing themselves because they are missing the overall view. The interconnection of all matter in this world, which is pretty obvious for us, cannot be described by matter itself. Continuity is something spiritual as also are the ordinal numbers proceeding as they do from 1 to infinity. They can be limited but they still belong together and they are inseparable. They are like waves in a vast ocean, they seem to be separated and still they are one.

We experience space and time as being something continuous.

From a scientific point of view, however, this is unthinkable. Basically every human being should disintegrate within every split second down to the last detail and then instantaneously come into existence again. Everybody will call this nonsense, and I agree with them.

Our life, time, space through which we walk, they are all continuous only for us. In fact, every kind of matter in this world, and that includes us, consists only of countless particles crushed together in the smallest space, which does not really mean that the particles possess continuity.

Continuity *cannot* be a product of the physical world because it does not exist in the physical world as such. For us it is, however, something real; we experience it in our daily lives and deservedly so.

We are only able to do so because there are two sides to it and by nature we simultaneously belong to both sides of this world, to the spiritual and the physical. The same applies to any creature, but it is only we humans – at least on this earth – that are aware of it and can think about it.

It is the continuity of numbers which gives us this perception and thus the illusion that all things in our physical world are interconnected.

It is only the continuity of infinite numbers in the infinitely large space as well as that of their inverse value in the infinitely small space which really structures the physical universe and everything belonging to it.

In this way the real and infinite immaterial spiritual number space generated around every finite point expands along the squares of all ordinal numbers. This is the result of the two-plane geometry (x^2y^2-geometry) because if projected on to just one plane (xy-geometry) only the infinite sequence of all simple ordinal numbers is relevant.

In contrast to this, effects projected into space become weaker, of course, also solely controlled by numbers: e.g. the intensity of light and gravitational forces decrease in the four-dimensional infinite space due to its two-plane geometry (x^2y^2-geometry) along the squares of the inverse values of all ordinal numbers (i.e. $1/r^2$). According to the great English physicist *Isaac Newton 1643-1727)* this is known as the "inverse distance square law".

Any effect directed into infinite space is thus always limited. Since it is encoded by infinite numbers, however, it remains infinite and eternally detectable because its information of BEING, the number "1", remains intact in eternity. Nevertheless, it becomes smaller and smaller. Its total quantity, however, e.g. the total intensity of light, is infinitely large in the end, as is the sum of all fractions from 1 to infinity.

If we place a source of light between two opposite mirrors we create our own infinity because everything between these mirrors, e.g. the light of a candle, is reflected infinitely often. However, the light will never become infinitely bright.

The German physician, *Wilhelm Olbers(1758-1840)*, once claimed that our universe must be finite since in an infinite universe an infinite number of stars would make the sky at night infinitely bright. This statement was accepted as proven fact until the 20th century. But the theory was based on a fallacy. Since infinite quantities of finite objects do not exist the number of stars cannot be infinite – not even when the universe itself is infinite. Then the universe can only be infinite because it is controlled by other principles and not by finite factors, i.e. its limits cannot not determined by *mere physical* particles.

Space and time are, in my opinion, continuous things and, therefore, of purely spiritual (immaterial) basic configuration.

They are both the two opposite sides of one and the same coin.

Wherever we perceive space as accessible, time is an irreversible arrow in flight. This is our present lot: we live in a world which is physical on its outside and we can physically walk through space in its dimensions.

On the other hand, the dimensions of time remain inaccessible for physical matter, such as our bodies. If, however, we withdraw to the purely spiritual part of ourselves, e.g. by meditation, then the situation changes profoundly. Then we are able to walk through time and to relive things of the past realistically. However, the space in which our body exists at the time remains almost the same although it alters slightly with each passing second.

Later in this book I will explain the polar-symmetrical relationship of time and space in more detail.

In our physical world the progression of time is linear and thus it follows the number ray of all ordinal numbers from 1 to infinity. Space is primarily also something spiritual since it is structured by numbers. This structure is of cyclical nature resembling the skins on onion following a rhythm of 24. Since time and space are something primarily spiritual they are continuous.

A ray of light is also considered to be something continuous. Since *Max Planck (1858-1947)* and *Albert Einstein (1879-1955)* we now know that light must possess the nature of particles (quanta), it is quantized.

Since the universe does not possess any (physical) medium, i.e. there is no "ether", which could transport the particles of light, it was assumed that light also had the property of waves. Ever since, light has been considered to be both a particle and a wave at the same time.

All observations made until today seem to support this assumption, although it is still rather difficult to understand even for modern scientists today.

Nevertheless, the question arises as to whether this explanation is really imperative. I do not believe it is!

That light acts in the same way as a wave does not at all mean that it must be a wave, especially when we can detect no medium in the universe.

Without doubt, light possesses *some kind of wave character*. This is undeniable. My alternative response derives from my intellectual model in a very simply way. We know that light particles have no mass of their own. And they become light only when they hit something which registers these particles, absorbs or reflects them.

Let us consider these light particles from a completely different point of view. Every particle of light is the smallest information unit of the universe. It is the information that something EXISTS, the information of its BEING. A particle of light has no mass because it is mere information just like a number is information. It follows that a light particle is something spiritual or, better: it has a spiritual side to it. On the other hand, it also has a physical side since it is a building block for matter when it is moved. Energy forms matter. Matter is frozen energy, but energy, as I call it, is "moved information". In adequately equipped laboratories[29] scientists have already been able to generate the smallest components of matter by bombarding light particles, known as photons – some call them pure energy – with each other. From a

---

[29] In 1998 already matter was created from photons in a number of experiments with the Stanford particle accelerator in California, USA. In this context it is often incorrectly mentioned as a "creation out of nothing". Here oriental wisdom is often quoted in an attempt to prove by means of an incorrectly interpreted comparison: "Nothing" as the translation of "not-being" is, according to Lao Tzu (7th century B.C.), by no means really nothing but more the intangible, invisible counterpart to the physical existence. He calls the latter, therefore, "being" and the former "not-being".

mathematical point of view each particle of light (photon) becomes the smallest unit of information "1".

If we imagine the universe as being an information plane around every initial circle – cyclically structured by ordinal numbers – which becomes an information space due to two infinitely intersecting perpendicular planes then the information "1" of the light particle is as 1^2 multiplied by every number around this circle and thereby expands itself into infinity.

In reality the photon obtains its wave character only because space is structured by means of concentric number shells whilst it obtains its continuous movement by the multiplication of its true quality, being the mere information "1", with all square-numbers of the true spatial structure.

No observation need be disputed since it is only the interpretation which changes thereby allowing completely new conclusions to be drawn.

If a linear continuity is a spiritual property and its cyclic conduct is a secondary result of materialization then we cannot use the cyclic factor as a criterion for describing purely spiritual things.

An old Indian proverb says: "Everything happens in circles." This supports the observation that spiritual information appears in a cyclic form in our world. The universe itself, as I see it, is structured in a circular form. The underlying spiritual background is something else: spirit develops and differentiates in a straightforward, linear way. Nature does not waste the time which would be necessary if the development were circular. It needs the cyclic factor only to structure the physical world efficiently.

We find a clear indication of this in the evolutionary history of all life on our earth. Whilst in the course of immense periods of time life has developed taking detours, making turnings and suffering setbacks and repeating well-known and previously approved forms there is a central constant which appears to be different.

By that I mean the nervous system which is obviously the physical mediator of the spiritual in all (advanced) creatures. Early on in our evolution new neuronal structures were generated which have been used for the transfer of information. At first, communication took place *within* these living structures, later it was carried out *between* single beings and also between different species. Over time the nervous system became increasingly complex and complicated. The development was slow at first, but I picked up speed later and with the start of mankind it almost exploded.

At some point in time this development stopped. The "hardware" reached a certain standard and nothing really new was added, at least up to now. In contrast to the development of the mere physical attributes the nervous system took a uniquely straight, linear course by increasing acceleration.

While the neuronal hardware seemed to be technically mature the spiritual, emotional and cultural development only now started. Blatant differences between *single individuals* became obvious and a completely new evolution appeared.

The species mankind was a new entity among the diversity of species which opened out to new multiplicity and demonstrated a different level of quality, that of the spirit.

The spiritual development of the cosmic whole, which took place in the background, was an absolutely linear procedure. The essential anatomic "tools", the hardware such as the brain and the spinal cord with their countless nerve cells and fibres did not undergo a cyclical development but they became, step by step, of ever better quality and higher functionality.

The world consists of two different components, a spiritual one and a physical one. The spiritual side creates the physical which it needs for its own further differentiation. It proceeds straightforward linear to an ever higher level, which can be circumscribed as maximum perfection with the largest possible diversity.

The physical side is structured cyclically and all physical matter approaches maximal disorder, chaos, in contrast to the spiritual.

The physical world is in the last instance only a necessary vehicle for the spirit. Without the physical world nothing would work since both parts became the flip sides of the same coin at the moment of creation! As long as the spirit creates new matter everything falls into place. Since numbers are an important regulating spiritual principle and progress into infinity, spirit will eternally differentiate to achieve the largest possible diversity and the highest possible perfection and it will continue producing matter for this purpose. The universe is, therefore, infinite and will exist in eternity.

Since the spiritual development of the whole proceeds in general in a linear fashion into eternity, irrespective of whether or not it is cyclically orientated due to physical connections, this applies also to any individual spiritual development.

This means: the spirit of every single human being came into existence at the very latest when s/he was born or at some time during pregnancy, in the same manner as the finite point, the smallest circle, the starting point for all matter. Once generated, this individual spirit develops incessantly further, even if the initially necessary physical environment, i.e. the human body, deteriorates into chaos when it dies.

Therefore, there is no turning back for the spirit, e.g. by means of a new body as the currently fashionable belief in reincarnation wants to tell us.

Spirit and body are two sides of one and the same coin just like linearity and circularity. Spirit always proceeds straightforwardly, bodies are inevitably structured circularly.

2.16) What Pythagoras Obviously Already Knew

The numbers 3, 4 and 5 have for thousands of years been the basis for the time scale divided into seconds and minutes[30] as we know it today and which seems quite rational. However, the majority of scientists still believe that this time scale goes back to number mystical origins of ancient times, without it being based on universal reality.
If we take a look at the numbers, we notice that we can group them together, as pointed out by the German natural scientist *Peter Plichta (*1939)*, into three infinite sequences. The first is the group of prime numbers, in the second all numbers can be divided by 2 and the numbers of the third can be divided by 3. Thus the numbers 3, 4 and 5 represent all three groups. Furthermore, they are the first Pythagorean numbers because they are the first integral numbers with which the three sides of a rectangular triangle can rationally be defined.
Every student knows the theorem of *Pythagoras (approx. 580-496 B.C.)* well enough which lays down that $a^2 + b^2 = c^2$.

The number 345 is also the sum of the numbers 273 and 72, whereby in 72 we have 3 x 24.
We recognised the number 273 as the universal limit of feasibility, whereas the number 24 organizes the expansion of all ordinal numbers around any smallest physical unit like onion shells into infinity.
And the number 3 plays a special role: it encodes the (spiritual) expansion of space (see Part 3). In Chapter 2.12 I already demonstrated how closely it is connected with natural constants such as that of the velocity of light.
Not only the number sequence 273 but also the sequence 618 is of decisive importance: it is the measure of perfection, of the optimum, and represents the "Golden Section". If we add these values the result is: 273 + 345 = 618.
According to Pythagoras's theorem it is: $a^2 + b^2 = c^2$.
Thus the three number sequences 273, 345 and 618 may be considered as being the planes of three squares which surround a rectangular triangle. The three numbers 3, 4 and 5, which together represent one plane are, as mentioned above, the three smallest integers which as side lengths fulfil the

---

[30] 60 minutes = 3·4·5; 3600 seconds = $3^2 \cdot 4^2 \cdot 5^2$ (see Chapter 1).

geometry of a rectangular triangle and are, therefore, known as Pythagorean numbers.

The area of the enclosed triangle is 153 (see illustration below).

If we take a closer look at this number sequence just from a *numerological* perspective we notice that it contains the "1", the symbol for an omnipresent and omnificent power in the world or, expressed in Christian religious terminology, for the spirit. The "5" in the middle is a number symbol for the very principle of life, but also for God and love. The last number on the "other side" of this 153 is the number "3", the quintessential dimensional unit for all three-dimensional objects in the universe.

It only asks for a little more fantasy to recognise in this centrally positioned new number sequence 1-5-3 a connection to the Christian Trinity with the highest central figure of God the Father, with the Holy Ghost on one side and, symbolized by Jesus Christ, physical humans on the other side. Of course, something similar applies to other religions since the trinity is not found in the Christian faith alone.

From a more *scientific* point of view, the number 153 represents again the physical expansion of matter (81) and the expansion of space (3) in a concentric number space with circles in a rhythm of 24. The addition of different things is mathematically a total.

Therefore: $153 = 81 + (3 \times 24)$ /[31].

These three number sequences control optimal conditions in our world – and that without placing overdue emphasis on religious and numerological aspects. The Pythagorean theorem interconnects them *geometrically*, in the same way as Albert Einstein's famous equation interconnects *arithmetically* the universal increase of mass with the sequence of all ordinal numbers.

By squaring the equation $E=mc^2$ we obtain $c = 3^4 \times (10^8) \Rightarrow E^2/m^2 = 3^4 = 81$.

As shown, the fraction 1/81 leads us into the sequence of all ordinal numbers from 1 to infinity (see Chapter 2,8, page 86) by a simple arithmetic process.

Without realizing it himself with his equation Albert Einstein supplied the mathematical prove that finiteness and infinity are the flip sides of the same coin, that both exist and control the world.

My representation, however, provides a new enclosed triangular plane whose value 153 again includes space and quantities.

The four values, 153, 273, 345 and 618, can be derived completely from the already mentioned four numbers each of which is also an important key

---

[31] The brackets are really superfluous since mathematically multiplication and division have priority over addition and subtraction.

number in our universe and that is the number 3 as well as those of the "three Musketeers" 10, 24 and 81 (see Chapter 2.8).

On the strength of these interrelations I already went one step further and claimed that we have to assume that the decimal system, as well as the cyclical order of 24, form the basis of all processes and events in this world, as does the number 81 by which the expansion of space over all ordinal numbers and the expansion of matter is encoded (see chemical elements and the genetic code). And it is exactly for this reason that they are probably the decisive keys in our universe *because* they can be described with the help of the first four ordinal numbers as their sum, their product or a combination of their product and power, as follows: $1+2+3+4=10$, or $1 \times 2 \times 3 \times 4 = 24$, or $1^2 \times 3^4 = 81$.

The four geometrically interconnected numbers 153, 345, 273 and 618 can be described exclusively with the help of the first four ordinal numbers, i.e. without any prime numbers in the form of $(6n \pm 1)$, for $n=1$ to ∞. /[32].

Only the three positive arithmetical operations are needed which are addition (+), multiplication (x) and the exponential (power).

We can see that in these four numbers alone all basic arithmetical operations are embodied in our world since from the three positive arithmetical operations the three opposite negative operations, i.e. subtraction (-), division (:), evolution ($\sqrt{}$) are derived automatically.

The sum and the product of the first four ordinal numbers, these being 10 and 24, and also the combination of product and power of these four numbers, this being the number 81 (see Chapter 2.12), define the three prevailing conditions for our universe. We can assume, therefore, that this is valid also for the exponential function itself.

But this is trivial, since the result of 1 power 2 power 3 power 4 ($=1^{2 \times 3 \times 4}$) remains 1. /[33] And the number "1" is the most awe-inspiring of them all. It is the real key number to the entire world.

Another important aspect to remember is the following:
In the (physical) world the numbers 273 and 618 do not occur as integers but always as irrational decimal numbers with an infinite number of decimal

---

[32] It is also true that:
 $153 = 81+72 = 3^4 + 3 \cdot 24 = 3^4 + 3(1 \cdot 2 \cdot 3 \cdot 4) = \underline{3^4 + 1 \cdot 2 \cdot 3^2 \cdot 4}$;
 $273 = (81+10) \cdot 3 = (3^4+10) \cdot 3 = \underline{(3^4+1+2+3+4) \cdot 3}$;
 $345 = 273 + 72 = (81+10) \cdot 3 + 3 \cdot 24 = (3^4+10) \cdot 3 + 3(1 \cdot 2 \cdot 3 \cdot 4) = \underline{(3^4+1+2+3+4) \cdot 3 + 1 \cdot 2 \cdot 3^2 \cdot 4}$;
 $618 = 273 + 345 = \underline{(3^4+1+2+3+4) \cdot 3 + (3^4+1+2+3+4) \cdot 3 + 1 \cdot 2 \cdot 3^2 \cdot 4}$;

[33] The natural order must of course be observed.

positions. The same applies to the arithmetically calculated results 153 and 345. They are all transcendental numbers[34].

In my attempt to consolidate mathematics, all the natural sciences as well as philosophy and religions, it must be allowed to evaluate this aspect again just from the *numerological* point of view: due to the inherent infinite number of decimal positions all these numbers are an inseparable part of the infinity of our world.

Illustration by Alexander: "Geometry of the Universe", schematic illustration: Important key numbers of natural science, principles of the creation and the expansion of mass, spatial structure and the expansion of space; all ordinal numbers, the decimal system, the dimensions of space, transcendence of numbers, circle constant π, squares as perfect examples for all quadrangles, the rectangular triangle as a perfect example for all triangles, the circle with all its forms as the basis of all

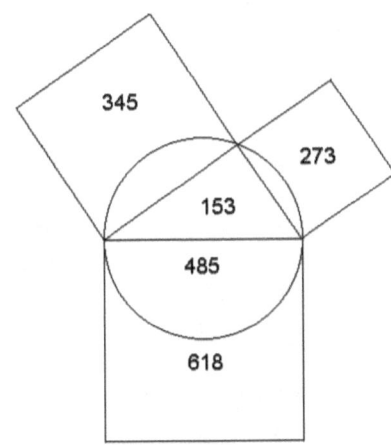

geometric constructions – all things are connected here in a simple manner.

We can construct a circle around the rectangular triangle shown in the illustration which is at the same time the internal circle of the largest outer square, i.e. it is the internal circle of the square on the hypotenuse. The area of a square divided by the area of its internal circle is always 1,273.

Only with precisely these dimensional relationships does this number sequence 2-7-3 equal the area of the square on the shortest side of the triangle exactly.

The area of this circle is in itself also interesting: it is also a transcendental value and without decimal places it amounts to 485.

It follows that 485 – 345 = 140.

We have already seen how the number 345 is arrived at with the aid of universally important numbers.

The number 140 closes another gap. It follows:

$140 = 1^2+2^2+3^2+4^2+5^2+6^2+7^2$.

In some of my previous books[35], I suggested, as I did here in chapter 2.14, why it might be that the electrons of all elements are to be found on a

---

[34] Since they cannot be described by an algebraic equation with a rational coefficient.
[35] See List of References.

maximum of 7 shells whereby the seventh shell is only partly occupied. The maximum number of electron pairs supportable by each shell is equal to the square of the relevant ordinal number (i.e. 1^2 pairs on the *first* shell, 2^2 pairs on the *second* shell, etc.). I have derived the maximum limit of 7^2 solely from the fact that it is impossible to draw a regular heptagon into a circle. Another argument is based on the cyclical spatial structure in the 24-rhythm to which I will return in part 3.

It becomes increasingly obvious here that the geometrical connections of the most important universal numbers alone encode this limit *directly*.

As the previous illustration shows, all important arithmetical and geometrical basic principles of the universe can be encoded in a simple diagram. That all this should be governed by pure coincidence seems to me quite ludicrous especially as in the long run it always loses its effect.

In my previous books I dedicated whole chapters to the subject of "coincidence". Here, only two examples should be sufficient.

First of all I want to remind ourselves of Galton's famous board of nails. At the top it has a funnel, in the middle nails are arranged in a square; beneath the bottom row of nails are little open boxes. If small pellets are fed into the funnel they hit the nails on their journey down and their path is regularly altered to the left or the right. On each and every *level* it is *impossible* to predict in which direction a pellet will continue its fall. If we allow enough pellets to go through the funnel, however, we will notice how the famous picture of the *Gaussian distribution*[36] also known as *normal distribution* is formed.

The same happens without the board of nails if we tip out a sack of rice. In the middle the heap will be highest, decreasing towards the sides in a non-linear fashion. The curve progression is also non-linear. Rice grains and pellets seem to "know" where they are supposed to go in order to be distributed as a whole in the right way. Of course, no grain of rice knows anything! Yet it always happens in the same way and may be repeated as often as desired. Coincidence bears chaos. Sooner or later, though, every chaos leads in an impressive manner back to a new order which the founder of the so-called chaos research, the Polish mathematician *Benoit Mandelbrot (*20.11.1924)*, termed *"fractal geometry"*.

We can also show that all thermodynamic processes, and that means in principle all physical events in this universe which are normally accredited to coincidence, must operate in exactly the same way. The so-called chaos game,

---

[36] Carl Friedrich Gauß (30.04.1777-23.02.1855); German mathematician and astronomer.

invented by a German professor of mathematics, gives a good example here. In an equilateral triangle the apexes are numbered 1, 2 and 3.

Outside the triangle there is a minute ball, e.g. a single gas atom. A random selector which can only choose between 1, 2 and 3 shows the first number and a line is drawn between the ball and the corresponding corner of the triangle. However, the line is stopped half way and another random number is established by the computer.

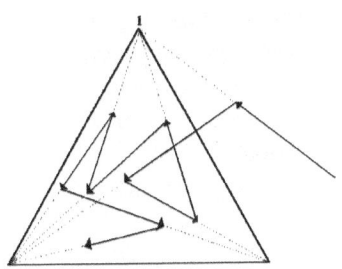

From the stopping point to the newly established corner (which could just as well be the same again) another line is drawn but again stopped half way and again a random number is selected, etc.

This game can be continued for as long as the players wish or at least about 1,000 times in order to obtain a sufficiently large number of randomly selected numbers and thereby new directions in our game.

After only a short time the ball or the gas atom will find itself within the triangle whence it cannot escape since each new direction runs from the inside towards one of the corners. In the end all three corners are approached equally often. The only condition is that the number of random single results is large enough.

Instead of coincidence the mathematical basic principles of our existence are laid out here.

I was the first to write about these interrelations in my previous books "Key to Eternity" (1999) and "A Better History of Our World, Volume 1, The Universe" (2000). Nevertheless, I am meanwhile convinced that the great thinkers of ancient times, primarily perhaps *Pythagoras* and *Plato*, must have known about these principles.

However, they did not have the possibility of recognising the presumably higher sense of these specific number sequences since only today do natural scientific observations help us to put them into the right perspective.

There may have been countless numbers of pupils and teachers over the generations who learned and taught this important geometrical basis of our physical world without ever recognizing its real importance.
This very thought is quite fantastic.

All numbers and number sequences which so prominently occupy important key positions in our world and control the construction and expansion of all things are without exception *two*-dimensional.
In other words: even if we consider just *two*-dimensionality everything already seems explainable.
However, we live in *spatial surrounding* which we perceive as three-dimensional since we ourselves possess three-dimensional bodies.
Yet this discrepancy allows only one reasonable, logical conclusion: the three-dimensional space of our universe is not what we all assume it to be.
In reality cosmic space is *four*-dimensional which is also logical, since a *closed three*-dimensionality necessitates a higher four-dimensionality to enclose it.
Furthermore, the real four-dimensional space must be connected very closely with two-dimensionality because its entire plan is laid down there. For logical reasons alone cosmic space can only really be imagined plausibly as consisting of two infinite, perpendicularly interconnecting *two*-dimensionalities.

Whilst the *three*-dimensional space, which we experience in our daily life, consists of an "xyz-geometry" (3 axes) with the measuring unit (e.g. meter) in the third power, the *four*-dimensional space has a "x^2y^2-geometry", derived from the two perpendicularly intersecting planes. Its measuring unit is raised then to the fourth power. This space is infinite since it is generated and controlled by the infinite sequence of all ordinal numbers, and it is organized in a circular order in the rhythm of 24.
Real cosmic space is thus an information space structured by numbers. This may sound extremely abstract at first, but this space is just as real as the numbers themselves. Meanwhile we should already have gathered some understanding for these relationships since we experience numbers everywhere in our world as a kind of familiar controlling force for everything. Numbers define the prevailing rules in the universe and for all life. They seem to be exactly what *Lao Tzu (* approx. 604 B.C.)* meant with his *Tao* which he was unable so to describe during his lifetime.
Yet how wise he was to recognise these connections intuitively 2½ thousand years ago is shown by his following poem:
"There is one thing that is invariably complete. Before Heaven and Earth were, it is already there: so still, so lonely. Alone it stands and does not change. It turns in a circle and does

not endanger itself. One may call it 'the Mother of the World'. I do not know its name. I call it TAO³⁷. Painfully giving it a name I call it 'great'. Great: that means 'always in motion'. 'Always in motion means 'far away'. 'Far away' means 'returning'. Thus TAO is great, Heaven is great, Earth is great and Man too is great. There are in space four Great Ones, and Man is one of them. Man conforms to Earth. Earth conforms to Heaven. Heaven conforms to TAO. TAO conforms to itself."

In this cosmic connection this poem for me is absolutely magnificent.

Plichta was the first to postulate such a space for our universe, although from a completely different intellectual approach.

The derivation I described, however, which is based solely on the logical construction of numbers and simple geometry and which I started publishing step by step in several books since 1999, seems much easier to understand and is much more plausible.

In the end we arrive in principle at a similar result, and indeed, how could it be otherwise.

In Part 3 I will explain in detail the cyclic spatial structure and the consequences arising from it.

---

[37] In 1910 Richard Wilhelm translated it into German and used the word "Sinn" which could be translated into English as the "intrinsic meaning", also "the way, the direction". He wrote that it must mean "work without action" – just as Lao Tzu describes it himself.

Part 3:

Our Cosmos

3.1) Pure Materialism

Over the last few decades the vision of a Big Bang as the initial spark for the development of our universe has become firmly accepted by scientists.
For many, especially in popular scientific media, the Big Bang and its related perceptions are already considered as proven knowledge. Due to the enormous amount of information flooding us more and more in ever shorter periods of time normal people are unable to give all these publications a reasonably critical evaluation.
The conclusion arising from the present state of scientific assumptions regarding the creation and development of our world, life and the origin and quality of the human spirit, is absolutely demoralizing and frustrating for any kind of religion or metaphysics. Only that which can be sensually experienced and is thus physical is recognised and everything is somehow governed by the same physical laws.
For scientists neither God nor a disembodied spirit exists and, of course, no life after death. For them a human being is some kind of insignificant breeze in a gigantic storm which, without reason and possibly also without sense, occurs, passes by and owes his short existence exclusively to coincidence.
I must say this so harshly because experience shows that in some religions people still foster hope to find some tiny loopholes in the alleged knowledge of our time in which their faith can find its place. For some religious groups the theory of the Big Bang turns into one of the columns of Christianity and people overreach themselves in order to accommodate their religious belief[38].
In fact, science leaves almost no space for religion and scientists are sooner or

---
[38] e.g. in Philberth, B., "Der Dreieine", see List of References

later keen to fill the tiniest gap with the results of their research. These are the sober facts.

On the other hand there are lines of religious thoughts which distance themselves completely from scientific perceptions and continue to teach their ancient fundamentalist ideas verbatim in a very dogmatic way even in our present time. Scientific knowledge makes no difference even if it is considered correct.

As long as such groups refrain from missionary work or even spreading their dogmas by violence this does not pose a severe problem. Unfortunately our world today is different and such developments are, in fact, very dangerous and threaten mankind as a whole.

Scientists must realize that they are largely to blame for this development. In human history it has never paid to act against the human heart, against intuitive perceptions and convictions, even against human nature in general with words and deeds. The same applies to many politicians who, in disregard of the individual, praise misanthropic forms of life and society and who help the government to become overpowering.

Scientists may object and ask what they can do about it if religious perceptions go against any scientific knowledge. But is this so?

Do scientists really always offer more truth than religions as a whole? I do not think so!

Unfortunately modern natural science suffers under a deficit of the corrective influence of philosophers who should endeavour to implement comprehensive views of the world in natural philosophical tradition.

Science should leave enough space for profound intuitive human experiences, which include myths and religions, in their three classical manifestations. This includes:

1) The belief in the existence of a personal God or of an adequate divine dimension superior to ourselves and the physical nature of the universe.
2) The belief in the existence of an immaterial spirit and a spiritual level and
3) The acceptance of the possibility that physical death might be survived.

If we take a closer look at the present standard of knowledge we are bound to counter this in three points.

1) Much information labelled as accepted knowledge especially by the overwhelming media is in fact not confirmed. On the contrary, regularly published information is full of subjectively distorted and in fact completely uncertified interpretations of at best small kernels of knowledge.

2) Most of the so-called "knowledge" has not been compared with that of other fields of research. Looking beyond the end of one's own nose, as I recommended in Chapter 1.3, is the exception rather than the rule.
3) A large number of observations do not fit existing theories. Often theories are adjusted retrospectively to the observations by using a few manipulative tricks. Some are just passed over, neglected or ignored. It is not uncommon to find the motto in practice: what is not allowed does not exist.

3.2) The Universe Today

In this chapter I will at first deal with present perceptions concerning our universe and primarily cosmic space. According to this perception, the universe was generated about 13-15 billion years ago by the Big Bang, some kind of gigantic explosion of a unbelievably tiny, really almost *infinitely* small point (so-called singularity) of simultaneously unimaginably high density.
Within an extremely short period of time – within split seconds – a huge ball of fire developed with an extremely high temperature. Caused by the cooling down process a thick soup developed consisting of the smallest components of matter and electromagnetic radiation (e.g. light). In the course of immense periods of time, first clusters and much later gigantic piles of matter were generated due to the constant collision of radiation particles. In the end all celestial bodies and galaxies were formed including our solar system.
Due to the Big Bang explosion large and small celestial bodies, e.g. all the galaxies, have been flying further and further apart ever since. Our universe is expanding – as is believed today – faster and faster, which is supposed to be proven mainly by the redshift of light. In the physical spectrum of visible light red light has a lower frequency and thus a wider wavelength than blue light. It is now assumed that light follows the Doppler Effect, named after the Austrian physicist *Christian Doppler (1803-1853)*: Imagine you are standing in a street and an ambulance approaches you with a loud siren. As long as the ambulance comes towards you the tone you hear is high which means that the frequency of the sound waves is increased and the wave length is decreased. The sound generated by the siren makes the air vibrate whereby waves are generated. When the vehicle comes towards you more and more waves approach you and are compressed in front of your ear. Therefore, the distance between the waves, the wavelength, becomes shorter and the number of waves, the frequency, increases. The moment the vehicle passes you and drives away from you fewer waves arrive at your ear and the distance between the waves becomes longer. The wavelength is increased and the frequency is

decreased. The sound of the siren becomes deeper. Let us now transfer this effect from sound to light.

We receive light from distant celestial bodies, such as galaxies. We observe that this light shifts further to the red spectrum the further away the galaxies are.

Already in 1924 the American astronomer *Edwin Hubble (1889-1953)* proved that there must be many billions of stars and at least many millions of galaxies in our universe. In 1929 he discovered a phenomenon which he called at first the receding motion of the nebulae and later he himself termed it the redshift.

In the same way as the deep sound indicates that a sound generator is moving away because the deep sound means that the sound frequency decreases and the wave length increases, the redshift of light coming from far away celestial bodies is supposed to indicate, as cosmologists assume today, a lower frequency and thus prove that they are moving away from us. The universe is, therefore, expanding further and further and, as is assumed due to other observations, the expansion is accelerating.

Another phenomenon also seems to support the Big Bang theory. Everywhere in the universe a very slight deviation of the temperature to the absolute zero point (0°K or -273°C) is detectable.

If this background temperature were exactly at the absolute zero point no movement would be possible, everything would be completely set solid.

This universal temperature which is also known as heat radiation or microwave radiation at exactly $2.73°K$ lies slightly above absolute zero.[39] It fills the entire cosmos with amazing uniformity in all directions a status known as isotropic.[40] Cosmologists assume that this background radiation (BGR) is the direct result of the cosmos having cooled down over the few hundred thousand years after the Big Bang.

Based on these observations the Big Bang theory sounds rather plausible but it does leave a number of questions unanswered.

First of all we must ask what was there *before* the Big Bang or why did the Big Bang happen. Scientists usually do not permit the first question, they argue that time as we know it was generated by the Big Bang itself, therefore, a "before" does not exist.

For the second question scientists give the following answers: the Big Bang happened out of *nothing*, which, according to quantum physicists cannot have been a total nothing because even in the "nothing of the quantum world" there are still unimaginably small, rather "virtual" particles, which could suddenly emerge. Quite by chance there could have been concurrences of

---
[39] ± further digits after the third position after the point.
[40] Only smallest differences (fluctuations) of less than a 30.000th degree have been detectable.

many such so-called quantum fluctuations like those in a chain reaction, for example, which could then have caused the Big Bang.

However, if the universe were generated in such a way it would inevitably be finite and must at some time disintegrate again since none of these quantum fluctuations could possibly provide the essential infinite quantity of energy if the cosmos were indeed infinite.

On the other hand, scientists claim that the Big Bang was generated by a so-called singularity. And here that means an *infinitely* small point.[41] This *infinite singularity* will henceforth just be called *singularity* in contrast to the *finite* ones.

In this case we must allow the criticism that the materialistic down-to-earth physics now finds itself in a "metaphysical" world which it normally despises, since infinity does not exist for finite, i.e. physical things, neither do infinite quantities of them exist – not even if the things are galaxies.

Everything which is divisible, and this includes any kind of matter, is in the last instance finite.

Today's most famous cosmologist, *Stephen Hawking (*1942)*, who has sadly been confined to a wheelchair due to a terrible disease, says in this connection: *"In the transition from nothing to being the key to God's Plan lies hidden".*[42]

If anything Hawking's words are rather loaded with sarcasm.

For me, at least, what we are confronted with as a whole seems to leave very little space for the "divine". However, we should bow with humility before the "divine" irrespective of what we understand by the term (and I try to keep this in mind every day). Even such an *(infinite) singularity*, this hazy nothing, must already contain all information essential for creating the entire cosmos, for everything that was ever needed, for any kind of life, for the spirit of humans and for everything else.

Another problem appears: the second law of thermodynamics says that all matter strives from the greatest possible order towards disorder. Therefore, as I have already explained in Chapter 2.15 a china cup which falls off the table cannot be restored to its former state and put back on the table without utilising additional energy (e.g. work, glue, painting and picking up, etc.). Looking at the universe today we still find that it is keeping an amazing order for its age. This means that at the moment of the Big Bang this order must have been even far more orderly. This would contradict, however, all Big Bang descriptions. For me it seems to be a rather absurd assumption that at the time of the Big Bang the greatest possible order was prevailing.

And what caused the Big Bang? A significant force in the cosmos is gravitation. Although it is the weakest of all postulated forces it is effective

---

[41] Physically a singularity is an infinite point for which the laws of physics are no longer valid.
[42] Discussion with Stephen Hawking, published in the German magazine "Der Focus", 36 (2001)

over huge distances. Where was it at the time of the Big Bang and during the early expansion?

How aptly the Russion physicist *Jakov Zeldovich* put it when he said: *"Cosmologists are often mistaken but never tormented by doubt."*

3.3) Critical Questions – Plausible Alternatives

For me the Big Bang theory, which I still consider to be a mere hypothesis, seems very questionable, or just plain nonsense. The very fact that this highly complex world can only exist because the extremely narrow limits of natural laws and nature constants are strictly followed always and everywhere (see Chapter 2.21) is an argument against the Big Bang theory.

In plain words, it seems more likely to me that every inhabitant of the world since the beginning of mankind had won the lottery jackpot every day of his life than that we could really have come into existence in the way which is currently assumed.

The head of the research centre of the Max-Planck-Institute of Astrophysics in Munich-Garchinger, *Gerhard Börger*, said in this context that "the age-old question: where do we come from? And where do we go to? are of even more pressing importance today than ever before".[43]

In addition to other unexplained or at least not unequivocally explained questions such as the asymmetry of matter and anti-matter[44], etc. doubt seems to be cast on the "key proofs" for the Big Bang theory. Above all, we have to record the fact that the temperature of 2.73 ... degrees Kelvin of the background radiation (BGR) is extremely constant and is subject only to minute fluctuations.[45]

Of course, particular attention should also be given to the number 273, which is the area quotient in my simple creational model which starts with the smallest thinkable finite existence (see Chapter 2.4) and which obviously represents the universal limit of feasibility (see Chapter 2.6). From this point of view the BGR is the lowest temperature which is necessary to prevent the universe solidifying in the cold. According to my explanations a different

---

[43] Professor Dr. Gerhard Börger in a conversation with Thomas Bührke. In: Spectrum der Wissenschaft-Spezial: Forschung im 21. Jahrhundert (Research in the 21st century) see list of references

[44] Even if some new explanatory models exist today the problem still remains unsolved and is not explained by observations.

[45] The COBE space telescope could only detect fluctuations of a mere one thirty-millionth of degree. The latest experiments with balloons (Boomerang and Maxima) showed even significantly smaller fluctuations. The background temperature is completely isotropic, i.e. absolutely even in all directions of the entire cosmos!

BGR than 2.73K is unthinkable. This undermines one the important fundaments of the Big Bang theory.

Let us go back to the redshift of light arriving here from distant galaxies. Today cosmologists are able to visually penetrate vast distances into the cosmos. The frequency of redshifts which they thereby measure are so large that the celestial bodies which emit the light must be moving away from us at the speed of light, or even faster. This is impossible since matter travelling at such a speed would become infinitely inert and, therefore, possess infinite mass.[46] Furthermore, it seems that Einstein was right when he defined the speed of light as the constant upper limit so that light cannot be overtaken by any kind of matter. There also seems to be a reason why a photon, in my opinion the "interface" between the spiritual and the physical world, does not possess mass. Even the smallest particle of mass would become infinitely "heavy".

If we consider the physical aspect we would again be confronted with infinities which cannot exist for finite bodies.

Cosmologists manage to eliminate this problem by simply altering the calculation basis for increasing velocities of expansion.[47] I certainly do not exaggerate when I say that, in my opinion, this is a manipulation serving the sole purpose of saving their outdated world model from the scrapheap!

After all, we know that the distribution of cosmic matter in galaxies is by no means as even as it would be if it were due to a Big Bang. The astronomer *Vera Rubin (*1928)* discovered this fact in 1954 already. However, the Big Bang was the "in" thing which is probably partly due to the succinct English wording "Big Bang" which is also very effectively used in the media which is reason enough not to lay it to rest. Of course, Rubin's discoveries were not accepted. But in 1986 the American astronomer *Margaret Geller (*1947)* was able to prove that our universe is rather like a big sponge.

Almost completely empty cosmic bubbles of different sizes are surrounded by galaxies whence their sponge-like character is generated. They form the structure of the sponge. Viewed from afar it all looks fantastically homogenous, but not exactly as a typical Big Bang induced pattern.

The Big Bang theory raises more problems with regard to determining its age. According to the unanimous perception of astronomers the Big Bang is assumed to have happened about 13 to 15 billion years ago. However, it would have taken many billion years after that to form complex celestial bodies. As recently as 2004 the American astronomers *Daniel Schwartz* and

---

[46] According to Albert Einstein and Hendrik Lorentz, Dutch physicist.
[47] By altering the so-called Hubble constant with growing distance.

Shanil Virani of the *Harvard Smithonian Center for Astrophysics* discovered a super massive, so-called black hole containing about one billion sun masses.[48]

This object – whether a black hole or not – seems to be 12.7 billion light years away from us and must have been generated about one billion years after the Big Bang. This is not the only object discovered by astronomers which is that old. Meanwhile huge piles of galaxies have been discovered which are more than 10 billion years old.[49] On the other hand it is assumed that all galaxies were generated within a comparatively identical phase after the Big Bang. Recently American and Russian astronomers discovered on pictures from the Hubble space telescope, e.g. the galaxy "I-Zwicky18", which may well be only about a mere 500 million years old.

During the congress of the International Astronomic Society in Sydney in 2003 the American *Debra Fisher* of the *University of California* explained why no planets could have existed shortly after the Big Bang. At the same time *Steinn Sigurdsson* of the *Pennsylvania State University* reported that in our very own Milky Way Galaxy he had found a complete planetary system in the cluster of stars M4 which must already have existed about 1.3 billion years after the Big Bang. With the current Big Bang theory this is inexplicable – or at least very difficult to explain. Yet no one seems deterred from continuing to pronounce this theory as allegedly confirmed knowledge.

The ingenious and rightly famous German physicist *Albert Einstein (1879-1955)* discovered a four-dimensionality with his relativity theory. He interpreted it as a four-dimensional space-time continuum. Included are the three dimensions of space and an additional fourth dimension as a single-dimensioned, directed axis of time.

Time, however, is relative as Einstein proved, i.e. depending on the velocity of the object from which it is *experienced*. The same applies to objects which are attracted by gravitational forces. Of course, it is correct that we all experience time as something that is one-dimensional and directed. We cannot relive the past. The question now though is whether this single-dimensionality of time regarded objectively is not just as relative as time itself as an objective quantity. In other words: is there a situation when time is of a higher dimension, just as space is for us?

I have already pointed out – and I will come back to this later – that this is probably the case, since time and space are symmetrical and polar to each other. They are exact opposites in the same way as is every number to its

---

[48] Catalogued under no. SDSSp J1306).
[49] More recently also the cluster XMMU-J2235.3-2557 which consists of many large galaxies.

reciprocal value – or as is a horizontal line to a vertical. Time and space are the flip sides of the same coin.

From such a perspective time would also be three-dimensional, whereas space would only appear as one-dimensional – exactly as time appears in a three-dimensional space.

Keeping these thoughts in mind, we can see that Einstein's four-dimensionality is in fact no longer a combined four-dimensional space-time unit but a real four-dimensional space (4-D space).

This would mean that the space of our universe is not three-dimensional, as currently still assumed, but really four-dimensional.

As far as I know, *Peter Plichta* was the first to explain and publish the theory of a 4-D space, although his explanations were based on a completely different chain of arguments. I thankfully took up his line of thought and later on I was able to show[50] for the first time that this kind of spatial structure inevitably results when we apply the laws of elementary logic – in the same way as many prevailing conditions everywhere in our world. This would, however, require that we are prepared to explain the generation of the universe on the basis of a *completely new model* which, of course, should not exclude any really confirmed knowledge, but which completely reformulates a number of current interpretations (see Chapter 2.4).

Einstein's incorrect assumption that a four-dimensional space-time continuum existed caused scientists to predict the curvature of cosmic space.

In this context we must remember that, according to previous perceptions, space is limited by the expansion of light, since nothing can move faster than light. In other words: if we assume that a Big Bang did indeed occur about 15 billion years ago, then our cosmos should have the size of a "three-dimensional balloon" with a radius of 15 billion light-years. Even so, a while ago some American astronomers published an estimate that the universe has a diameter of 156 billion light-years. This is difficult to understand and seems to contradict all logic.[51]

Einstein correctly assumed that the path of light must be curved by the gravitational forces of large celestial bodies. This would *simultaneously* mean that space itself is also curved.

Meanwhile we can look far into space. In fact, however, although cosmologists have been able to detect a curvature of light they have as yet been unable to detect the slightest curvature of space.

The universe appears to be absolutely flat and plane (Euclidean). Yet, scientists observed decades ago that the path of a ray of light passing a large

---

[50] My book "The Universe", Monologue, Chapter 5, "Straight to the Point".
[51] From the magazine FOCUS, June 2004

mass, e.g. the Sun, is indeed curved. Therefore, it is accepted today that at least *local* curvatures of space itself must happen.

However, if it were true as I claim, that light and space are not absolutely congruent, space being something else developing in a different way as previously thought, then the deviation of light does not necessarily mean that space itself must also be curved. This perception is usually not taken seriously; what else should expand space and determine the limits of space? What else should be the nature of cosmic space if not a kind of "cone of light" generated by an unbelievable Big Bang?

Modern cosmologists assume that the galaxies are moving away from each other and that the entire universe is expanding.

The laws of gravitation are supposed to curve space but, wherever we look, it is indeed absolutely flat. This makes cosmologists search ever more fervently for new explanations leading them to invent, for example, dark matter, currently thought to be extremely small but simultaneously immensely heavy. And recent findings of an ultra-far-away gigantic light-ring seem to support the existence of such "dark matter". The light is supposed to be curved since dark matter should act as a gravitational lens. But, as I will try to explain shortly, the curvature of light is not necessarily caused by dark matter at all.

Another theory invents matter–penetrating so-called "wimps". Nobody has seen them yet but scientists are already evaluating the possibility that they are the cause of background radiation. Anti-gravitation forces are invented which are assumed to be the cause for the fast expansion of the universe after the alleged Big Bang and there is blithe speculation about a so-called field of inflatones, which disintegrated after the Big Bang. Nothing of the kind has yet been found, of course – and, as I claim, because none of these "magic things" exist to be found at all!

Meanwhile, the fundamental problem remains that fewer and fewer observations seem to fit the initial hypothesis and that nobody is prepared to reject them and search for adequate alternatives.

Therefore, everything is adjusted to the new observations and a hypothesis – already promoted to a theory – is explained and increasingly corroborated. With my comprehensive alternative I offer something completely new which seems far more plausible.

Up to now no serious astronomer has challenged the current model although so heavily encumbered with deficiencies, continual enforced speculations and profound contradictions. It seems to me that they worry too much about possible career setbacks and the cartel of defenders of antiquated perceptions is too strong. There seems to be a good reason for the adage that new knowledge cannot be appreciated before the defenders of the old have died out.

Gravitation seems to be something especially "mystical" for cosmologists. *Isaac Newton (1643-1727)* explained *how* it works: he established the "inverse distance square law" according to which the attraction between two physical quantities decreases with the square of the distance between the sources of gravitation. This is pure mathematical law found in abundance in our world.

Unfortunately, most scientists today believe it most unlikely that *these* laws themselves could be anything real or even be the underlying reason for many observations and for the properties of our world. More than two thousand years ago things were quite different as we can see in the works of *Pythagoras (approx. 580-496 B.C.)* and *Plato (approx. 427-347 B.C.)*.

For more than two thousand years scientists were convinced that the universe was filled with some kind of ether since the famous Greek philosopher *Aristotle (384-322 B.C.)* was unable to imagine a completely empty universe and talked about the "horror vacui", the fear of the void.

It was over a hundred years ago, however, that two American scientists *Edward Morley (1838-1923)* and *Albert Michelson (1852-1931)* supported by their experiments ruled out that there existed any kind of cosmic filler material.

The universe is, apart from some drifting atoms which are very few and far between[52], absolutely empty outside the innumerable celestial bodies with their gigantic masses. Our cosmos is in fact a near vacuum. This knowledge finally led scientists to accept our present perception of light:

Isaac Newton already realised that light must be composed of smallest particles, and the famous German physicists *Albert Einstein* and *Max Planck* among many others confirmed this perception.

In communication electronics today, we experiment and work with light particles such as *photons*, for example. All types of radiation consist irrefutably of particles or, in general, of *quanta*. They possess no mass and are, as I already explained in Chapter 2.14, an interface between the really existing spiritual world and the physical world as we know it. Basically they are a smallest information unit representing the information of BEING, i.e. they give the information that something exists. From a mathematical point of view they correspond to the number "1". They are the simple opposite of nothing, of zero.

It is also true to say that in a vacuum such as the cosmos, light cannot move freely as a pure succession of such massless particles. If there is no medium, no ether, in the universe, then light itself must be something more than just a number of particles. This cognition led to the presently accepted perception

---

[52] It is assumed today that there is approx. 1 atom per cubic metre in the cosmos.

that light must possess a wave-particle duality. Light, and any other kind of electromagnetic radiation (EMR), adopts thus a kind of hybrid existence: it is assumed to consist simultaneously of *particles and independent* waves.

All observations lead us to conclude that this perception must be correct – although it is difficult even for some physicists to grasp.

Nevertheless, in my opinion, this perception is wrong! The simple reason for my almost blasphemous allegation is that the basic premise is wrong. The following descriptive comparison may support the reason for my doubts (illustration by Martin):

When throwing stones into water we create waves. These waves, however, are not the waves of the stone but those of the water, the surrounding medium. If we shout into a room we clearly cause waves again.

It is not, however, the waves of our vocal cords but those of the surrounding air which cause the sound. In both cases waves are generated by the vibrations of the surrounding medium.

Evidently, such a medium – the famous ether – does not exist in the universe. This fact has given headaches to generations of scientists who came up with the presently accepted theory that light consists of waves and particles simultaneously.

Significant difficulties also arise with regard to the end of the cosmos: the debate about the latest results of cosmological research[53] leads us in a roundabout way to the until recently unbelievable conclusion that the universe is flat and extends into infinity (inflationary universe, but also steady state). Finally, at some unfathomably distant point in time, it will thin itself out and will practically disappear into a disconsolate obscure void and become completely inert. For a long time scientists assumed that the universe will collapse again eventually when its expansion terminates and it will then be regenerated by another Big Bang (fluctuating universe).[54]

The quanta fluctuations as a model conception as mentioned above, which supposedly brought about the Big Bang, would thus be relegated to obscurity by this new concept of an infinite expansion and inertness, since the infinite amount of energy needed at the beginning could not possibly have been available. This would, however, have been a precondition, if we stick to the Big Bang theory. In spite of this old-new idea of an infinite expansion of the universe, we still seem to be unable to imagine infinity in a plausible way. The

---

[53] **These perceptions were established in 2001.**
[54] Based on the models of the Russian physicist Alexander Friedmann (1888-1925).

reason for this could be that in the presently accepted theory the limits of cosmic space must be marked by some kind of matter, light in this case.

Furthermore, a "flat universe" already denotes two-dimensional planes, whereas limits induced by light would, according to common perception, mean that there is a (physical) "frame" which would contradict any theory of infinite expansion.

It seems to me that cosmologists indeed find themselves entangled in a self-induced web of contradictions from which they can hardly escape - a situation due entirely to their own inability to refute their unbelievably fantastic but obviously incorrect hypotheses.

Some of them, among others the English physicist *Stephen Hawking*[55], whom many regard as a genius, possess the impertinence to believe that they are "at last" very close to describing an all-explanatory world model.

In my previous books I already defended the theory always supported by famous scientists that only simplicity can hold the truth: Simplex sigillum veri est.[56]

Again, I claim that our universe, too, with all its present complexity, adheres to a ingeniously very simple, i.e. divine, plan.

For this reason I was the first to develop years ago a small intellectual experiment. I explained it in an even simpler and more comprehensive form.

The starting point is a *finite* point, which, be it as small as we can possibly imagine, is still a circle. The only two pre-requisites are:
1) Strict orientation to God's "biblical call" to "be fruitful and multiply" and
2) Observation of the laws of symmetry and polarity which are obviously found throughout the world and which we experience daily.

By merely mirroring and enlarging the initial circle, strictly observing these two clear specifications, new definition points develop automatically. We then obtain after only a few steps four new circles and by connecting their central points a new perfect unit in multiplicity is generated: the square.

This first expansion of a finite point into an area (two dimensions, mathematically: *xy-plane*) automatically creates all important ideal basic geometrical patterns and certain number constellations which are in principle independent of the chosen calculation system. In addition to the circle (start: smallest infinite point) and the square (new unit in multiplicity formed by connecting the central points of four initial circles) we also find the rectangular triangle and the equilateral triangle.

---

[55] However, I do not consider it as being impertinent or arrogant that in a reader's letter to the German magazine FOCUS (38, 2001). I described him as the greatest fairy-tale teller since the Grimm brothers.
[56] Latin: Simplicity carries the stamp of truth.

If we juggled about with numbers we would start with "1" which stands for the circle and via "2" and "3" we would soon arrive at "4" which stands for the square made up of four standard circles.

If we add up the numbers **1, 2, 3** and **4,** by means of which the square can be obtained by creating a mirror-image of the circle, we arrive at the number **10**.

If we multiply these numbers by each other we arrive at the number **24**. And by a rational combination (see Chapter 2.8) of multiplication and exponentiation we arrive at the number **81**. Furthermore, in the decimal calculation system[57] the number sequences **618** and **273** are also automatically generated – **618** denotes the Golden Section and is simultaneously the measure of perfection and **273** is the measure of physical feasibility.

To expand this two-dimensional plane into a three-dimensional space and if we intend to follow the strict logic of my successive and continuously controlled development, we must again mirror the plane. Hence we obtain two perpendicularly intersecting planes whose geometries ("xy") must, therefore, be multiplied. Thus we obtain the x^2y^2-geometry of two intersecting planes or areas perpendicular to each other.

It only takes another small step: my entire intellectual experiment is based solely on the first four ordinal numbers. Imagine now that numbers are just as real as we are ourselves. Imagine further that numbers, which are pure information, are the spiritual data "ether" of our universe. Let us now assume that already at the start of my creational game these really existing numbers as information are behind the development of the first finite points, the smallest circles. Then we can easily imagine that these numbers continue to run autonomously once the sequence has been "set in motion". After the 1 has been generated the 2 follows suit, and then the 3, etc..

This development has always progressed to infinity since numbers can be imagined as being infinite in contrast to finite, i.e. physical, things with which we are familiar.

As I explained in Chapter 2.15 we can assume that there exists an expansion of (spiritual or informative) numbers structured in a rhythm of 24 around every smallest finite point. It would follow these two planes into infinity. Since these two planes are perpendicular (symmetrical and polar) to each other and intersect each other, a "really four-dimensional" infinite pure number space, or in other words, an *information space* is generated.

This perception enables us to find answers to all cosmic problems in the simplest possible way: the universe, imagined as a number-structured space of

---

[57] The calculation system is basically of no consequence since the numbers are derived from geometrical relationships (see part 1).

two infinite intersecting planes, would be infinite, thereby conforming with the latest assumptions of cosmologists.
In addition the expansion of space would no longer be congruent with the expansion of light, i.e. they could be imagined as being independent of each other.
Although light is curved by the influence of large masses this would no longer mean that space is also curved. Even if light does consist of massless particles, as an interface between the spiritual and the physical side of our world, it would still possess its own physical part which would mean that it gains very little mass solely due to its moving through space. So, as I call it in many lectures, energy is moving information and motion creates mass. In contrast, the (static) "number information" for our space structure is of purely spiritual nature. It follows that gravitation cannot affect it whilst it indeed influences the moving particles of light. Light becomes an effect of space, light is generated and participates in forming it, but it does not frame it.
Space would be exactly what all the latest observations confirm – to the amazement of many cosmologists – absolutely flat, *plane*, or Euclidean. There would no longer be a necessity for anti-gravitational forces, and cosmologists could stop looking for dark matter.
Space would (at long last) possess a medium again, the "ether", although not a physical one. The new "ether" is generated exclusively by the really existing numbers which means: *structural information*.
It follows that light would no longer be considered as having a problematic dual nature. The waves of light would no longer be "real" light waves, but they would rather originate from the transport of light particles (photons), which takes place over spherically arranged number shells emanated by every finite body into infinity. Light becomes the information of BEING or, from a mathematical point of view, as the number "1" it is multiplied by all numbers.
The wave length of the light curvature of a photon would then be derived from the distances of the numbers, or the number shells responsible for transporting the light. This distance depends on the size of the finite point, e.g. the atom, or the number and density of atoms, which combine to form matter from which light is emanated.
I will come back to these details when explaining why the redshift of light is *not* proof for the expansion of the universe.
As we see, all physical observations and results remain unimpaired in my model – even the accepted wave-pattern remains intact. It is just no longer the wave of light itself. In the end it is only the interpretation of the pattern and its derivation which has altered. Exactly this is the important point, however,

since in my model the existence of a spiritual dimension becomes possible and is inseparably connected with the physical world.

The present perception of cosmologists completely excludes the existence of such a dimension.

Gravitation too could thus be understood as an effect of space with finite velocity – just as *Albert Einstein,* as opposed to *Isaac Newton,* predicted. Both the velocity of light and that of gravitation would, of course, be identical and their constant limit would be determined by the "purely spiritual", i.e. number controlled, spatial expansion.

All this sounds rather crazy at first – I know – but let us go on "spinning this yarn": the space of our universe would now be something spiritual since in reality it consists exclusively of really existing numbers. Our cosmos would be nothing more than a *field of information.*

Although light and gravitation could lag behind spatial expansion if, for example, they were decelerated, something successfully achieved in recent experiments, they cannot hurry ahead, i.e. they cannot be faster than the expansion of space, since it is the expansion of space which limits both effects. The "purely spiritual" spatial expansion and the expansion of the "physical-spiritual duality" light are indeed two different kettles of fish.

The number "4" stands for the real *four*-dimensional *infinite* space and we term all *finite* objects which are inside this space "*three*-dimensional".

Therefore, it stands to reason out of purely theoretical considerations to connect the *finite* velocities of light and gravitation with the number 3. Of course, the number 3 must then also be the measure of the number-controlled spatial expansion and thus its upper limit.

This idea is merely an obvious indication but it is not a scientific proof.

In fact, we have already known for a long time that the *experimentally measured* velocity of light is only slightly lower than 3×10^n. [58]

Furthermore, American astronomers measured the velocity of gravitation with a radio telescope in Effelsberg in the Eifel in Germany a few years ago and came up with the same value.

All this sounds rather crazy at first – I know – but let us go on "spinning this yarn" of my alternative view of the world:

Cosmic space is something purely spiritual since, in reality, it consists exclusively of really existing numbers. As already expressed in less religious-philosophical but rather modern-practical terms, our cosmos is an unimaginably gigantic *field of information.*

---

[58] The exact measured value of the velocity of light in a vacuum is $2.9979 \cdot 10^8$ m/s, which is a mere 0,069% deviation of the ideal 3×10^n (see Part 2, Chapter 12).

The spirit, our traditional expression for "organized immaterial information", has returned to our world – long overdue in my opinion! To crown it all, and very much to the chagrin of all disciples of materialism, an especially important role is (again) allocated to it! Having arrived at this point, it is only a very small step to the notion that really existing numbers are not everything and do not represent the entire spirit. In fact, they are only a (small) part of the entire really existing, spiritual information field which seems so unfathomable to us.

Exactly the same applies to a number of ideal geometrical basic forms, to the actual spiritual raw material for any kind of physical manifestation but also of any number development. They provide all essential basic conditions for the world – and that completely independently of the calculating system.

I think I can claim quite rightly that I have (re-)discovered a plan for our world – a spiritual absolutely "divine plan".

Finally, another small step:
My smallest point is a circle. As such it is the smallest and *ideal* representative of physical matter. Any arbitrary circle can be exactly defined by three bits of information on the circular arc. A mathematician may say that two bits of information would be sufficient, if they were the coordinates of the central point and one point on the circular arc. This may be true but for me it is too vague since in addition we would have to explain what it is that these bits of information define. And that would at least be one more bit of information.

In other words, such a circle could never be found unlike the one in my three-point model. Again we recognise that nature chooses the unambiguous and safe way. That is exactly why its genetic code for the synthesis of protein has 84 positions, of which 81 are effective. This makes the genetic code rather smart and not at all degenerate as many biologists claim today (see Chapter 2.9). All this information is, of course, something purely immaterial. The logical deduction can only be that alone something spiritual generates physical matter directly. In religious terms this is known as creation.

The first verses of St. John's Gospel tell us: *"In the beginning was the Word – and the Word was with God and the Word was God"*. It was surely for a good reason that the message of this first and most important opening sentence of this gospel was spread over exactly three paragraphs. Furthermore, the choice of the term "word", which is also repeated three times, is in my opinion a clear symbol for immaterial information.

The biblical account of the creation takes on a completely new meaning and importance, provided we are prepared not to take it literally, but rather as being of symbolic value as other biblical tenets or in the same way as in other religions.

Information is spiritual material in the same way as atoms are physical material.

Something physical – depicted in my example in a simple way as a finite point, the smallest imaginable circle – is created by information and thus by spirit. And such information is also a component of each new circle. Due to its physical existence everything in this world adopts the character of a coin with two symmetrical and simultaneously polar sides. The physical side is always connected with a finite expansion and finite existence and the immaterial spiritual side with an infinite expansion and eternal existence.

If numbers, being part of this really existing spirit, really exist themselves, then they form a kind of eternal spiritual or "informative trelliswork" around any kind of physical existence in our world. The information concerning the "BEING", mathematically the number "1", of any "physical matter", however small, will use this trelliswork to grow forever into the vast space of the increasingly physical world which stretches into infinity.

In other words, an infinite sequence of really existing integers is set into motion around every finite, i.e. physical, point, always being structured in a rhythm of 24 (see Chapter 2.15). In fact, there are two number sequences around every finite existence since we are dealing with spatial bodies, one over each of the two perpendicularly intersecting circle areas *(x^2y^2-geometry)*.

Therefore, we must consider the expansion of numbers proceeding *in squares* – or in other words: we should imagine an information space which is structured by the squares of all ordinal numbers. This is infinite in its expansion and eternal since the numbers by which it is formed, really exist and proceed into infinity.

It forms the *"spiritual corset"* of each and every physical point in our universe.

3.4) The Cosmic Onion

As already mentioned, I believe that the natural scientist *Peter Plichta (*1939)* was the first to envisage such a number space in the 1990s. I was intuitively attracted to this notion. But I believe that this model has only been given a conclusive logical meaning by my simplified intellectual experiment based on the growth and propagation of the smallest finite point while taking account of the rules of symmetry and polarity.

Over many months *Plichta* and I kept in close contact. Many of our discussions were very fruitful as I still believe. After publication of my second book "Key to Eternity" he broke off all relations to me in January 2000 since, seemingly he considered me as unwelcome competition. I very much regret that, for this reason, he was unable to become acquainted with my plausible additional line of thought and my models by first-hand knowledge and to discuss them with me.

The natural development of all ordinal numbers around any finite point, i.e. around any arbitrary physical component, progresses in circles.

As I already mentioned in Chapter 2.9 an ancient adage of Native Americans says: *"Everything comes in circles."* Any information space structured by numbers – simply termed number space – consists of an infinite number of many concentric circles arranged like onion skins. My creational game plausibly suggests that each one of these shells contains exactly **24** (= 1x2x3x4) numbers. This is in accordance with *Plichta's* perceptions, who assumed the same, based on his earlier but completely different intellectual approach (see below).

Schematic representation of number-structured concentric circles around a finite inner circle, drawn by my son Martin:

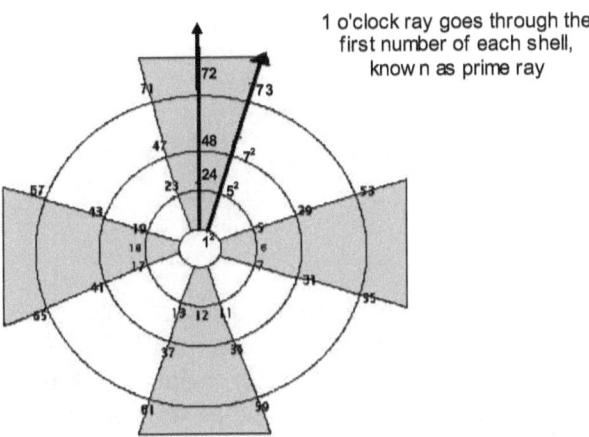

Starting from the finite internal circle all ordinal numbers are ordered in a rhythm of 24, like onion shells, and proceed into infinity. The two arrows denote two number rays one at 12 o'clock and the other at 1 o'clock. If a pure information space is generated around a finite object and is structured in this manner, than it can be assumed that the entire information is hidden within which is important for the development of this space, i.e. which exactly determines all essential conditions and basic parameters. I will come back later to these two number rays in detail.

Here I would like to point out something interesting: all prime numbers can directly be read off in this number space within the cross pattern shaded in grey. This cross pattern equals the Maltese or St. John's cross. The question certainly arises as to whether the vague knowledge of the mathematical basics of this world has been part of the intuitive human experience since time immemorial.

First of all let us take a look at the prime number ray or, more simply, the prime ray as *Plichta* call it. The following schematic drawing by my son Martin shows it at 1 o'clock (direction of the arrow). It proceeds through the first number of each "onion skin".

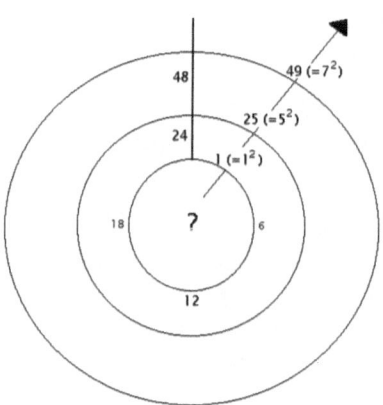

What importance does this have? It seems that observations have been made in our universe which are closely connected with prime numbers. Prime numbers are well suited as code keys. Practically all intelligence services use them for encoding secrets. Why should nature not do the same?
If we imagine the inner "onion skin" of the concentric circles structured by numbers in a rhythm of 24, which surround every smallest finite body, to look like a clock with 24 hours, then the number 24 would replace the number 12 at the very top.
On such a clock all prime numbers can be read off directly on 8 rays (Maltese cross, see page 157. In the position of the 1 on a normal clock we also find it

in the first cycle. The first number on the second shell is the 25 or 5^2, i.e. a prime number square. On the third shell in the same position we find the 49 or 7^2, another prime number square.

5 and 7 are adjoining prime numbers or prime number twins. We can easily recognise that an outwards directed ray is generated on which in addition to simple prime numbers the squares and the products of all imaginable prime numbers are positioned, beginning with 1^2, 5^2, 7^2 etc., according to the formula "6n±1". In between there are shells with simple prime numbers. For example on the third shell we find the number 73 and on the fourth the number 97, both simple prime numbers whilst on the fifth shell we find the prime number square 11^2. On the sixth shell we have a prime number product 5x29, then on the seventh shell with 13^2 again a prime number square. With increasing numerical values the number of *prime number twins* decreases, as the French mathematician *Jacques Hadamard (1865-1963)* already proved in 1896.

This decrease follows a constant, known as *Euler's Constant "e"*. It describes all growth and disintegration processes in nature and equals – with only a slight deviation – the square of the "Golden Section" (see Chapter 2.12). Between the prime ray and various processes, which are quite common in nature, there is a close and demonstrable connection.

The decrease of prime number twins with the increasing distance from the point of origin seems to be of great importance as I will explain below.

3.5) Light and Space

Light[59] consists of small single particles, known as photons. A resting photon is massless. Taking this perspective into account light is not really something physical; it seems to be *neither* fish nor fowl. Nevertheless, light particles are part of our physical world since we are able to perceive them, we work with them every day and we can watch them with physical devices. Light is an *effect* in our physical world. In my opinion, light is in one respect *both* "fish *and* fowl". Yet again, I think that light possesses a completely different form of dualism than that so unanimously claimed by physicists. As I already explained in Chapter 2.14, I consider light to be an *interface* between the physical part of the universe and its spiritual origin and eternal background; without mass every photon is actually first of all an *information* point (spiritual, informative effect). Simultaneously it "shines" (physical effect) because the sensitive cells in the retina of the eye causing nerve impulses to be triggered which are

---

[59] Light in this context stands for all electromagnetic radiation.

processed by the brain. The eye in this context stands for all kinds of technical devices. If there were no sensory, nerve or brain cells, if there were nobody who could "see" the light, then light would have no meaning. The universe is dark. We make it light because we can see (or measure).

So, being the interface between spirit and matter light has two aspects. As resting spiritual information it has no mass, as a moving physical energy quantum it has no continuity. For this reason alone it cannot simultaneously be a wave. On the one hand light is subject to the known physical laws of nature in the cosmos such as the law of spatial expansion. This means that light cannot be faster than the spatial expansion.

But in my opinion space is a spiritual or informative space. The same applies to gravitation. Gravitation is an effect of matter within space (see Chapter 3.12). Light and gravitation influence each other. In contrast to the present state of knowledge I believe that light does not create space und does *not inevitably* form its limits, although it *could* do so. Light and spatial expansion must rather be seen independently of one another, whereby the expansion of space defines the upper limit of light and limits its velocity. The actual constant is thus not the velocity of light but the expansion of space. Light cannot be faster than that but, on the other hand, it could indeed be slower.

The massless particles of light correspond, mathematically, to the information "1". This information is transported by means of the concentric onion skins of cosmic space where it is multiplied by every number of the infinite number space. In this context I recall Chapter 2.8. Important universal cornerstones are the numbers 10, 24 and 81. They are all derived from combinations of the first four ordinal numbers which form the basis of the number space. While the number 10 is the sum and the number 24 is the product of these four numbers, the 81 is derived from what I call a sensible combination of multiplication and exponentiation of these four numbers ($1^2 \times 3^4 = 81$).

Although the factor 1^2 is in principal completely superfluous, it is nevertheless very sensible to include it because *this* is what indicates the underlying character of any kind of physical existence in our universe. Everything contains the information of BEING, represented by the number 1 or, for three-dimensional bodies in the four-dimensional space, by the factor 1^2.

The light particle or photon is the smallest imaginable existence with two sides, a physical and a spiritual-informative one. However, since it does not possess mass it is not really matter. *Plichta* calculated that the sum of the numbers on each "onion skin" including the first and last number[60] is a multiple of 300 ($= 3 \times 10^2$):

---

[60] This follows from the geometry of concentric circles and corresponds with the theory about omnipresent interfaces.

The sum of the first shell is 300, (= **1** x $3x10^2$), that for the next shell is 900 (=**3** x $3x10^2$), and that of the third shell is 1500 (=**5** x $3x10^2$) and that of the fourth shell is 2100 (=**7** x $3x10^2$). The basic value 300 (or 3×10^2) increases from shell to shell alongside the infinite sequence of all *odd* integers. Therefore, *Plichta* calls them *extension numbers*.
If we add the first two sums (300 and 900) we arrive at 1200 or 300×2^2. If we add the first three sums the result is $2700 = 300 \times 3^2$. The next result is 300×4^2, and then 300×5^2 etc.
The increase in the *amount* of numbers on the shells of the "space onion" which expands outwards around every finite body is actually a square increase of volume alongside all ordinal numbers by the factor $3x10^2$.
Let us go back to the *extension numbers*. The sum of the first 10 extension is 100 1×10^2, the sum of the next 10 is 300 (= **3** $x10^2$), the sum of the next is 500 or **5** $x10^2$, etc.
Thus another, and this time even higher, order of extension numbers is generated which again is encoded by the *odd* numbers.
Finally we can say that by filling in a circle with 24 numbers (i.e. in the position of 12 o'clock) a mathematical model for its expansion is generated which is defined by the number 300 (= **3** $x10^2$) or a multiple thereof encoded by the sums of the *odd* numbers. We could also write:
$3 \times 10^2 \times 10^2 \times 10^2$ etc.

When we multiply powers the exponents are added together. Thus we obtain the general formula for the spatial expansion: **3 x 10^n**.
In fact, we usually calculate the speed of light as being 300.000 km/s, which equals **3** x 10^8 m/s. The actually measured value of the velocity of light which was nearest to this number was 299.792,458 km/s. The difference to the "ideal" is merely 0,069% (see Chapter 2.12). This means that spatial expansion follows a square law and is encoded by the number **3**.
The famous *Isaac Newton (1643-1727)* discovered that the force of gravity diminishes by the square of the increasing distance (r) from an attracting mass, and similarly increases with the decreasing distance. It is called the inverse-square law of distance. It is simply: $1/r^2$ /[61]
Gravitation is an effect *within* space just as light is.
The intensity and thus the brightness of the massless light *particles* which expand into infinite space, diminishes also with the square of the distance from the source of light. The light becomes weaker.
Gravitation, which is exerted by any kind of matter – objects with very large masses such as celestial bodies have an especially strong gravitational force –

---

[61] Known as Newton's "inverse distance square law".

makes light grow stronger again according to the squares. Light becomes brighter again. This is what can be observed from a great distance as the *curvature of light*.

Since the limits of light and space are two so completely different things for me as chalk and cheese, the increased brightness of light (= attraction of photons) does *not* indicate a curvature of space. If we accept that there is an immaterial spiritual number space, a curvature of space is quite impossible, since space consists of two infinite perpendicularly intersecting planes. They are, as the word says, plane and not curved.

By using this model it becomes very easy to explain gravitation. Light and gravitation are effects within space. Light consists of photons which can leave their source; gravitation has an effect on masses. Light is basically pure information and consists of particles. Although they do not possess mass and they are not really matter they are indeed a kind of preliminary stage of matter. Gravitation particles do not exist, i.e. gravitation is not transferred by information particles. Its effect is based on the expansion of space alone as is that of light, i.e. it is encoded by numbers. Light and gravitation thus have the same characteristics. This is why I again go into more detail and recapitulate simultaneously. From the laws of symmetry and polarity it follows:

Light is something primarily "spiritual", i.e. pure information. Mathematically this is represented by "1" and is the information of BEING, the smallest existence. Light as the interface between spirit and matter, has a physical part, or a physical side. What is meant here is the quantisation in (discontinuous or discrete) massless smallest particles.

Whilst space is generated by the development of *all numbers,* from 1 to infinity around every smallest finite object, light consists exclusively of a sequence of "1"-information bits. They are multiplied by the numbers of spatial expansion whereby every particle of light is transported into space.

If the light particle, the information "1" of BEING, is primarily something *spiritual* then there must be a polar-symmetrical *effective counterpart* on the "*physical*" side. By this I mean an effect which is exerted by any kind of mass but which also possesses an informative, i.e. spiritual and, therefore, now *continuous* side. However, this excludes the existence of particles which would convey this effect.

Gravitation fulfils these requirements. It is exerted by every mass. And Newton's discovery that gravitation seems to function according to a simple basic mathematical principle, the "inverse distance square law", can now be explained in a plausible way by the squared construction of number space consisting of two planes and governed by ordinal numbers without the necessity of particles which exert this effect. It follows that the search for so-called gravitons which might exert or mediate gravitational forces, becomes obsolete. Such particles do not exist. Another idea that gravitation is in fact the result of the pressure exerted by smallest invisible particles, the neutrinos, which completely at random flit through space, is nothing but science fiction. According to this the pull of gravitation is really gravitational pressure. This idea, presented as something new, really goes back to the Swiss physicists and mathematicians *Nicolas Fatio de Duillier* and *Georges Louis Le Sage* (beginning to middle of the 18th century).

3.6) The Big Bang is buried

What does all this mean for the Big Bang at the beginning of our universe?
The background radiation (BGR) of **2,73** degree Kelvin above the absolute zero point of **-273°C** is very important evidence for scientists that there was a Big Bang. It is considered as being some kind of aftermath due to cosmic cooling. The fact that it is so extremely homogenous in all directions of the cosmos – known as being *isotropic* – and that it shows only very slight deviations (see Chapter 2.6), engenders hardly any doubt in any of the opinion-forming cosmologists today about the Big Bang theory. On the contrary, when in the 1990s tiniest deviations of the BGR were found in the dimension of about one thirty millionth of a degree, it was considered to be a confirmation of the current view of the world. However, it is evident that the world is equipped with ideal basic parameters, in the same manner as a circle seems to be finite. It is only when physical laws are applied, which of course include the application of mathematical rules; that inevitably very slight deviations from the ideal occur. The circle constant π is no rational value either.
Does nothing strike you about the BGR? The number sequence **273** is one of the early results of my creational game about the propagation and growth of a finite point, the smallest circle. It is derived from the quotient of the areas of the square and the initial circle (see Chapter 2.4). By an arithmetical transformation of a universally valid geometrical relationship an irrational number is generated.
It shows that the infinite is inherent in finiteness and it explains in a simple way the smallest deviations between the physical AS-IS state and the spiritual ideal.
Wherever we look in this world, and especially in important key positions, we will regularly find the sequence 2-7-3.

It defines the limit of feasibility (see Chapter 2.6). In the same manner as the circle constant π is irrational because it is the inadequate attempt to realize and describe a geometrical ideal, a spiritual perfection such as a circle with the methods of the physical world, we will find only similarly blurred values for all natural laws and constants.

In fact they all arise from the "physical implementation" of perfect patterns and prototypes designed by an omnipresent spiritual world in the background. This is why we find the number sequence 6-1-8, the measure of the "Golden Section", throughout the world in places where we expect to see something optimal and perfect. It follows that the number 273 is in reality no indication of the Big Bang.

The redshift of light is for cosmologists the second most important piece of evidence for the Big Bang hypothesis.

However, for this we have also some alternative explanatory models which I was the first to propose already in 1999. I would like to reiterate here in short the important key points of my ideas.

The universe is a pure information space, something purely spiritual, which is generated around every finite point, i.e. around every physical body be it ever so small.

Its geometrical structure is four-dimensional infinite and consists of two perpendicularly intersecting infinite planes. The universe is thus completely flat (plane or Euclidian).

The information units which structure the universe in an unambiguous way are the ordinal numbers from zero to infinity. The smallest finite point within the plane is a circle. The spatial expansion around this point occurs in concentric circles similar to onion skins.

My simple creational model concerning the growth and propagation of a smallest circle suggests that each one of these "onion skins" is progressively encoded by 24 numbers. With this model spatial expansion and the slight loss in the velocity of light are explainable in a plausible way.

Since this is a number code it should already be indicated by the specific arrangement of the numbers. Thus the redshift of light must also be hidden in the number space.

The first concentric number shell ends with the number 24, and each succeeding one with a multiple of this number. If we draw a connecting line through these end points of each shell pointing outwards then we can encode the constant measure of the spatial expansion by way of the number 3, educible as a code in the form of 3×10^n (see previous chapter, page 161).

This upper limit corresponds exactly with the constant limit of the velocity of light as calculated by *Albert Einstein*.

All measured values are actually only a fraction below this measurement.

If the number ray which runs through the *last* number of each "onion skin" is of fundamental importance we might also expect something similar of the number ray which runs through the *first* number of each shell. The first ray is generated by prime numbers, their products and the prime number squares (see Chapter 3.4, page 158). *Plichta* termed it the conductor of the number space, probably without knowing how literally we should take this term with regard to the characteristics of light.

The first number on this ray is 1^2, the first number on the second shell and thus the second number on the prime ray is 5^2, the third number is 7^2. As we can see there are three consecutive prime number squares. The 73 and then the 97 follow which are simple prime numbers. Then on shell five we find again a prime number square with the 11^2 on the prime ray, thereafter a prime number product ($145 = 5 \times 29$), etc.

The further we proceed outwards the less often *prime number squares* appear. In other words: the distances between consecutive prime number squares increase.

I assume that the *velocity* of light is encoded by the constant of spatial expansion on the number ray which runs through the *last* number of each onion skin. It follows that another physical value of light, namely its frequency, could be defined by the ray which runs through the *first* number of each shell. If we assume that the photons are transported into infinite space not over each single circle shell but only over those which are defined by prime numbers then the light frequency could be encoded by the distance between the *decreasing number of prime number squares*.

The consequence would be that the frequency of light would diminish in accordance with the growing distance to the source of light or, in other words, that light would show a redshift due solely to the great distances.

The actually observed redshift of distant celestial bodies would prove to be a natural phenomenon which is due solely to immense distances.

To put it in simple words we could almost say that light somehow "grows old" because its frequency decreases over long distances.[62]

The age of a celestial body alone would cause the redshift of the light it emanates. And this is a fact that all cosmologists already know. However, if we assume that there was a Big Bang then the celestial bodies and galaxies which are close to one another should not be so hugely different in age. But this is exactly what is observed. Therefore, it is much more sensible to assume

---

[62] Of course this is not really a process of ageing. If we translate the frequency to human behaviour and compare it with youthful hectic then the frequency decrease is comparable to the serenity of the old age.

that they race apart at different speeds. In a universe without a Big Bang, however, in which something new is constantly generated, such age differences are no problem at all.

Here is a typical example. Astronomers have discovered *quasars*[63] which probably are very distant galaxies. They show a very high redshift which cannot be explained by the Doppler Effect. Its interpretation would become absurd and the "velocity of light" as the upper limit would be questionable.

Therefore, scientists are looking feverishly for other alibi explanations.

It is remarkable that there are quasars which must be in close spatial proximity to certain galaxies or which are even connected with them all of which seem to be of equal distance away from us.

Nevertheless, the redshift of light of exactly these objects varies tremendously. As a classical example I would like to mention here the *Galaxie NGC4319* which shows a redshift that would indicate an escape speed of 1,700 km/s. It is, however, connected with the *Quasar Markarian 205* over a bright light bridge whose redshift indicates a much faster escape speed of 21,000 km/s.

Furthermore: when prime number squares, which become less frequent with the increasing distance from the starting point, are a hidden number code and control the frequency of light then this alone would imitate a constant spatial expansion, since the distances between them increase. The result is comparable to the often quoted balloon on which a line is drawn which becomes longer when the balloon is inflated. In this manner an actually observed expansion of the so-called light curvatures is also explainable.

Now, the cause for this is something quite different: the stretching of light curves is induced by a really existing square number code which produces the real spatial structure.

We can attribute the redshift of light mainly to the immense distances between the objects whereby many rather paradox phenomena in the sky might be simply explained as the above example with the galaxy and the quasar demonstrates.

If the redshift can be explained in a completely different way then hitherto, by the presently fashionable one, i.e. the Doppler Effect and the expansion of light curves as a consequence of spatial expansion, then the most important argument for the expansion would become obsolete. The Big Bang theory would lose ground.

---

[63] Quasars = quasi-stellar objects or radio sources, i.e. star-like objects, possibly dying galaxies.

I have no doubt at all that all celestial bodies in the cosmos move around with high speed and rotate around various axes – but we cannot assume that they are racing apart with ever increasing speed.
Under such a premise the Big Bang is no longer a necessity.
I believe this would be a much better starting position for explaining our universe and for avoiding contradictions.
Another example: Some time ago a star was discovered which is only 36,000 thousand light years away and which must have been born as some kind of prematurity some 15 billion years ago, according to scientists, which means very shortly after the alleged Big Bang.[64]
However, the whole assumption has a flaw: due to its very low content of iron this star has such a low mass that it could not have developed at such an early time.
Furthermore, with the Big Bang being backdated to about -13.7 billion years, as it is done today, its existence does not fit into the picture at all.
Without the Big Bang theory, which is doubtless very handy, very media-effective and thus money making, we would be much more open to think about a different start for our universe – at long last! One joint beginning for everything, which must already include every object that comes into existence later, would no longer be an issue. Alternatively we could imagine many small beginnings which keep creating "space within space" and occur simultaneously in many places. Such a scenario would, of course, be completely unspectacular which would be far more consistent with the biblical descriptions. Accordingly the world was created over a period of several days. The Hebrew expression "jom", translated with "day", really means long, undefined periods of time.
We could rather imagine a continuous creation which is not necessarily over yet.
Matter is obviously still generated today. It condenses to form stars and galaxies and it moves restlessly through the cosmos and perishes at some time or other by disintegrating into its components. Surely we all recall the most impressive pictures of gigantic star factories which the *space telescope COBE*[65] transmitted back to us for the first time.

---

[64] It is known as HE0107-5240.
[65] COBE = Cosmic Background Explorer, since 1989 in an orbit around the earth.

3.7) Shedding a new Light on Creation

But what is the substance of which this matter is made in these breeding places?
It is electromagnetic radiation (EMR) or, in one simple word, light.
The real origin of light is spirit; since light has two sides but is primarily information. Like any kind of spirit, light is fundamentally pure information (see Chapter 2.14).
The physical side of light emanates from its quantisation and its movement, or as I like to say: (physical) energy is moving information. In fact light consists of single discrete particles, known as photons. Each one of them is the information "1" which is something completely different to zero, nothing, and which is, from a mathematical point of view, multiplied by all ordinal numbers of the number space. This kind of "movement" also results in a very, very slight decrease of velocity. Then, particles mean discontinuity and that is exactly the nature of all physical matter. In contrast to this, the nature of the spiritual is continuity. The differences are comparable to desert and ocean. If we look down from an aeroplane we see both as an impressive, seemingly homogeneous coherent vastness. But the desert consists of an immeasurable number of discrete grains of sand. The ocean has waves and there are small puddles of water on the beach but no drop is really separated from the one next to it.
Its particle nature, caused by "flitting single 1-information-units", turns light into an interface between spirit and matter, whereby it belongs – unlike gravitation – primarily to the spiritual side.
It was only much later, in the course of the evolution of all life, that some general, undifferentiated pieces of information combined to form ever more complicated and increasingly complex yet still inseparably interconnected differentiated information conglomerates.
With the "energetic" aid of complex physical structures, a spirit – rather undifferentiated at the beginning – slowly becomes more and more differentiated. You will find more on this in Part 4.

Everything I have explained above has for years given me the clear recognition and deep conviction that only a completely new view of the universe can give us a balanced picture of our world and really explain it to us in a comprehensive way. Such a model of our entire cosmos not only includes something spiritual, but is actually based on something spiritual. First and foremost, this spirit offers the decisive framework and simultaneously the controlling background for an infinite and eternal cosmic existence.

Apart from that, this "primal spirit" itself in the "early stage" seems to me to have been rather "spiritless". It was rather "empty, with meagre content" and "undifferentiated". It developed slowly like an embryo prior to birth.
With my completely different alternative perception, creation and the creator not only remain possible but they again become essential.
The creator and creation become again an essential and important part of our infinite and eternal world and make it simultaneously transcendent.
If now a creation and a creating being exist which together make the universal spirit transcendent, then the world can only be understood as the awakening of the spirit and its finding of the way to itself via the universe.
The spirit, originally undifferentiated, seeks not only any kind of manifestation in and with this world.
No, it actually needs *its own* physical manifestation in order to materialize itself within and with this world, and to grow and to prosper. In this way the spirit creates everything it needs and makes use of it thereby developing itself further with the highest perfection in the greatest possible diversity in its own world. The spirit creates life and is the source of all life. Life is the purely spiritual quality which marks the difference between a complex heap of matter, which we may call an animal or a human body, and something we may call a rock.
No number sequence, no information, no spirit and no life — all of them purely spiritual qualities — could ever come to an end or disappear in this infinite and eternal cosmos. For all these death does not exist.

3.8) The Polar Symmetry of Time and Space

Everything in this world has two sides. The two sides of the same coin demonstrate symmetry and polarity.
One side creates the other. Let us simply take a look at the development of mankind. Humans only exist as man and woman; they are also "polar-symmetrical twins". The female part stands at the beginning and the male part develops from there — not the other way round. In simple words: the male is created via the female.
Space and time are also two polar symmetries. Of course, they belong together and are inseparable after they have been generated. Therefore, it is not incorrect to speak of an interconnected space-time, but not in the sense that Albert Einstein meant. For him the world consists of one dimension of time and three dimensions of space and all physicists have parroted this ever

since. Since space and time are two polar-symmetrical sides of one and the same coin they are both four-dimensional in themselves.

Here we have to differentiate between important details. Space only develops secondarily through a finite new creation – in short: through matter. And it is something spiritual since it is structured by the infinite sequence of ordinal numbers. In cosmic space the spirit manifests itself again. We can recognise how the same procedures are applied later to life and to the differentiating spirits of living creatures. Space also possesses a *physical* side because it is generated by two planes, i.e. two two-dimensionalities. Both planes are polar-symmetrical to each other since they intersect each other perpendicularly. This x^2y^2-geometry is not automatically infinite. It only becomes so due to its inherent spiritual part, i.e. due to the concentric circular structuring numbers (see Chapter 3.4).

With the finite point, the smallest circle, Spirit practically creates the "first matter". At the beginning this is "matter" on a plane. It is only in the further process that a four-dimensional space over two planes is developed (see Chapter 2.4). It follows that three-dimensional finite bodies are secondarily created within it. Both planes of the four-dimensional space are controlled by numbers, integral components of the spirit, into infinity. The spirit has once again thus manifested itself through its physical creation. In the same way as the four-dimensionality of space is generated by means of two polar-symmetrical planes, so too must the four-dimensionality of the spirit itself possess an internal polar symmetry. It only unfolds itself with the development of the space which is polar-symmetrical to itself, i.e. in the moment of creation of matter. Spirit without its physical creation is a timeless blank sheet. When space comes into being due to the creation of matter, then the past and the present are developed as the two dimensions of the spiritual event-horizon and the future and the infinity are developed as the two additional polar-symmetrical dimensions which are inseparably connected with the spatial expansion.

I will explain this in detail below.

Continuity and discontinuity are two additional symmetrical opposites. Space and time seem continuous for us.

In fact, there is no continuity in our physical world. Everything we find in the universe can always be further divided. In the last instance the smallest particles remain – atoms, atomic nuclei and quanta. Everything is divided down to the last particle, i.e. it is discrete or discontinuous. Time also seems to be discontinuous since it is inseparably connected with light and its velocity. And light is quantised; it consists of single particles, photons. We have already adjusted ourselves to that and since 1967 we have measured one second as the defined number of 9,192,631,770 periods of the electromagnetic radiation of the caesium atom (Cs atom clock).

Discontinuity is the essence of all finite things and is thus the basic concept of the physical world. However, this does not apply to our perceptions and observations. According to these time is continuous as is all kind of life. We live over a longer period of time and do not keep dying every split second and regenerating again afterwards. This would be the inevitable consequence of a purely physical view of the world without its own continuity. The continuity of time must remain an illusion if we look for it in the physical world. In order to avoid such contradictions physicists invented the light *wave*. This is a scientific attempt to bring continuity into the world which has no physical properties. Albert Einstein tried to fight this construct; unfortunately he had no ready alternative explanation to hand and was forced to withdraw from the debate. Continuity and infinity belong inseparably together. However they are properties of a spiritual world.

Continuity is *not* a product of our physical universe which we can experience with our senses. We humans have a sense of time only because we live and we are animate and thus we naturally belong to both levels – the spiritual and the physical – of this world. Many living organisms, especially those which are more or less aware and, of course, all those being self-aware living creatures possess a spirit in their physical bodies. This even applies to those of us humans who ignore and fight this spiritual side of the coin of our existence in spite of our own daily experiences.

Where does it stem from, this continuity which we observe in phenomena such as time, life and spirit or animation everywhere in the entire universe? What causes this internal coherence?

Why was the light *wave* invented?

Continuity is generated in the physical world alone by processing all ordinal numbers from "1" to infinity. This is the spiritual background of all continuity. Numbers are something purely spiritual. They give us the illusionary impression of an internal coherence in the physical world. Cosmic space is thus continuous because it is structured by numbers. It is generated by two perpendicularly intersecting infinite planes. From a one-plane geometry xy a two-plane geometry x^2y^2 is thus created. Thereby the number structure of space becomes also a square and every information of BEING, which as "1" is multiplied by each ordinal number, becomes multiplied by 1^2 in space. Space is an essential property of the physical universe. Matter creates spirit whilst differentiating it. The physical universe, however, is an essential condition of a long existing spiritual level. It is absolutely essential as only so is the spirit able to differentiate itself over unimaginably long periods of time until it finally reaches utmost perfection in the widest possible diversity.

Without space there is no diversity and thus no perfection. All physical things can be traced back to something very simple and are generated on the basis of very simple ideal geometrical specifications provided by a spiritual world which initially defines the parameters. To do this, single pieces of information must be separated from the spiritual field. The "1" is, so to speak, separated from the field of infinite ordinal numbers and becomes independent. This does not alter the value of the total information of the spirit, because the "1" is separated by division.

Discontinuity is generated and thus the all decisive step towards a physical world is taken. Hence single pieces of information are "set into motion". They encounter one another which means they are multiplied by one another and by the continuous ordinal-number-sequence-frames. In our linguistic usage and thus projected into the physical perspective we would say that by splitting off single pieces of information quanta, photons, are generated. Their movement is energy in its most fundamental form: Energy is moving information.

Single quanta also collide with one another. Due to repeated collisions or, expressed in a somewhat softer way, due to the fusions of some of these at rest completely massless quanta, the "germs" of all matter is generated. Again formulated in a more mathematical way, three information units clearly define a circle and three pairs of information units define a sphere (see Chapters 2.4, 2.14 and 2.15).

Around every smallest finite creation an information space is then automatically generated which is structured through the processing of all ordinal numbers from 1 to infinity in an order of 24 and which inevitably stretches into infinity. Any information transport, e.g. the expansion of light, is the equivalent of the multiplication of one piece of information, i.e. the number 1 by the squares of each ordinal number of this number space, our cosmic space onion.

The universal law of symmetry and polarity is generated only because the spirit creates a second polar-symmetrical world which it needs for its own advancement to itself, as *Teilhard de Chardin* already termed it. Everything which is generated and developed from now on must, therefore, possess two sides of one and the same coin.

Even if cosmic space is information- and number-space and thereby something spiritual itself, it still has a physical cause and is only the newly differentiated spiritual aspect of that physical cause.

Without this first finite, i.e. physical, existence which itself is, of course, due again to a spiritual creation, space could ultimately not be generated.

Within this infinity of the four-dimensional number space the finiteness of three-dimensional physical bodies is generated.
In this way, every finiteness possesses an infinite aspect and vice versa.
In contrast, time is the underlying primal dimension of the spirit and is, therefore, only secondarily transferred to the physical world to be implemented in it in a very subjective way. Time needs subjectivity, i.e. time without a perception of time is quite nice but useless. Perceptions and subjectivities are in general not properties of the physical world.
Time is inevitably continuous and continuity is an essential property of spiritual space and thus also for the universe if we imagine it to be a spiritual information- and number-space.
The concept of space as we imagine it did not exist in the spiritual world before physical matter was created because basically it would not have made sense. The primarily spiritual space is a condition and not a space which could accommodate physical bodies.
Time is primarily a spiritual dimension. It is secondarily transferred to the space generated around every new particle of matter – and thus also to the universe as a whole. With the creation of physical matter and "its" space a concept of space emerges for the first time.
This new space concept is secondarily transferred to the spiritual world and so becomes existent in the spiritual perception.
Time is relative as Einstein already so impressively demonstrated.
Relative time *perception* means that time can also be subjective.
Albert Einstein once imagined travelling on a ray of light. This made clear to him that, even when measured objectively in the physical world, time is not absolute. Therefore, ever since we speak of its relativity. In a similar manner we can easily envision the subjective relativity of time. For example, every human being perceives time in a different way. Psychologists say that we feel the first 18 to 20 years of our lives to be just as long as the remaining 50, 60 years or more. Everybody knows from experience that retired people have less time than anybody else, although they should be the ones with so much more time on their hands since they do not have to work.
If we are looking forward to an imminent holiday or a party time cannot run fast enough for us. But the holiday or the party are over far too soon.
There is also a biological time. Different people grow old in biologically different ways; some look like 50 when they are already 80 years old, others look like 50 when they are only 30 years old. People who look old in their

appearance may "internally" be much younger, for example, if they remained young in spirit – especially if they never stopped learning. Especially responsible assignments require and encourage people to remain younger than their age. An example is the former German Federal Chancellor *Konrad Adenauer (1876-1967)*, who came into office when he was already rather well advanced with his 73 years, or *Pope John Paul II, (1920-2005)*, who even after surviving life-threatening injuries in an assassination attack and in spite of his other serious physical illnesses kept on travelling the world for many years, was still very active and mentally fit and significantly involved in the termination of the "Cold War".

We should go a step further, therefore. It is essential to remain mentally active in order to live longer. This is a fact. We have even better chances of surviving otherwise deadly physical diseases for a longer period of time. The very famous words of the French philosopher *René Descartes (1596-1650), "Cogito ergo sum"* (I think, therefore, I am) could have a much more far-reaching meaning. *Only because* I think, or in a transferred sense, *because* I am *still* mentally active I am (still) alive.

This thought does not contradict age induced illnesses of the brain such as Alzheimer's disease or dementia, both are not illnesses of the spirit but only of the brain. The term "brain disease" may in most cases be more precise.

Time is – viewed subjectively – valued completely differently.
Even objective time measures are – depending on the speed – different. The velocity of light relativises time. If light quanta are primarily information and thus something spiritual then the "subjectivity" and "relativity" of light are practically the same and they point to the true origin of time as the basic dimension of the spirit. The same does not apply to space. Space is not relative. Distances and dimensions are identical everywhere – from a completely objective point of view. A subjective space does not exist in the physical world, but only in our imagination, i.e. "in the spirit".

In order to overcome longer distances in cosmic space we really have to struggle. However, if we travel "mentally" into the past and relive experiences which are long gone by, this is an easy exercise provided we have enough time for peace and contemplation.

Twenty years in the space time concept is the equivalent of a light distance of nearly 200 trillion kilometres. That is the distance which light travels during this period of time.

We could more easily travel through time than through space.
Of course, you will retort that we are (only) travelling "mentally" and by that you probably mean the brain. But this is not correct. Travelling through time

happens "in" as well as "with" our spirit. Although this also has something to do with the brain, as I will explain in detail in the fourth part of this book, it is only so to a limited extent.

Time is continuous only because it was originally a spiritual dimension. Its projection into our physical world requires a medium. This is light or, in general, electromagnetic radiation (EMR), whereby time finds access to the physical world.

Due to the "1" "dropping out" from the world's inherent information field, or put religiously from the divine spirit, time loses its continuity.

Since it is motion-dependent, i.e. speed-dependent, this turns it into a relative physical quantity. Its newly acquired, now physically oriented objectivity is again polar-symmetrical to its purely subjective character in the spiritual world.

Space, on the other hand, becomes continuous because it is structured solely by spiritual components, namely ordinal numbers.

Space and time are two sides of the same coin. Space is captivating due to the finiteness of every single three-dimensional body and the simultaneous infiniteness of its own real four-dimensional space structure. Time is also finite on the one hand and that means for all three-dimensional bodies which are spatially limited anyway. On the other hand it is infinite, i.e. eternal. Time is infinite because, as a polar symmetry to the four-dimensionality of space, eternity must exist as the fourth dimension of time. Furthermore, it is essential for the infinity of the four-dimensional space since the infinity of numbers and the eternity of spirit represent the same spiritual background.

Units of information – in physical terms light or, in mathematical terms, the "1" – manifest the primarily purely subjective characteristic "time" of the spiritual world in the physical world which it generates itself for this purpose and then structures it, thereby filling it with purpose. Time receives at first an objective complexion. The original subjectivity is now expressed in motion-dependent relativity. Nevertheless time soon returns to its very own real subjectivity:

After aeons of years it manages to do this due to the maturing of life and consciousness with the aid of innumerable, adequately matured neuronal structures (see Part 4). The constant interactions with their underlying spiritual background make it possible in the end to perceive real continuity in general and consequently also continuous *temporal* processes in particular.

In the physical world time still remains discontinuous, fragmented and disconnected. We keep measuring one second as the billion-fold periods (frequencies) of the caesium atom, in the same way as a movie consists of millions of single pictures which *we* ourselves connect to a continuous film because only *we*, i.e. our spirit, perceives the pictures as being continuous.

The Austrian philosopher *Karl Popper (1902-1994)* once discussed death and a possible life after death in the 1970s with the brain scientist and Nobel Prize winner *John Eccles (1903-1997)*. For Popper the prospect of "eternal life" was unbearable because it would probably be unbearably boring. This was why he could neither imagine eternal life nor believe in it. Eccles, however, was of a completely different opinion; he was as convinced that the human personality remains in existence after death as I am.

If we follow my arguments that time is primarily the dimension of a spiritual world since time does not exist as something continuous in the physical universe and, furthermore, since it is something purely subjective on the spiritual level, then Popper's basis of argument with regard to the unbearable boredom is pointless. An "after death eternity" is also something purely subjective and will have nothing to do with our imagination of objectively measured relative time, as measured by those of us, who happen to be physically manifested on earth at the moment.

Time is a dimension of the spirit. It is polar-symmetrical to space which is the dimension of the physical world.

Cosmic space seems to be four-dimensional in reality. Time is also four-dimensional. Space possesses four real dimensions which are generated by erecting a two-plane geometry, i.e. by exponentiating the number 2. Two real spatial dimensions develop during the process of "materialising" in the same manner as 1^2 is generated from the simple information "1" (see Chapter 2.10). The four-dimensionality of space in the sense of a x^2y^2-geometry only makes sense if it is infinite. Cosmic space is probably infinite.

Infinity is, however, not a property of the physical world. It is brought about by something spiritual which structures it by processing all ordinal numbers of the two perpendicularly intersecting planes of the four-dimensional space into infinity. The spirit which creates and structures space by means of physical matter also provides its infinity. This means simultaneously eternity; for eternity is a term for spiritual infinity. In the physical world space seems to be three-dimensional. In fact, it is four-dimensional. Time seems to be directed in one dimension. It proceeds from the past over the hardly comprehensible present and on into the future. That which already has three different real dimensions in the spiritual world merges together in our perspective. The four-dimensionality of space is generated by two dimensions unfolding from a two-dimensionality on which they are based. In the spiritual world we might again expect a polar symmetry of this. Analogue to space we find two open time dimensions and another two which still have to unfold. The past and the present are already open whereas the future and eternity still have to unfold. Since space cannot exist, the mere concept of space as we perceive it can find its way into spiritual subjectivity. Therefore, when we are in it, space seems to us to be three-dimensional. In both cases a five-dimensionality results. The number "5" has been the number of all living things in all myths and religions since time immemorial; it is the connecting number, the number of love or a divine number. This seems to be reflected here. In fact, a five-dimensionality does not exist.

The physical world is an objective world with subjective "spirits" which populate and evaluate it in the course of time. It is four-dimensional and possesses a one-dimensional time arrow. The spiritual world is purely subjective, a world in which we perceive the two dimensions past and present as separate entities existing in parallel. In addition, we experience the three-dimensionality of space.

For us living in our present time various actions happen simultaneously in spatial vicinity. For example, while I am writing my book you are somewhere else on this earth working, sleeping, relaxing, playing with your children, taking care of your parents or maybe eating something. While you are reading this book I may be writing my next book – discussing something completely different. At every one of these various places where we are doing different things at the same time an immense number of actions have already taken place in the past.

Only for us time has raced in one direction and earlier events have left no traces at these places today. Once upon a time....
In our physical world gigantic sequences of events happened at one and the same place at different points in time. The place has changed due to these events, but it has not changed its position within its parameters.

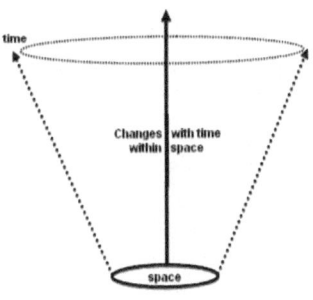

Let us imagine that we have been transferred to a spiritual dimension where all past events up until today exist in parallel in the same way as all places in the physical world. A place for us in the physical world is equivalent to time in the spiritual world.

As for us time passes by continuously in one direction, the three-dimensionally perceived space does the same in the spiritual world. It is constantly changing in the same way as we perceive time. As we are carried forward in the tidal wave of time in the physical world, where seconds, minutes and hours change continuously, so space carries us away in the spiritual world and we change continuously the place of event, since space is continuously changing.

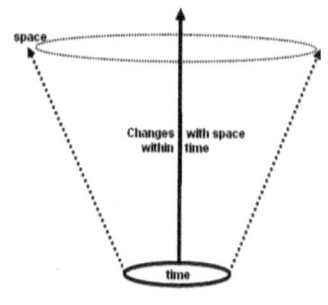

In our physical world we cannot be in different places at the same time. We can, however, be at the same place at different times. We cannot influence our past even if it happened at the same place because we are there at a different time.

In the spiritual world we cannot be in different times simultaneously just as we cannot be at different places in our physical world. We can, however, visit different times at random – as we can visit the same place here. Here we have a different time, in the spiritual world a different place, which gives us a new perspective. In this way we can never influence past events – we remain spectators.

If we revisit the past in the spiritual world a new and changed place has "happened" in the same way as a new time has started in the physical world if we change the place. Here and now we only experience the place at the present time without experiencing the events of the past. There, and at some time in the spiritual world, we can observe the events as they happened in their time but from the perspective of the present new place.

When we travel in the physical world we cannot influence the past because during our journey the time has changed, as the popular German cartoonist and poet *Wilhelm Busch (1832-1908)* describes it so vividly: "*One, two, three, time is fleeting and we race along*".

In the same way as we cannot really change places without living in a new time so the journey into a different time is automatically connected with changing places in that world.

In our physical world an immense number of events have taken place within a certain now existing area since the beginning of all existence up until our present time. In the spiritual world, where time takes the place of the physical area, everything that happened since the beginning of the world in this area, has its place within the time which *exists* there at the moment.

Our temporal future in the here and now is inseparably connected with the further unfolding of space in the future.

Future is thus not only a question of time but also a question of space. The same applies to all future events. Space *and* time change and together they form a joint future.

Therefore, our future can *not* be forecast exactly.

When we philosophise about future expectations we only look at the time which has not yet happened and we forget the space which must still be generated for the future. If we remember that space should not only be seen as a whole but rather as something that keeps developing anew around each and every smallest finiteness, the fundamental significance of the inseparable connection between space and time becomes clear. That we *cannot* forecast our future in principle does not mean that, depending on the perspective, there are no rather significant and certain probabilities which indicate future events.

Here is a simple example: if you were to claim that you could immediately fly away without any means of support, the probability of doing so would tend to zero and insofar I can forecast your future.

In the spiritual world all former events exist in parallel, just as in the physical world all places exist in parallel. In this world we can visit other places and perform new activities. However, we cannot influence old events although the place of action is the same. Time has changed in the meantime. And since some time elapses during the journey any action is a future event if viewed from a point of time before the journey started.

In the spiritual world we can revisit all former events; we are able to travel freely in former times. However, we cannot influence past events because the place has already changed as soon as the time travel starts. If we want to take action it will always happen in a different place. It is impossible to breach the logical course of events. We cannot travel back into our past and kill the hated grandfather whereby our own existence would immediately be deleted. This is something for science fiction authors. This is a paradox imagination based on a small error in reasoning.

Now we must think another step forward, however. Spirit creates matter and spirit penetrates or encompasses matter. This is the last step in the expansion of the levels of existence. And with their aid spirit itself develops further.

Spirit can exist without matter but not matter without spirit. However, the spirit does not enjoy its existence without matter because without matter it cannot progress further.

Of course, at first the spiritual part in lifeless matter is confined to its inherent simple information "to be", i.e. the information "1" of BEING represented by the photon. The "1" marks the smallest (finite) particle of which something consists and it is transported along the infinite information or number space which is emanated by itself and which is structured by numbers. It "radiates".

In living creatures the spiritual part increases dramatically and reaches its maximum at least for the time being in us humans here on our planet. My reflections about time and space are, of course, based on the view of someone who lives here on earth and includes thus matter *and* spirit. From the view of a purely spiritual being existing in a purely spiritual world two other aspects are significant.

The first aspect is that of a mixed perception which is due to the above-mentioned physical-spiritual perspective. It is the result of the polar symmetry of time and space with which we have made ourselves familiar.

In addition, with the growing distance from the physical world, or, if primarily no knowledge of physical relationships has been obtained, we would increasingly or even a priori adopt purely spiritual perceptions and emotions.

Then time and space would not longer bear any significance, since space would be missing or the "recollection" of it would diminish so that a real difference in time would no longer be perceivable. Consequently everything will become more and more purely subjective and from this perspective simultaneously timeless while, of course, there would still be an objective albeit relative period of time in the physical world.

We find a beautiful picture for the simultaneous temporal existence in a spiritual world in the opera "Parsifal" by the German composer *Richard Wagner (1813-1883)*. The young hero Parsifal is guided into the Castle of the Holy Grail by the knight Gurnemanz to participate in the holy act of unveiling the grail. The decorations of the stage settings slide past the slowly proceeding hero. Parsifal is amazed and says to Gurnemanz: *"I hardly walk but still I feel as if I have walked far already."* And Gurnemanz answers: *"You see my son, time becomes space here."*

In the spiritual dimension it is possible to visit any earlier point in time within the current event horizon determined by space and time. They all exist in parallel in all these places which are flowingly merging into one another, almost "racing away". However, since we are already outside the place we visited – as we are in our world in the same place at a different time – past events can only be observed passively. This is similar to a movie where we are also in a different present room which is separated from the room of the film story.

Future here means the opening up of the room for something new and simultaneously the unfolding of a new time.

For everyone in this spiritual world, regardless of the *time* whence s/he comes, the same applies.

What is for us our only real, i.e. physical, space is fundamentally also something spiritual, since it is a pure information and number space. However, since it has been secondarily generated by the creation of every smallest finiteness and was later "filled up" with matter and for our perception "illuminated" by light, we exemplify it and it becomes the central dimensionality of the world and thence of our level of perceptability.

Time on the other hand remains a spiritual dimension which can in practice only be simulated in the physical world. The same, the other way round, applies to our space which is a form of simulation in the spiritual world and which presupposes that it has been experienced as a real dimension.

We can consider this as being another indication that the development of the spirit, or, as I like to describe it, its "differentiation to maximum perfection in the highest possible multiplicity" necessitates the creation of the physical world.

Time is thus a priori indeed something coherent, something continuous for which no adequate counterpart exists in the physical world. Its continuity, its flow[66], is solely due to a thinking subjective spirit. Since in our physical world time is never absolute but always objective, and is, therefore always relative for us because it is regulated by gravitation and velocity, it requires commonly accepted perceptions among "subjective spirits", i.e. among us thinking beings – and this means again it requires our existence.

We are the ones who turn time secondarily into an apparently real physical dimension.

However, due to its continuous character it remains a simulation in the physical world. It will always remain dependent on gravitation and velocity and, therefore, remain objectively flexible. As we all know the relativity of objective time measurement was discovered by *Albert Einstein*. The higher the velocity and the stronger gravitation, the slower time "passes", which is measured by means of the vast number of frequencies of the caesium atom[67].

---

[66] "Panta rhei", Greek: Everything flows. This wisdom came from Heraclitus, the Greek philosopher Heraklit (approx. 544-483 BC).
[67] Since 1967, the basic unit of time is one second defined as the length of time taken by 9.192.631.770 periods of electromagnetic radiation generated when the two hyper-fine structures of the caesium isotope ^{133}Cs alter between their normal energy levels (caesium clock).

It can easily be imagined. Maybe you have seen the television adverts for batteries where a large number of toy rabbits play on a drum in front of them. As the batteries grow weaker, the drumming becomes slower and slower. We could also say it just becomes more difficult for them. It is as if they had to play the drums with the same power of performance against an increased resistance – such as, for example, a higher force of gravity.

Then, too, it would become more difficult for them and they would have to slow down. When the force of gravity is increased, therefore, the clocks slow down as well.

Imagine on the other hand you are flying very fast, at half the speed of light perhaps. *Einstein* thought deeply about this and developed his intellectual experiment with the light clocks. Light, travelling at maximum speed in a back and forth motion inside a huge vacuum tube, must travel a further distance if the tube itself moves through space.

Since the maximum speed of light is constant, however, i.e. it has an upper limit, the only logical consequence can be that *time* itself must have changed, or more exactly, that time has been extended. Einstein talked about a dilation of time.

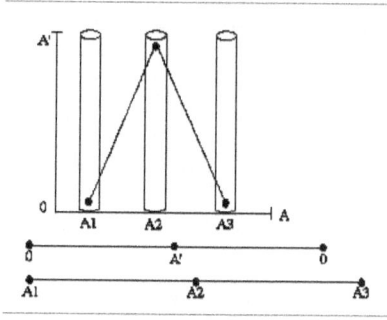

The illustration on the right by my son Martin describes the dilation of time:
Light moves from 0 to A' and back again in a vacuum tube.
At the same time the tube moves from 0 to A. Therefore, the light has to cover a further distance. If the velocity of light remains constant, time must be dilated.

As already mentioned there is nothing really continual in the entire physical world. In the last instance everything can be explained by the interaction of single particles and, even in the case of light, by the interaction of photons (commonly known as quanta) with their *"1"-information*. When talking about *time* we mean a continuity which does not exist in our physical world.

The only real continuity in our physical universe is generated by the sequence of ordinal numbers in number spaces which form around every finite point. They are, however, something immaterial. All numbers are spiritual. And their sequence going from 1 to infinity gives the impression of space possessing continuity.

The information and number spaces are the spiritual expansion of matter. Any kind of matter possesses also something spiritual. This becomes more understandable if we consider matter itself as being the product of something spiritual. Spirit and matter are obviously interdependent, just as the famous and age-old principles, *Yin and Yang,* of ancient Chinese philosophy suggest for everything in the world (see Chapter 2.10, page 99).

The sequence of single events which is in fact always really discontinuous throughout the universe is made to appear continuous merely by the number frame of space and is thus due to something spiritual.

To a degree depending on their level of awareness, only living beings are able to perceive time as something really continuous. And we humans are receptive not only due to our higher consciousness, which enables us to comprehend such relationships, but also to our ability to think in an abstract manner – both being again based on spiritual principles. –

Without life and its thinking beings, time and continuity would make no sense.

We humans are able to develop a perception of time in our physical world without any kind of physical correlation. This alone must certainly strongly indicate the independent existence of a spiritual level in which time is of the same fundamental significance as is space in the physical world. And it is this spiritual background which, much later, ensures that – over and above the numbers – further even more complex and differentiated spiritual contents are manifested in our physical world thereby enabling their own development to continue. These purely spiritual contents are life and spirit.

The creation of life is still an absolute enigma. It is still an inexplicable phenomenon. Life can only be generated by life. Having experienced the various steps of life, it leads in the end to an ever more self-aware and complex spirit (see Part 4).

Time is not merely the fourth dimension in Einstein's model of a space-time continuum. Practically all scientists have accepted this view without criticism. The (only) four-dimensional space-time is, in my opinion, an inappropriate human concept conceived at a time and age when it was fashionable to consider materialistic aspects alone as being true.

Of course, it is indisputable that a time arrow exists which points from the past into the future and leads to ever more chaos (entropy). This is established by the second law of thermodynamics. Time, then, really resembles a one-dimensional line with a clear direction. However, this is merely the *physical* side of the whole truth. If we also take the spiritual side into consideration – provided that we accept its existence – then everything looks completely different. Therefore, to end this chapter I will take another look at the essence of time alternately from both sides of this world. First we view it through our normal *physical* spectacles, through which *space* appears to be *three*-dimensional and time seems to be *one*-dimensional and directed.

Some years ago I already discussed a rather apt example with my two sons. It started in 1995 when we all stood on top of the Table Mountain in Cape Town (South Africa) together with my father and enjoyed the fantastic view. Unfortunately my father died a year later. In 1997 we visited the same place and remembered him with love and affection and talked about him and all the nice things of the past became present in our minds again.

In our physical world we were at the same *place*, i.e. at the same place in space.[68]. Although we were able to change the *place* at random in the meantime, *time* travelled in only one direction. In 1997 my father was no longer with us. What belongs to the past has passed *here* by.

Looked upon this scenario from a spiritual dimension, *space* becomes what *time* is for us now here "on earth".

Although space also appears three-dimensional to us, it appears as a kind of *spiritual line*. However, since time immemorial past and present events happen simultaneously. The future, however, can be considered as a new room which is constantly being generated anew in the same manner as future time in a physical space. The two visits to the Table Mountain mentioned above still exist in the spiritual world side by side. They can both be "visited" again; however, we will never really take part in the event because we look upon it from a different spatial point of view similar to viewing a movie film.

In the spiritual world we can relive all past situations up to the present, yet we cannot interfere with them at any point. "Here" we can visit the same *place* at different times. However, we experience a *temporal* limit. We cannot relive the actual experience. In the spiritual world we can effortless revisit past times, but we experience a spatial limit. Therefore we cannot influence the past.

I am convinced that *space* is infinitely open and four-dimensional. The infinity of space is the consequence of the infinity of time. We call it eternal. An infinite *space* and an eternal *time* possess and remember *continually and eternally* the information of all events in their original as well as in their constantly changing full complexity. Everything exists in reality and is also eternally preserved in its dynamic. Everything which is able to act will retain its capability to do so eternally. It will never be possible to violate causality. Although all *times* exist side by side and can each be "visited" in the spiritual world, the *place* will always be a different one.

---

[68] It is negligible for understanding this example that in fact the earth is meanwhile no longer in the same position in cosmic space as it was then.

One of the big problems of our time is that we still have not yet freed ourselves from our materialistic viewpoint and that we are not prepared to do so.
It still represents the spirit of our time and age. Therefore, we are unable (or no longer able) to recognise the nuances.
This is the reason why so many people on our earth are dispirited and helpless, and why some are driven to follow radical-fundamentalist dogmas. Both are sad state of affairs.
Only a new and better view of the world will provide the long overdue key to a better world. This is at the same time the *only* key to a future world with a chance of survival!'

3.9) Where is the Antimatter?

From space and time to antimatter? Do you think this is a big jump? Not at all!
The two probably most important elementary basic rules in our world are: everything is polar-symmetrical and nothing can emerge from nothing (see Chapter 2.11)
The acceptance of a really existing polar symmetry of space and time with their two aspects of finiteness and infiniteness are important for the comprehension of the entire world structure.
When scientists today attempt to fathom why there is matter and antimatter, or left and right versions of amino acids $(AA)^{69}$, or why there are men and women, or why we have two arms and two legs, then the answer is: for symmetrical reasons this is inevitable. Even if one day we should come into contact with other creatures in this universe we will surely notice that there is not and cannot be an exception to this polar symmetry which is intrinsic in our world. And I have no doubt at all that "Aliens" exist, the only question is whether we can and will ever make *physical* contact with them due to the immense distances involved. I rather think not!
It is remarkable, however, that in some cases almost exclusively one form exists with only solitary polar-symmetrical variations, whilst in other cases both possibilities are found almost as frequently. Why is that?
Symmetry and polarity are, of course, already implemented on the spiritual level which is the blueprint and the basis for the creation of the physical world. Spiritual values, such as good and bad, love and hate, justice and

---

[69] One of 20 biologically relevant amino acids has no optical centre. It can be structured left as well as right. The remaining 19 AAs are optically active and are structured either left or right.

injustice, beauty and ugliness or harmony and disharmony, etc. already exist within it.
Here a decisive difference is already outlined:
Whereas in the *dis*continuous physical world everything is strictly polar without transitional forms, e.g. matter *or* antimatter, left *or* right configuration of amino acids, etc. the continuous spiritual world always shows transitional forms between antipodes. This becomes especially obvious in the case of men and women. Considered from a purely physical respect they are of clearly different gender. Considered from a spiritual, i.e. from an emotional respect uncountable numbers of transitions exist.

Furthermore, the rule becomes apparent that it depends on the strength and the duration of the spiritual influence exerted on the single object to determine to what extent purely physical or purely spiritual aspects are finally manifested. If the generation of something physical takes a longer period of time, then the subjective influence of the spiritual world is stronger than in those cases where something is generated fast or indeed very suddenly. The longer this influence is exerted on the object the more significant is the time-dependent conversion process later. Objects which are generated spontaneously and suddenly are not subject to a temporal development process. They always manifest themselves in either one *or* the other form, and that form once generated is practically never or at least very seldom changed later. This is the crucial reason why so obviously only matter exists to the total or overwhelming exclusion of antimatter and why almost only left configurations of amino acids exist and practically no right configurations, even if both forms were theoretically possible. Antimatter is the mirror image of matter. Therefore, antimatter as well as "right-configured" amino acids can meanwhile be produced but only in traces and with an immense effort. The natural existence of larger amounts of antimatter would certainly be problematic because a collision of matter with antimatter could possibly destroy both.

If we consider the natural and also stable elements and the number of left-configured amino acids (AA) in our universe the following facts become apparent (see Chapter 2.9): the 20 biologically relevant AAs are divided in 19 optically active and 1 optically inactive AAs. The 80 chemical elements, following hydrogen as the leading element, can be arranged, according to various criteria, into four groups with 20 elements each, which can always be depicted in the form of "1 + 19" again. As an example I would mention the group of 20 elements which appear in a so-called "*pure* form". They are also known as *pure* isotopes. The first pure form is beryllium with 4 protons. It is an *even*-numbered pure isotope. The remaining 19 pure isotopes possess *uneven* numbers of protons and all of them without exception are *prime numbers*.

Plichta was the first to point out that there are exactly 81 natural and stable elements in the whole cosmos. I was the first to point out that the crucial order principle of the genetic code lies in the exact number of 81 code positions essential for protein synthesis. On one side there is a leading element, hydrogen, on which all other elements are based, and on the other side there is *one* single nucleotide or a code word which starts all protein production. In most cases this is the AUG (see Chapter 2.9).

The core elements of animate *and* inanimate matter use the number 81, a number which can be derived from the first four ordinal numbers in a smart and uncomplicated way (see Chapter 2.8).

Among the other things already discussed in Part 2, the sum of the first ordinal numbers provokes the thought that the decimal system might be the universal calculating system. In this place value system the next place after the number 10 ($=10^1$) is the number 100 ($=10^2$). The difference of 100 minus 81 is 19, a prime number. Prime numbers seem to have special significance in our world, as *Plichta* already pointed out.

This includes, for example, the control of light frequency which decreases with the increasing distance from the light source, which is probably the real cause of the redshift of light from faraway stars and galaxies, as I was the first to discover and describe some years ago (see Chapter 3.6).

From all this we may assume that elementary structures in our world always appear in the form of "19 + 1". According to this there should be about 5% antimatter annihilated by the same amount of matter. The same applies to left and right configured AAs and for all the other things of which only *one* variant exists in nature today. The probably randomly favoured and now prevailing variant was able to survive in always sufficiently large quantities and numbers, due to those circumstances discussed above.

3.10) Symmetrical Differences betwen Spirit and Matter

Everywhere in nature there are two basic variants of symmetry: we have to differentiate between the fundamental principle and its physical forms or peculiarities.

Spirit and matter are fundamental structures as are time and space, or finiteness and infiniteness. They are polar-opposite to each other and they are always generated in perfect symmetry. The same applies to the male and the female aspect, i.e. in humans, for men and women.

Perfect symmetry always indicates the fine thread through evolution in our world. Every basic principle can then develop and shape itself further. In inanimate matter, for example, single elements are generated and within these isotopes are formed. In organic matter gene code positions and amino acids are generated. With respect to the details of the basic principle or, as I call it, its various forms and shapes, the "law of symmetry" demands that *both* possible variants are realised. Although they were both generated at the same time, they could do more harm than good to evolution under certain conditions.

For this reason they are controlled by simple mathematical specifications in accordance with other factors – those of an asymmetrical manifestation. In the case of simple physical basic building blocks which do not possess a further differentiated spiritual part, the two mirror images probably eliminate each other, as is the case with matter and antimatter. Absolute symmetry would be counterproductive in these cases.

Due to a purely mathematically controlled "asymmetrical" symmetry only one variant remains with the aid of which everything else can be constructed without risk.

This form of polar symmetry is found at all further levels of evolution. Here I choose deliberately an outstanding example – homosexuality – which seems to me far too often to be the cause of excessively heated discussions within our society today. It is nothing more than a natural variant of sexual orientation which is, by the way, not found exclusively in humans, but also in animals.

From the reproductive point of view it is counterproductive, of course. Therefore, it appears asymmetrically in nature. Today we know that about 5% of the human race is homosexually orientated, a number which confirms this assumption. Homosexuality is neither a disease nor is it misconduct due to education or other circumstances. Those concerned cannot help it, their orientation is simply the result of a completely natural variation of nature by which they are affected and others are not. Modern humans who have the sense to discover and also to understand such phenomena should finally learn to fully accept and not to villainise these people.

The same message should also be addressed to some representatives of various religions when they praise above all the love of God, Allah, Jehovah, etc. – or however s/he, the personal divine dimension may be called – but overlook that "this magnificent divine" loves *all* its creatures in their *natural form*.

The stronger the purely spiritual and thus the emotional, the ethical-moral or in general the cultural and the aesthetic aspect advances due to further

differentiation within the evolution of this world the more it is that time influences the symmetry of certain values and patterns of behaviour.
It is changed by a constant developmental process. This is the most important reason why we humans look into our future full of optimism and hope, and why it is that we are allowed to assume that the bad will turn into good in the course of time and that injustice will become justice and hate will become love, in spite of all wars, crises and self-induced problems.
This first applied to the development of mankind as a collective process of evolution on this earth – but not anymore. We cannot compare mankind with animal species which are largely homogeneous collectives; rather, we are a large number of immensely important single individuals unlike any other species on earth. Therefore, this requirement no longer applies just for the whole; that would simply no longer be sufficient. Only if every single part of the whole, i.e. when every single person as an individual part of the whole of mankind, can anticipate this development with optimism, only then can mankind achieve the same as a whole.
However, humans as physical creatures do not live long enough to achieve this as individuals in the course of one lifetime.
Even if future humans get closer to these ideals as a whole, the humans of today are very far, much too far, away from the goal as unfortunately we all experience every day.
However, my demands make no exceptions for us, the "ancestors of the future". All of us, and that really includes all humans without exception, must and will personally undergo this development to the positive.
Only this will "redeem" mankind as a whole in the real sense of the word.
This can only be achieved if life is "prolonged" on an all-penetrating and all-encompassing spiritual level – or as religions in the Far East assume, by continuous rebirth into a multitude of different physical lives. I do not believe in the latter, because logic contradicts this (see Chapter 2.15).
Thus the assumption that we continue to exist as single individuals in a different world, a spiritual world, remains inevitable.

I have explained repeatedly that infinite space is directly generated from the finiteness of every physical point.
Each single atom provides an infinite information space. The entirety of all these single spaces make up the universe as we perceive it which is constantly changing with the highest level of dynamic.

This notion embodies the source of an eternal and infinite information store of everything and everybody. [70]

In the same manner the differentiated and increasingly personal spirit lives on. It is the product of the differentiation due to the mutual interaction between physical finite bodies (brains) which have become competent to do so, and the initially undifferentiated spiritual field which penetrates them. The then differentiated spirit corresponds with the soul in religious terminology. It is an individual and independent whole as well as part of a bigger and all-encompassing whole.

An infinite spirit differentiates itself with the aid of the finite physicality of matter. It is not always aware of its eternal existence which distinguishes itself by means of its subjective time perception and by its temporal as well as spatial boundlessness.

The spirit is not an independent substrate as *René Descartes (1596-1650)* postulated, but, due to the interaction between matter and the surrounding spiritual field, the spirit develops and becomes a differentiated individual product. A mature spirit is generated by the increasing interaction between competent matter and an initially immature spiritual field. The interaction starts as soon as competent structures have been developed by matter which needs a fairly long time (see Parts 4 and 5). This purposeful evolution requires a continuous and consequential spiritual control based on quite simple mathematical rules (see Part 1). Development takes place only where life exists. Life itself, however, and I will explain this in the following part, is already the result of a spiritual development and is not some kind of automatism inherent in inanimate organic structures.

After a very long lead time matter becomes mature enough to start a noticeable interaction with the spirit in an efficient and later conscious and even self-aware manner.

Due to such self-awareness humans have reached another, higher level on the ladder. From there the spiritual maturing process accelerates at unexpected speed and efficiency. This process needs humans who have finally become aware of natural laws and interconnections on which this development is based.

At the same time when physical order regresses into disorder, a process which is irreversible (in physical terms: positive entropy), an ever more complex and more organized and higher developed spirit is simultaneously generated – as the other side, the mirror image, of the same coin.

---

[70] This seems to me to be the intuitively-religious basis of the so-called → Akasha-Chronicle. This term goes back to Sanskrit and means something like "space, ether". It means some kind of "world memory", in which everything that ever existed is supposed to be recorded.

Due to the perfect symmetry inherent in all basic patterns of the world, it strives to achieve the highest possible differentiation of an initially completely disorganized and undifferentiated spiritual field.

The highest possible perfection requires the highest possible multiplicity. The spirit which finally differentiates itself, or matures, is not a collective spirit. It is a complete collection of perfect individual and differentiated spirits; it is the sum of all souls.

Perfection in multiplicity makes the notion of a physical space mandatory. If the notion of the existence of a progressing spiritual being is to stand up to scrutiny we have to accept that the experience of space is essential for its differentiation, its maturation. It follows inevitably that a physical dimension must be generated as the real counterpart to the eternal spiritual temporality. The existence of differentiated spiritual personalities in eternity with their subjective time perception requires a spatial concept. Only this allows us to transform an initially spaceless condition into some kind of playground in which spiritual maturation becomes possible.

If the spirit itself, as the counterpart to matter, which evidently strives towards ever more disorder, were to strive towards ever more order and more differentiation or maturation, i.e. to the highest perfection in the highest possible multiplicity, this would have consequences which would support my optimism. Here is another consideration to this end.

This world can only exist if the initial absoluteness becomes the only absoluteness on the one hand and simultaneously the absolute good, the absolute goodness and the immeasurable love on the other. If there were a counterpart, the absolute evil, nothing at all would ever have had a chance to develop. The absolute evil would exclude not only everything positive but also any other form of existence right from the start. Nothing would be able to exist next to the absolute evil which would otherwise not be absolutely evil. If we conscious humans could not believe in something positive and believe in love, then we would be unable to bring children into the world.

Since the spirit is striving towards the highest perfection within the highest possible multiplicity this must be accompanied by the quest to turn the bad into something good. Therefore, we can be optimistic and assume that in the long run injustice will turn into justice and hate will turn into love. This is exactly what religions teach us if we were only prepared to listen carefully.

We can rest assured that inanimate and animate matter are again the flip sides of the same coin just as are matter and spirit or finiteness and infiniteness. Of course, finiteness means decay and infiniteness stands for eternity. It follows logically and consequentially that life and death are also the flip sides of the same coin. In this sense death stands for the inevitable decay of any three-dimensional body, it does not, however, apply to its inherent potentially infinite spirit, its soul (see Chapter 2.14). Although death is the temporal termination of any physical spatiality it is not the end of life itself, because that would relate to spatial and temporal infinity.

Since life itself is again a coin with two sides, matter and spirit (on whatever kind of level), it must become evident to anyone that death only terminates the finite three-dimensional physicality. Thereafter follows the infinite and eternal, non-physical continuing life of the spiritual aspect. Non-physicality does not at all mean that there is no physical body. The dimension is only slightly shifted.

3.11) Electricity and Magnetism and the Standardisation of the Four Elementary Forces

Electricity and magnetism are two phenomena which modern scientists can describe but cannot exactly explain.

In my opinion they are again the two sides of the same coin and thus they belong together and are inseparable. Of course, both phenomena must be explainable with my perceptions. Therefore I will try to explain it in the following manner. Electricity is due to the existence of two polar charges, which we arbitrarily describe as (+) und (-) and which we term electric poles. Poles with the same charge reject one another; poles with opposite charges attract one another. Forces interact between them, an area known as the electric field, which almost "cry out" for being explained by the number space. In the 19th century the English scientist *Michael Faraday (1791-1867)* discovered that every (total) charge is a whole number multiple of the smallest quantity of charge, the so-called elementary charge. It follows that the total charge is proportional to the number of charge carriers. If the charges are moved or temporarily changed another force *field* is generated, the magnetic field.

The electric field and the magnetic field are two manifestations of one and the same field, the electromagnetic field. We talk about fields without knowing any details. Basically, this is a form of magnetism caused by electric charges.

The following applies: the value of the attracting or rejecting force is always directly proportional to the total charge.

This already results from that mentioned above because the more charge carriers there are, i.e. the higher the total charge, the more powerful is the force between the oppositely charged poles. This force also depends on the distance between the two poles.

The following rule applies: if the distance between the bodies increases, or more precisely, if the distance between the centres of the charges is increased, then the force will always decrease by the squares of the reciprocals of ordinal numbers. If the distance between the poles is decreased the force grows by the squares of all ordinal numbers. However, if the poles draw closer together, the force increases by the squares of all integers. You will notice immediately that this is *Isaac Newton's* "inverse square law" all over again which also applies to the decreasing force of gravity or the diminishing of light in space. The squares of all ordinal numbers also control the *effects* of (electro-) magnetic forces. Solely responsible for all this is the real existing number space around each finite body.

Now we still have to explain what it could be that causes the different charges. We already know that any finite existence, i.e. any three-dimensional body within a space, exerts gravity due to its very own number space. If many finite bodies are densely packed then the force of attraction is correspondingly stronger.

According to *Faraday* practically the same rule applies to (electro-) magnetic forces which, however, are far stronger than those of gravity. This means, however, that the *structure* of finite bodies, or their "naked" existence, alone *cannot* explain electromagnetic force.

Therefore, I believe that, apart from the structure, *function* also plays an important part. *Function* means here rotation. Any finite body, small or large, can rotate around its own axis whereby the same direction of rotation denotes the same elementary charge. If two bodies rotating in the same direction and thus possessing the same charge approach one another they will repel one another in the same way as one rotating cogwheel does not harmonize with another next to it rotating in the same direction.

Every finite body, small or large, can rotate around its own axis. If the bodies rotate in the same *direction* it will mean that they have the same *elementary charge*. I was the first one to suggest this in my book about the universe.[71] If two bodies with the same direction of rotation and therefore the same elementary charge draw close they reject each other in the same manner as a rotating cogwheel cannot harmonize with another one rotating in the same direction.

Within every atom there are tiny electrons rotating around their own axes *(spin!)* whilst also orbiting the nucleus. The far larger protons only rotate around their own axes but in the opposite direction to the electrons. The neutrons do not seem to rotate at all.

Thus different elementary charges are generated which usually compensate each other within the same atom. To the outside, therefore, the atom appears

---

[71] "A Better History of Our World, Volume 1, The Universe" (August 2000).

to be neutral, i.e. electrically uncharged, if it carries exactly the same number of electrons as protons, i.e. an equal number of particles each rotating in opposite directions. Only when one electron is removed – by friction, for example – does the atom become electrically charged.

The name "electron", by the way, is Greek and means "amber". The ancient Greeks already noticed that a piece of amber develops an ability of attracting other bodies, such as hairs or feathers, after having been rubbed against fur.

An electrically charged atom which has one electron too few or one too many *(an ion)* always strives to discharge, i.e. to become neutral.

For this reason, electrons move from places with an excess of electrons (negative pole) to places with a shortage of electrons (positive pole). We say that an electric current is flowing. We are observing here the incredibly fast transport of particles and information from one atom to the next.

The number spaces of the atoms involved are thereby *continually frequented* again and again and are probably strengthened due to the constant "renewal".

Thereby a condition is simulated as if far more atoms were closely packed together than there really are. This brings about a noticeable increase in the force of "simple gravity" and electromagnetism is generated. It has the same effect as gravity but is much stronger.

Gravitation is the "basic force", generated and controlled by the real number space around every finite point. It is exclusively the result of the "naked" *existence* of any finite *structure*.

The electrical charge is an expression of *additional movement* and thus the external sign of an additional *function*. Different charges are the direct consequence of *different directions* of movement.

Electromagnetism is the direct consequence of this function "movement" which concentrates "simple" gravitation into an electromagnetic force in a similar way as a lens focuses light. All these forces are controlled solely by the numbers of the infinite real number spaces.

The word "magnetism", by the way, is derived from the place where chunks of certain iron ore which attracted other metals are said to have been found for the first time. The name of the place is *Magnesia*, today called *Manisia*, which lies north east of the Turkish town of Izmir in Asia Minor. Certain metals such as iron (Fe) or Copper (Cu), for example, always possess *two* apparently "loosely connected" outer electrons.

Expressed in simple terms we could say that these electrons move easily between such atoms even when the metals themselves are still in a solid state. There is a natural transfer of particles which is why metals are especially good conductors of electricity. These "loose" outer electrons prevent the creation of a firm connection between two such metal atoms to form a molecule. They

support the formation of a dense mesh structure in which the atoms come to lie in close proximity to each other. I suppose that it is due to this spatial proximity that the two outer electrons orbit two adjacent atoms in the figure of eight whereby their orbits run in opposite directions.
The illustration below by my son Martin describes this clearly:

In this way stable pairs are formed which possess two poles of equal intensity but with different charges. We call them dipoles. Since they are the smallest units between which an exchange of electrons takes place they are known as molecular magnets. Fe = iron, N = North pole, S = South pole.

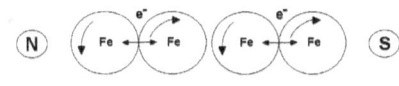

If the dipoles are distributed randomly, their magnetic effects are compensated.
But if they are well ordered in one direction then the whole object becomes magnetic. We then have the typical magnet with stable north and south poles. This means that in natural magnets we also find a "flow of electrons". The two poles of the dipole form two number spaces which overlap in the middle and, therefore, mutually compensate their effects there, whereas towards the poles, of course, their effects are strengthened again. They control the extension and the direction of the magnetic force.

Magnetism and gravity are very similar since magnetism has the same effect as gravity, however, gravity is solely the result of a *structure*, i.e. the consequence of any "naked" finite existence, which generates an infinite cyclical number space around itself.
Such a number space then controls the behaviour of other masses and effects. Magnetism is built up from this base. It is the result of the *function*, i.e. it is due to the rapid movements such a structure can exert.
Magnetism is much stronger than gravity because its effect is practically focused due to the continuous movement of particles whereby the number spaces are constantly renewed.
In principle all these effects obey in order and extent solely the numbers. Structure and function together determine *what kind* of force is generated. The numbers then determine *how* this force takes effect.
All four of the known elementary forces can be understood and easily explained alone by the terms "structure" and "function" and by using the infinite cyclical number frame around each finite point.

"Structure" always means here the pure or naked finite existence of every finite body itself and "function" means the movements of this finite "being", sometimes also its order.

In the next two chapters I will look at some specialities in the fields of physics, mathematics and cosmology which can also be explained very simply and plausibly with the world model I introduced above.

3.12) Physical Oddballs: the Double Slit Experiment and the Aspect Experiment

Following my explanations we conclude: light consists of particles and has *no* simultaneous wave character. This perception which may sound rather antiquated at first, is in fact rather revolutionary and I know that it completely contradicts the current level of knowledge of modern physics. It is almost shameful to say this, but I think I am right.

I published my perceptions for the first time in 1999, and I think I explained them plausibly. Meanwhile many years and five more books "have gone by" and I have the strong feeling that my point of view has been confirmed. The wave character of light seems to have strong proponents, but, alas, they suffer from illusions. The observable wave phenomena we are told are the result of some kind of cosmic ether, the non-existence of which was already a proven fact 100 years ago...

Nevertheless, it does indeed exist we are told, but it is no longer the kind of ether it was assumed to be for several thousand years. The real ether is *not* physical nature, but, in my opinion, something spiritual. It is pure *information* within an *infinite information space* – comparable to the world encompassing and all-penetrating cosmic internet. It is structured by all ordinal numbers which is why it is known as number space. Viewed from the physical side, light particles, photons, are transported through it. However, each photon is basically a single piece of information. From a mathematical point of view this corresponds to the number "1". For this reason I call it the "1-information".

The "1" is the information of a smallest existence or, as I call it, the information of BEING. Therefore, it is the *opposite* of zero, of the non-existence or the real nothingness, but it does not originate from it. The "1" is, therefore, not polar-symmetrical to zero because that would be the "-1". It follows that the "1" and the zero are not mutually dependent as are the "-1" and the "+1" (see Chapter 2.10).

If light particles are transported through cosmic space it means that their real essence, the information "1", is multiplied by every ordinal number from 1 to infinity in an infinite number space which is generated around every finite body.

With this completely new alternative perception, which can be derived in a plausible manner from my very simple intellectual experiment about the growth and propagation of a smallest finite point, the smallest circle (see Chapter 2.4), all these observations in our world are explainable.

My idea of the true nature of light also enables us to explain effectively some phenomena which have occupied physicists' mind for many decades and which up until today are still waiting for a really satisfying explanation.

One of them is the so-called "double-slit experiment". In simple words this means:

If we shine light through *one* slit in a screen onto a wall a typical pattern of light will appear which we know as the "Gaussian normal distribution"[72].

This means that the light has passed through the slit in the form of single photons, i.e. massless "light particles".

If, however, light passes through *two* adjacent slits in the screen, the pattern on the wall will change to a so-called "interference pattern"[73].

This seems to indicate that light must have passed through the slits in the form of "waves".

In order to verify the results scientists sent single photons through the slits. This did not change the result: with one slit there was only one light point on the wall behind the screen, with two slits there were always two points of light on the wall.

The experimenters wanted to be very smart now and decided only a split second after they had "fired" a single photon[74] whether to use the screen with one or with two slits.

However, it was demonstrated again and again that light cannot be outsmarted.

In the meantime the same experiment has been carried out with electrons and even with atoms which are all still incredibly tiny but in contrast to photons they are not massless.

---

[72] The light photons passing through the slit are distributed in accordance to the bell curve established by the famous mathematician *Carl Friedrich Gauß (1777-1855)*. Most photons hit the middle, towards the left and the right the probability of hits diminishes exponentially to both sides.

[73] Interference = is the phenomenon to be observed if two or more waves are super-imposed whereby the crests of the waves either interfere constructively (the resultant wave amplitude is increased) or destructively (the resultant wave amplitude is decreased).

[74] We have to keep in mind that this means a light particle or, better, a "1"-light information has been severed from an atom, i.e. from a finite point.

The explanation given by modern physicists sounds rather weird to me, although it has become a natural scientific manifest today.

According to this light must be *particle and wave simultaneously*. This is known as the particle-wave dualism. It may also depend on the experimenter himself – in some way or other – *how* light, whether as a flow of photons or only as a single photon, really behaves in the end. Others even assign some kind of subjectivity to light itself. The famous Danish physicist *Niels Bohr (1885-1962)* thought that light departs as particle and arrives in the same form. In between, however, it travels in the form of a wave. Only when measured or, in general, due to the observations of an experimenter the "wave function collapses".

I believe that this problem can be solved in a much simpler and more plausible way if we take into consideration the existence of an infinite information space which is structured by numbers and is generated around every finite point.

Every finite point, which means specifically every single atom as the *biggest* thinkable small finiteness, generates an infinite number space around itself which is structured by the processing of all ordinal numbers from 1 to infinity (see Chapters 2.45, 2.13, 2.15).

This number space always transports the *smallest* possible information of our universe, in mathematical terms, the number "1", into infinity through the entire universe simply by multiplying it by every one of these ordinal numbers.[75] All number spaces really exist, were they not existing finite points would also not exist and vice versa.

Whether light is emitted as a strong flow of photons or merely as a single photon – it always means the same. A source of light is essential and that consists of finite particles, of atoms. The emission of light or of single photons then means that the information "1" on its own or consecutively in large numbers is multiplied with every ordinal number (i.e. square number) of the number space generated by the light source. At the same moment the "1"-information is in fact present *everywhere* but on an *immaterial pure "information wave"*, the number shell of the number space. Insofar Bohr was right. However, it is not the light itself which becomes a wave; the wave exists independently of whether light is transported or not because this is a permanent (informative) space wave.

The rest of the experiment can be explained in a rather trivial way: all space waves, i.e. the onion skins of the number space, allow a "1"-information to pass through any hole which presents itself in their infinite expansion. If there is a hole, there will surely be either a photon behind it or the normal distribution curve if there is a flow of photons, i.e. a flow of particles. If there

---

[75] To be exact this is the 1^2 for three-dimensional bodies in the two-plane geometry of space.

are two holes in the screen we will find either two "1"-information units on the wall behind it or two normal distribution curves.

For a scientist who measures them with special instruments or who can even detect them with his eyes, the "1"-information units are, of course, photons, because they interact with the receiver cells or regions of the relevant tool or the retina of the eye. This is then known as the exchange of energy.

The apparent wave of light is in reality only due to the "1"-information being multiplied by every ordinal number of an infinite number space which is generated around every ever so small finite point.

Here a bit more information especially for "cosmos freaks":
The "EPR Paradoxon" can be explained in a similar manner and thus "Bell's Theorem" and the so-called "Aspect Experiment" as well which was carried out later to prove it.

However, let's take it step by step. The physicists *Albert Einstein, Boris Podolsky* and *Nathan Rosen* (the abbreviation "ERP" consists of the initials of their family names) did not believe in mere coincidence for the occurrence of important events on an atomic and subatomic level as postulated in quantum mechanics. At a conference with the great physicists of their time in Brussels in 1927, Einstein made the famous remark: "God does not play dice".

In 1935 together with his colleagues mentioned above Einstein published a scientific paper[76] in which they summarized their doubts about quantum mechanics being a correct and complete theory of nature. Einstein was of the opinion that its explanations must at least be incomplete since he was still convinced of the profound lawfulness of all cosmic events. And I am convinced that Einstein was right.

However, at the time he was heavily criticised for his pertinacity and even today his perceptions of quantum mechanics are widely accepted.

Anyway the three scientists mentioned above saw great discrepancies which went down in history as the "ERP-paradox".

About 30 years later the Irish physicist *John Bell (1928-1990)*[77] was the first to perform an experiment which was supposed to clarify many contradictions in quantum mechanics, such as the example concerning the question of "wave or particle".

It was left to the French physicist *Alain Aspect (*1947)*, however, to be the first to carry out a practical series of tests in 1972. In principle he blasted off a pair

---

[76] Title of this paper: "Can Quantum-Mechanical Description of Physical Reality be Considered Complete?"
[77] John S. Bell, see List of References.

of so-called twin photons with differing polarisation from an atom which simultaneously shot in different directions.

We might imagine this as if each one of these photons possesses a small "arrow" in addition to its "1" information, whereby one photon carries a horizontal arrow and the other a vertical arrow.[78]

This results in a constellation different from the double-slit experiment explained above, in which only the naked information "1" was emitted as proof of the existence of the smallest unit of "being". Here now we have some further information, namely the polarization. The scientists of the group around *Aspect* emitted two differently polarised photons simultaneously. After a defined distance (in the experiment only a few metres) both photons were detectable again. For this purpose so-called polarization filters were used which selectively collected only those photons with the appropriate polarization. In other words, one filter could only collect photons with the horizontal arrow, the other only those with the vertical arrow.

The following paradoxical results were established:
If the filter "only for horizontal arrows" sought to catch a photon, the horizontal photon was caught automatically. The other photon was then found in the filter "only for vertical arrows". Trials to catch it with an additional filter for "horizontal arrows" always failed. The same result would have been achieved if the distance had been several million kilometres, if so much space had been available. That was clear for every scientist.

Now another trick was tried. Even when the photons were emitted first and it was *only later* decided which filter to use on which side to catch the photons, the result remained the same. If it was decided to use the horizontal filter on one side after the differently polarized photon had been emitted then the other photon on the other side could only be caught by the filter for vertical arrows.

However, how were the photons to know *which* filter was actually used *after* they had been emitted?

This very simplified description of the experiment *apparently* underlines the perception of quantum physicists that, analogous to the double-slit experiment, the photons do not really possess an existence of their own but only some kind of "probability".

---

[78] This example should only facilitate a better imagination. The direction of the arrows and their position is in principle arbitrary.

They would really manifest themselves if an external observer – in this case the experimenter – by a conscious action – in this case by measuring the photons – were practically to decide from the outside how the protons should behave.
Other scientists assigned a kind of consciousness to the photons which enabled them to adjust their polarisation in order to outsmart the amazed experimenters; I can hardly express it in a better way.
Other scientists believed that a connection faster than light must exist between the differently polarized photons which, at the very moment when the experimenter decides which filter to use for one photon, the other reacts with high speed and behaves in the opposite manner.
Everybody who reads this will realize why some things in quantum mechanics cause so much uneasiness and incomprehension even among many scientists. But the fact remains, up until today we still have no better explanations than this.
Later this "probability wave" was happily promoted to become a dogma, since for many it was the most sensible solution even if often not really understood. Einstein, by the way, kept opposing this perception until he died, but in the end he was overruled by his overpowering colleagues.
As so often, the following applies here as well: to belong to a minority does not necessarily mean you are mistaken. Already in 1999 – 44 years after his death – I was the first to try to rehabilitate Einstein with the following solution which I published in my book "Arguments for a Life after Death and a slightly different View of the World". In 2005, 50 years after his death, it was almost a necessity for me to do so in the German original of this book.

I hope physicists will bear with me, for I attempt this explanation without being a physicist myself and I am indeed aware of this chutzpah.
This time it is all about photons. Both twin photons are in principal purely massless particles, where the term "particle" is almost an exaggeration. In the last instance this concerns only the smallest information units of everything in this world, of all energy and thus of all matter. And as I do not stop repeating, they are not independent waves. Considered from a mathematical point of view they are basically the number "1" (or 1^2), transported into infinity and multiplied by all ordinal numbers which structure an infinite number space which itself is automatically generated around every smallest finite point.
The two photons in the Aspect Experiment possess two information units; they carry the information "1" as well as the information "arrow horizontal" or "arrow vertical".

Mathematically, these additional information units can be expressed very simply by differing algebraic signs, i.e. + and − . Thus the two photons become now "+1" and "-1".

If they are sent off on their journeys simultaneously they are also simultaneously transported through space according to the spatial expansion constant. If the experimenter were now to decide – regardless of how far away they are from their starting point – to use both appropriate filters for carrying out the measuring, he, of course, decides by his choice of filter the existence of that information unit, either "+1" or "-1", which he wants to prove.

Both information units are simultaneously detectable because they are both primarily a pure "1"-information and as such, of course, simultaneously multiplied by all numbers of the infinite number space and that happens with the speed of light.

Due to this "energy exchange" only one of the two photons or "1"-information units can manifest itself in the end so that, for a further energy exchange, only the other information unit remains available. Therefore, it is indeed left to the experimenter to decide which polarization is measured, but for a completely different reason than that which has been previously assumed by scientists.

One of the two photons does not manifest itself because it alters its form or adopts the appropriate information at the very moment when it is supposed to be measured. It is rather so, that the observer wants to measure exactly that specific photon whilst being completely unaware that, due to the number structured information transport of the basic information "1" through the infinite "onion skin space", he could in principle *always* measure both polarizations.

In the experiments of the Aspect group it was *not* the *non*-locality of the photon which was in principle measured, as the astrophysicist *John Gribbin (*1946)* claims, but rather its *pan*-locality.

The photon is in fact *everywhere simultaneously*.

For the observer it is impossible in to change the objective existence by a subjective intervention. Supported by mathematical laws the two information units are always everywhere at the same time and the researcher can only choose which one of the two possible objective information units he actually wants to measure.

This is only possible because they are the smallest information units in the world and thereby of all electromagnetic radiation (EMR), i.e. in the last instance of all matter.

That everything functions in this manner is, therefore, due mainly to the "materials" with which the experiment is carried out. Had the scientists chosen apples and pears instead of photons the result would have been different.

3.13) Why Pierre de Fermat was Right

It may be that within this alternative space model lies hidden the real secret of *Fermat's* "Last Theorem".
The famous French amateur mathematician *Pierre Fermat (1601-1665)* was a judge and also a typical loner. All his life he enjoyed poking fun at his mathematical colleagues and every time he found some new mathematical theorem, he always claimed that he was able to prove it. But he very rarely did, and when he did, his proof was incomplete. He loved to keep his colleagues guessing by dropping discrete hints. Before we come to his famous "Last Theorem", recall to mind the Pythagorean theorem, which I already discussed in detail in Chapter 2.16. In my opinion this theorem is of the utmost importance if we want to understand our physical world. It simply says: $a^2+b^2=c^2$, i.e. in a right-angled triangle the area of the square on the hypotenuse is equal to the sum of the areas of the squares on the other two sides.
The first three integers fulfilling these conditions are the numbers 3, 4 and 5, which are known, therefore, as the Pythagorean numbers.
Pythagoras was able *to prove* that there is an infinite number of integers which fulfil this equation.
It was Fermat's idea to investigate how many numbers would fulfil the equation if the exponent were increased at random, e.g. to $a^3+b^3=c^3$. Figuratively speaking, this would no longer involve squares but cubes.
His question became therefore: are there two whole numbers the cubes of which add up to the volume of the cube of a third whole number?
He posed this same question, of course, for all kinds of higher exponents, so that the equation could be generalized: is there an integral solution for the equation $a^n + b^n = c^n$, if "n" is higher than 2?

Fermat established in the end that *no single whole number* higher than 2 would fulfil this equation.
For the equation of Fermat' famous theorem ($a^3 + b^3 = c^3$, or generally speaking with exponents higher than 2) there is indeed no integral solution. Figuratively speaking again there are no two cubes which together result in an appropriate third cube. There are, however, an infinite number of exponents

which are only *slightly off* the mark as the illustration by my son Martin shows below with cubes which have an edge length of 6 and 8:

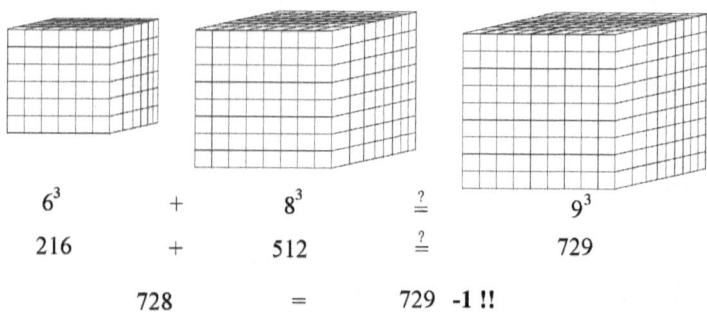

Of course, Fermat also made it known to all his colleagues that he was able to prove all this but, alas, he did not reveal his proof. Until a few years ago nobody has been able to prove his theory in spite of avid research. Over a period of three hundred years the mathematicians of this world have racked their brains in vain. At long last, in 1993, the English mathematician *Andrew Wiles* produced a mathematical proof for Fermat's famous theorem. The derivation was written on more than one hundred printed pages, as the scientific journalist *Simon Singh* explains in his excellent book.'
You will certainly ask now what all this has to do with the alternative world model.

Well, first of all, is it not absolutely amazing that for the exponent "2" an *infinite* amount of integral solutions exist yet for all higher exponents there are *none* at all but many "close" solutions.
That reminds me again of *"Miss Smilla's Feeling for Snow"* by *Peter Höeg*, the book from which I already quoted in Chapter 2.2.

Nature repeatedly confronts us with manifestations which clearly remind us that they are based on an optimal program which actually never fully materializes. On the other hand it reminds me of another mathematician, *Leopold Kronecker (1823-1891)*, who once said *"natural numbers were made by God; everything else was made by humans!"* And Mr Kronecker believed that the entire field of mathematics could be traced back to integers.

If the *program* for our physical world is indeed *two*-dimensional and thereby subject to the law of symmetry and polarity, by which a *four*-dimensional (infinite) space is generated from a plane by the reflection over a right angle, then there is *only one* possible solution for Fermat's equation.
Only the exponent 2 (or those below, i.e. 0 or 1, but this is a triviality) fits into the *two*-dimensional *program* on which our world is based.
That means that nothing can exist that extends beyond the Pythagorean theorem since a *three*-dimensional space as we know it is only a "reduced" part of the *four*-dimensionality which is itself due to the development of all physical things.
Every closed *three*-dimensional body already demands the existence of this *fourth* dimension of space for logical reasons. A *one*-dimensional line can only be imagined on a two-dimensional piece of paper which needs the environment of a *three*-dimensional space. It follows that space needs a real four-dimensionality which encompasses it. We could spin this further eternally if the *four*-dimensionality were not also *infinite*.
Therefore a higher dimension of space can be ruled out.
This is exactly what I attempted to demonstrate by imagining the infinite four-dimensionality of space as being generated by two perpendicularly intersecting infinite planes. The infinity for this is provided by numbers. *Plichta* was the first to develop this space structure. I was the first to develop a plausible concept as to why it has indeed developed in this very simple and completely logical and no other manner (see Chapters 2.4, 2.10, 2.11, 2.13 and 2.15).
Although I never read the mathematical proof of Fermat's theorem by *Wiles*, and would probably not even understand it if I did – here I provide an understandable and logical explanation which is also pragmatic and supports my alternative perceptions about our world as it probably really is.

3.14) Epilogue

Our present cosmic view of the world is by no means based only on the exact results of observations and experiments.
It is rather developed due to various interpretations which are based on many exact results.
In contrast to exact results interpretations are, however, of a subjective nature and depend on various circumstances in which the spirit of the age also plays an important role. To interpret something against the spirit of the age can indeed ruin a career and put a premature end to a scientist's academic life. Some physicists and cosmologists have already experienced this.

To me the present cosmological view of the world seems no more coherent than the geocentric world view of *Ptolemy (approx. 100-170 B.C.)* according to which the earth is orbited by the sun and all the other stars.

This incorrect view of the world was maintained by the Catholic Church as the authoritative cultural institution of the occident for more than one and a half thousand years. People with different views were often prosecuted and even killed.

The new perception of the world was already known long before church officials finally relented to it. Today the situation very often seems similar.

At least the people with different views have a better chance of survival.

Part 4:

Life and Spirit

4.1) Numbers Play a Role Again

Back in 1999, I was the first to be able to demonstrate that the genetic code seemed to be a universal *positional* code based on the number 81.
We have already come to know the number 81 as being the measure for the amount of all stable and natural chemical elements in the entire universe. The 81 is derived from the first four ordinal numbers by means of a mathematical connection which appears initially strange but which is actually logical, and this is $1^2 \times 3^4$ (see Chapter 2.8).
According to popular doctrine the genetic code is the all decisive instruction for the construction of all organisms.
Every living being goes through a development phase before being born. This is known as the embryonic development.
Based on a number of experiments, e.g. with chickens and mice embryos, the famous English biologist *Lewis Wolpert*[79] came to the conclusion that it is the *exact position* of a certain cell within its embryonic tissue which mainly decides how that cell later develops, i.e. how it is differentiated and how it matures.
In the final instance the development of a stem cell depends on the place – or the *position* – which it takes within the cell structure at the beginning of the development and which decides whether it will be a cell in the forearm or in the hand, whether it will be a liver cell or a muscle cell.
No biologist knows today, *where* this information to take a certain position originates and *what* it is that this information really contains.
Of course, the important relationships are again expected to be found *in* the genes, i.e. in the sequences of nucleotide triplets (see Chapter 2.9) which together determine the external characteristics, the phenotype.

---

[79] L. Wolpert, "The Triumph of the Embryo", see List of References.

More precisely, this information should only be found in the biochemical structure of the genotype. I expect this again to be a dead end, especially since numbers are almost self-imposing when "*positions*" again play a role.

To explain this phenomenon *Lewis Wolpert* looked only for biochemical indications and causes. He was able to show that at a very early state of development of organisms very often *two perpendicular development axes* (!) are generated around which then the three-dimensional cell structure is built. Wolpert's perception seems to come very close to my intellectual model of the development of finite points (see Chapter 2.4).

The cells at the ends of both perpendicular axes become two opposite poles. Between them an obviously very finely tuned concentration gradient of cell fluid (cytoplasm) develops which seems to be responsible for the information concerning the positions. Here certain substances seem to play a role as mediators.[80] They have the effect that only special genes can be read. In this manner the appropriately encoded proteins are generated (see Chapter 2.9).

These block or support the reading of other genes. Hence the cells are increasingly differentiated and each cell specializes. In the very moment as it is differentiated to a higher level, the development of other cell types is blocked although, initially, each arbitrary cell did possess every appropriate piece of information to become any kind of cell (pluripotency).

The important question, however, is, *how* is this finely tuned cytoplasmic concentration gradient generated which attempts to define these exact positions?

The term "positional information" alone already indicates, in my opinion, that the answer is directly related to integers.

The growth due to exact positional determinations is surely universal; at least it applies basically to all living beings on earth in a similar manner.

With regard to amphibians, *Wolpert* was able to show that the positional values must be arranged like the numbers on the face of a clock with the number sequence 12, 1, 2, 3, ...9, 10, 11, 12 and a second time round to 12 again, i.e. a total of 24 must be arranged around an extremity. Only if these positional rings are complete can growth proceed and even the regeneration of complete parts of extremities can take place. For example, we can identify various positions on the shinbone (tibia) of a cockroach, which is well able to regenerate, which we may number arbitrarily from 1 to 10.

If the large middle part between the positions 2 and 9 is removed, and the short end stubs with the positions 1 and 10 are connected, then the missing middle part marked 2 to 9 is formed again so that in the end the normal

---

[80] e.g. the so-called retinoic acid, a vitamin A.

shinbone is regenerated as the following illustration by my son Martin, modified according to Wolpert, demonstrates:

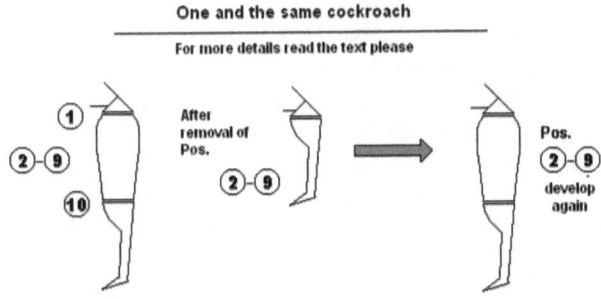

If the short end part after position 10 is cut off and the long remaining part is connected to the equally long part of another cockroach leg cut off at position 1, i.e. rather close to the upper end, then the positions 1 and 10 are reconnected but in reverse order.

We would normally expect the body to remove the superfluous tissue to arrive at the much shorter normal length again.

But, in reality, the opposite happens: In fact the shinbone grows longer because the missing positions 2 to 9 have been regenerated as you can see in the following illustration by Martin, modified according to *Wolpert*.

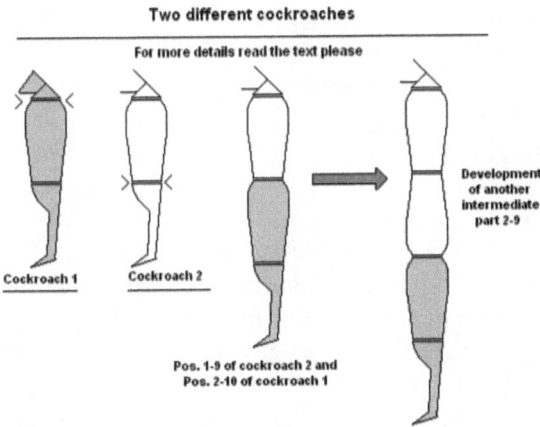

Wolpert believed that the cells were apparently not reacting to just any kind of general stimulation which would determine the length of the shinbone, but only to local stimulation. An important principle begins to emerge; if some cells are put near other cells which are not *natural* neighbours then the *missing positional values* are always regenerated between them. All experiments show conclusively that cells do actually possess such positional values. Other experiments also show clearly that growth and regeneration do in fact follow an exact graduation which is encoded by ordinal numbers.

The English biologist *E.L. Grant Watson*, for example, described some peculiar details observed during the pupation of swallow-tail butterflies as follows[81]:

In the pupa *'a breakdown of tissue takes place'* in the process of which nearly all organs of the caterpillar are reduced to *'some kind of non-cellular mash'*. However, *'form and position of the butterfly organs are marked on the pupa during this stage. The markings are on the outside while on the inside nothing has yet formed which would correspond with them. Although there is nothing inside but the deteriorating old body of the larvae, on the outside of the pupa we can already detect the outline of the entire insect with wings, legs, feelers, etc. in their correct positions and where we will later find the organs which have not yet been formed'*.

The pupation of the caterpillar to the butterfly is a metamorphosis, i.e. a transformation, going hand in hand together with the further development. In the process the cell tissue disappears while certain forces are clearly at work maintaining the continuity of *life* and, based on very specific and apparently abstract immaterial information, are determining its further progress. "Immaterial development programs" really do seem to exist. The English development biologist *Lewis Wolpert* thinks they may and must consist of very simple instructions, although they often adopt very complicated forms. He compares it to *Origami*, the Japanese art of folding paper, whereby the instructions only describe some very simple moves, such as the folding and unfolding of paper. But the forms which are created are very complicated, e.g. a paper bird or a beautiful flower. He himself believes that such "biological instructions" are given by means of differences in *chemical* concentrations which brings us automatically back to my initial question, *how* and *by what* is such a gradient determined.

Let us go back to humans. In appraising the numerical structuring of the arm and leg bones we will notice a similar pattern: *One* bone in the upper arm is followed by *two* bones in the forearm, in the wrist we have *three* bones in the first row and *four* in the second row, followed by *five* fingers (phalanges). The leg is structured in the same way: *one* femur is followed by *two* bones in the lower leg, *three* bones in the back of the foot in the first row (ankle bone, heel bone and navicular bone), *four* bones in the second row (three sphenoid bones and one cuboid bone), followed by *five* toes. This progression towards the

---

[81] Quoted by Adams, G. (1979) and Bischof, M. (1995)

extremities can be found in most living beings and is so clearly orientated to the first *five ordinal numbers*. It seems to be the real secret behind embryonic regulation – which means:
Numbers also determine the development of all life.

And I have already pointed out several times the significance of the paired appearance of five, i.e. the number 10:
The number 10 is the measuring unit of the decimal system – the naturally preferred calculation and counting system in our world, *because* it is the sum of the first *four* ordinal numbers.
Regarding the number of phalanges (i.e. the number of fingers and toes) at the end of extremities which in all (higher) forms of life[82] are arranged in pairs, the number *five* seems to be a pre-set natural limit[83]. At first sight this should be quite astonishing since for purely logical reasons we might expect a further numerical division in anatomy, especially since all phalanges consist of two or three bones: *five* mid-foot or mid-hand bones might conceivably have been followed by *six* proximal phalanges with maybe *seven* mid-bones and *eight* end bones. But this is not the case. A structure of *six* does occur occasionally (*six* fingers or toes in the distal area) – but it is a very rare exception. And a seventh member is even more seldom and when it does appear it is only a rudimentary stump at the end.
It seems very obvious to me that here again something purely spiritual is at work, namely the really existing immaterial sequence of ordinal numbers which is the determining force in the background. In other words: the ordinal numbers determine *what* is developed and *how*. It seems to me that they alone are able to effect such finely and precisely quantified graduations in the cell environment. Yet, no one has ever looked for such a simple information transmitter based merely on ordinal numbers although a large number of really amazing numeric parallels suggest the merits of such a model. Today, famous developmental biologists are finding ever more indications that it is especially the *positioning* of each single cell in a narrowly limited environment which determines the basis for its further development.
Furthermore, the development of different species seems to depend very often on relatively minor gradual changes (e.g. asymmetrical growth) in otherwise identical conditions.

---

[82] This does not apply, for example, to insects. Their form is, of course, also determined by numbers, but follows a structure which is directed towards the interior; however, this cannot be discussed in detail here.
[83] The development of two toes in even-toed ungulates (e.g. the cow) or of one single hoof as in the horse, for example, are, of course, functionally necessary "retrograde" developments from a five-fold structure which is still recognizable in these animals.

At the beginning of the 20th century the British biologist *D'Arcy Thompson*[84], used simple cartographic drawings with which he demonstrated how easily the different forms of whole species are achieved. Wolpert wrote: *"If we were to draw the outline of an animal, e.g. a crab or a fish, into a rectangular system of coordinates, then – by slightly distorting the axes – we depict the form of related fish or crabs. It is similar if we draw the outline on a highly elastic fabric and then stretch the fabric in different directions or distort it in any other way."*

The following drawing by my son Martin (modified from Wolpert) illustrates this:

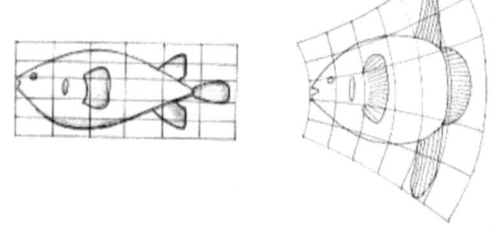

The drawing to the right shows a fish drawn into a right-angled coordinate system. By slightly distorting the axes a new phenotype of fish is generated.

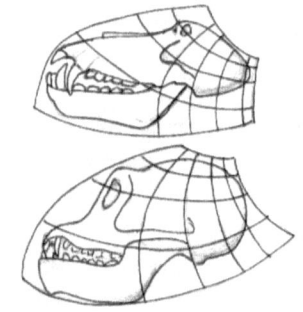

This can also be done with various forms of skulls from mammals to humans.
The drawing to the right by my son Martin, modified from *Wolpert* shows the skull of a red-bridged nose baboon, e.g. a mandrill (above) and an orang-utan

If the spherical fish is the result of a distorted system of coordinates then it must also exist in reality.
Wolpert himself did not warm to this theory. For him the reason for the difference in shape lay in the differing growth rates of the various areas in the same system of coordinates. Questions as to *how* and *why so precisely* such growth is coordinated and controlled can hardly be answered plausibly. Yet, systems of coordinates are nothing but *mathematical position maps*. These obviously universal concepts are good circumstantial evidence that the ordinal numbers used for establishing such map systems are really at work in the

---

[84] According to Lewis Wolpert, "The Triumph of the Embryo", see List of References.

background. This could also mean that such distorted systems of coordinates control development and not the other way round.

Certainly our genes carry an enormous amount of information; but probably only part of it is *biochemically* structured.

Far more information may perhaps be stored *physically*. The reason for this lies probably in their three-dimensional spatial structures. I will discuss this in detail later. However, regardless of whether anything is stored biochemically or physically, there is always a spiritual programme behind it.

This we can again consider to be *one* coin with *two* sides. One side of the spiritual programme is impressed with the infinite sequence of really existing ordinal numbers. This represents the purely *objective* component. The other side stands for the *subjective* component and contains that which I usually describe as "spirit".

The following applies here: The earlier a species appeared on the stage of life, the more significant is the part which the "objective component" has played in its development. The development of all life is known as phylogenesis.

The same applies to individual development (ontogenesis): The younger an organism, the stronger is the influence which "objective components" will have in its development. The later a species appeared on the stage of life or the older the individual organism is, the stronger and more substantial is the influence exerted on it by the purely "subjective spiritual". In this manner phylogenesis and ontogenesis are controlled.

Seen from this point of view, humans, being the first creatures on earth which are actually conscious of themselves and their environment, can indeed be considered as a "masterpiece of creation" – not least because they are the first species able to become aware of these interconnections.

And this is by no means arrogant as *Gerd Binning*, winner of the Nobel Prize for physics in 1968, stated in an interview.[85]

4.2) Mutations are Not the Only Explanation

During the 19th century at the very latest natural sciences became more and more central to our thinking and formed the basis of a firmly materialistic view of the world.

In principle this is still true today at least in western cultures.

This is also known as *monistic materialism*. According to this everything in our world is based on matter which is the real and all-engulfing basic principle. Even the human spirit, our consciousness and our own free will are mere

---

[85] "Wirtschaftswoche", 24 (2001)

features of the system or products of matter, so-called epiphenomena. Modern biologists and brain researchers try to make us believe this principle. In the following chapters I will take a very critical look at their ideas. To clarify my position right from the start, I assure you unambiguously that I believe that a purely materialistic view of our world is utterly wrong in every respect.

The famous French mathematician and astronomer *Pierre Laplace (1749-1827)*, replied to *Napoleon's (1769-1821)* ironic question as to where in his book *"Mécanique céleste"* he could see a place for God in the universe: *"Sire, je n'avais pas besoin de cette hypothèse"*[86].

For me *Laplace* is the epitome of arrogance which we can still see in those of our contemporaries today who are no less well educated and who never doubt themselves.

The major supports within the structure of modern knowledge are the evolution theories established by the British naturalist *Charles Darwin (1809-1882)* which are no longer seriously challenged.

His ideas were psychological dynamite in the 19th century, because they caused such a stir when they were published wherein the most shocking detail was the assumed direct human decent from apes. *Darwin* himself, by the way, never suggested this.

Between 1831 and 1836 Darwin travelled the world on his ship *"Beagle"*. In 2005 I followed in his traces whilst I was aboard a ship passing through the Beagle channel, named after his ship, in Tierra del Fuego between Argentina and Chile. During his travels Darwin studied the animal kingdom very carefully, especially on the Galápagos Islands in the Pacific Ocean to the west of South America. His later studies, which were based on the knowledge he obtained on his sea voyages, concentrated especially on the changes to which species are subjected and the formation of new species. In 1883 his main work *"On The Origin of Species by Means of Natural Selection"* resulted from these studies, a work which is still acknowledged today as a masterpiece of modern biology. This and other works by Darwin led to a completely new ideology known as *Darwinism*.

His theory is a pure *selection theory*. When discussing *Charles Darwin's* theory people always talk about "the battle for survival" or even of the "rights of the strongest". However, *Darwin* himself never used these expressions, he talked about *"the fittest"* which really means the "best suited" or "the best adjusted", which is by no means always the strongest. There are other possibilities of qualifying oneself to be the "best suited", such as the ability to cooperate, all of which play an important role as well. However, the realization of this has

---

[86] From the French, translated: "Sire, I never needed this hypothesis".

only recently gained ground. Meanwhile scientists believe to have recognised that even microbes such as bacteria communicate and cooperate with one another. The struggle for life, as Darwin called it, is by no means a fight between creatures of unequal strengths.

Stricter interpretations of the selection principle such as this stem more from his scientific successors, e.g. the German biologist *Ernst Haeckel (1834-1919)*. He and some of his contemporaries became the founders of *neo-Darwinism*. Although Darwin already took coincidental changes into account he still did not know how they worked. Genes and chromosomes were still unknown.

With the science of genetics the mutation of the genotype became the all important coincidental reason for the formation of new species.

Logically an organism should in some way adjust to its environment before the commencement of the selection process. However, descendants only benefit from the changes which an organism undergoes for environmental reasons if they indeed inherit such a change. According to the currently accepted view this is only possible through the biochemical genotype which scientists of the 20th century are increasingly able to describe. The fact that a camel, for example, gets horny knees due to its having been forced to kneel in the desert, changes nothing for its descendants. The famous French naturalist *Jean-Baptiste Lamarck(1744-1829)*, one of Darwin's scientific ancestors, assumed that adjustments to the environment would indeed be passed on to the following generations. And his idea does indeed seem quite plausible. In Lamarck's time the science of genetics did not yet exist. We know today, however, that Lamarck cannot have been correct, just as long as we know of no alternative to the genome as the only known medium for passing on genetic information. A change in the external shape of a creature, the phenotype, acquired in the course of its lifetime, is *not* manifested in the (biochemical) genome and, therefore, cannot be passed on to the offspring.

Since the discoveries of *Gregor Mendel (1822-1884)*, or at least since 1953 when the British genetic scientist *Francis Crick (1916-2004)* together with the American *James Watson (*1928)* recognised and decoded DNA as the actual construction plan for all creatures on earth, it seemed to have been established beyond doubt that every change must first be manifested in the *genome*, before being passed on to succeeding generations. The horny knees of the camel must also have been manifested in the genome first.

But how did that happen? How could the genome know, without being able to think, that for its "master", the camel, horny knees would be useful?

Even today, biologists say: pure *coincidence*. According to them it is impossible to create anything useful deliberately or even detect a purposeful direction pointing to convenient changes. Only after a distinguishing feature has been developed could we say in hindsight that horny knees, to stay with this example, are quite useful and, therefore, they stayed and did not disappear again.

Being something "suitable" it survived the challenges through which this creature had to go over millions of years in its struggle for life. But the fact that these horny layers on the knees did indeed develop happened due to an accidental *mutation* in the genome of the creature "camel".

According to modern evolutionary biologists, who, by the way, no longer talk of neo-Darwinism but of "synthetic evolution theory", only a mutation of the genome can be the instigator of anything new. We know that such mutations can indeed lead to the generation of new and different proteins. Nevertheless, there seem to be very effective mechanisms which tend more to diminish than to propagate the effects which such mutations may have on the generation of new cell structures (protein biosynthesis).

Apart from the starting codon and the three nonsense triplets, there are exactly four times as many base-*positions* available in the genetic code (80) as there are amino acids (20). It is interesting to note that with 4:1 we again have a whole-number ratio. Small defects, therefore, that may occur due to the mix up of single nucleotides do not automatically lead to a change in the amino acid sequence (see Chapter 2.9). In addition there are also other protective mechanisms which seem rather to diminish the effects of mutations.

Most of the important proteins essential for supporting the so-called construction and maintenance metabolism consist of very long chains with 20 so-called α-amino acids.

We can compare some of these proteins to construction workers or tools working inside the bodies of humans and animals. They are known as *enzymes*.

Enzymes are needed for producing other important components, e.g. new tissue, which contribute to the healing of deep wounds. An example for a very important enzyme which we need for our respiration is the "cytochrome C".

Its protein consists of 104 amino acids (AA), of which 70 could easily be exchanged without resulting in any functional disorder or in any change of function at all. To create something here by mutation would require a large number of coincidences. In fact, as I see it, mutations are a rather blunt instrument.

In other words: many mutations lead to dead ends.

Nature, or however we want to name whatever it is that is actually working here so constructively, obviously does not like mutations much and protects itself against them. This should be no surprise, since we read every day that mutations tend more to threaten our health than help us reach "higher orders". One of the most dreaded diseases today is cancer. Many kinds of cancer can be traced back to mutations brought about or caused within normal cells, for example, by solar radiation (→melanomae), viruses (→lymphomae) or a number of dangerous materials such as benzene, asbestos or nicotine (→bronchial cancer).

Mutations indeed often seem to be more harmful than useful; and it is hard to imagine that their influence on germ cells should be any different to that exerted on normal body cells. This does not at all mean that they are always and without exception harmful. Certainly not; they can and sometimes do play an important but rather complementary role in the formation of new and useful features or capabilities, or in the further development of existing ones.

Let us reflect on this by returning to the horny knees of camels: if every mutation were subject to a strict selection then it would only survive if the next generation already benefited from it. Should the mutation however merely give a push in a certain direction of development but not yet reach perfection, well – according to the generally accepted expert opinion – it would disappear as suddenly as it had appeared, since selection by definition means choosing the most suitable and discarding anything which is imperfect or which must be considered unsuitable or "not suitable enough".

Of course, in a specific case, such as that of the horny knees of camels, an instant "selection-stable" improvement by mutation within the genome may be plausible. It becomes difficult, however, to accept the notion that all the different species on earth, and thus the entire evolution in the animal world up to human beings, was *exclusively* achieved by random mutations and subsequent selection of the "most suitably mutated".

This contradicts any logic, and even the stereotype reference to the immeasurably long period of time which has elapsed since these processes began on earth, one or two billion years perhaps, does not help, in my opinion, to explain anything.

The biologist *Wilder-Smith* put it into words in 1978 very succinctly, in my opinion, and with the necessary bite: *"If, with the aid of mutation, a worm is to survive as a worm, then the mutation must transform it into a 'better' worm – and not into a more developed creature on the next level of animal life, because at the start of the next evolutionary level it will automatically be poorly suited to being a worm. Natural selection will therefore not lead to a higher species but will stabilize and improve the already existing species."*

Random mutations occur constantly, of course, and have doubtless played an important role in the history of evolution. I do not contest that at all. However, I do not believe that they play such a decisive role in evolution as that presently credited to them. The importance of mutations – as also of our genes and our brain by the way – is vastly overrated; of that I am convinced. I will come back to this point later.

4.3) Evolution by natural selection

According to the neo-Darwinists, who today call themselves representatives of the synthetic evolution theory, mutation is the basis and the driving engine for any kind of evolution. Mutations are coincidental changes in the genome which are passed on to the next generation. Should a mutation bring any advantage for its carrier, then it will resist the current possibly adverse environmental conditions. This advantage may be marginal at first but in the long run it *could* cause the descendants of the mutated variant to prevail. It may also happen that such a mutation leads to a change which shows neither advantage nor disadvantage but which is nevertheless passed on to the following generations yet still remains hidden. The environmental conditions for this creature may change at any time and the mutation which up till then had only been carried passively all of a sudden proves to be very suitable. The offspring of such a variant will later prove themselves to be the better adjusted species and they will survive. I already discussed the plausibility of what I have explained here in the previous chapter. Let us now simply assume that it is as I say. The mechanism explained here is known as "selection". For biologists it is the second most important and, after the initial mutation, the most decisive mechanism in evolution.
Basically the idea of evolution by selection goes back to *Charles Darwin*, but whilst Darwin himself still adhered to *Lamarck*'s ideas – according to which beneficial adjustments to a changing environment *acquired* over a life-span are *somehow* passed on to the next generation – such ideas are no longer accepted today, although very recently a new branch of biolological research seems to have materialized which supports Lamarck's ideas in quite a different way: epigenetics.
I will come back later to this very new and interesting approach (Chapter 4.9).
If new genes, generated by mutations, have no effect at all but are still continuously passed on to following generations, modern evolutionary biologists accept this without doubting their theories. They call this "anticipating adjustment" and they take it as a given fact. However, in my opinion it seems quite amazing that, for example, flies carry a gene which is responsible for the formation of an inner ear, which flies do not have, of

course. But when implanted into mice which, due to a gene defect, do not possess an inner ear, it in fact induces the generation of one.

By and large contemporary opinion believes that evolution *mechanisms* may be finally explainable by the terms "mutation" and "selection" and may in fact be complemented by "communication" and "cooperation".

I am of a completely different opinion although I do not question these fundamental principles. It is just that I do not believe that these explain everything – on the contrary, it is at this point that the whole thing starts to become truly fascinating.

I also claim nothing less than that, *in principle*, Lamarck was right when he stated that certain environmental conditions can have a lasting and significant influence on subsequent generations. At this point some biologists may start twitching their noses and put this book aside. But they would be too hasty.

Lamarck wanted to explain why it is that successive generations of many kinds of animals have developed continually improved characteristics, properties or abilities. Every living being is in general able to influence the usage of certain organs or its physique and to neglect others through the *"exertion of its inner senses"*. Due to such constant influences over a long period of time, organs or other parts of the body become newly formed, regressed or, in general, are changed. These newly acquired properties are thought to be passed on to the next generation. A recurring example usually quoted in this context is that of giraffes with their long necks. Stretching the neck constantly over many generations in order to reach leaves on high trees is supposed to have resulted in an elongated neck which was then passed on from generation to generation. According to the accepted opinion among biologists this could never have happened. The German neo-Darwinist *August Weismann (1834-1914)* put paid to this idea over a 100 years ago with his doctrine that the germ plasma (known today as genome or genotype) governs the body functions (somatoplasm, known today as phenotype), but never the other way round.

In fact, no well accepted indication exists up until today that physical changes acquired in the course of a life-span could be manifested in the genome as we know it today by some kind of biochemical means, thereby leaving a lasting impression on later generations. Therefore, with respect to the evolutionary mechanisms hitherto described, merely the first chapter of a book concerning evolution can be considered complete. It is high time that we start writing the rest or at least some additional very important chapters, because I believe that heredity involves much more than the mere passing on of genes by means of purely biochemical information. In my opinion, heredity is more an extremely complex term which embraces other mechanisms presently not even considered or whose existence is generally and categorically disputed.

I am talking about mechanisms which are based on the real existence of a level which may be described roughly as *"immaterial spiritual"*. Phenomena such as instinct and consciousness are examples. I do not at all consider these two as merely accidental, and more or less welcome, (by-) products of their physical basis, the brain, but as in principle completely self-reliant and independent, hierarchically-graduated, immaterial influencing powers.

This transforms heredity into a much more complex subject than it has been assumed to be up to now. On the one hand, of course, it still takes place on the acknowledged physical level due to physical triggers and mediators. On the other hand, however, it is considerably and constantly influenced by a completely independent and yet really existing immaterial spiritual level.

This hypothesis is compatible with the really proven knowledge we possess about our world if we separate observation from interpretation and consider them without emotion. The large number of numerical congruencies with respect to the most important basic values and key positions in chemistry, genetics and cosmology should alone convince any unbiased observer of the real existence of numbers and geometrical forms as the spiritual controlling instruments. In doing so, he would at least in principle be accepting the real existence of a spiritual dimension.

In the following chapters I will offer a number of further indications to be found in biology and medicine which support this.

If numbers and geometrical forms indeed play an important and realistic role in the background of evolution then the emergence of giraffes could be explained as being a result of the slow adjustment to high sources of food by their ancestors; Giraffes could be portrayed in the same way as fish or primate skulls, by mere proportionally distorted systems of coordinates (see Chapter 4.1). The long neck does not need a completely new development.

A constant environmental stimulation merely exploits the available latitude of existing hereditary factors in which numbers already played such an important role. The following illustration by my son Martin in which a comparison is drawn between the African short-necked giraffe, the *Okapi*, and the typical (long-necked) giraffe, may make this clearer.

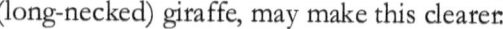

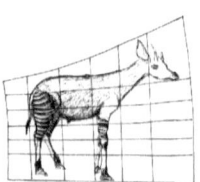

One last point at the end of this chapter:
The argument most often used for supporting the theory that mutation and selection alone have been sufficient to bring about evolution is the unfathomably long period of time over which evolution took place.
Critics of these common theories are accused of searching for other explanations merely because they are so impatient and cannot think in such vast time frames. For us they are as abstract as a huge amount of money, for example when (understandably) government budgets are being discussed.
This is made clear when we observe the indifference of most people – including those in our own country – towards the horrendous and sometimes completely unnecessary and excessive debt of a bloated state machine.
Such an argumentation, however, is much distorted. An exact calculation of the time spans involved shows that they were far too short for mutation alone to have been the decisive motor of evolution. Furthermore, in the meantime, zoologists in the USA and Australia have discovered that completely new animal species may develop within amazingly short periods of time.
This can only mean that coincidence cannot be as important a motor of evolution as previously assumed. We can read, for example, in the highly respected science magazine *Science*[87] that a certain species of salmon[88] accidentally marooned in a lake only 60 years ago has split already into two different lines which are no longer able to cross breed. Exactly this characteristic is typical for the existence of two different species of animals.
Insects very often show the formation of completely new species within even far shorter periods of time. Two related species of Australian flies[89], for example, altered their sexual attractants within only nine generations to such an extent that cross breeding was no longer possible simply because males and females of these two new species could "no longer stomach" each others smell.
Mutation and selection doubtless remain two very important engines in the evolutionary history of all living beings. But, and here I like to repeat myself, they are both certainly only one part of the whole truth and maybe even only the smaller part.

---

[87] Science, Volume 289
[88] (Oncorhynchus nerka), which were marooned in Lake Washington between 1937 and 1945. Over only 13 generations distinct differences developed which clearly separated the species.
[89] Fruit flies Drosophila serrata and Drosophila birchii

4.4) Evolution and Theodizee – a philosophical approach

Since evolution theories cannot at all be explained in a plausible way as yet they alert critics who often take more steps back than jumps forward.
Three evolution models, partly judged as being rather controversial and prejudiced, are competing today with the scientifically acknowledged "synthetic theory of evolution" in the discussion concerning the essence of evolution. Especially in America and in Australia there are several very active groups, known as "Creationists". They believe in the exact wording of the biblical history of creation according to which the world was created in six days. They are not satisfied by merely establishing that there is a God or some kind of personal divine dimension at the beginning and as a supra intelligent background to basic cosmic laws, as the representatives of the so-called "intelligent creation" attempt to do. The latter are rather moderate critics who have well-founded doubts that the presently accepted theories of evolution are indeed finally and sufficiently explained for them to be believable.
The doctrine of the "intelligent creation" does sometimes but not invariably also include biblical notions. The famous Greek philosophers *Sokrates (469-399 B.C.)*, his student *Plato (427-347 B.C.)*, who I hold in especially high esteem, and the student of the latter *Aristotle (384-322 B.C.)* were already advocates of the intelligent creation.
Today there is also a modern, purely scientific orientated group of critics who in principle relinquish all religious perceptions. They support the "intelligent design" theory and attempt to find a suitable path between coincidence, necessity and intelligent design on the basis of scientific methods alone to arrive at a possibly all-encompassing alternative perspective which might also include other fields of science.
I myself see the solution as lying somewhere in the middle – whereby I soundly reject the creationistic perception as mistaken belief – where, at the same time it can hold its ground compared to all the others. Not one of us can only remotely imagine the whole truth, but we can choose the right direction. A drawing by my son Martin, which he once prepared for a presentation in natural philosophy, may illustrate this: All humans searching for the truth are standing around a mountain. Its summit represents the truth. Some are nearer to the summit, some are further away. Some are already turned towards the summit whilst some must still turn around. Like the American philosopher *Ayn Rand (1905-1982)* I am convinced that there is an objective truth. And humans have the sense to recognise it.

Every one of the theses or theories mentioned here represent some part of the truth but none of them contains the whole truth.

Nor do the religions do not because they do not possess any scientific or historical authenticity. However, religions represent an intuitive access which obviously lies at the core of the evolution of human beings, and which is unfortunately ignored by many scientists today, some of whom even treat it with contempt. Yet it is precisely this human intuition, i.e. the origin of all religions, which is the all-important thread leading us along the path to cognition.

Practically all religions and many myths always include the same three key theses[90]:
1) the existence of a God, something divine, a divine dimension
2) the existence of an independent spirit, a spiritual level
3) the further existence of the spirit or the soul in whatever manner after physical death.

The "intelligent design" – or in short "ID" – theory will never be in full possession of the truth either, mainly because it rejects the divine factor altogether. Nevertheless, it is severely attacked by representatives of "classical scientific theories". Pressurized by the scientific fraternity, a German biology professor at Cologne University had to close down his homepage for a while because he associated himself with the concepts of the ID theory. Otherwise he would have risked disciplinary action. This reminds me of the Catholic Holy Inquisition during the Middle Ages. The very fact that the ID theory has raised hardly any or no doubt at all on the current *cosmic* view of the world is in my opinion a problem; if this view is incorrect then the theory on which it is based must also be incorrect. And I already explained in Part 2 and 3 why this view cannot be correct.

Creation theories bring back the divine factor, but they do not necessarily cling to the literal sense of religious traditions. For me, however, they often go too *far*, since they too often imply the incessant divine omnipotence and creation of everything. The question of divine omnipotence and omnipresence also induces *theodicy*, a severe criticism of religions. According to this the examples of unfathomable crimes of humans committed on humans, such as that of the Holocaust by the Nazi regime, must be an argument against the existence of God or the divine. If there were a God as the absolute good then "she+he" would never have allowed this to happen.

For me such thinking is far too short-sighted. I am convinced that the world, in spite of the creation of a number of basic parameters and conditions,

---

[90] Detailed explanations in my book: "Nobody Ever Dies!" (2003)

remains in the general state of "creative emergent", i.e. it keeps developing and generating itself.

However, what does the term "world" include?

For modern scientists it includes nothing more than physical matter, the entire physical world. For them nothing else exists. I am convinced, however, that a polar-symmetrical spiritual world exists which actually preceded the physical world and which itself was generated by it.

It is even more important, that they both permanently and constantly exchange information. God's presence becomes evident initially in the creation of the numerous first things, regardless of whether they are of spiritual or physical nature (see Chapter 2.10-2.13). God's activity is also reflected in the "construction" of the absolutely ingenious basic parameters and conditions which are recognizable everywhere in this world if we are willing to recognise them.

Certainly, God's influence is always exerted in the entire world in the course of its further development. This is noticeable as a more subtle spiritual influence based on interaction. Therefore, all human beings can and will experience it in the course of their *lives*. But what does "life" mean in this context?

I believe that the debate concerning theodicy can even be construed as indirect evidence of a "creative emergence" in our world. God's omnipresence and omnipotence do not become evident in the prevention and elimination of all problems and encumbrances during people's lives. It is rather shown in the people's determination that their lives will be successful and their goals will be achieved.

"He+she", God, the divine, cannot and should not do this because such habitual intervention would prevent any "creative emergence". It is only the constant innovation due to this "creative emergence" that will lead to the highest perfection in the highest possible multiplicity and thereby permitting the objective of the world to be achieved.

If this is true, then it follows inevitably that the term *life* should be used in a different sense than it is commonly used today. Viewed from the divine perspective, the path of life is for each individual something completely different from what *we* believe it to be. This means that our view is incorrect. All of our lives continue after our physical death. Death only means that our life trajectory experiences a turning point which might be compared to a change of school. From here on humans start a higher education.

Physical life is only a small part of the real "time" we all have available. Justice which we do not directly experience on earth we will no doubt experience later.

My ideas and my world model which I will explain in detail in Part 5 of this book draw on all kinds of theses and theories whereby they approach the summit of truth because they are integrative and holistic, i.e. they are interlinking and comprehensive.

4.5) Curiosities of Evolution

The nice movie "Beautiful People"[91] presents in a remarkable and very humorous way scenes from the daily lives of a number of animals in the Namibia Desert in Africa.
This desert region stretches for 2,000 kilometres along the Atlantic coast from South Africa's northern Cape Province across Namibia to southern Angola. Let me start this chapter with some examples from this film and ask "*How could this have been brought about?*"

First, let us take a look at an expert snake hunter, the mongoose, drawn here by my son Martin. It opens snake eggs by propelling them beneath its body and smashing them against a stone where they break open.

This is a very complex procedure which is certainly not induced by a simple mutation of genes. It is probably something that young animals learn by imitating their parents over generations thereby learning it afresh.
However, how can it be explained that some animals, which never had a chance to watch their parents and imitate them, still show the same patterns of behaviour?
Consider the desert duck that seeks to protect its ducklings against an approaching hyena. First it tells its ducklings in a kind of duck language by a violent and probably very distinctive cackle to keep absolutely quiet and look for a safe hiding place above water. This instruction is given very quickly and takes only a few seconds. The ducklings obey immediately.
Then the mother duck turns to the hyena and imitates an injured and helpless duck. The hyena is thus quickly distracted and follows the mother duck to the water without paying attention to the ducklings. This complicated and concerted pattern of behaviour between parents and youngsters against predators somehow seems to be programmed in these ducks. I cannot

---

[91] by Janie Uys (+1996), South Africa 1970.

imagine that this behaviour might only be due to *biochemical* reasons found in the genotype of ducks – I will come back to this later.

It seems that only animals living in the same biotope have mastered this pattern of behaviour even without their ever having experienced this specific

dangerous situation. After mating, the rhinoceros auklet, here drawn by Martin, keeps its female for several months in a hollow tree which it has walled-up with clay. There the female hatches the eggs.

When the chickens are hatched the male bird opens a slit in the bark of the tree just wide enough to put his beak through. Through this slit it feeds the chickens which never soil the nearly enclosed and thus almost inaccessible nest. The chickens know right from their hatching onwards what is expected of them. They are house-trained and position themselves in such a clever way that their excrement is ejected through the slit.

It is impossible that they could have *learned* this behaviour. The genome contains no genes either which may induce this specific behaviour.

The symbiosis between the honey badger and the honey cuckoo is also very interesting. The cuckoo shows the badger the way to a beehive. The badger is immune to bee stings, the cuckoo, however, is not. Therefore, the badger takes charge of robbing the beehive. It drags the honeycombs far enough away from the danger zone so that it can eat the honey in peace. But it only eats part of the prey leaving the considerable remainder for the cuckoo.

As long as lions have had enough to eat, zebras will drink together with them peacefully at the same watering-place. Other animals too seem to sense exactly when it is possible to drink with the lions and when it is better without them.

Should other predators approach the watering-place the "Go-away"-bird will raise the alarm and warn those present of animal or human predators.

Here are another two examples from the ecological system of the underwater world of the Great Barrier Reef off the North East coast of Queensland,

Australia. There we find rather strange cylindrical creatures with a prickly skin, here drawn by Martin, known as sea cucumbers. These animals, which crawl along the sea bed, are completely blind and live alone. They do not know each other, so they are certainly not aware of the existence of others of their kind. The interesting thing is how they mate: At precisely the same time, as if moved by invisible strings, they all stand up on their backsides, stretch their cylindrical bodies further

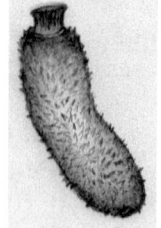

and further upwards with strange circular spinning dance movements finally ejecting an egg or sperm in a high arc into the water. Of course, the probability that an egg meets a sperm and is thus fertilized is all the better the higher up they stretch and the further they eject their eggs or sperm by their spinning movements. What causes this exact temporal synchronization? Patterns must exist here that could not possibly have been tried out and synchronized with each other. These creatures have existed since time immemorial. Their entire existence seems, after a short development phase, to have been stable and unchanged.
They are simply perfect within their scope of possibilities.
The same applies to the corals of the reef. They all eject their spawn into the sea at exactly the same time of year where it is mixed and fertilized. This all happens, very carefully synchronized, with all species.
There are numerous creatures living on earth which have never adjusted their appearances for many million years because they are sophisticated and perfect. One of them is the horse-shoe crab which lives on the American Atlantic coast, here animated by Martin.

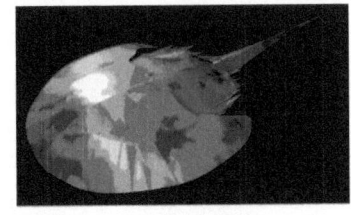

This animal has lived on earth for about 500 million years (Cambrian). It also mates only once a year, in early summer. And all the animals come together for the mating session as if they were following a command.
Some beautiful examples from different ecological systems show here complicated and amazingly well and extremely exact synchronized patterns of behaviour. Some of them are even exercised together with animals of completely different species at the same time which is equally helpful for all those participating. They very often follow intricate patterns which even more highly developed species can hardly employ consciously. A consciousness can only be present – if at all – in a very rudimentary form in only a few of the animals mentioned above.
For years scientists have attempted to decode the genotype of animals and humans and they expect to find explanations in the genes for such patterns of behaviour. However, we have to realize that, in the genotype at least, the biochemical differences are far smaller than scientists had expected and had previously assumed, even between species which are as little related as humans and flies. The genetic differences between humans and anthropoids amount only to about 1%, possibly even less. And a genetic difference of less than 0.1% to 0.2 % can hardly explain the myriad of human features – if we try to explain this in a conventional manner.

Furthermore, latest research reveals that our human genotype consists of only approximately 30,000 genes which encode proteins and thus contribute to necessary construction processes as well as to physical characteristics. This is far less than previously expected.[92] The first plausible explanation for this apparent contradiction seems to be that genes must control not just *one* but several characteristics simultaneously. The question then arises as to what it is that gives them the necessary assistance in reaching the decision? In my opinion there must be more as yet unknown information mechanisms within the cells or in the genotype itself to account for this. I will offer a plausible solution in Chapter 4.10.

There are probably other quite different hereditary mechanisms too which are still not being taken seriously by today's materialistically orientated scientists.

Meanwhile, I am certain that an immaterial influence is involved in the evolution of all organisms which comes from a parallel world, a spiritual world, whose existence is just as real as that of our own world. In the course of this book I will attempt to corroborate this idea which unfortunately sounds rather absurd for most contemporary biologists.

A plausible explanation for the examples from the world of plants and animals mentioned above could be that, depending on the stage of development, random patterns of behaviour are developed, tried out, trained and then optimized and thoroughly learned in the same or over a few successive generations. If other species are involved a careful coordination takes place.

That which is new, good and thoroughly learned will be much easier for succeeding generations to "rediscover", further develop and learn again as if they already had a "premonition" of the innovations. Coincidence seems to play a decreasing role from generation to generation. Each successive generation improves and perfects the existing pattern and refines the cooperation between all animal species involved.

Over many generations an optimized complex process emerges which is securely retained in each cooperating species and from then on the pattern of behaviour is passed on to the following generations without their having to rediscover, redevelop and learn again. However, how should all this happen if learned abilities evidently cannot alter the genotype in its biochemical formation?

Modern biologists generally reject the concept of improvement and coordination by mutual coordination on an informal base, the plausible suggestion I just outlined above, as nonsense.

---

[92] Even if there were 100,000 genes, as was previously assumed, it would make no difference. I will come back to this later.

They stick to the idea that every change has been caused by random mutation and is, therefore, manifested in the biochemical genotype and has later been developed further by selection in a very difficult and time-consuming way.
I believe therefore that there must be other hereditary mechanisms and that they actually do exist. A number of observations seem to support my ideas. Even the famous American geneticist *Craig Venter*, who is accepted today as being one of the top researchers in the decoding of animal and human genomes, said in an interview with a German magazine [93]:
"I am convinced that there are even less than 30,000 (...human genes). A fruit fly possesses 13,000 genes, a thread-worm 20,000. The number of genes apparently says little about the complexity of a creature. The discovery contradicts the genetic deterministic way of thinking so widespread today." And further on in the same interview he states very clearly: *"We only found 300 genes in the human genome for which there is no equivalent in mice."*

4.6) Spiritual Fields in the Service of Heredity?

In 1920 the scientist *William McDougall*, a Scotsman and later an American by choice, started an experiment at *Harvard-University* with pure-bred white rats. Under laboratory conditions they were bred over 15 years engendering 32 generations of pure-bred rats. The animals were supposed to learn to escape from a specially constructed water basin by swimming through one of two passages leading out of the water. Since the animals usually avoid darkness, the "wrong" passage, the dead end, was marked by a bright light, whilst the "right" passage, which led out of the water, was left in darkness.
At first the rats tried of course to leave the water tank by the bright but "wrong" passage. In addition, at the dead end, the rat received a powerful electric shock.
The training was aggravated insofar as both passages were alternately lit but the dark passage always remained the "right" one. The number of wrong decisions taken by a training rat until it had learned to leave the water by the alternating dark passage was the measure by which the speed of learning was determined.
After a various number of trials, all the animals learned to use the dark passage to leave the water although this was changed constantly.
Whilst the first generation of rats needed an average of 56 trials, the rats of the 32nd generation only needed an average of 20 trials. At the same time the rats of the later generations became much more cautious.

---

[93] "Focus" 8 (2001)

When the Scottish scientist *F.A. Crew*, a critic of *McDougall*'s results, wanted to check them, he performed the same experiment with a later generation of *McDougall*'s rats.

In addition he had a control group of other rats trained whose ancestors had never participated in the earlier experiments.

Crew also carried out a long-term experiment. The amazing result was that the first generation of *Crew*'s rats needed only as many trial runs as the 30th generation of *McDougall*'s rats before swimming directly to the correct passage. Obviously Crew's rats already knew something which they had not previously learned. And this success was completely independent of the group of rats to which they belonged. Even Crew's control group whose ancestors had had no prior training achieved the same result. Similar experiments were repeated again in a far-away country by *W.E. Agar* in Australia. Agar's untrained rats learned just as fast to swim to the correct passage as those rats whose ancestors had been trained for many generations.

Something must have happened here which has not yet found its due acknowledgement in biology: Clearly, it must be possible to inherit or pass on knowledge other than in the known biochemical, genetic ways.

S.A. Barnett[94] wrote in 1967: *"Whatever it was that induced the improved performance it was not the training" (...) "Many observations are still unexplained; some seem to be the result of unintentional changes in the diet."* Barnett too seemed very surprised by the results of these experiments. The reason he gives for them, however, makes me laugh. It seems to me that whenever the reason for something is unclear, it is always the diet which is made responsible. *How* are we supposed to imagine this in a plausible way?

The famous British biologist, *Rupert Sheldrake (*1942)*, also made a number of similar observations which showed him clearly that it must be possible in some way to pass on learned knowledge to distant descendants. These observations led Sheldrake to the notion of the so-called *"morphogenetic fields"*. This expression had already been introduced by some evolutionary biologists after having conducted several similar experiments. Originally the term "field" is used in physics and was coined by *Michael Faraday (1791-1867)*. According to him space itself is a source of energy.

Later, the term "field" was restricted to electromagnetic phenomena such as light – however, *Albert Einstein* extended it to express the power of attraction between masses, i.e. gravitation. In my opinion the term "field" ought to be modified since every field possesses something uniform and continuous.

I believe, however, that in general in this world continuity is always and exclusively an *immaterial spiritual* characteristic. Therefore, every field must be

---

[94] Samuel Anthony Barnett, former zoologist at Glasgow University, see List of References.

something purely spiritual. This includes cosmic space itself with its structured expansion along the squares of all really existing ordinal numbers. The universe is thus an informal spiritual space (see Part 3).

In the 1980s *Sheldrake* postulated the existence of really existing, immaterial and purely spiritual fields which represent a kind of species memory. All creatures of the same species form this species memory and in continuous resonance, independent of time and space, they exchange (unconsciously) experiences and influence one another.

The entire *"integrated"* and *"self-organizing character of systems, as simple or as complex as they may be"* is based *"on the influence of such fields"*.

He tested his "field theory" with an experiment concerning the organization of termite colonies. Sheldrake points out here that the idea of organizing fields should by no means diminish the relevance of normal sensory communication; we know today for a fact that many animals and insects – and thus also termites and ants – use various methods to communicate such as sounds, smells, mutual touch and the sharing of food. He gave his special attention to the construction of arcs in termite's nests as the following drawing by Martin shows:

First the workers construct several columns at a distance from one another. They stay open at the top until the termites start building the arches like a bridge, where both sides are bent further and further until they meet in the middle.

Termites are completely blind. The workers working on one column cannot see the other column or the workers that work on it. Neither do they crawl along the ground to measure the distance between the columns.

Sheldrake writes: *"It is very unlikely that they are able to perceive well-defined sounds from the other column which might be transmitted via the ground in all that hustle and bustle."*

Their sense of smell *"is scarcely sufficiently developed to explain the overall set-up of the nest or the position of each single insect within the community as a whole."*

Rather *"they seem to 'know' what kind of building structures are necessary; they seem to be controlled by an invisible plan"*.

Sheldrake suspects that the colony as a whole possesses an organizational field and that the plan is a part of this spiritual field. Such fields *"must be able to penetrate physical structures such as magnetic fields*" and to "*coordinate the activities of different groups of termites even when no normal sensory communication is possible*".[95]

In Part 5 of this book I will explain in detail why I am absolutely convinced that a purely spiritual world exists. On the one hand, it creates the entire physical world while, on the other hand, it completely envelops and penetrates completely the physical side.

Every living being belongs simultaneously to both parts of this world by virtue of its being alive.

In the course of its own life every creature helps to differentiate and to perfect the originally undifferentiated or immature spiritual field.

The higher the spiritual evolution of all life advances – up to an individual spirit, which is aware of itself and has a conscious perception of its surroundings, such as the human spirit – the more the spiritual field will become diversified and personally structured and will no longer remain a merely collective field. It is exactly at this point where finally my opinion differs from that of *Rupert Sheldrake*.

4.7) Convergences: Strange and Unexplored

Very interesting and rather strange phenomena in nature are convergences. This means the appearance of identical, or at least very similar, characteristics in unrelated plants and animals as a means of adjustment to the same or similar external environmental conditions.

We find convergences in many regions on earth which are separated geographically by great distances. We can usually say for sure that the creatures concerned have not had, or could not have had, any contact whatsoever with one another.

We also find convergences in different periods of time. We know of plants and animals possessing very similar or even identical characteristics and patterns of behaviour which lived at different times during the history of the earth. These general similarities are to be found among these animals or plants although they are not related to one another at all.

The currently acknowledged theories hardly provide us with a plausible explanation for convergences. Even very special external forms, anatomical constructions, functions of body parts or organs, or even behaviours of entire species, keep re-occurring in exactly the same shape and form. How could this happen if the real engine of evolution were coincidental mutation?

---

[95] Quoted from R. Sheldrake, "Seven Experiments That Could Change The World", see List of References.

Does it not give one the impression that nature keeps drawing on a well-known pool of ideas? Here is a comparison: Many fantastic buildings have been constructed by humans. Legions of workers and machines have probably been necessary to carry out the innumerable work processes over years and decades. In the construction cells of every organism certain proteins, known as enzymes, take over these functions. According to *Lüth* there is a probability of 10^{-130} or 1 to 10^{130} that such an enzyme be produced accidentally, even if it were a small one consisting of only 100 amino acids and possessing only one amino acid which could not be exchanged without changing its entire function. In other words, if we were to play dice to find the right combination for this special enzyme we would need more throws than there are atoms in the entire universe as we know it today. Although such calculations can be somewhat qualified by some counterarguments they cannot be refuted. And it becomes even more difficult to contradict this notion if we assume that one single enzyme is not really helpful since it takes more than one swallow to make a summer. It is rather that, for the generation of identical complex characteristics, numerous enzymes and processes are necessary.

"Mister Coincidence" cannot help much here.

I would like to give some more examples to further clarify the phenomenon of convergence:

About 200 million years ago there existed pterosaurians whose bones were very light and who had elongated bones in their hands between which wings could develop. Only after this species had long since disappeared did other species emerge with exactly the same characteristics, e.g. birds and some mammals such as bats and flying foxes.

The Australian ant eater, the North American armadillo, the South American ant bear and the African pangolin are not related but they look very similar.

They all have long beaks or beak-like jowls and even longer sticky tongues with which they catch insects, their food. In addition they all have strong claws, which enable them to dig up anthills, and a very robust stomach which can digest poisonous and chitinous food.

Many evolutionary biologists try to explain such parallels by maintaining that it is the "similarity of food" which leads to similar evolutionary development (see Chapter 4.6).

For me such explanations are simply not good enough. When we keep asking "why" and "how" convergences occur we get nothing but violent head-shaking from most scientists. Such questions are considered as being unscientific.

In his very interesting book "Überleben in Eis, Wüste und Tiefsee" *("Surviving in Ice, Desert and Deep Sea"), Walter Kleesattel* describes some interesting examples of convergence.

However, he also avoids making any concrete statement as to possible reasons for this amazing phenomenon. He mentions, for example, water-storing plants of the spurge family in the Namibia desert in South Africa which have a close similarity to some cacti in North American deserts, or the way in which the African miniature puff adder moves sideways in the same way as does the American sidewinder rattle snake:

Due to their specific methods of locomotion they both touch the hot desert sand for only a very short time and with only a very small part of their skin. All these animals have one feature in common and that is that they are not related to one another.

There are countless other examples of convergences. Apart from identical or very similar construction and functions even identical patterns of behaviour can be found. Some of them even seem absurd because in the specific environment in which they are exercised they may be rather harmful or possibly even dangerous. The well-known argument that after multiple mutation such animal behaviour was generated accidentally from preliminary stages and selected due to a supposed advantage in the battle for survival, sounds rather bizarre. I would like to give two examples of completely different and geographically separated species: One is the arctic musk-ox, the other is the takin from the Himalayas, a mixture of sheep and goat which is difficult to classify. Both of them display almost identical defensive behaviour: both form a kind of "body fortress" as an external defensive circle against enemies and intruders. They lower their heads towards the outside thereby protecting their calves within the circle. Takins, however, inhabit dense vegetation. Their body fortress is not at all effective. It would be much better to run away in the face of looming danger.

Confronted with such questions biologists have a quick and only apparently plausible explanation at hand: there must have been a common ancestor at some time. Today, however, affinities of races can be established by gene analyses. The result definitely contradicts these arguments. The musk-ox is no more related to the takin than it is related to us humans.

The German paleontologist *Edgar Dacqué (1878-1945)*, a refreshingly lateral thinker, pointed to the following peculiarities. A certain level of development *beneath* the evolution of mammals produced the pouched marsupials such as pouched lions, wolves, bears, badgers, rats, mice and also bats. More precisely we should say: lions, wolves, bears, badgers, rats, mice and bats already existed as pouched varieties. The same species of animals appear again, this time on a higher level of evolution, as mammals. We all know them as lions, wolves, bears, etc.. Maybe this explains the long neck of the giraffe. The same pattern is found many millions of years earlier in dinosaurs, e.g. the brachiosaur.

Convergence is, in my opinion, a phenomenon which almost compels us to accept my belief in the existence of a spiritual construction plan behind the evolution of all kinds of life. *Plato* would probably have called it the real existence of a "concept" for *all* creatures. This would enable us to imagine that certain basic patterns exist as absolutely real spiritual construction plans according to which certain features, functions and behaviours are repeatedly realized at new levels of evolution. However, I would like to emphasize, that – for my feeling – Plato's ideas go much too far; he believed in the real existence of all *complete* concepts in a kind of "spirit world" from which they merely had to manifest themselves. I consider this, in complete accordance with *Laplace's* logical objections, to be certainly wrong. It would also contradict the logic of a best possible world with no restraints on *creative emergence*. Nevertheless, I am convinced that "concepts for certain basic patterns" as well as "structural conditions for their realization" really do exist.
They could on a spiritual level – similar perhaps to *Sheldrake's* description of morphogenetic fields – always be adjusted to the actual conditions of life and environment, or they could even be actively modified by means of learning processes. Thus evolution in the end remains *emergent*, i.e. self-creating and organizing as the Austrian philosopher *Karl Popper* suggested.
One last example at the end of this chapter: Camels and nurse sharks posses the same characteristics in their immune systems. They lack two so-called light antibody chains which other creatures have. Even a fleeting glance tells us that these two species can hardly be related. But why are they so similar in this specific feature?
Such phenomena can by no means be explained understandably and plausibly by common evolution theories.

4.8) Apes and Humans: Who is Descended from Whom?

I do admit that this headline is rather provocative.
But it is not that simple to answer the question.
The German naturalist, philosopher and paleontologist *Edgar Dacqué*, mentioned in the previous chapter, established during the first half of the 20th century that the various periods in the history of our earth did not simply house all known kinds of creatures at the same time.

Each period rather had certain forms of life which were characteristic for that time. Some basic tendencies seem to reveal themselves: walking upright developed *steadily*, as did the ability to fly. Later on I will show that mental capabilities as well as consciousness were also part of this development.

Different periods possibly "demanded" specific features or specialization. Dacqué wrote: *"It seems as if nature needs 'certain' forms of animals in certain places and develops them from 'other forms' which are available in those places"* (accentuations '...' by me).

From his studies derives the comparison of the large principal similarities between the forms of a number of pouched animals and mammals (see Chapter 4.7). *Dacqué* recognised as well that during evolution the supposedly higher form did not always simply develop itself from the supposedly lower form which, however, contradicts the basic theories of evolution propagated today.

The German sociologist and physician *Paul Lüth (1921-1986)* wrote in his beautiful book[96] that it indeed seems logical when something complicated or higher always develops from something simpler and lower – if only simplicity were really so simple. Anyone who has studied unicellular organisms in their environment knows how complicated they actually are. In their minute bodies we find miniscule organs known as organelles which can only be seen with a microscope – and even smaller, sub-microscopic structures are also visible.

In 1924 the biologist *Viktor Franz (1883-1950)* wrote: *"Higher plants, unicellular plants and unicellular animals developed from a kind of 'primeval cell'"* (accentuations '...' by me). For *Paul Lüth* the latter are to be considered as a dissociation from unicellular plants which were unable to spread further. The same applies to animals and to us humans when we look at the development of germ cells.

Everyone knows that the female egg and the male sperm are the basic ingredients for the generation of a new human being or animal. In principle both germ cells are unicellular organisms which are generated from a complex multicellular organism "animal" or "human being" by means of the so-called reduction division or *meiosis*. These unicellular organisms both possess only half a set of chromosomes (a haploid set) without any loss of genetic information. When, during fertilization, the two unicellular organisms fuse together, a new cell with a complete set of chromosomes (a diploid set) is produced, from which a multicellular organism is quickly developed by means of simple division. If there were no meiosis, monster organisms with huge sets of chromosomes would develop which would be unable to survive.

In fact, it seems easier and less complicated in nature to develop multicellular organisms than to develop unicellular organisms and it is probably the latter

---

[96] "Der Mensch ist kein Zufall", see List of References.

that are produced from the former rather than the other way round. This observation, however, makes it even more difficult to understand the present perception of the evolution of life. It is not always the case that something higher develops from something lower, and indeed different times keep producing forms of life which are coordinated afresh but continue to appear similar. They develop on their own specific level of development which we have come to know as convergence.

This leads us to suppose that for each form of life in nature there could be one common, central basic form. This should not be considered as a merely abstract idea, but as an *empiric* fact, i.e. based on experience. There may seem to be a large number of absolutely real ideas about organisms or of their basic principles. They exist independently of one another and they develop constantly further on their own. We could compare them to the seeds which bring forth various bushes and trees. The result, that is the individual form which the tree or bush will adopt, can never really be predicted exactly. Such a bush could grow and become really big, or it could remain rather small; it could have many ramifications, or it could stay rather thin and meagre. Just as the most various bushes and trees grow from their seeds, so do the most different and varying forms of life develop almost "over and above" the really existing ideas of all life, i.e. their basic principles, by specializing and adjusting to the environmental conditions prevailing during their specific life times.

The central, principal form itself, however, never strives for specialization. Nevertheless, I suspect that the central, principal form possesses one very special and fundamental property, which is why I will go into detail here. Even the most varied anatomical and physiological forms seem to keep repeating themselves at various levels of evolution throughout the animal world and are obviously following fixed patterns.

However, there is one especially important structure of the body, our own included, for which this does not apply and that is the nervous system. In contrast to the evolution of body features, which were reiterated, went round bends and followed several zigzags and diversions, only the nervous system has advanced in all forms of life at all times and everywhere in the world steadily in a straight line from a lower level to an increasingly higher level. The nervous system becomes an important constant of evolution, a remarkable fact to which I will come back in detail later.

The nervous system found on each successive level of evolution is always, without exception, an improvement on the predecessor from which it developed. Later forms of life which emerged from a (lower) principal form are characterized by ever higher and better qualified neuronal structures. The visible conclusion of this evolution on earth is the human being. It seems reasonable to conclude that, by physical specialisation and further perfection in the course of the earth's history, all creatures separated from this principal form which in the end produced the human beings.

The end products of this evolution, humans themselves, are physically rather unspecialized, but they are distinguished by their brain which matured towards perfection. We may say, therefore, that all creatures on Earth "derived from humans and their line of evolution" which is solely determined by the nervous system and which developed in a straight line. And it was not the other way round, as previously assumed, namely that humans developed from some preliminary animal stages. This could also explain why the thrust of evolution has noticeably receded since humans appeared on the scene and why the variety of species is decreasing.[97] So, in the last instance the apes evolved from the humans and not the humans from the apes. This could serve to explain the famous and among biologists well-acknowledged rule established by the German biologist *Ernst Haeckel*. He maintained that the human embryonic development, the ontogenesis, is a shortened version and a repetition of the phylogenesis, i.e. the evolution since primeval times.

Biologists know that during their embryonic development humans possess certain structures which, for example in a fish, develop to gills. In the human embryo they develop to parts of the face, ears and the auditory canal. However, in contrast to common theories, these parts do not actually develop from gills. This suggests that no human embryo ever went through a fish phase. The human embryo merely went its own way, prescribed since medieval times, to become a human baby. Its specific structures, which later developed into a face or an ear, became specialized in the case of a fish and developed into gills at an earlier stage in the history of evol

The fish, therefore, is the finished product of the as yet unspecialized principal form "human" which had at that time not yet been recognizable as such.

This can best be compared to a tree *trunk* (see illustration by Martin) whereby human evolution is represented by the (inner) trunk, right up to the top *branch* at the crown, which stems directly from the trunk. All other branches grow from the sides of the central trunk.

---

[97] The two other forms of life, plants and insects, which basically have a completely different structure, must be excluded, however. I refer to my first book, "Plädoyer für ein Leben nach dem Tod und eine etwas andere Sicht der Welt", *(Arguments for Life after Death and a slightly different View of the World)* (not translated into English yet), see List of References.

And now the crucial significance: just as, in this analogy, the tree consists of two different parts – the wooden trunk and branches, and the foliage – the "human" tree *trunk* may be visualized as an "imaginary tree" or a "tree of ideas". Branches, which can also be considered as ideas for the physical specialization of single creatures, grow from its sides.
The branches are covered by leaves growing from them. This foliage corresponds with the physical manifestation of all forms of life.
This central trunk of ideas communicates with its physical environment, i.e. the conditions on this earth, or to put it simply, to the outside through its nervous system which develops lineally into ever more complex structures. The wood itself corresponds in this metaphor to the nervous system which is nourished by roots and countless capillaries. It is ideas that nourish this tree and they are the basic principles for all creatures. This nourishment is something immaterial, something spiritual. It is taken up by the roots which correspond in this analogy to the countless number, millions upon millions, of tiniest ramifications of nerves in our cerebral cortex.
The central tree of nerves of which I am talking here stands on its head since the "roots" are *at the top*. These are anatomically and functionally important facts which I will explain in detail later.
The top of the tree, and thereby the pride of place at the crown of my tree is occupied by humans. They get something back which they themselves have increasingly contested over the last two hundred years: to be something special in this world.
The renaissance of the recognition of their real importance on this earth should be enough to induce them to be more careful in handling themselves, their brethren and their environment.
Just as the nutrients which every tree needs and its wood and leaves are very real yet still different, so are the ideas and basic principles of all life and their physical manifestations in this world, both real and yet completely different. The central nervous system thus becomes an interface between the physical world, which most of us accept as the only real world, and a spiritual world which is actually no less real. The nervous system, which means primarily the youngest and hierarchically highest developed part, the brain, possesses a physical as well as a truly spiritual aspect. By many scientists, even renowned brain researchers, this aspect is repudiated today and argued away. This does no justice to the truth and it is social-politically very dangerous. I will also discuss this later in more detail.
Human beings may well be at the centre of the animal world.
Their specialization is not purely physical. Their physical side is represented by the development of an optimizing brain.

This is, however, merely the hardware which enables something "greater" to be attained. The cerebrum is an extremely complex and hierarchically highly developed "hardware" which enables us humans, to develop an enormous versatility, both in regard to quantity as well as quality. The most prominent feature in this development is a spirit which, for the first time in evolution, becomes fully self-aware.

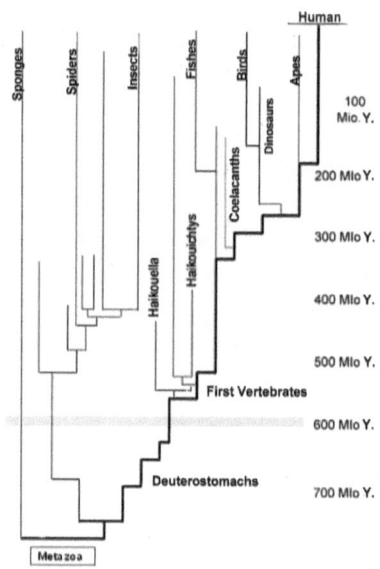

Illustration to the left by Martin: Conventional diagram of the family tree of all creatures on our earth up to humans.
According to this, humans developed as some kind of late "offshoot" from animal ancestors and occupy thus an unimportant side line.
Really important seems to me to be something else:
There is a central constant of evolution, the nervous system (see illustration by Martin below).
It developed in a straight line directly from lower to ever higher structures and levels.

On different developmental levels of the nervous system more and more new species are generated which are characterized by physical specializations (see illustration to the right).

At the end of the central line which marks the evolution of the nervous system stands mankind. Humans are in no way especially physically specialized. Instead they are going through a new purely spiritual evolution.

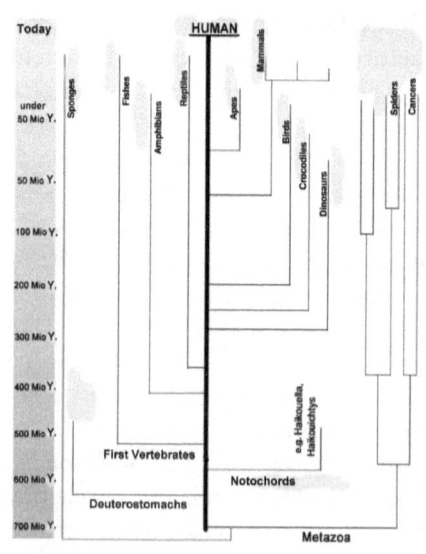

The vital question now is: what is this spirit? Is it in the last instance just another physical product of the brain made tangible by research and experiments, or is it something immaterial which utilizes the optimized brain for its own purposes?

In my opinion it is the latter and in the following chapters I will support this perception as the only really imaginable and reasonable solution. Let me say it in the words of the famous brain researcher and Nobel Prize winner *John Eccles (1903-1997)*: *"It is the spirit which controls its brain"*.

And the spirit is *"from another world"* in the words of the physician, author and moderator of a German science TV programme *Hoimar von Ditfurth (1921-1989)* who was very popular in his lifetime.

And indeed not only humans have a spirit. All forms of *life* are imbued with spirit. Life is animated. It is probably the spirit which really differentiates between a living creature and inanimate matter (see next chapter).

Many of the phenomena, for which we normally cannot offer a reasonable explanation, will now start to make sense:

How else could be explained, for example, the fantastically beautiful appearance of many creatures, an aesthetic optimized over long periods of time? In fact, beauty neither offers special advantage in selection nor a better chance in the struggle for survival. This becomes all the more apparent when such aesthetic perfection is found in places in which there are no eyes to admire the beauty, e.g. in the darkness of the deep sea.

Every form of life seems to strive for "its very own" perfection. Sometimes this indeed improves its chances of survival. Very often, however, it could all be pure luxury, certainly in those cases in which it is just aesthetical perfection. In such cases all known explanations are simply useless.

This is especially true in the case of *symbioses* in which living creatures are of great use to one another and the survivals of both species even depend on it. In such cases the simultaneous development of both species is essential – or at least the purposefully "directed mutual development".

In a few instances this may even be possible without mechanisms of superior control, but not with the vast numbers, the variety and, most of all, the complexity of such mutual relationships in reality. And the imitation of other species, known as *mimicry*, can only be reasonably explained in this way.

I would mention here *Paul Lüth's* example of a certain mussel ("Lampsillis ovata ventricosa") which produces a peculiar form along the rim of its shell, i.e on the soft part of the shell-opening, which looks exactly like a fish. Illustration to the right by my son Martin.

This fish imitating structure has eyes, a tail and it moves wave-like several times a second. If a fish wants to investigate the supposed fish on the mussel and moves too near, the mussel suddenly shoots out a cloud of larvae which are automatically drawn into its gills with the next breath.
By means of this very clever method the mussel reproduces itself.

Although fish are rather easy to deceive and a much simpler dummy would have been sufficient, nature takes the trouble to design an elaborate, complex and perfect model of a fish which looks remarkably like a real fish and is accurate in every detail.
Many plants use mimicry as well. Some orchids have developed flowers which look and even smell like insects. The imitated animals are attracted by these flowers which then "misuse" them for pollination.
The orchids and the females of the pollinating insects give off identical scents after they have been fertilized.
This not only repels the males from their female partners but also from the flowers so that they search for other objects, i.e. the pollination of other orchids.[98]
Also very interesting is the perfect deception made possible by the imitation of a special kind of behaviour. We all know that male lions, when taking charge of a new pride, very often kill the already existing cubs. The lionesses of the pride are then quickly prepared to conceive again.
Baboons show the same behaviour but their females have a special trick when meeting the new boss of the tribe for the first time. Usually the backsides of the females are bright red and swollen when they are ready and willing to conceive. If now a new male takes over the tribe, those females of the tribe, which already have a young one, show the same signs although they are not at all ready to conceive again. The male seems to be so impressed that his mind is distracted and he forgets about killing the youngsters.[99]
At the end of this chapter let us look at an example of creatures which are mostly disliked and yet belong to the most extraordinary helpers of evolution: highly specialized *parasites*.
They form a huge independent world of their own. Parasites possess the ability to use completely different, in many cases even several, species within the food chain as intermediate and main hosts.
They are able to use for their development a combination of different animals— and in some cases this unfortunately includes humans – by means of extremely clever and sophisticated manipulation techniques which enable their

---

[98] from Oecologia, 3 (2001)
[99] Source: American Journal of Primatology 52 (2000)

own species to survive. A number of such peculiar interconnections is mentioned in the very interesting book *"Parasitus Rex"*.[100]
Parasites do really amazing things with their hosts in order to ensure the survival of their species none of which can be explained by coincidence and selection alone. For example, the larva of the small liver fluke moves into the brain of an ant. There it manipulates the mental control centres of its host so that the poor ant avidly climbs up a blade of grass and falls prey to grazing sheep. But that is not all: to make it even easier for the sheep, - after all they could fall down again – the ant suffers a bite cramp at the top of the grass blade and is unable to let go. The sheep only has to pick the ants up.
I think the time has come to take a closer look at the expressions "life" and "spirit" and at their "interactions" by means of an optimized "hardware", starting with the organelles of the cells, followed by the organs of the body and finally the nervous system right up to the brain. This will be the subject of the next chapters.

4.9) Life, Spirit and their Hardware

Quite a number of scientists believe that it is only a question of time before we are able to create life from inanimate organic matter.
From a mixture of organic substances, cells could be created which are equipped with all the properties a cell needs to reproduce and to move. This would mark the beginning of a man-made evolution.
Scientists at Zurich University seem to be on the way towards solving a special problem as to how to create suitable membrane structures for cell walls. However, even so, no living cells could be created if the concoction were not mixed to a significant degree with the finished parts of already living cells.
The salient point remains the question: why is dead material all of a sudden alive? How are the cells brought to life?
Living cells are made of organic substances. Chemistry differentiates between organic and inorganic substances and compounds.
Of course, organic compounds consist of the same atoms as inorganic substances. But organic compounds consist, however, of mixed, complex, very versatile and often very long chains of molecules. Proteins are important components of our cells. They are constructed with the assistance of other proteins, known as enzymes, according to genetic specifications.

---

[100] Carl Zimmer, "Parasitus Rex", see List of References.

The *construction* proteins and the enzymes, or, so to speak, the construction materials and the construction tools, and also the craftsmen and the architects must all be at the building site *at the same time* if anything is to be achieved.
Furthermore, they have to be constantly informed of the progress of the construction and the state of affairs.
The various tasks at various construction sites must always be finely tuned to one another and well coordinated.
Here, a third group of organic compounds comes in. They are the nucleic acids which consist of long chains and represent our genotype, the genome.
If we imagine the genome as an encyclopaedia with several volumes, then each volume would be one chromosome. Each entry in the encyclopaedia is explained in more or less detail.
Each such explanation acts as a building instruction for one specific characteristic of a certain cell or multi-cellular organism. It is known as "a gene" (see Chapter 2.9).
So we have three strictly separated groups of extremely complex organic compounds. Obviously they must have existed simultaneously right from the start which enabled them to prepare the necessary physical preconditions for the development of life.
On 15th May in 1953, the young American scientist *Stanley L. Miller (*1930)* seemed to have won a decisive victory for the large army of materialists. In the biochemical institute at Columbia University in New York he simulated for the first time the terrestrial primeval atmosphere in a simple glass retort. He filled it with methane, firedamp found in mines, and, after adding ammonia, water and oxygen, he heated it all up to 80°C and bombarded this mixture with electric lightening for one week. Afterwards he found not only carbon monoxide (CO) and carbon dioxide (CO_2), but also – and that was the sensation – a large quantity of organic compounds, primarily amino acids which are the construction components for proteins. Miller's experiments were repeated very many times and meanwhile even the production of nucleic acids has been detected.
Scientists believe that, if the necessary basic construction components are available, the way to the creation of cells or even multi-cellular organisms is sufficiently prepared. The Belgian biochemist and Nobel Prize winner for chemistry in 1977, who was born in Moscow, *Ilya Prigogine (1917-2003)* seemed to support this theory with the results of his research.
Prigogine was able to prove that a steady supply of energy in sufficient quantity can cause organic compounds to reorganize from an originally chaotic state to a new previously unknown ordered one. Such a change of state occurs as suddenly as, for example, certain metals, the bimetals, bend

suddenly when a certain temperature is reached. However, if the supply of energy ceases, they return immediately to their previous chaotic state.[101] The further supply of energy could even cause a cascading sequence of ever higher levels of structures. But there are narrow limits.

Still, it is surprising to realize what an immense number of synchronized coincidences must have occurred to have given life on this earth a chance at all. The probability of coincidence for the development of the building blocks of life is very remote. Already one single relatively small protein with 100 different amino acids possesses 20^{100} (with 20 AAs) or, in mathematical terms, about 10^{130} different combinations, i.e. a 1 with 130 zeros. This is probably already a much higher quantity than the sum of all atoms in our entire known universe. A coincidental construction of the essential building blocks of life is hardly imaginable.

If we assume that the earth is about five billion years old and over the last three billion years one protein has been generated per second then only about 10^{60} different proteins could have been generated. That is only a 10^{70}th part of the just mentioned 10^{130}, and thus only a negligibly small amount which would be available for building perhaps a required protein.

Furthermore, the "right" proteins must join together because only they fit together. Even if we assume that the environmental conditions are optimal it is grossly unlikely that the appropriate proteins are generated at all if the probability for this to happen is so remote.

If all accidentally produced proteins were spread in a layer around the earth the layer would be one meter thick and in every single square centimetre there would be about 10 million proteins. That two "fitting" proteins meet in this layer if one lies perhaps at the north pole and the other at the south pole is extremely improbable. Coincidence makes no sense.

Admittedly, according to mathematical considerations from which certain restrictions derive, we must acknowledge that not necessarily *all* available possibilities have actually been tried out during the generation of proteins. More than 30 years ago scientists were able to prove this with the tobacco mosaic virus. Nevertheless, it remains far too improbable that complex life could have been created by pure coincidence. Here a nice quotation from the article *'Life force'* by the renowned scientific magazine *'New Scientist'*, where it says so aptly: *'Throwing energy at amino-acids will not create chain molecules, just as putting dynamite under a pile of bricks won't make a house'*[102].

---

[101] Theory of the so-called *"dissipative structures"*, see Glossary.
[102] Edition of 18.09.1999. My friend, Ship's Master *Klaus Müller*, was so kind as to send me this edition from Scotland.

The next question arises here as to where on earth life could have started. Some scientists assume that life started in the water. However, a chemical law, the so-called "law of mass action", contradicts this theory. Substances which were produced from the primeval soup, such as nucleic acids and amino acids, are supposed to have reacted with one another in the water and have thus facilitated the production of ever more complex substances, such as proteins. During this process, known as condensation, water is set free. A mechanism – and especially a cascade of reactions, in which water is set free – could never have occurred in an environment with a surplus of water. The generation of life in *free* water was, therefore, impossible. The only explanation might have been the existence of water-free zones in the ocean, e.g. protected recesses and caves produced by under-water volcanoes, where a sufficient supply of dry crust could be found along their rims. This is exactly what many scientists assume today.

However, the temperatures in the neighbourhood of masses of lava would be far too high and thus incompatible with life. A number of unicellular and even some multi-cellular organism do exist which can resist higher temperatures, but for most organisms, especially for the more complex ones, high temperatures inevitably lead to death.

In my opinion, this explanation seems rather unlikely and implausible, at least as a universally applicable explanation for the evolution of immensely diverse and complex forms of life.

Next to water, light is also a very important prerequisite for the production of organic material from inorganic preliminary stages.

Sunlight is only able to penetrate water if the water lets the light through. Water is, of course, in general translucent. This is, however, rather amazing since the so-called absorption spectrum of water[103] is such that only a small spectrum of radiation, only visible light, is allowed through. Everything else is absorbed and, therefore, cannot penetrate water – neither radiation with a higher nor a lower frequency than visible light. Underwater volcanoes are primarily found in such depths of the ocean which are never reached by visible light.

Another theory claims that the earth was fertilized from outside, for example by comets out of the cosmos (panspermia).

This explanation seems to me more realistic than all the previous ones. It has some additional appeal because it presupposes that there is life on some of the myriads of celestial bodies.

---

[103] It shows which "wavelengths" of radiation are absorbed by water and which pass through. The spectrum of visible light passes through water.

Many people claim that the mere concentration of substances necessary for the existence of life already is life. But this is not true.
Firstly, these substances must all have been available in a well balanced and coordinated quantities right from the start.
All forms of life, no matter how small they are or how simply they are constructed, already have a specific way of harmonizing and functioning with one another.
Nearly all forms of life, even the simplest, already involve sexual propagation. Even small crab-like mussels have a rather "dynamic" sexual life. To reach and fertilize a female partner they possess an immensely long penis. Furthermore, they change their sex at will and can achieve up to 500 copulations within 75 minutes.[104] Even unicellular bacteria propagate sexually: there are male and female individuals, the "donor and the acceptor cells".
Some organisms are hermaphrodites: they are bisexual either simultaneously or they change sex just like the above-mentioned mussel. Sometimes this happens due to a close dependence on environmental conditions, or due to hormonal influences for whatever reason.
For a sexual propagation a reduction division, or meiosis, must take place in order to convert one cell possessing a double set of chromosomes into two cells with half a set with no loss of basic information. Even unicellular organisms are already rather complicated and harmonize with one another in diverse ways.
In short, it is impossible to be a bit alive, just as it is impossible to be a bit pregnant. Either a structure is alive or it is not alive. There is nothing in the middle. Even the often quoted virus, which has been pronounced a bit hastily a "half-alive organism", is no such thing. Viruses do not have an in-built metabolic system and they cannot propagate on their own; to do that they need other multi-cellular or unicellular organisms possessing such properties and which "do the work" for them. Nevertheless, viruses could not exist without their host organisms which would suggest the conclusion that they have developed as parasites from more complex organisms by "regression", by retrograde steps, and not by more complex organisms having been developed from them. Finally I should mention that living organisms are characterized by movement, by locomotion and by the internal transport of information.
It is always life itself which creates new and higher forms of life.
Only when life already exists can new life be created. The biologist K. *Wacholder* wrote more than 50 years ago that life alone sets *"the generation of multiple graduated levels of organic order structures"* in motion.

---

[104] Journal of Zoology, Volume 253

Life is generated only when the necessary organic components have reached a sufficient degree of complexity.

Prigogine's findings confirm this. The complexity of the single parts necessary for the generation of life may be explained by reaction cascades occurring under a sufficient supply of energy.

The higher self-organized levels of molecular biology are thereby generated. One theory as to why such processes are set into motion is, as we already heard, that it is pure coincidence.

I dismiss this categorically. *Coincidence* doubtless plays an important role, but it still leaves the question unanswered as to "*how* exactly" something develops later in detail. I cannot believe that coincidence ordains "*the principle*" and the general direction of a certain development. *That* anything is developed at all and *that* it proceeds along its almost inexorable path to development and perfection, will only be marginally influenced by coincidence in the long run. In other words: the development of life accepts coincidence as assistance, I am convinced of that, but life is not the result of coincidence.

Coincidence already modulates – i.e. in the spirit – existing, that is pre-existing perceptions of "fundamental principles" in this world, and also of life.

These "pre-existing perceptions of fundamental principles" are thus *not* identical with *Plato's (427-347 B.C.)* perceptions or his *"ideas for everything being"*. They rather allow an immensely creative *emergence*, as the Austrian philosopher *Karl Popper*, for example, also believed.

In one of my previous books, I described everything in our world as being "*teleologic* and yet *emergent*, as well as being *deterministically* and yet *indeterministically* orientated", which roughly means: There are, to a certain extent, clear outlines and predetermined conditions for all existence in this world. These indicate a purposeful direction which is hardly comprehensible or even recognizable to us, but which is there nonetheless. Within the scope of these possibilities everything can unfold and develop freely and creatively".[105]

Life is, therefore, a spiritual principle and not merely the product of a complex organic structure.

It is the purposeful manifestation of a really existing spiritual world by means of sufficiently developed and structured organisms, the hardware, with the firm aim of consistently perfecting itself.

With the aid of life an initially undifferentiated but completely real spiritual field develops itself further into a differentiated, matured intelligence.

---

[105] Explanations for the words "deterministic, indeterministic and teleologic in Part 5.

Evolution, life and the organism necessary for it can be compared to the radio engineer and the radio he has constructed. The engineer is neither identical to the radio nor to the program it transmits. But he knows that he can receive radio programs only with a suitable radio.

He knows that he can only receive radio programmes with an appropriate radio set. He experiments with the components available to him until he succeeds in constructing a rather primitive but functioning radio set.

Only after it has become sufficiently "complex", i.e. when there are enough parts which have been assembled correctly, and that means "knowingly", will it function properly.

In other words: if only one screw were missing the radio would not work. Just throwing transistors and switches into a box does not lead to success either. In the same way as the finished radio is not the "programme" the programme cannot be found in the radio set itself. Neither is the program a product of the radio – just as life is not the product of cells.

To bring something to life a sufficiently complex organic structure must have been generated beforehand. For its generation it needs a construction plan, a specific and spiritual construction plan according to the principles to which it adheres. The resulting construction which has developed itself far enough starts to live because it is now able to receive and transmit programmes. The living being now participates automatically in the all-encompassing spiritual field which penetrates the entire world. The activities are effective in both directions right from the start: every living being is simultaneously receiver and transmitter, whilst the radio in my understandable but inefficient comparison is always only a receiver. An organism becomes immediately inter-active because it is alive. Any further self-organization from that point onwards consists in the further differentiation of the rather empty immature spiritual field I postulated. Initially a small, and later an increasingly growing, part is differentiated further, i.e. in a species specific, individual and at some time even "personal" way.

In return, the now living structure can participate in the growing amount of information this spiritual field possesses – at least insofar as its own specific possibilities of access allow depending on various, mostly general but also individual possibilities. Such access possibilities, if regarded from our perspective, lead to the development of well-known phenomena such as drive, instinct, intuition, seventh sense, etc. And now we know from actual neurobiological investigations at the University of Alabama, USA, that our experiences can also influence some recently discovered control-molecules. They sit on DNA-helices especially those in our brains and can switch a veriety of genes on or off, which can even lead to hereditary transmission of the newly created gene-constellations. This may give us a bridge between spiritual influence acting on the brain and the hereditary influence of so gained experiences. Scientists call this – for more than hundred years an unimaginable result of research – epigenetics. So, Lamarck's ideas are being revived (see Chapter 4.3).

The possible interactions with an assumed spiritual field bring us back to the morphologic fields as envisaged by the Englishman *Rupert Sheldrake*. In one important point, however, *Sheldrake's* spiritual fields differ significantly from the spiritual field I postulated. In my theory consciousness also consistently takes an enduring and important position at which it arrives after having progressed due to the matured physical possibilities which have been generated during the life of a higher organism.

In other words: the differentiation of the all-enveloping spiritual field I postulated progresses continually. It includes complete information on everything that has ever been and preserves it for ever. Since it is something spiritual and continual it represents the polar symmetry to the discontinuous physical world.

If time limits everything physical then the spiritual must exist eternally (see Chapters 3.8 and 3.9). It can at any time influence the presently physically embodied creatures by an initial but very subtle and constant interaction and can thus codetermine their development. And such interactively experienced information might then even be transmitted to the next generation e.g. by epigenetic mechanisms as just mentioned.

In contrast to Sheldrake's perception, however, the subtle influence diminishes as the single individual increasingly develops its own consciousness and the ability to recognise itself in the course of time, thus facilitating the exertion of a more purposeful influence. At first consciousness may be an inhibiting factor for the spirit as a mechanism for evolution since it is still immature and any kind of immaturity poses a risk.

Nevertheless, it will enforce its effects. This only makes sense if the chance it offers outweighs the risks right from the start. Such cognition requires an already existing consciousness. Consciousness may be an opportunity if it recognises and understands the relationships between the physical and the immaterial, interactive, spiritual world to which it has always belonged right from the start. Only here does it stand a chance as is increasingly shown – sadly enough – by the deadly dangers which are self-induced on this earth by consciously performed human deeds.

Consciousness may thus introduce a new form of independent evolution, an evolution which is of purely spiritual nature without it having to generate other physical sections or further specialization. At the same time all developed forms remain preserved with all their facets as an important factor in this spiritual world for ever.

With the growing consciousness, the importance of the collective and thus that of the species as a whole diminishes. Consciousness strives for individuality. An immense number of single and ever more diverging states of consciousness become apparent, for example, in humans.

The process of "individualizing" is an elementary part of this new evolution on a higher, the spiritual, level. This enables a far greater – an almost unfathomably – wide variety to be generated than that created by the purely physical achievement of sexual propagation.

Humans, as the first representative of this new generation of evolution, must learn to recognise this as being a clear concept of this world.

Powerful ideological currents, especially during the last two centuries, profoundly failed to recognise this development causing great harm to mankind. And unfortunately this seems not to have found an end yet.

Many social problems of our time could be solved and a more harmonic cooperation could be achieved if humans would at long last become aware of the real basic principles of their existence. One of the biggest problems is that of intolerance towards the most diverse but peacefully executed religious denominations and political convictions.

Frequent but always inappropriate discriminations against minorities which maintain a peaceful way of life but which may be somehow different from that of the majority or the norm is sadly another.

The individuality of the "new" evolution has nothing whatsoever in common with an (egoistic) individualism.

As is true with *life*, the *spirit* is not a product of anything physical. Suitable organic structures are essential to facilitate their unfolding and to instigate their continuous and lasting development. The spirit matures due to the interactive communication between a sufficiently suitable organic structure and a spiritual field which envelops and penetrates the whole world, or, better still, which ultimately generates it.

This constant omnipresent interactive communication leads on to an indescribable evolution of the entire spiritual field and is instigated expressly by the enormous number of individually-thinking and self-aware creatures.

This alone makes the world into a kind of *"God in Emergence"* as *Teilhard de Chardin (1881-1955)* suggested.

4.10) There is Light in our Cells

In the last chapters I described a few phenomena which only allow one conclusion: the storage and transmission of information must take place not only in commonly accepted ways by means of chemical substances or of weak electrical currents, but it must be possible in other ways a well. The question then arises as to what kind of ways are we thinking of?

Perhaps the Bible could show us the right track. It starts with the words: *"And then God said: 'let there be light': and there was light"*[106].

The German physicist *Erwin Schrödinger (1887-1961)* pointed out several decades ago that it is not only the energy content of light but also the information and the order it contains which seem to play an important role.

Since *Max Planck (1858-1947)* and *Albert Einstein (1879-1955)* we definitely know that light like all electro-magnetic radiation is quantized. From this theory it follows that light is not really a continuous beam but that it consists of a sequence of a countless number of tiniest particles none of which possesses any mass of their own.

These photons race around the world at various frequencies. Within a second, varying numbers of photons dart through space one after the other. Each single photon also seems to have its "own frequency". We can measure it by its varying number of wave crests and troughs per time unit. From a measuring-technical point of view, we have a *ray* of light which travels wave-like. This is only logical, as the Danish physicist *Niels Bohr (1885-1962)* once stated in a telegram to *Albert Einstein*, for if light and any other electro-magnetic radiation would consist only of particles the telegram could never have reached Einstein.

The theory of the "wave-particle-dualism", which is still difficult for many people to understand even today, was born during the first half of the 20th century. It introduced a completely new kind of physics known as quantum physics or particle physics. I have already pointed that any kind of radiation really consists just of particles and has no wave character (see Part 3). Even the term "particle" is rather exaggerated, since each is in fact merely a massless "point of light" or better single information units. Thus photons are interfaces between a real spiritual world and a physical world which we can perceive by our senses. On the one hand they are "physical" points of light if they hit something which can measure them by energy exchange or which can perceive them. On the other hand, and that is their real character, they are single "spiritual" information units of being. Expressed in mathematical terms, every single one of them represents a "1".

---

[106] The Bible, Genesis, 01.03

Of course, the wave character of light moving through space is a provable phenomenon. It is a really existing phenomenon and this is why physicists, all too hastily, like to smile about my ideas.

The so-called wave character of light is not due to light itself being a wave. It rather travels as a quantum (particle) through a real, onion-skin-like concentric but informational or spiritual space. It is spiritual because it is infinite and eternally structured by all ordinal numbers from 1 to infinity (see Part 3).

The distances between these onion skins must vary according to the characteristics of mass, size, structure, density and behaviour of the various atomic structures and their close connections (see the heavy-black central circles in Martin's illustration). Photons (quanta) are emitted, due, for example, to radioactive disintegration caused by thermo- nuclear fusion in the sun or by radio-transmission from pulsars. They are transported over the variably large real and concentrically structured infinite number spaces which represent the infinite space of the universe as we know it.

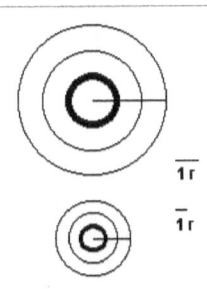

In mathematical terms the number 1, or 1^2, is multiplied by every number of the number space (see Chapters 3.4 and 3.5). That is why we, who live and work within this system and are thus part of it, inevitably perceive the phenomenon of continuous waves. In reality, however, this is *not* a "wave-particle-dualism" of the light, since light continues to consist merely of massless information *points*. But now we do recognise a *spiritual-physical dualism*: this is the real double nature of light, in my opinion: here the point of light in the physical sense when it hits something which can recognise it and there the pure information in the spiritual sense – the real character of light.

Scientists today recognise increasingly the enormous potential light will have in future as a carrier of information.

We are already able to use laser light as a safe and enduring medium for transporting and storing digitally encoded information.

Of course, we still like to believe that we have *invented* new technologies. As so very often, however, I am convinced that we have only *rediscovered* a part of something that has existed in our world from the very beginning and has been perfected right down to the last detail. It is especially interesting to note that when transmitting information by laser light it is especially weak lasers with a low intensity which are the most suitable ones.

The German scientific author *Marco Bischof* wrote an interesting book about this, in which he reports in an easily understandable way of a number of findings concerning radiation in organic tissues made mainly by *Fritz Albert Popp*, professor for physics who presently works in *Neuss,* Germany.

In 1922 already the Russian physician and biologist *Alexander Gurwitsch (1874-1954)* discovered that the living cells of onions emit a weak light. *Fritz Popp* has been able to prove by modern methods that all living beings store light in all their cells, thereby demonstrating that this is a universal phenomenon.

Cells seem to emit especially strong light during the process of cell division, or when they are damaged (probably due to repair mechanisms) and when they are *dying*. When a cell is *dead* it *no longer* radiates light. This phenomenon, which Popp called "bio-photon-radiation", could be proved in the meantime in a strictly scientific way. It is also certain that this is not a kind of "thermal radiation", i.e. thermally effective photons which, according to *Bischof* hardly disperse at all, i.e. they have an exceedingly high degree of coherence which goes far beyond anything we presently know about technical lasers.

This renders it at least probable that bio-photons also perform a biological function and are utilized as the basis for communication within the cell and between different cells. It follows that we should attach more importance especially to the three-dimensional structures of cells and their components, such as complex proteins and nucleic acids. They are probably ideal resonance bodies for the amplifying and storing of information transmitted by light. It seems also to be proven that bio-photons are closely connected to DNA which carries the biochemical genetic information within the cell nucleus. Therefore, it seems probable that DNA acts as a main storage for bio-photons. In future we may possibly come to recognise that bio-photons, i.e. the light in our cells, play a key role in the hereditary mechanism.

Which frequencies are especially important and how the various imaginable bio-photon controls work, remain as yet still unanswered questions.

Critics of these theories claim that bio-photons are merely a form of spontaneous light radiated by chemical substances and are caused by a spontaneous chemical luminescence. Others claim that they are incoherent, indeed rather chaotic and are, therefore, not suitable for the transmission of information and are biologically absolutely insignificant. Meanwhile this criticism for the theory of bio-photons was clearly refuted long ago.

4.11) The Nervous System and the Brain

The renowned Californian neuro-biologist *Kenneth A. Klivington* wrote in his extremely interesting book "Brain and Spirit": *Nothing is as complicated as the human brain. Its working method is one of the greatest mysteries we know."* Although he tends to take rather the materialistic point of view he added later: *"Brain research is so exciting because it is possible to interpret discoveries in completely different ways".*

The brain is the highest and surely most complex part of an enormously wide-ranging and, on the whole, complicated nervous system, and yet, it is relatively easy to explain roughly what is really known today about the brain and its functions. First of all, it is surely worth mentioning that a large number of organisms exist without any kind of nervous system and they obviously get along just fine. This includes plants and a number of simple multi-cellular organisms and all unicellular organisms, including bacteria. The French scientist *Jean-Claude de Tymowski* of the *Alliance Médicale Internationale* in *Paris* said that this fact does not at all prevent them from possessing highly developed structures or of being quite clearly outstandingly well-adjusted to their environment.

Apparently, it is not absolutely imperative to possess such a nervous system as communication network in order to guarantee the existence of many different forms of life and their constant further development over aeons of time – in short to be successful in this world.

At some time during the evolution of life on earth, however, such a nervous system appeared. Whilst life on earth has taken some large detours and gone round bends and is still doing so, the nervous system has continually developed in a straight line to higher levels. In the course of time it has become increasingly more complex and has been converted into something that strives continuously toward an ever higher hierarchical order. Each newly attached area is strictly "downward compatible", i.e. it is able to work together harmoniously with the hierarchically lower and usually older sections.

For the last few thousand years, however, the development of the human brain seems to have come, for the time being at least, to a standstill. We may now say, without considering interpretations for the phenomena "thought", "consciousness" or "emotionality", that humans have attained an intellectual, psychological, cultural and emotional degree of development incomparable with any other creature on earth. Only humans possess such an infinitely diverse and complex, individual consciousness and a self-awareness with such emotional richness not to be found anywhere else. In addition, only humans have the infinitely expandable ability to think and act in abstract and differentiated ways whilst also possessing an incomparable memory. These abilities seem almost to explode during human development, although this passes no judgment on their individual qualities...

Two general hypotheses can be drawn from this cognition: First, the spiritual capabilities have escalated over many thousands of years while the anatomy of the brain, i.e. the physical factor, has not developed any correlating important new features. In his final statement and after having appraised the results of these examinations carefully *Klivington* also believed that *"the proof of the existence of structural differences within human brains is extremely difficult to deliver"* – *"even in the case of extremely pronounced differences in intelligence or other characteristics (or a completely different cultural background)"*.

Secondly, the history of evolution seems to have changed the paradigms. Immediately prior to the appearance of humans on the scene, the thrust of evolution, which towards the end seemed strongly orientated to the creation of ever more new and physically specialized varying species, definitely receded, even if we disregard the often destructive effect humans have on their environment. In return we see an unbelievable diversity of human individuals with ever increasing spiritual, cultural and emotional variations.

Evolution has switched horses. What, however, did it do to the spirit?

What constitutes the new, much greater and almost unrestricted spiritual evolution? Is it in fact the mere expression of an increasingly complex brain with ever more interlinked circuits as many media-orientated brain researchers very effectively want us to believe today? I do not believe it: spirit is something completely different. This already follows from the statements above, since human brain anatomy and spiritual diversity are not congruent. The spirit, which increases almost explosively only in humans, has a different quality than the brain and I believe it can only mature by continual inter-active experience *with the brain* in the course of every single life. It follows as a logical conclusion then that the spirit, being absolutely independent from its brain, is not inevitably bound to die with it.

Our intellectual capacities and all our emotions are part of our personality and, therefore, also part of the spirit, but they are not part or product of our brain. This fundamental statement needs to be explained and supported in detail since it is grossly incongruent with the notions of some brain researchers today.

At first I will give you some important anatomical-physiological basic explanations. The basic unit of the nervous system is the nerve cell, the neuron depicted in the following illustration by my son Martin.

Each single nerve cell is a living biochemical factory and has the ability to process and store information.
Neurons possess various appendices which facilitate communication with adjoining neurons.

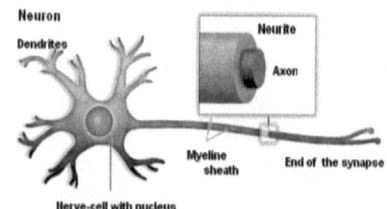

256

We can discern a receiver part which consists of many, probably up to a thousand short appendices, the dendrites. They transmit information from other cells to the neuron. Furthermore, there is *one* longer appendix, the axon. This has an "internal transmission wire", the axon, which can transmit information over longer distances to other neurons.

Between the dendrites and axons of adjoining cells there is a small gap which is only about one thousandth of a millimetre wide, it is known as the synaptic junction. The point where the two cells meet is slightly bloated. It is known as the synapse.

For the mature human brain we may give the following – rough – approximate quantities: the human brain has about 1 trillion nerve cells with about 1 quadrillion connections between adjoining cells.

If we were to connect all nerve cells of one human brain into a long chain we could wind the chain around the earth a few thousand times. That alone is for many people explanation enough for the incredible efficiency of the brain-dependent spirit as they see it. But this is a hasty and superficial judgement.

Let me give you now a rather rough description of the brain-function: the transmission of all information within the nervous system is based on electric currents, so-called impulses. In this way the stimulation of the skin by stroking it softly, for example, stimulates such electrical impulses. For such stimulation to be transmitted to the brain thereby enabling us to become aware of it, it must possess a certain intensity. If it is too weak nothing will happen, and if it is too strong it does not achieve anything *additional*. This is known as the "all-or nothing-law".

A current remains a current – its strength does not vary in the nervous system; there are no varying electric degrees of an impulse. This principle remains unchanged even if the intensity of the stimulation is increased by increasing the frequency of the impulse. This, however, merely increases the number of connections and it facilitates a finer adjustment. To each single connection the "all-or nothing-law" applies. In contrast to all known scientific doctrines I believe that nature attempts here again to reduce risks or misinformation to a minimum, which is also important for genetics (see Chapter 2.9). Circumspection of nature is the reason for this form of information transmission according to the "all-or nothing-law" in my opinion: it is simple and absolutely safe. Either an electrical impulse is transmitted, or it is not – there is nothing like a bit more or a bit less like in the same way as there is nothing like being a bit pregnant.

As already mentioned, there are two different kinds of nerve tracts: the receivers (dendrites) and the transmitters (axons). The currents with which our immense number of neurons communicate always travel *in only one* direction which is anatomically determined. Dendrites and axons are always one-way streets. At their ends, the docking stations, the electrical impulse must be transmitted from one nerve cell to the next or to the target organ. In rare cases this is achieved by an electrical impulse, in most cases it takes place by chemical means. At the synapses a chemical messenger substance known as the transmitter is released by an approaching impulse. The transmitter then crosses over the very narrow synaptic gap and may either trigger a new impulse on the other side or inhibit the formation of such a new impulse. Here again the same rule applies: either a new electrical impulse is triggered by the chemical messenger substance or it is not; there is never just a bit of an impulse. It is not yet known why there is such a large number of transmitters when just two would be quite sufficient for inhibiting or transmitting impulses.

My guess is that – quite apart from a more focussed selection of the desired impulse receivers – a better gradation between the desired impulse receivers is thereby facilitated, in the same way perhaps as with press-buttons in a telephone system: when I push one button I may only reach *one* specific receiver, whereas if I use another I reach *several* receivers at the same time – I may even start a chain of telephone calls. Whenever I push such a button it always causes *at least* one telephone to ring – either the button is pressed or it is not.

Of course, there could be defects due to transmitters being produced in an insufficient amount or with inadequate functions resulting in defective impulse transmissions at the synapses. An example of such a defect is Parkinson's disease which is also known as "shaking palsy".

Sensory perceptions from our body periphery are transmitted by means of sensitive or afferent tracts to centres such as the brain. The reaction patterns which originate there are sent to the relevant peripheral target organs via efferent or motor tracts. These, too, are always one-way streets.

Each single strand of these neuronal cables is well insulated. Damage to the insulation can lead to fatal electrical short-circuits. One example for this is the severe disease "multiple sclerosis".

In the following I will describe some details concerning the general construction of the brain before I turn to the *most important tiniest details of the cerebral cortex*.

In the hierarchical order the oldest and now the lowest part of the brain, the hindbrain, stands above the spinal cord. Thereafter follows the midbrain and then the interbrain. All these parts are covered by the cerebrum, or cortex. The cerebellum occupies a special position with regard to its location and function. All this together is known as the central nervous system.

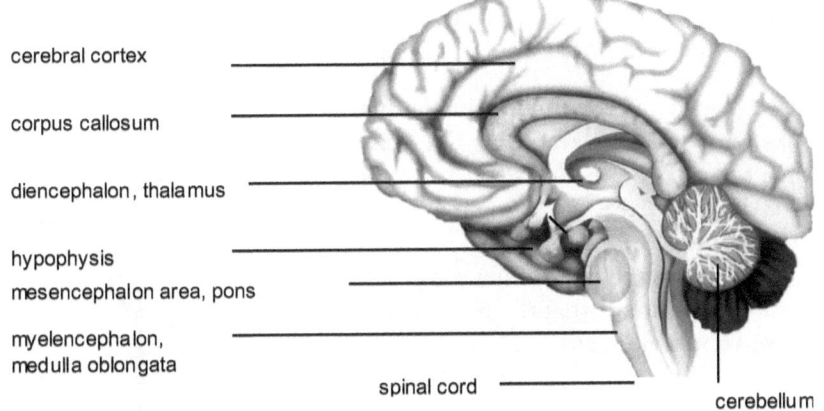

- cerebral cortex
- corpus callosum
- diencephalon, thalamus
- hypophysis
- mesencephalon area, pons
- myelencephalon, medulla oblongata
- spinal cord
- cerebellum

If we take a look at a cross-section of the cerebrum a grey layer and a white layer can easily be discerned. The so-called grey substance contains an immense number of neurons, nerve *cells*, which is why this is referred to as the grey matter. This layer is found on the *outside* and thus directly on the surface of the brain. The surface area is considerably enlarged, especially in humans, by its many convolutions and grooves.

In comparison to the class of mammals one step below in the hierarchy, the large number of cells and of connections between these cells in the human brain *alone* appears like a "quantum leap" in brain complexity.

The white substance lies beneath the grey matter and consists of the most varied conduction pathways. Thinking, feeling, memory and consciousness are situated in the grey matter according to today's prevailing opinion – either *in* the cells of the cerebral cortex or in mostly island-like groupings, so-called cores, in the sections of the brain beneath.

Such concepts are usually either based on various electro-physiological experiments or on observations of changes in human or animal behaviour after brain surgery.

In addition these perceptions are supported by studies using brain imaging methods, such as *MRI* or *PET* and by contrasting substances such as sugar, which is fed into the active centres of the brain, or with radioactive xenon.[107]

In spite of this "evidence" I will demonstrate that the common conclusion, namely that conscious spiritual and emotional actions are *situated* in the brain itself and are initiated by it, is hardly sustainable.

---

[107] MRI = magnetic resonance imaging or nuclear spin resonance tomography) and PET (positron emission tomography) see Glossary. Xenon is an inert gas.

The famous *John Eccles* most persistently pointed out, we should pay special attention to the *micro*-structures of the cerebral cortex, i.e. to those structures which can only be seen under the microscope.

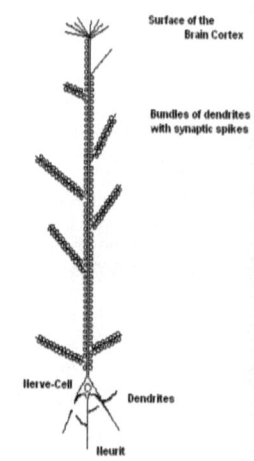

The following aspect is very interesting in this context (see illustration by Martin, according to Eccles):
Each nerve cell (neuron) possesses many ramifications, such as the dendrites, the "receiving masts", and the neurite, the "transmitter mast".
It we look at the arrangement of neurons in the cerebral cortex, we notice that the many dendrite arms of the neurons point upwards and outwards like antennae. Like hairs on an upright brush they point to the surface of the brain and approximately every 100 of such vertically upright striving dendrites are bundled together into one functional unit, the dendrite.
In one single important section of the cerebral cortex alone, for example the motor-centre which is responsible for body movements, the human brain has approximately 40 million such dendrites compared to only approximately 200,000 in the brains of higher mammals.
Each single one of these "bristles" is in addition equipped with approximately 5,000 spikes, the free synapses, i.e. docking stations for the appendices of the nerve cells. Here we find literally trillions of synapses which grow like ivy up to the surface of the brain without touching another single nerve cell.

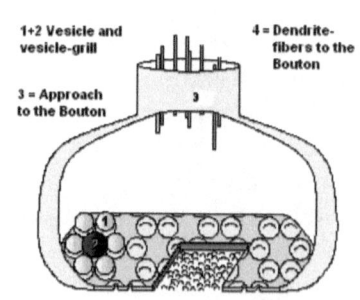

The spike synapses are swollen at their ends (see illustration by Martin, according to Eccles). We also talk of a button-like extension, the "bouton" (= French for button). There are small bubbles inside, so-called vesicles, which are full of transmitters and which are arranged 30 to 50 at a time in honeycombed *hexagonal* meshes of vesicles. If we *want* to take a really close look we find all in all many billions of antenna-like nerve tracts arranged next to one another perpendicular to the surface of the brain.
Each of these "antennae" possesses several thousand points of contact, the synapses with their *free* buttons, each one of which carries a mesh of vesicles.

Even without a great deal of fantasy we may compare them to flat parabolic mirrors by means of which every living being, e.g. all mammals and primarily, of course, humans, can receive or transmit.

John Eccles, who was awarded the Nobel Prize for his work on synapses, describes this in the same way. He assumes that due to their extremely low weight[108] the transmitters within the trillions of vesicles could be set free by purely physical "quantum processes" as the result of thinking processes carried out by an immaterial spirit, which could then cause brain actions to be followed by physical reactions.

It seems important to me to point out again, that all tracts of a nervous system, in whichever direction they go, are one-way streets. And all impulses which run along these tracts follow the all-or-nothing law. These strictly defined regulations help to reduce errors within the reaction chains to a minimum.

In all highly developed creatures on Earth, and especially in humans, an immensely large number of "transmitter and receiver stations" standing upright like "antennae" are to be found at the hierarchically highest end, and yet simultaneously the youngest end from the evolutionary standpoint. This must have a special meaning!

I believe that the anatomy of the nervous system and especially that of the brain with its "antennae trees" is indeed similar to trees in the open countryside. This could surely lead us to the reasonable assumption that all living beings with a cerebrum are in constant interactive contact with a mostly unknown – since not recognised – outer world, in the same way as the leaves on trees absorb light energy. It is the world of an immaterial, all-enveloping and all-penetrating spiritual field. We all take advantage of it and personally claim a small part of it just for ourselves, which we differentiate in the course of our physical life by learning and collecting experiences. This limited spiritual field is the personal *"intranet"* of a "spiritual internet" which generates the whole world and sustains it eternally and develops it further continuously.

It also includes the species-specific morphogenetic fields of *Rupert Sheldrake*. Only, for creatures without self-awareness, it must always remain an unconscious and collective intranet. Due to the development of an individual consciousness and self-awareness alone it becomes an individual part of an immeasurably large whole. And this part can become aware of it at any time.

In the hour of physical death at the very latest every single one of us becomes aware of it. Here and now it becomes clear that brain and spirit are not the same – they cannot be.

---

[108] A transmitter molecule weighs approx. 10^{-18} g (= one quadrillionth or an atto-gramm)

Therefore, it is time to deal with these manifold conclusions which still seem to keep most brain researchers enmeshed in their materialistic way of thinking.

4.12) Brain and Spirit

Without doubt brain research has made great progress over the last years. Some renowned brain researchers assume now they are on the right track when they identify all previously unexplainable but "somehow spiritual" activities as products of the brain. They do not even stop at our daily experience of the "Ego" or the "free will".

Spirit, consciousness and thinking with all its facets become a product of our brain, an epiphenomenon similar to a secretion, like perspiration from a sweat gland.

According to this the free will is pure illusion, as is the Ego and thus our entire personality. Such perceptions lead to fateful social political consequences. We would no longer be personally responsible for our deeds if we are no longer self-determined but totally controlled by our brain which dictates to us to take actions which we only notice later and which we accept in hindsight as self-determined decisions made by our personality. The brain becomes a mega-computer which controls itself and everything else and humans are nothing but very complicated automatons of their own brains.

Such new approaches are incessantly spread around today as already proven knowledge by means of modern media. In order to increase the impact the same scientists are repeatedly cited – such as the American *Antonio Damasio* or the German brain researchers *Wolf Singer* and *Gerhard Roth* – but there is indeed no real proof as yet. The whole matter is further complicated by the fact that just as many renowned scientists do *not* agree with this perception. Their ideas are, however, of little interest in a materialistic orientated world – not even if they are published by Nobel Prize winners such as *John Eccles (1903-1997)*, who died only a few years ago. They do not fit the spirit of the age and, therefore, they are not given space in the media.

Some years ago the human brain was compared to a kind of telephone switch board which could receive all kinds of messages from peripheral installations such as the sensory organs. In the brain, the centre of our nervous system, all information is collected, processed and then, just as the operator used to do in the old days, the correct connections are made as far as possible. Suitable ideas, actions and reactions could be prepared, redirected to other specific cables and then transmitted to the peripheral target receivers.

Exactly *how* the central processing was expected to work, i.e. *what* really happened in the brain, remained a mystery, of course. Nevertheless, for some brain functions this explanation may indeed still be correct and may provide a descriptive aid.

Nowadays the brain is rather compared to a trainable computer. But still it is reduced to a pure information-processing machine. As such it continually receives countless pieces of information from its environment, filters them, processes what is necessary and stores them as memory. By means of programs which are capable of learning, this machine calculates and modifies everything that happens in the course of its life and ensures in the end that the best ideas, actions and reactions are implemented through peripheral installations accessible by means of its immense cable network which is extremely fast and effective.

The American neurobiologist *Kenneth Klivington* admits, however, that it is becoming increasingly apparent that *"the brain does not really function like a computer, at least not like the ones we know today"*.

For me, however, technical computers seem to be another helpful though insufficient model when attempting to explain the functioning of our brain. However, neither telephone switchboards nor the diverse computer networks communicating *within* the brain are sufficient to give a reasonably satisfactory explanation for the reality. Above all, it is the incredibly large number of cells and connections with which our brain is equipped which seems proof enough for many people for rejecting any assumptions about a purely spiritual, i.e. immaterial, influence *on* our brain. The human brain probably consists of approx. 30 billion nerve cells. Every single process of memorizing activates 10 million cells simultaneously.

About 4 billion electric impulses can be exchanged per second between the two halves of the brain over the corpus callosum, the great band of commissural fibres (see illustration in the previous chapter and the following illustration in this chapter).

Our nervous system possesses about one hundred trillion synapses (10^{14} synapses). The number of possible combinations of all synaptic connections in a human brain seems to be even higher than the number of atoms in the entire currently known universe[109]. The sheer number of brain cells and their configuration already inspired some popular scientific book authors compare them to stars and galaxies in the cosmos. Some believe, therefore, that the universe is some kind of gigantic brain of an even more gigantic, immense "super being".

---

[109] Numbers from K. and St. Kunsch, "Der Mensch in Zahlen".

Let me describe to you now some classical experiments und examinations which have been carried out with animal and human brains and explain with their help interpretations which are very effectively spread by our media. We know for sure that the brain of a worm is hardly more than a kind of electronic control system and that flies possess indeed tiny, perfectly functioning calculating machines which are, as the German professor *Valentin Braitenberg* of the *Max-Planck Institut für Biologische Kybernetik (Max-Planck Institute of Biological Cybernetics)* in Tuebingen, Germany, describes them, perfect auto-pilots.[110] It is also a fact that in principle the human brain is made of the same components as those in the brain of a fly. Nevertheless, as every child who was ever allowed to play with a unit construction system knows, completely different objects may be constructed from identical basic components, even objects of varying complexity and those being technically ambitious. It always depends on *how* and with *what additional* details something is constructed.

Take another example: aeroplanes, ships, trains and many other large pieces of machinery such as the mammoth brown-coal excavator which I see frequently in our neighbourhood, are all basically made of identical materials. You will never succeed, however, in making the excavator fly or the train travel over water. In the end *Valentin Braitenberg* also accepted that *"there is nothing degrading about being convinced that something as complicated and amazing as the human brain is in the last analysis made of insignificant basic components. What counts is the manner in which these components are connected with one another".* The same applies to the living cell as I already pointed out.

Of course, humans also have centres of rather complex and autonomic-controlled actions which might allow the conclusion that mechanisms are actually working here which are processed and stored *in* the relevant control centres, even if it remains a complete mystery as to how this is achieved. In such cases the relative size of a brain area is also decisive for the extent of a specific qualification. For example vultures and other scavengers possess a relatively large olfactory brain area. Thus they are able to smell dead meat over a distance of many kilometres. The tyrannosaurus rex also possessed such a relatively large olfactory area in comparison to its brain size. This is one of many indications which possible point to the T-Rex as not having been such a dangerous predator, as it is still made out to be in countless books and movies, but that it was merely a scavenger. Obviously, there seems to be much scope for readjustments in palaeontology as well.

It is also possible that mathematical control circuits play a role in the processing and storing of information in the control centres of the brain

---

[110] Quoted from Kenneth A. Klivington, "Brain and Spirit".

which influence these processes by subtly graduated concentrations of chemical substances. A very good example for this is the very complicated, extremely exact and also forward-looking cooperation of our various digestive organs which work without our conscious intervention. Every human possesses regulatory processes which start to function as soon as he sees or smells food. With unbelievable precision everything necessary for digesting the amount of food which the body needs at that moment is brought together in the digestive tract.

At the same time a deeply-rooted reflex, which can hardly be influenced, is controlled in such a way that only such food is selected which the body expects and which is best suited to it.

The notion that numbers can also control the performance of our central nervous system is supported by the example of the processing of sounds different frequencies in the brain and the ears. Sounds are processed alternately by the left or the right half of the brain when they have a frequency of the exact multiple of 40 and 60 Hz.

With the aid of simple digital codes, which influence various physical processes, it can be explained why it is that we can differentiate between two slightly different notes although in our internal ear, the cochlea, they induce practically an identical stimulation. There are also some biological rhythms which are also very good examples in this context. All mammals and humans follow a daily rhythm which is absolutely independent of the prevailing environmental conditions and covers 24 to 25 hours. Mice and rats have a rhythm of exactly 24 hours and 16 minutes for which one of the so-called "grey cores" in the brain, i.e. an internal cluster of nerve cells, seems to be responsible.[111]

The psychologist *Richard F. Thompson* of the *University of Southern California* in *Los Angeles/USA* gave rabbits behavioural training.

As with the famous dog of the Russian physiologist and neurologist *Iwan P. Pawlow*, which after similar training produced gastric juices if a bell started ringing even when no food was forthcoming, Thompson conditioned a blink-reflex in his rabbits provoked by *one* single tone. Meanwhile, due to other experiments, it has been established that a certain area in the grey matter (a so-called "core") in the cerebellum is responsible for this behaviour.[112] When this area was removed, the conditioning disappeared whilst the normal blink-reflex remained. For many people such an experiment, which has been repeated in similar form many times since, is a clear indication (if not even proof) that the home of the trained reflex observed here must be stored *within* the grey cells

---

[111] Nucleus suprachiasmaticus
[112] Nucleus interpositus

of the cerebellum. This may be a logical conclusion; but it should be made absolutely clear that what we are looking at here is only a rather simple reflex arc and not an intellectual performance. Furthermore, such a core does not lie on the surface of the cerebral or cerebellar cortex but is hidden deep inside the brain tissue. These are not the typical anatomical characteristics of the micro-structure of the cerebral cortex which I described in the previous chapter and which for me clearly indicate contacts to "the outside".

Nevertheless, even in this case a different explanation could be plausible: by removing this area of grey cells the electrical circuit necessary for the acquired faculty is impaired. It is like connecting a hose-pipe to a water-tap in your garage in order to water the plants in your garden while a lawn sprinkler is also connected in-between. Imagine you have a visitor who has never seen such a device before. When he observes how water also comes out of the sprinkler he may be tempted to think that the sprinkler itself may have something to do with the water supply. Then you disconnect the sprinkler and forget to reconnect the loose ends of the hose-pipe again. If now no water for your plants comes out of your hose pipe then the statement of your visitor may be that this is only to be expected because the water is *produced in* the sprinkler which may at best cause you just to give an embarrassed smile. This example may sound a bit shallow but the principle of it is illuminating.

In the meantime it has become accepted knowledge that hardly any complex mechanism or sequence of movements is stored *in only one* place. Even the presumed highest brain centres are no exception to this rule. There is an area in the cerebral cortex known as the "motor cortex" which is generally accepted as being the highest centre for conscious movement. When, in experiments with cats, this area was cut off, the cats still went about their "normal business" as usual without any perceivable restrictions.

They were even able to give birth to kittens and to take proper care of them. Such behaviour might be explained by certain automatisms which continue to be controlled via the more menial centres of the brain. Other attempts to exert influence consciously, which may suddenly become essential, could still be achieved by means of higher centres which we should not consider as being the domicile of these consciously exerted influences but merely as mediators for them.

We should consider them rather as being a communication centre between the physical brain and a really existing brain-independent spirit.

In comparison to humans, cats are a species of relatively low self-awareness and the "spiritual exchange" takes place with the spiritual "cat field" which has evolved during evolution – a kind of typical species-specific intranet, as *Rupert Sheldrake* postulated it with his "morphogenetic fields".

This deep communication ensures the "proper", i.e. the species-approved patterns of behaviour such as giving birth to kittens or the provision of proper care for the kittens when the actual centre for specific patterns of behaviour fail.

The biologist *Stephen Rose* experimented with chickens.

On the day they hatched, a certain behavioural training started. At the same time they were injected with radioactive substances which could be detected in the brain and with which the effect of the training was to be examined. It was established that, in comparison to a control group of untrained chickens, in the trained chickens the nerve cells of a certain region in the frontal lobe of the brain, especially in the left hemisphere took up higher concentrations of the radioactive substances.

These experiments show that the growth and the development of nerve cells in the frontal lobe are activated by learning. Similar studies with other creatures, e.g. monkeys, confirm this observation. Now we might hastily conclude that a learning process is stored in a typical manner *in* a certain region – however this may be possible.

But slow down: after the specific region of the brain in which the radioactive substances had been stored was removed, the chicken had *not* forgotten its training. We can only say for sure that these regions of the brain must have had something to do with the learning – but we cannot say that they themselves are the memory bank for these lessons. If in fact only these centres are active because they had absorbed the injected radioactive substances, then we can at least exclude with some certainty that other centres are also involved in the learning process. If now the active regions were surgically removed and the learned lessons remain intact, then, I think, this leaves only one plausible answer: the trained abilities must have been manifested outside of the brain and if they are needed they can be recalled via structures of the brain suited to the task. In contrast to the conditioned, relatively simple, and – in any case – autonomous blink-*reflex* of the rabbit which in fact was probably stored *in* one of the "grey cores" in the "depths" of the brain, it was not a reflex here which was the object of learning but a much more complex, even if comparably simple, pattern of *behaviour*.

Therefore, it was processed through the cerebral cortex in the *frontal* lobe of the brain, in a region which many assume to be the typical "communication organ" for contacts "to the outside".

A number of esoteric, mystical and East Asian religious teachings claim the frontal lobe to be the communicator for a spiritual outer world – an assumption based on pure intuition.

Some very important experiments, the results of which *seem* to support the materialistic perceptions of many a brain researcher, were carried out on humans by the American neurophysiologist *Benjamin Libet* of the *University of California* in *San Francisco* (USA). *Libet (*1916)* became almost an icon for "materialistic brain research".

His experiments were aimed at clarifying the connections that exist between the brain activity of a test person and his conscious decision. In short, it was to be established whether humans have a free will or whether this is just an illusion. For the experiment Libet measured electric currents in the brains of his test persons who were asked to execute certain rather simple, intellectually undemanding actions.

By using special time measuring methods he found that approximately one third of a second before a certain action was carried out, an electric current could be detected in the frontal lobe, the so-called readiness potential. This was only to be expected, since the brain activity must start *before* the order of the test person goes to the relevant muscles to bend his finger, for example. It seemed surprising, however, that the test person himself only became aware of his decision to bend the finger a third of a second after this readiness potential had been registered.

In the meantime, these experiments have been repeated frequently, and they always showed similar results. Benjamin Libet and many of his followers believed that even personal decisions must already have been finally concluded *in* the brain before the *Ego* itself (wherever that may be located *in* the brain) thinks it has just made the decision.

Hence, for Libet the human free-will becomes a pure figment of the imagination. He comes to the conclusion that the intention to act is merely the result of pure brain action and that the necessary mechanism for setting this action in motion is not at all part of our conscious perception. It is the brain itself which autonomously initiates the action of which we *later* become consciously aware.

However, I believe that Benjamin Libet was very much mistaken in this as were his followers who were just as keen to experiment and were too uncritical by far!

First of all, each test person knows, of course, beforehand *what* he is expected to do during the ensuing experiment, e.g. to bend a finger at a moment of his own choosing.

The responsible areas of the brain are, therefore, already prepared, since the bending of a finger is hardly a great intellectual or emotional achievement. And we know already that one of the specific characteristics of the entire nervous system, including the brain, is to prepare and delegate future actions in fine nuances, as and when required.

We experience something similar when driving a car, for example. When we start to learn to drive a car we have to give our full attention to the task, whereas experienced drivers hardly register all the details and the "ins and outs" of driving a car. Some people drive for many kilometres without really being aware of what is happening around them. They drive subconsciously. However, at any time consciousness is prepared to take control again should some sudden unexpected changes occur. If we ask the driver what he noticed along the way or how many cars have passed by he will hardly be able to tell us.

Even if the bending of a finger in Libet's experiments is supposed to be a conscious action, it is still a simple *pattern* of movement which each test person has made automatically for many years and decades. For the brain this is not a challenge. We can definitely assume, therefore, that the required basic pattern of movement is already *stored* on some brain level or other. We can also assume that in such or similar experimental situations the previously planned action is set in motion from a "trained" level even if it is meant to be a conscious action. We may compare this to a sprinter who makes a false start because he expects the starter's gun to fire. The start is already stored on the appropriate brain level. The pattern of movement necessary for a start is stored once and for all and is only waiting for the action to begin – just as the bending of the finger in the experiment of the brain researchers. Or, for example, during a presentation in front of an audience when we must concentrate and think in advance not to loose our thread, it could happen that an (immaterial) thought turns up before its time or that an idea is rejected immediately after it turned up. In these cases we experience a "slip of the tongue". The so-called Freudian slip can thus be explained.

The philosopher and sociologist *Jürgen Habermas (*1929)* said something similar in his acceptance speech when he was awarded with the Kyoto Prize in 2004, which next to the Nobel Prize is one of the highest awards for science and culture. Habermas described the research question as being some kind of spiritual-intellectual artefact, because *"no freedom of action is manifested in the naked decision to stretch out the right or the left arm since there is no connection with a reason which for example would motivate a cyclist to turn off to the right or the left. Only with such a consideration the space of freedom is opened up, because the sense of considering lies in the fact, as Ernst Tugendhat*[113] *points out, that we can act in this way or in a different one."*

Habermas adopted the argumentation which *Immanuel Kant (1724-1804)* already used trying to defend the idea of the autonomous human spirit against

---

[113] Contemporary German philosopher

scientific attacks over 200 years ago when he said that an action is controlled by reason even if biological laws determine the course of functions.

At the beginning of 2005 the German brain researcher and neurosurgeon *Detlef Linke (1945-2005)* died. I knew him when I was a student during the 1970s. In his book which was published posthumously, *"Die Freiheit und das Gerhirn"* (Freedom and the Brain), he vehemently contradicts the interpretations of his colleagues as being excessively influenced by contemporary notions. To examine fourteen billion neurones and one quadrillion synapses for possible indications of self-determination would be as if we wanted to determine the inner values of a person by means of an intestinal probe. For *left* wing people freedom is subject to reason. Nature, however, knows no reason, only causes.

The difference lies in the question and how it is posed. Scientists usually ask *what?* (causes) but not *why?* (reasons). Therefore, they usually only receive limited answers.

Libet discovered that his test persons were able to stop the action within a split second after they had become aware of the impulse. He found *his* theory supportedthereby. I, however, see *my* perceptions supported since this seems to prove that consciousness is indeed a kind of *"guardian"*, as *Klivington* believed, but not over the *"intentions generated by the brain"*, as he also wrote. It rather guards the movements which are previously planned by the brain-*in*dependent consciousness, and which are then initiated by the brain according to plan and independently, since they are already well-known and well-trained and intellectually not demanding. The brain is a marvelous butler for the spirit.

There is, however, a completely different possible explanation:

The readiness potential in the frontal lobe, which is always there and which precedes all conscious actions, must also be present when a brain-independent spirit influences the brain by means of vast numbers of small "parabolic antennae" known as the vesicle mesh on the brain's surface (see Chapter 4.11).

The frontal lobe seems to be some kind of portal, in the same way as a modem facilitates the communication between a computer and the internet. This perception, however, is not even considered by those brain researchers all too often quoted in the media today since the idea alone that something immaterial spiritual could exist contradicts their own basic principles. What does "to become aware of something" mean in this *alternative perspective?*

For an outsider such as the experimenter, the test person must express himself in some way – by an action perhaps, a remark, a blink or maybe a smile. All these expressions themselves need an interaction between a possibly brain-independent spirit and its brain and, therefore, as an expression of the consciousness "attracting attention"; in this physical world they are measurable only with delay. This interaction probably happens through the same portal at the same time. As *John Eccles* already discovered, practically all interactions seem to induce this readiness potential in the *frontal lobe*.

It was already established a long time ago that this part of the brain especially plays an important role in the development of human *personality*. During the 1950s the frontal lobes of many people were intentionally destroyed as a treatment for *schizophrenia*, a split personality. Such people underwent dramatic personality changes due especially to a separation of their feeling and thinking. This was certainly *not* due to the fact that relevant autonomously working centres were positioned there, but rather because the connections with their (brain-independent) spirit had sustained lasting damage.

Let us go back to *Libet's* experiments. It was impossible for Libet to establish the exact moment at which the test person believed that he decided to bend his finger; to do so it would have been necessary to communicate in some way and each form of communication being an independent action in itself would be encumbered again by a corresponding temporal delay.

The fact that every kind of conscious action is preceded for a split second by a readiness potential *supports* the assumption that there must be an interaction between the brain and a brain-independent spirit belonging exclusively to this specific person. Only if we reject this possibility *right from the start* do we inevitably arrive at the materialistic interpretation of a non-existent free will and oppose personal experiences in daily life. According to *Detlef Linke* the view of the world, developed by his much quoted colleagues, must put up with the accusation of being trivial and naïve. Becoming aware of an action is in itself an interactive process, by the way, since during our (physical) lifetime our immaterial spirit usually exists only in connection with our brain.

The brain is another one of the many interfaces between the spiritual and the physical world as I have already explained here and in several of my previous books.

As such it connects the just as real spiritual world with the physical world which we know. And the readiness potentials preceding the "physical" actions induced by it are the electrical substrata of its interactions.

I think it is irresponsible to support the unfortunately widespread opinion that the human free will does not in fact exist, not even to the rather limited degree determined by its physical surroundings, since, in my opinion, this perception is based on unsound premises. Such perceptions lead to profound misapprehensions; just think, for example, of the possibly fateful consequences this could have in the field of crime and punishment.

Electrical brain potentials are neither *causally* responsible for the "intention" nor for the memory. They could be an indication of brain-dependent stored automatic actions as well as for conscious interactions between spirit and brain.

In 1951 the renowned brain researcher *Wilder Penfield (1891-1976)* suggested naming certain regions in the temporal lobe of the brain the "memory cortex". During the 1980s he said: *"...I explained that the memory storage must be located there in the cortex close to these points where the stimulating electrode can induce an experience reaction. That was an error...! The storage is not to be found in the cortex!"*[114].

Up to now, all attempts to locate *complex* traces of memory *in* the human brain and to isolate it as a physical substratum have failed. There is a very simple reason, in my opinion, as to why nothing has yet been found in spite of the intense efforts: there is simply nothing to be found!

It is also wrong to assume that deep emotions such as love or mourning are located *within* the brain. What the pineal gland was for Descartes is the limbic system for modern brain researchers. Even if we believe it has been possible to transplant emotions in experiments with animals this is only true to a limited extent. Up until today it has only be possible to transfer basic reflex-like emotions such as rage or fear to other creatures. I do not agree with Klivington when he claims that *"if due to a stroke or another kind of brain damage the ability is lost"* to perceive such feelings then we would have *"the proof that they are also caused by the activities of brain cells and not by the unfathomable property of a non-biological spirit"*. But no surgical operation can position emotions such as love or mourning which are triggered elsewhere.

The limbic system is only involved in the *transmission and mediation* of deep emotions or memory activities in the same way as all parts of the brain are involved in other complex actions. They are certainly neither positioned nor produced there. Impairments in these highly complex structures will scramble the communication just as damaged aerials and atmospheric disturbances disturb the reception of radio programmes. The programme is not located *in* the radio set.

Since humans are unable to express themselves directly by means of the brain but only through the physical periphery of their bodies it is essential that the various appropriate physical interfaces for "igniting" emotional reactions or very deep emotional conditions are kept intact. The loss of this specific interface, which has become specialized in the course of the individual development, must logically entail at least a partial loss of the personal abilities to express oneself. But then we cannot tell whether the emotions themselves are lost when the hardware is damaged. In my opinion, nothing significant has

---

[114] Cortex = Greek: bark, Penfield quoted by R. Sheldrake.

been lost at all because all complex emotional qualities are only to a very small part, perhaps with very narrowly defined and indeed very personal-specific reaction patterns, actually "idiosyncrasies", manifested *within* the brain. The major part is of immaterial-spiritual nature, and that which becomes apparent in the end, is the result of an interactive communication.

Another examination method by which brain functions are supposed to be explained in a better way is that described by personality changes in patients if, due to an accident or a disease, certain parts of the brain have been destroyed, damaged or surgically manipulated.

I have already described damages to the frontal lobes. Another typical example is that of patients whose corpus callosum has been severed, that great band of commisural fibres, due to the affliction of severe and chronic *epilepsy* which could not be treated by drugs (*Split-brain-Syndrome*, see illustration by Martin). The great band of commisural fibres (Corpus callosum) is a broadband cable which connects the two hemispheres of the brain and their circuits. Superficially, even weeks after the operation, no significant changes in the personality of the patients are noticeable, which is certainly also an indication of the 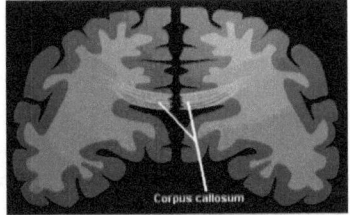 compensatory attempt of the *spirit* to maintain the unity of brain functions.

A more thorough neuropsychological examination, however, suggests, far too hastily in my opinion, that *two* completely separate "consciousnesses" have now materialized.

This results in actions incompatible with one another: for example, one hand pulls the trousers up, while the other tries to pull them down.

Such studies are also used to identify the differences in the specialization of the two hemispheres of the brain, both of which complement each other, but whose dominances differ.

Right-handed people, for example, usually have a causal-logically analyzing left brain hemisphere and a more analogue-creatively working right hemisphere. The right half seems to be superior in recognizing faces and is "responsible" for emotionally negative perceptions and emotions.

The left half is responsible for the more positive emotions. But this is not the place to go into further detail. On the one hand there are indeed distinct differences in the functions of each brain hemisphere.

On the other hand, the full significance of such differences only becomes apparent if the connection between them is *suddenly* severed. If the processes progress very slowly, taking even years, a complete compensation is indeed possible. As an example I would like to tell you of one of my greatly-appreciated employees of long-standing in my surgery. When she was over twenty years old a computer-tomography of her skull was taken because she suffered from recurring headaches. To everyone's amazement it was discovered that almost the entire left half of her brain was squashed. Due probably to a congenital disease, the internal hollows – the ventricles – started to grow, slowly at first but in the end they were dramatically enlarged. The pressure within her skull increased so much that she started suffering from headaches. Nevertheless, she never experienced any loss of functions nor was her intelligence or intellect or her speech or other mental capabilities impaired in any way. Even more severe was the damage coincidentally found in a 55-year old truck driver who was taken to hospital in Oxford, England, after a car accident. An examination of his head in the CT revealed that both frontal lobes and a large part of the temporal lobes and parietal lobes, in short large parts of his cerebrum were missing. He had probably suffered a severe stroke already in the uterus. This man showed no significant peculiarities; also his intelligence, which brain researchers like to locate *in* the frontal lobe, was completely average.[115] Only because in the first case it was such a slow-progressing process and in the second the damage happened at such an early developmental stage was there sufficient time to compensate for it (plasticity of the brain); everything seemed to be in perfect order. If, however, the decrease in available space or the stroke had occurred to such a grave extent suddenly as it could happen with a brain haemorrhage with subsequent violent bleeding, severest enduring damage or, even more likely, instant death would have been the result.

One obvious conclusion which may be drawn from the observations of the "split-brain-syndrome" is that with progressing age many sections of the brain become more and more specialized. This specialization probably has genetic reasons – it is inherited.

The specialization of brain sections does not mean, however, that all information is actually stored *within* them. They should rather be considered as a "device within a device" which in fact facilitate the storage of fundamental recurring and simple automatisms and probably also of circuits controlled by ordinal numbers. Furthermore, with their aid, "external" interaction becomes possible thereby opening up more possibilities for communication and information processing.

I should add here again that all these experimental results are only *describing* facts; they are purely descriptive. They will never explain *how* or *why* the observed patterns of behaviour or personality changes indeed take place. These things for me are of the very essence.

---

[115] From the magazine GEO 05-2004

Unfortunately, most of the accepted interpretations of such observations are of materialistic nature, according to which the brain itself, its two hemispheres or the various sections, *produce* all thoughts, intentions and in general all mental content.
This makes them identical to the spirit (identification theory).
For example, if after a stroke the bleeding in one of the speech centres in the left hemisphere causes certain impediments such as the inability to find the right words or loss of speech it does not at all mean that speech was primarily *generated* there. Nor does it mean that speech, words, sentences, grammar or other contents are stored there. Nor can it mean, of course, that any kind of storage would be impossible there.
I believe that in general only well-known activities, trained and automatic actions are really stored locally in the brain itself – even if we still do not know *how* this takes place.
Everything new and more demanding, on the other hand, needs a purposeful interaction with the brain-independent spirit. I see no proof at all that the will to formulate words and to generate speech is located *in* these centres.
All we can say at the moment is that these sections of the cerebral cortex are involved in these mental performances.
Something similar happens when you have a telephone conversation with a friend. Nobody would assume today that your friend is actually sitting in the telephone receiver. If you came across a tribe of people which was completely untouched by civilization somewhere in the jungle, however, and they saw you telephoning your friend on your mobile phone, I am convinced that such natives would assume exactly that, since they would not know what a telephone was.
The telephone is only an instrument and if it is broken you will be unable to call your friend with it. This does not change his continued existence, however, and the fact that he might be thinking of you. The same applies to all higher "grey" brain areas and the failures attributed to them in the case of disease.
To a certain extent our brain could be viewed in the following way: if one hand of a "split-brain-patient" wants to do the exact opposite of the other then this is still *no* argument against a *uniform* consciousness. In the end they are only "devices within a device" supplying contradictory pieces of information. Due to the specialization they once acquired, and the fact that the processing of certain activities was once delegated to them this must result

in quite different reactions whilst the spiritual command that activates them (from outside) remains unchanged.[116]

Another little analogy: English and German typewriters differ in the layout of the keys. Furthermore the English language does not use "umlauts" or the letter "ß". The German keyboard is called the *"QWERTZ"* and the English is called the *"QWERTY"* keyboard. A secretary using a touch-type system must adjust when changing from one system to the other. At the beginning she will make many mistakes when writing letters.

I can write almost as fast with my right hand as with my left. With my left hand, however, I automatically write in mirror-writing. For me this is nothing extraordinary although a young lady won a lot of money with this ability in a very popular TV show some time ago.[117] This is an automatism and is caused by the specialization of the two halves of the brain but has nothing to do with the spirit which induces the action. I reckon that many people are able to do this without knowing it since they have never tried it yet. This ability is probably genetically determined if we have inherited the genes for left *and* right handedness. To change this automatism special concentration is required, i.e. a conscious deliberate action.

However, since my corpus callosum is thankfully still intact, I think I can claim to have only *one* consciousness and that it is *my* consciousness.

Critics will say that I only believe this and that in reality I just leave both "consciousnesses" to roam around freely. They will add that these "consciousnesses" are of course merely two functional parts of my brain or consequences of its neuronal activities.

I am of a completely different opinion. In the course of the individual human development certain areas of the brain underwent an extensive and rational specialization of certain brain areas by their interaction with an originally undifferentiated almost fallow spirit which must still be structured and differentiated.

We could now perhaps compare the personal spirit to a kind of spiritual *intra*net of a global all-enveloping, all-penetrating spiritual *inter*net, the "world spirit".

The further developed the device "brain" becomes the more complex and specialized are its "devices within the device" which are able to communicate constantly with the "world spirit" in an interactive sense. Only then, over the course of an individual human life by means of the sum total of all

---

[116] In a similar way the influence of genetic or other chemical (medical) factors need to be considered. Due to new different basic conditions identical mental commands may be channelled in different ways.

[117] In the TV programme "Wetten dass" with Thomas Gottschalk, ZDF, beginning of 2005

experiences gathered and events experienced, will we mature or, as I call it, will we differentiate our very own, personal, self-aware and eternal part of this "world spirit" which is permanently accessible only by ourselves.

4.13) Evolution from a Different Viewpoint

All forms of life have surely developed in the course of evolution's immensely long history. There is no scientific sustainable corroboration of the creationistic theory.
Genetic innovations due to random mutations of germ cells have been just as important as the constant selection of the most suitable. Insofar *Charles Darwin (1809-1882)* and many of his followers are right. On the other hand, for me this seems to be only one part – and maybe even the smaller part – of the whole truth.
Yet the much greater part of evolution is probably made up of "experiences". By this I mean that the continual adjustment and specialization of species due to their "experience of life". They start with common patterns for all and everything which usually lead to more perfection on the chosen course later.
It also seems that no matter what kind of improvements have been achieved over single generations – e.g. appearance, structure and function as well as species-specific cooperation or even cooperation between different species – practically none has ever been discarded.
Everything is collected and used again for the further improvement of the entire species, possibly after some modifications here or there. The basis of evolution is significantly extended and becomes much more extensive. This cannot be explained satisfactorily by genetics alone. Meanwhile it has been discovered that there are only about 30,000 effective human genes which are responsible for all human characteristics. Even this number fades into insignificance if we consider the fact that there are comparatively primitive forms of life on Earth which possess far more genomes than humans. There are species of lilies, for example, whose cells possess thirty times more DNA than human cells. A phenomenon becomes apparent here which has also been observed in the brain. Anatomical and biochemical structures may be proportional to the size and number of their biological specializations – however, they are *not* proportional to their non-biological, i.e. their spiritual, specializations. For example, the olfactory brain of animals with an excellently developed olfactory sense is relatively large compared to the total size of the brain. The brain of a feeble-minded but otherwise healthy person is not significantly different from that of Albert Einstein.

The idea that life-experience and changes to the external physical appearance of living beings, caused by their adjustment to the environment, have the effect of modifying their germ cells, thereby altering the genotype, was ruled out for a long time. Recent findings of "epigenetic mechanisms" might lead to an albeit limited revival of such ideas (see Chapter 4.9). However, the (biochemical) genotype is probably the most important playground for coincidence; even if it is kept at bay by some very effective safety precautions (see Chapter 4.2).

I will try to unravel this problem as *Alexander the Great (356-323 B.C.)* attempted to do with the *"Gordian knot"*. I am convinced that there are completely different evolutionary mechanisms at work *in addition* to those usually accepted by scientists today. I even believe that there is a cascade-like evolution of evolutionary mechanisms. The key is probably the phenomenon of biological "communication".

Presumably, all living beings receive outside information by means of light – and for those not possessing their own nervous system there is probably no other way. Photons provide exactly what single species additionally need in order to adjust to the world and to develop further in an appropriate way. The chlorophyll of plants may serve as an example here. Chlorophyll is a three-dimensional giant molecule and is thus a molecular hollow body. *Four* organic substances are arranged in *pentagons* around a central magnesium atom, i.e. a metal, which practically acts as an "antenna" for receiving the sunlight necessary for photo synthesis.

Any hollow body is a kind of resonance body. It is suitable for amplifying and storing information. Examples of this are all musical instruments. A small organ-pipe with only a small resonance body emits a high tone with a high frequency. A bigger pipe emits a lower tone with a lower frequency. Photons of light, being the important "physical substrata", are in fact digital information. Each photon is the information "1".

Photons are simultaneously the really existing basic building components of our whole world. Both properties show the two sides of their coin and announce their origin, since as massless units of information they are part of an all-enveloping and penetrating spiritual world. In the course of the evolution of life further structures have obviously been developed very early on which facilitated new, additional and, moreover, even further differentiated forms of information-transfer.

A nervous system was soon developed which was not only able to transfer information within the organism itself but which could also contact the "external spiritual world"[118], which in turn differentiated itself in an increasingly species-specific harmonious way. The precondition for this communication is a sufficiently highly developed hardware. Any kind of nervous system consists basically of identical components in the same way as simple radio sets, multiband receivers, television sets or computers are all made of a handful of similar components. Nevertheless, there are tremendous qualitative and quantitative differences of performances between these devices. Depending on the equipment the environment can be contacted in various ways. Radios can receive passively, but are unable to transmit. Well-equipped computers already enable the user to interact directly with other at least equally well-equipped computers or with the virtual and yet real data network, the so-called *internet*.

The general anatomical construction of all species has indeed continually changed in many ways throughout the history of evolution. But it has always stuck more or less to certain basic principles and this fact alone would suggest that a basic construction plan exists. There are a number of clear indications that such a notion should be taken seriously. One of these is certainly the large number of anatomical and functional developments which are orientated to the first four ordinal numbers and their interconnections by addition, multiplication and exponentiation. Not least phenomena such as convergence, mimicry, symbiosis or parasitism which still remain a mystery for evolutionary biologists, belong here as well (see Chapters 4.1-4.7).

In contrast to all the "physical only" developments, however, the nervous system has been generated in the course of time as a completely different structure developing from low to high complexity in a straight line. It took no significant detours and there were no dead ends. The nervous system has become a central constant of evolution. Of especially great importance are the microscopic structure of the hierarchically youngest and the simultaneously highest level of this system, the upper crust of grey brain cells or, generally speaking, the cerebral cortex. As already explained in the previous two chapters, it can only be plausibly compared to a large number of smallest antennae or parabolic reflectors.

Technically such installations transmit and receive data. Meanwhile, biologists have experienced something similar. It was recently discovered that green sulphur algae, which also practise photosynthesis, exist 2 kilometres deep in the Golf of Mexico. However, at such depths it is pitch black. As the American biologist *Robert Blankenship* of the *Arizona-State-University* established, they collect the light of an extremely weak geothermal radiation by means of

---

[118] This "external spiritual world" is probably equivalent to the "internal world" sometimes mentioned in certain cultures, in myths, in psychology or esoteric doctrines.

microscopically small "satellite dishes" and use it for the production of sugar (carbon hydroxides). A form of biologically useful information is collected by means of "parabolic reflectors". This is a proven fact. Why should the brain not do the same?

John Eccles (1903-1997), the famous Australian brain researcher who was awarded the Nobel Prize for his discovery of the brain synapses, vehemently promoted this idea all his life in the face of harsh criticism. He was by no means the only one, although the majority of today's opinion-shaping brain researchers do not really accept this idea.

I believe *Eccles* was right in principle. As an interface between its immaterial spirit and our physical environment the cerebral cortex takes on a new and immensely important role. It becomes the higher developed engine of evolution.

It becomes a central receiver for basic information from the spiritual world which was especially needed for a long period of time for the development of the *species*. Later, when the brain itself reached a level of sufficiently high perfection it began to receive, mostly subconsciously, information useful for the *individual* development within the same species.

Therefore, the book about the evolution of all life needs to be completely rewritten and is by all accounts by no means complete yet. Although *Darwin's* theories remain an essential basis, they represent the contents of the first chapters. I believe, however, that the Neo-Darwinists are on the wrong track. By establishing dogmas, which are based on Darwin but which interpret his theories too narrowly, i.e. materialistically, they become responsible for the book of evolution being considered as closed.

Evolution is a never ending story which continually needs explanations and amendments and the time is gradually becoming ripe for the next chapter.

In this chapter the most important role is certainly played by the nervous system. It probably is, due to its purposeful development, not the consequence of but rather the prime reason for the evolution of all higher forms of life. It is the spirit which, being increasingly differentiated and structured, influences the nervous system directly and purposefully by means of the brain, thereby guiding evolution in the right direction without the loss of its creative emergence.

This new perception enables us to explain the *"missing links"*, i.e. the missing transitions, between various species on different levels of evolution, e.g. between humans and their animal ancestors. They are not missing because they never existed, they are missing only in the sense that it is impossible today to find their traces. If the brain as the interface between spirit and matter possesses another, as yet unknown, key function in evolution, then it must have been this organ through which the key information of the development of new species and of higher levels was transmitted. The physical manifestation of this "message" occurred later.

If palaeontologists today are unable to find such transitional forms either in the genotype or in fossils, it is for the simple reason that the genotype does not play such an outstandingly important role as has been attributed to it and that fossils only reflect the manifestation of information long after the information has been already transmitted.

We will never find any missing links since the relevant structures of the nervous system were only adjusted *after* the spiritual information essential for further development had been transmitted. The structures of the nervous system, however, consist of soft tissues which perished long ago.

And since the data on which the evolutionary steps were based were of purely physical nature, no evidence remained for later generations. It follows that there must always have been missing links.

However, they were primarily *neuro*-anatomical intermediate steps and not other physical characteristics such as the slowly elongating neck of a giraffe.

4.14) Human Individuality is Unique

There are good reasons for assuming that at the end of a very long and magnificent story which we call the history of the evolution of life, humanity was the only species – leaving aside for now the development of the nervous system as the central constant of evolution – which evolved without any physical specialization.

Strangely enough, of all physical developments the nervous system was the only one which took an unwaveringly straight course.

All the other purely physical characteristics and attributes took countless, sometimes extremely long detours, and were often even marked by distinct zigzag lines.

We can say, therefore, that the entire evolution of life on our earth has in effect been an extraordinarily qualitative and quantitative growth of nerve structures with ever higher forms of organization and complexity. It developed, by means of simple and always identical basic components, from the simplest of nerve fibres by way of an already rather complex spinal cord into an extremely multilayered and complex brain with truly excellent interconnections. After this level had been reached, however, evolution seems to have come to a standstill. The number of newly developed species all of which differ in their physical appearance, suddenly decreases. But it was just evolution switching horses again. In fact, evolution is still accelerating and will continue to do so for a long time yet on a purely (neuro-) anatomical basis at first:

The filigree structures especially, deep in the "depths" of brain tissue, are improving themselves enormously, whereby the size and the weight of the human brain is increasing in relation to the volume of the body. The already enormously increased number of nerve cells is now supplemented rapidly by an even higher number of new interconnections.

If we consider evolution from this point of view – i.e. allowing for detours and flourishes in the development of bodies, but maintaining a continuous straightforward development of the nervous system with ever more complex higher centres each based on those lower down and hierarchically compatible with them – then we must learn to accept that evolution does indeed have "a clear aim":

First there is surely the aim to develop an ever higher brain structure which is obviously combined with a qualitative and quantitative higher performance. Later more and more differentiated forms of consciousness and self-awareness develop so that they too seem to become the objective thereby replacing the former aim of evolution, that of physical development.

Most biologists today reject such a perception. They claim that all this is merely the consequence of undue purely retrospective observations, just retrospection.

But I see this in a different light. The above-mentioned differences between the "physical" and the "neuronal-spiritual" evolution are a sure indication that I am correct with my theory that the entire evolution of life is principally based on a kind of "spiritual construction plan". This plan defines the framework and the general aims but leaves the creative emergence free to roam. The last link in this development is as yet us humans.

It is interesting to note that the pressure of evolution seems to have eased off after humans appeared on the scene. Fewer and fewer new species have been created since then – as indeed was true even before humanity had spread in such a dramatic way as today. This is, therefore, not entirely due to our merciless treatment of the environment. Even if the results of latest research indicate that the mammoth fell victim to early human hunters, it is not human "action" which is responsible for the greatly reduced evolutionary pressure but rather the very "being" of humans alone.

From a purely physical point of view humans seem to be a rather final "product" of evolution which took a completely new direction from then on - it turned towards the further development and perfection of neuronal (brain) structures – specifically those which are spiritually active and establish something completely new, something which does not exist in the animal world – boundless individuality.

Expressed in our modern computer language, the human brain seems to be the first sufficiently qualified "neuronal basic hardware" which enables it to participate actively, consciously and with self-confidence in an all-penetrating and all-enveloping spiritual world.

Of course, this does not mean that further improvements of the hardware are no longer possible or necessary. More and more details are merely altered and improved – and to a lesser extent the basic and rough anatomic attributes.

There is an immense "immaterial-spiritual" difference between humans and any kind of animal, even anthropoids, which are the closest relatives to humans:

When an animal eventually reaches adulthood, it is finished – but this does not apply to humans. Nothing really sensible can be added to an adult animal, as *Paul Lüth* says, because there is nothing missing. *Lüth* describes it in the following way: *"An animal is without fate, like a sleeping baby."*

The (human) baby, however, will develop further and will soon leave the state of a *"vegetative semi-consciousness"*, and will consciously experience a personal, completely individual fate.

In contrast to any animal living on our earth, every human being possesses his own, unmistakable and individual biography. We can also attribute a biography to an animal – but this will always only be a subjective biography devised by humans *for* the animal, in most cases a pet. However, it will never really be an objective, unmistakable and unique biography. It is not a biography of the animal itself, bearing real significance for the animal, its community or indeed its entire species. Animals can never (re-)experience their own lives to the "full extent" consciously and self-aware, neither can they look back and remember the details nor are they able to control their own lives to any large extent or add any details. Even older anthropoids do not possess an individual biography which could be relevant for themselves or for whomsoever, whether living in a zoo or out in the wild. All their lives are, roughly, entirely interchangeable. For animals the individual and the individuality are of secondary importance and count less the lower we descend down the various levels of evolution. What really counts is the whole species. Animals are born, they live without being even remotely able to experience life as does a human – they eat and drink, they procreate and probably have fun doing it, at least on the higher levels.

At some time or other they die. Their life experiences are practically identical and they are indeed important – but of value only for the species as a whole.

In my opinion, here they are of great spiritual value (see Chapter 4.6). During their lives, however, there are no distinctive individual features.

Animals are characterized without exception by their *"being"*, humans by their *"becoming"* until they die. A poorly-developed animal individuality cannot at all be compared to that of any human being – not even to that of "primitive people" or to the ancestors of modern man (Homo sapiens sapiens) who are surely incorrectly described as being "primitive".

An animal is only unique if we attribute this feature to it – in most cases we do so with animals living as pets in our home in close contact with us. This is easy to comprehend if we consider the countless examples of the same species living anonymously in animal asylums.

Of course, many animals are also rather helpless for a shorter or longer period of time after birth and could hardly survive for long if they were left alone. Humans, however, are absolutely *un*finished when they are born and remain the most helpless species for quite a long time. A human would be helpless for many years and inevitably doomed to death if he were left without the constant shelter and protection provided by his social community or his family. It takes about two decades before a human being can be considered as being grown up, at least on paper and in a physical sense. But, as this slightly critical expression intends to imply, it takes even more years, sometimes many years or even decades before a human being becomes really grown up mentally.

Sometimes people never really become adults at least not during their physical lifetimes. *"Maturity comes with age"* is a well known adage which is certainly true but not very well liked by young people, neither in the past nor today.

The much cited "maturity" of a human is the result – never clearly defined but always expected – of a continuous development process which reaches its zenith not before old age when slowly (physical) death seems to approach. Only humans learn in such abundance throughout their lives starting at the moment of birth. Their syllabus is not even remotely comparable to that of any kind of animal. The subjects are more varied and complex than any animal will ever know.

They span a potentially infinite diversity of theoretical knowledge and personal experiences as well as an enormous range of practical capabilities which are needed to survive in this often merciless world. These qualities alone – which are completely new in this form, infinitely versatile, deeply emotional and completely unexplainable in an ethical-moral and scientific-materialistic way – have no pendant whatsoever in the animal world.

Such mental and emotional differences as those found between humans on the one hand and the entire animal world on the other do not exist within the

animal world, not even between mammals – be they dolphins, whales, anthropoids, pigs, dogs or cats. However, I must admit that I strongly believe that highly developed mammals, and even many birds, do indeed possess some mental and emotional competence albeit in a far more rudimentary way, but compared with any human capability it remains rather elementary.
Nevertheless, it includes the ability to express loving care and sadness not only as instinctive behaviour but also to a certain degree of consciousness and even self-awareness. Some birds (e.g. magpies) as well as monkeys and dolphins recognise themselves in a mirror, something cats and dogs cannot do.
If we take a look at the development of mankind and that of all other living beings on earth from a more "spiritual" point of view, then we will notice the following.
From this point of view all animals are quite comparable with each other. The individuals are all interchangeable; there is no such thing as real animal individuality. What really counts for animals is the "entire species". Each species of animal is basically a true collective. All animal life is concentrated on "being".
There is no real "becoming". The human species, however, consists solely of single unmistakable individuals in "being" and "becoming" and "becoming" grows increasingly important in the course of life.
It is only through immensely painful, social-political aberrations that humans have been and still are inadmissibly forced into collectives whereby their individualities are shamelessly and unnaturally suppressed. Many social conventions in cultural societies are difficult to comprehend when the individual has a different view on life and seeks to live in a different way. It is unacceptable when these conventions exert a negative influence on the lives of individuals thereby causing personal and emotional damage. It is unacceptable when the individual is expected to fight against his own personality just to be respected by his society and to be judged as someone leading a life worth living whilst all the time being subjected to a social or political dogma intent on keeping the chains in place. Of course, the basic premise must be upheld, namely that the unconventional life style of one individual cannot be allowed to substantially infringe upon the lives of others. *"Live and let live"* is the famous and appropriate adage. *"Every fool is different"*, and *"Each to his own"* is the folk wisdom whence I came in the Rhineland and there is a lot of truth in these sayings.
In the world of animals we notice immense differences between the different species also. Within the same species, however, the members are extremely homogenous thus representing a true collective.

Humans, however, display immense and dramatic differences between single individuals. This notion has nothing to do with individualism as some would criticise too hastily.

It is primarily nothing more than the bare statement that evolution began to take a different path when humans appeared on the scene – evolution simply switched horses. Evolution very clearly chose the path toward individuality. Not the collective species but rather each single individual has now quite clearly become the new target of evolutionary development. The further development of the whole species "mankind" now progresses always and exclusively through every single individual "human being".

Evolution thereby grants each single human the unique chance of becoming an important partner and of helping to shape evolution significantly. Culture becomes the sum total of single evolutions.

For the first time evolution is no longer something that has to be endured passively.

It has become a partner to its own creatures, something that can and should be utilized actively and with self-awareness. Humans as individuals, and not just as part of some collective conglomeration, become the focus of their own, their personal further evolution which is no longer merely pure growth or a kind of physical specialization as it is in animals.

No, the life of every single human being is an evolutionary process in itself – an evolution towards something spiritual. The personal spiritual development of every single human being becomes simultaneously the necessary precondition for true altruism, i.e. unselfish help towards the successful evolution of his fellow men.

Every single human being must first become aware of this fact. Every human being must be granted the chance to develop in the one unique way which he has decided to be the right one for him. Inseparably connected with this is his own duty to grant everybody else the same chance and not to harm others by his way of life. This is an individual responsibility which cannot and should not be taken away from anybody. Today, a number of scientific, often sociopsychological, and even legal notions and movements, tend to point in exactly the opposite direction.

I believe that such ideas are wrong and very dangerous because they are based on incorrect premises.

Every single human being must learn to become the driving force for himself as well as for his fellow men. From this point of view, every single human being has an extraordinary opportunity for self-realization – in a way that no other living being has on this earth, because for them this term has no meaning.

But at the same time, every single human being bears great responsibility: the assumption of responsibility for his own well-being and also for that of his fellow men. And society has to keep a keen eye to ensure that no single person does harm to another by misusing his own chances. This applies to private citizens as well as to politicians, for example.

The physical and mental integrity of each one of us must be paramount in all of us. Unfortunately, even in our country, people are sometimes excessively punished for offences, the culpability of which is based increasingly on inadequate or even random laws and rules. They are made by ever more undisciplined authorities who are getting out of hand and are growing ever greedier and tend to exert excessive bureaucratic power. These authorities even search for new paths to preserve their destructive and dishonourably bloated self-importance. One example is the abundance and sheer diversity of tax laws in this country.

In relation to this, people who kill or attempt to do so or who inflict bodily harm on other people are very often not punished sufficiently.

In my opinion this process is all wrong and it betrays dangerous excesses of a misdirected frame of mind and an abortive social development.

An offence against property, although being absolutely reprehensible, can in no way be compared to an attack on someone's life and soul, a crime which should always and severe rigour incur the harshest punishment for all the direct or indirect culprits. However, the death penalty, which is still imposed in many countries, is completely unacceptable simply because death cannot be a punishment. I intend to discuss the most pressing social-political issues of our time in more detail in a later or even my next book.

The realisation of our own opportunities and those of others, and the acceptance of responsibility for our own lives and for those of others, is what I believe is really meant in the Bible by the terms "love of God", "love of oneself" and "love of one's fellow-men" – and exactly in that order, too.

The "love of God" involves becoming aware that a human being is by no means merely an accidental creature in this world created at random, but that every one of us is unique and will remain so for ever, and that we must recognise our own opportunities and the responsibilities we have for ourselves, for others and also for the world we live in.

Only when we realize this have we created the right basis for helping others in a rational way and for being of service to them by doing so – not least in helping to save our beautiful Earth from its impending but self-induced destruction.

Every single human being must at some time learn to understand that the evolution of life entered a new, completely different and simultaneously incomparably higher level when it created mankind. For evolution itself this was a qualitative as well as a quantitative quantum leap involving both opportunity *and* risk.

We humans must learn to understand that this new form of evolution has also become our own individual evolution. We must recognise that this is our spiritual, ethical-moral, cultural and social as well as our emotional evolution which is far more sensitive and differentiated than any physical development.

We humans must all recognise that this new and individual evolution approaches its climax with advancing age and that weakness in old age is only physical but by no means spiritual and emotional. In this context I would point out yet again that most mental illnesses are in fact illnesses of the brain and not necessarily of the spirit.

If we realize all this then it becomes completely absurd to expect that the physical death of a human being should be the end of his personality. A hitherto continuous spiritual and emotional process will and must, of course, survive physical death. I already dedicated several books to death as being nothing more than the end of an important stage in human life.

4.15) Numbers Help in the Evolution of Life and Spirit

A truly four-dimensional space contains two square number sequences which determine our world. From all ordinal numbers beginning with "1" and reaching into infinity (∞) the square sequence with $1^2, 2^2, 3^2, 4^2, ... \infty$, is automatically generated. This gives structure to everything in the world towards the outside. It is *infinite* and simultaneously *unlimited*.

From the reciprocal values of all ordinal numbers from 1 to infinity the sequence of their reciprocal square values is generated, i.e. $1/1^2, 1/2^2, 1/3^2, 1/4^2,....1/\infty$.

This too is *infinite* but simultaneously it is *limited* in its expansion since, although it becomes smaller and smaller, it will never actually reach the value zero. There is always "space" between zero and 1.

Finally, the number "1" must be especially emphasized, since it is the intersection between all these number sequences and it follows that:
$1/1^2 = 1/1 = 1 = 1^2$.

The infinite and unlimited number sequence of the squares of all numbers structures everything towards the outside and stands for the expansion of everything that is *countable*, i.e. all physical *matter*.

The infinite yet simultaneously limited sequence of the reciprocal square values of all ordinal numbers, on the other hand, describes the expansion and structuring of *effects* in our universe.

Any kind of electromagnetic radiation such as light, for example, becomes weaker in the infinite spaces of our universe along the infinite sequence of the squares of all reciprocal values. The same applies to the effect of the forces of attraction, gravitation.

This means that physical behaviour is determined solely by mathematics.

Certain particles which are assumed to bring this about and for which scientists are searching today, such as gravitons for gravitation, are rendered obsolete by this perception. And in fact, no one has actually found them yet.

Gravitational forces also affect light, i.e. the information which is transported as massless photons through space.

Gravitation attracts and strengthens light thereby reversing the effect of the reciprocal number sequences which has initially weakened it.

Therefore, to a far distant observer, space would appear as if it were curved, since scientists still think that the expansion of space equals that of light. Space itself, however, is purely informational-spiritual and is structured by numbers: it is infinite and completely flat (see Part 3).

In contrast to the massless effects, all countable masses – and thus all physical objects – expand along the squares of all ordinal numbers into the universe. Since all matter possesses a second side which is its spiritual component, i.e. the information of its existence, all matter also expands informational-infinitely. In other words: everything – once in existence – remains in existence eternally as a complex information with all details. This does not apply to the finite aspect of the underlying original matter, i.e. its corporeality.

The same principle applies to the space of the universe itself, of course. Since it is equal to the expansion of all square numbers it is something spiritual and also infinite. Countable masses in this space, on the other hand, are always finite.

As an example I would like to refer again to the number of electron pairs which orbit an atomic nucleus (see Part 3). On the first shell we find a maximum of 1^2 electron pairs, on the second a maximum of 2^2, on the third 3^2, etc. Due to special number-theoretical circumstances (see Part 3), the maximum number of shells should be seven, i.e. theoretically there should be a maximum of 7^2 possible pairs of electrons.

Indeed, there are only seven shells and most of the outer ones are not filled to capacity by electrons. Nobody has ever discovered an atom, not even an extremely short-lived one, whose outer shell was filled with the maximum possible number of electrons and not even an extremely short-lived atom has been found as yet whose outer shell is fully filled with atoms. In practice such atoms would be extremely "top-heavy" on the outside and will probably never be generated artificially – not even for a split second.

There are only a total of 81 naturally existing and stable elements in this universe. According to the logical constellation I suggested, based on the first four ordinal numbers, i.e. $1^2 \times 3^4$ (see Chapter 2.8), it is impossible that there could be more.

It follows that the genome of all life is also connected with the number 81. In 1999 I already suggested that the genetic code should better be considered to be a positional code, because it could diminish failures, whereby we would also arrive at a total of exactly 81 code positions (see Chapter 2.9).

From this point of view the extent of randomly provoked defects, i.e. damage caused by mutations, is significantly restricted. Evolution thus obtains a new image.

These, in my opinion, universally valid and fundamentally important, number-theoretical aspects are applicable to all areas of life and evolution. If we consider the development of such an incredible number of different species within this immensely long process which we call evolution, we will notice the following:

Over a period of many hundreds of millions of years the variety of species increases slowly at first, then picks up speed and finally explodes. Right at the very end of this development humans appear on the scene.

At this point in time, I believe, evolution switched horses.

The immense proliferation of species slowly draws to a standstill. However, this does not at all mean the end of variety. On the contrary, variety is increasing no less dramatically, but now in a completely different way. Instead of new varieties of species, i.e. of collectives, whose single individuals are practically interchangeable and whose total number is in the last instance limited, a new, potentially infinite and simultaneously unlimited variety now emerges.

It is the unlimited variety of single individuals within only *one single* species, that of humans.

Humans are the intersection "1" of evolution.

Now no longer are large numbers of species generated in an almost "infinite" yet inevitably limited total number of varieties all of which have similar characteristics and whose appearances are easily confused with each other or which differ only in insignificantly small details.

On the contrary, there is now *one single* species which dominates all others and which becomes the main focus of evolution from now on: the human species.

And this is the first species to possess the infinite aspect of the infinite *individual* variety since this is something purely spiritual, something emotional and cultural.
And anything spiritual is infinite and unlimited since it cannot be counted.
If we consider next the development of the spiritual variety within evolution we see a similar picture:
Over a period of several hundred million years, the development of neuronal structures and connections starts off slowly, picks up speed and finally seems almost to explode. When at the end of this development humans appear on the scene, they are already equipped with a fully developed, mature cerebrum with very complex connections.
During the few hundred thousand years that humans have lived on Earth in their present form as "homo sapiens (sapiens)", the cerebrum has remained practically unchanged.
Evolution has switched horses again.
Although the immense variety of neuronal anatomic structures and their connections has reached a relative maximum and slowly grinds to a halt, this does not spell the end for the development of spiritual variety. On the contrary, in the absence of new adequate morphologic adjustments, a new development starts which is identical to that of the total number of neuronal structures.
Slow at first, but then picking up speed and finally, as we can see today, an exploding increase in spiritual variety *in one and the same type of brain* with almost identical equipment.
For a long period of time the variety of life, and thereby also the spiritual variety, was distributed over all species whereby each collective of species functioned as one unit and developed to perfection as such.
Now, however, the variety of life and spiritual variety are something purely individual and strive to perfection in one and the same species, that of humans.
The basis for all spiritual variety, i.e. the essential hardware for this in our physical world, is the uniform brain.
It has changed little over the last few thousand years. By using the human brain as a further intersection "between the two worlds of matter and spirit" the spirit expands quantitatively and qualitatively into infinity; spiritual and emotional variety are uncountable and have an unlimited effect.
Before humans appeared, the spirit was represented by millions upon millions of animal brains which remained comparable with one another within one species. The spirit differentiated itself in parallel with and proportional to the development of complex brains.

The human brain has, due to the "quantum leap" taken by its complex cerebrum, obviously achieved the character of an anatomical "final stage".
The spirit, however, is by no means in its final stage.
On the contrary, its evolution will continue unlimited into infinity analogue to the infinite sequence of ordinal numbers.
Mental capabilities continue to increase – and they often start doing so properly – after the anatomical basis, the hardware "brain", has stopped growing.
This applies especially to all mental qualities and emotions which are not directly represented by some physical substance of the body. This means language, for example, which is without doubt a mental faculty. But it is inseparably connected with the entire system of language-conveying body structures (e.g. tongue, mouth, lips, larynx, etc.).
All forms of thought (including later on the thought of language) as well as all deep emotions, such as love, grief, sense of justice, etc. are in principle independent of any kind of physical structure. These specifically are the ones which develop inordinately faster under the influence of a mature cerebrum.
It is not soleley the huge yet limited number of brain cells and their connections which are the essence of an almost infinite spiritual variety. Spiritual variety has no real morphological correlate.
It is indeed something truly unlimited; but all this is now concentrated in every single individual of *one and the same* species, the human beings.
For the development of the "world spirit", individuality now clearly gains far greater significance than a collective spirit. Only a spirit which is allowed to develop individually in every single human being in different ways can grow much faster and become much greater and will achieve more variety.
Humans with their brains are a kind of special interface of evolution. Although it is not only humans who belong to both sides of this world, the spiritual as well as the physical side, they are the only creatures on earth yet who are able to become aware of this situation and of their own uniqueness.

4.16) Final Remarks

How and when was our universe created?
Nobody knows yet. The most common and media-effective theory of a Big Bang seems to me rather doubtful when scrutinised closely.
Is our universe finite or infinite?
Until recently, the majority of cosmologists assumed that it is finite. Some years ago their great "alpha wolf", *Steven Hawking*, conceded for the first time

that its expansion might be infinite. But what happened to all those seemingly persuasive arguments which were intended to convince us of the opposite?
It seems that the same applies here as it does in politics: what do I care about my blabbering from yesterday?
Is light itself both particle and wave, does it possess such a physical double nature?
All experiments up to now seem to support this supposition.
However, such a notion would contradict all the basic principles of physics in other fields as well, such as the principles of acoustics, i.e. of sound. Here, sound waves are effects of the surrounding medium. But there is no relevant physical medium, no "ether", in the universe. Must, therefore, the interpretation of light as being simultaneously particle and wave inevitably be correct?
All these questions and many more I have already discussed in the first three parts of this book.
I made an attempt at providing answers which never contradict the confirmed results of scientific research.
Nevertheless, my answers to these questions are very often different to those you know.
First of all, however, they retrieve something which has sunk into oblivion and which seemed to have been lost for ever due to present scientific perceptions: the fundamental conviction that there really does exist an all-penetrating and all-enveloping spirit and the clear commitment to believe in a superior and creative power which Christians like me know as God, the Muslims as Allah, the American Indians as Manitou and the Hindus as Brahman.
And by and by along the way, due to my answers, death looses its horror image because it does in fact not exist.
I made a search for these fundamental convictions also in the fourth part of my book in the evolution of all life on earth. And I actually found them confirmed everywhere: in life itself, and soon after in an ever more fantastically operating, later conscious and self-aware spirit which permits deep feelings and might also spill a cornucopia of beauty and harmony if it were to decide to do so.
What fascinates me especially is the fact that this creative spirit – in contrast to all ideological attempts of countless adversaries, especially those of the 20th century which has just ended – has started out with a will to manifest itself equally within every single human individual and not to fizzle out as just another collective universal spirit.

If we finally leave behind us the blinkers of an absurd collectivism, deeply contemptuous of humans, which has been imposed on us for many decades, then we will all be able to see ourselves in a new light in future.

Every human being is a unique character in this world.

Every single human being is important for the success of the great entirety, the evolution of the spirit towards something indescribably higher, to *"Omega"*, a term which my favourite philosopher *Pierre Teilhard de Chardin (1881-1955)* coined as a synonym for *"God in emergence"*.

Each human individual is in fact *one* real centre point of this world and every single one matters.

The evolution of life is *also* an evolution of the spirit which, for this purpose, gradually installs its own essential hardware thereby enabling it to find itself again in the physical part of this world.

This path, which only seems elaborate, is really indispensable for finding the way back from an initially undifferentiated immature entirety via the inexhaustible and unexpected variety of spiritual individuality to a new higher and finally perfect differentiated and mature entirety.

Spirituality in this world is omnipresent at all times.

Even in the genotype, the genome, it is always the same numbers which are involved and which we already know from the universal basic principles of the cosmos.

Numbers and simple geometric forms are an important part of this spirit. They are the set of rules providing the decisive framework.

We must merely be prepared to accept their real existence in the same way as we accept love, harmony, mercy, justice or beauty.

We can detect interrelations on all levels of life which are based on numbers and are closely connected with them.

They are a crucial factor in co-determining the close relationships between life, spirit and evolution.

Even more extensive reflections on these complexities than those discussed in Part 4 are to be found in my trilogy "A Better History of Our World, Volume 2, Life".

Part 5

The World is an Integrated Whole

5.1) My Alternative World Model

At the very beginning, our world was created by "transcendental cooperation", an "origin" as *Thomas of Aquinas (1225-1274)* terms it, a "last cause" or a "last mover" as *Aristotle (384-322 B.C.)* believed. It is impossible to make a detailed statement as to the point of time when everything started. It most certainly was not a Big Bang, but rather a phase of continuous creation with some kind of beginning. This phase might not yet be over.
Nor can we describe in detail the transcendence of this primordial creation. The Bible tells us: "*You shall not make an image of God for yourselves*".
It is probably not allowed because it is simply impossible.
In the light of my own Christian tradition I will continue to name this transcendence "God", without wishing to discriminate against anyone having different perceptions or using different religious expressions. We are all right. God is certainly neither male nor female but inevitable both. God is certainly to be understood in a personal but also abstract way. God is the absolute and – in this respect – the absolute good, because otherwise nothing could exist. God is the highest form of love.
God created our entire world in the same way as, metaphorically speaking in mathematics, all being is created by numbers from the imaginary number "i" (see Chapter 2.10). The basis of our world is thus a divine creation which

underlies strict and clear rules. When they appear in the world, everything develops from there on in a creative and emergent manner, i.e. self-creating.

The world includes two completely independent and separately existing areas of being, which are nonetheless thoroughly interwoven and intertwined and which even create one another.

The most beautiful depiction of this primordial interconnection is the East Asian symbol of Yin and Yang which probably goes back to the great Chinese philosopher *Lao Tzu (*approx. 640 B.C.)* (see Chapter 2.10).

Everything generated can be considered as being the flip sides of one and the same coin. Both belong inseparably together because with only one side the coin is nothing. Nevertheless there is one aim.

This aim leads to the absolute which simultaneously again means unity and perfection. Every development along its path towards this aim must, therefore, bit by bit relinquish one side of the coin.

I will come back to this later.

Both sides of the coin are completely different. They are always symmetrical and polar-opposite to each other. The same applies to both areas of being in this world. They have the same relationship to one another as do the numbers "-1" and "+1".

In the same way as in mathematics at first the "-1" is derived from "i" and only then the "+1" from the "-1" the two areas of being are neither generated simultaneously but rather one after the other (see Chapter 2.10).

The first area of being entails the next. The construction of the entire world is reflected in this simple mathematical principle.

The first area of being is the spirit or the spiritual world. From our point of view this is a largely abstract spiritual field which is originally vastly undifferentiated with regard to its contents.

In the broadest sense in physics a field means the collective values which represent any kind of property at any arbitrary point in an area or a space. This space may be an abstract space with a randomly high dimensional number. Too often the term space means for us a three-dimensional space, because we experience it as such in our daily lives. However, we must free ourselves from this perception if we want to understand the world.

We must imagine the spiritual field as being completely abstract with regard to space because it possesses no spatial dimensionality as we know it. It is best described by the term "bodiless existence" as used by ancient philosophers. The Hindu term "Nirvana" describes this perception rather well, although in western cultures it is often incorrectly translated as "nothing" or "void". For me the term "space of condition" sounds rather apt. Here the main focus lies not on the spatial aspect but solely on the momentary condition of existence.

Neither do the Christian terms heaven and hell describe real places but rather certain positive or negative conditions in which someone may find himself depending on his conduct during his lifetime.

This space of condition includes all emotional terms such as love and hate, good and evil, justice and injustice, mercy, etc.! Expressed simply and only metaphorically we can compare it to our dream world. [119] It seems to be spatially limited, it measures time subjectively and it often seems to be real to us. Our dream world is, however, not real nor is it individually closed off and clearly separated from those of others.

In contrast to the dream world, the world of condition in the spiritual space is a joint world occupied by the entire spiritual field and everything which has ever existed within it. In this capacity it includes also all later existing individual "worlds" which are interconnected throughout, and which harmonize with and exert an influence on one another. Whereas our dream worlds seem real to us, although they are not real in the sense of physical matter, this world of condition in the spiritual space is even the actual reality behind everything.

The spiritual field is initially pluripotent. This means it possesses all possibilities to differentiate and specialize, to develop to the highest perfection in the highest possible multiplicity.

The term "development" implies what we understand as "time". For this reason alone the spiritual field is already something continuous.

In the same manner as an arbitrary distance is a measure in our physical space, so is time the measure of spiritual space. In the same manner as all distances exist side by side in the space known to us, so also exist all times simultaneously side by side in the spiritual field. Everything already existing exists simultaneously. Time is generated only together with BEING.

At the beginning nothing physical exists, there is "only" the spiritual field.

The gospel according to St. John describes it so aptly: *"In the beginning was the Word, and the Word was with God, and the Word was God."*

The spiritual world corresponds with "God's words", his rules and his framework for everything which is to be. Insofar it is *not* a field with already preformed ideas for everything, as *Plato (427-347 B.C.)* assumed – even if the spiritual field does of course include certain basic ideas. In our modern time with all its computers and information technology we could compare it perhaps to a hard disk on which only one kind of system software is installed which has just one set of rules and no other programs.

---

[119] This is, of course, already differentiated because when a human being dreams he has already made experiences which are then included in this dream world and which determine it, e.g. spatial experiences.

It is almost waiting to be programmed.

From here on I will call the primarily existing spiritual field suggested here, the "pluripotent" spiritual field and I will abbreviate it as PSF.

The dimensionality of the PSF is time. It is something continuous and originally to be thought of as "timeless eternity". The infinite is thus already primarily embodied. In BEING it obtains three further dimensions. Time becomes four-dimensional with the dimension of infinity (eternity), past, present, future. Time is primarily a purely spiritual principle and belongs to the spiritual world.

The PSF has two organization systems, one of which is a "spiritual construction plan", which I will abbreviate as SCP the other being a "mathematical construction plan" which fundamentally orders and structures everything, abbreviated MCP. Both are really the foundations of the PSF and are not generated by it or within it. They reflect the transcendent entity which is behind the entire creation and which I will always refer to here as God. As already mentioned, God is absolute and insofar also absolute good and absolute love. Were God not like this there would be no reason for this world, a world in emergence, to exist. As little as we humans would want consciously to bear children without love. We cannot describe God any more closely than this. We must see God as being the highest personal entity for us. At the same time he is the all-encompassing information and thus somehow remaining also impersonal. God is neither male nor female but both simultaneously, because by him and with him both are indirectly generated.

The real existence of the all-encompassing and penetrating spiritual field PSF also necessitated the existence of God because nothing can be generated from nothing (see Chapters 2.10 and 2.11).

The graduation of being necessitates the existence of God, and this corresponds exactly with the perception of *Thomas von Aquinas (1225-1274)*.

The spiritual field is the germ cell of our physical universe and of all life which inevitably develops within it.

That life itself is also a purely spiritual principle becomes apparent in that it is, like time, continuous. Life is, therefore, connected with time as the real dimension of the spirit.

Nowhere in the physical universe is time continuous.

Time is primarily not a dimension of physical space (see Chapter 3.8).

Life is the first manifestation of the spirit after at least parts of the physical universe have developed and conveniently matured in consequence of the spiritual construction plan (SCP). In contrast to this the generation of all inanimate matter and, with it, cosmic space follows solely the mathematical construction plan MCP. More to this I will discuss later.

After the physical universe developed and after life manifested itself, the second manifestation of the initially pluripotent spirit is reflected in the appearance of the spirit in and with living bodies which developed later. Slowly the spirit becomes able to interact and to initiate a feedback with the spiritual field. At the same time it differentiates parts of this field. In the course of time it becomes more and more independent, later conscious and at some time sooner or later even self-aware.

Karl Popper (1902-1994) and *John Eccles (1903-1997)* also support vehemently the idea of the independence of an immaterial spirit in living bodies. By means of the highest possible individual diversity with the highest developed physical complexity of its neuronal systems it strives to achieve its own perfection as a whole, but through individual diversity and not as part of a collective overall development.

Interactions between the spiritual field and the individual spirit need a sufficiently high order and complexity of the physical universe. This is why panpsychism – according to which everything even non-living matter, be it ever so small, must possess some kind of soul – cannot exist. My conclusion contradicts the perceptions of some of the great philosophers, such as the German *Gottfried Wilhelm Leibniz (1646-1716)* and the Dutchman *Baruch de Spinoza (1632-1677)*. If we prune them a little, however, they can indeed be discussed.

All kinds of matter are directly generated from the PSF and develop from there to form the "physical" space, the universe, as we know it.

The continuous spiritual field experiences an impulse, a "first" movement. Something starts stirring in the spiritual space of condition, comparable to a "flash of thought", the "divine spark". We could also speak of a tension within this information field. We can, however, not describe how this came about, whether there was a beginning and if so, when it started, or whether it is not rather an eternal and still lasting, informational stress field.

A Big Bang is very unlikely because it had to contain all the energy and the information for the generation of an infinite and eternal universe, as even traditional cosmologists assume today. However, this contradicts all logic.

Due to this "initial tension", single units of information were in a manner of speaking "torn-off" from the infinite information field. (Perhaps they had been previously duplicated in the same way as the genome of living beings is duplicated before new creatures are developed?)

Each single information unit corresponds with the number "1". The "1"-information units, which have broken the continuity of the spiritual information field, are simultaneously the direct preliminary stage of matter and thus in effect the first physical manifestation, since discontinuity characterizes this new world. Since every single information unit belongs to both worlds it is the first real interface between spirit and matter generated by it. And together with the generation of the first finite units, which symbolise a physical existence, physical space is generated simultaneously, since information units which can be separated from one another, and which are in motion and generate something new, need space.

The smallest "1"-information units in motion of the now first physical existence we call photons. Since, with single photons, the continuity of the purely spiritual was left behind, time is also discontinuous due to it being transmitted by them. The actual continuity of time is continually guaranteed by the spiritual field which now works in the background.

Of course, the subsequent physical space also needs continuity. This cannot be provided by single photons. The spiritual field and its mathematical construction plan are called for here.

Therefore, the continuity of space, as we correctly observe it, is thus again an accomplishment of the spiritual world. It is produced and guaranteed because every ever so small physical object, which consists of moving information units, surrounds itself with its own information space made up of numbers which unambiguously structure it. Thus, a gigiantic, never ending and eternal structured information field develops.

Yet photons, as interfaces between the worlds, are not really pure matter, i.e. resting photons are massless and possess no matter at all. From a physical point of view they are transmitters of electromagnetic radiation (EMR). Their movement is characterised by direction, frequency and polarity. Light is an important part of this EMR. It consists of frequencies which we can perceive with our eyes. To keep it simple in this book, I mostly use the expression "light" as a synonym for all EMR. Light is the quantized or disconnected counterpart to the continuous, i.e. not disconnected information field of the PSF. It was emanated by it and it is thus the first interface between the spiritual and the physical world. And God said: "Let there be light!"

The PSF is like water. Although there are single droplets of water[120], it is not possible to separate them in the water. Photons are like sand: even the biggest heap of sand consists of single grains. Water is like spirit, sand is like matter. And light possesses both aspects, depending on whether it is at rest or in motion. As massless information "1" it is an expression of the spirit, because the "1" is multiplied by every ordinal number and is thus part of the whole like a droplet of water. As a photon moving in space it remains like a grain of sand and is always separable.

---

[120] Of course water also consists of atoms, i.e. of finite particles, of matter; since water is part of our physical universe.

With the aid of light (EMR), space, our universe, becomes visible for *us* when quanta hit the retina of our eye or a technical device and react with the appropriate sensitive cells or substances. Otherwise our universe remains in darkness. Light is only pure information. *We* make it partly visible.

In contrast to the current perception, however, light does not *create* space since space is in reality a pure information space. It is "generated" by numbers. Light appears to us in space with a constant maximum speed, the speed of light (c). It is constant because it is mathematically limited by the expansion of the number-structured information space and differs from it infinitesimally. This is understandable when space consists of numbers and each photon as "1" (or in space "1^{2n}") is multiplied by every number of this space. The "1" cannot hurry ahead of the generation of space. There must be an upper limit, therefore, as Einstein was the first to recognise. However, light itself does not create this limit and this contradicts Einstein's perception.

The velocity of light is alone the result of a cosmic information space being structured by means of a mathematical construction plan (MCP) – here it is the processing of all ordinal numbers and their logical circular arrangement (see Chapters 3.4 and 3.5)

In the last instance, any kind of matter is generated by the spirit – matter which consists at first of the faintest of traces, even better described as "semi-matter", which are actually information units, namely photons. Nevertheless, we can already correctly talk of matter since these light quanta (photons) are quantized and are thus the discontinuous expression of information as such. The original equivalent of the purely spiritual side is the infinite continuous field (PSF).

Isaac Newton (1643-1727) already was convinced that light consisted of particles[121] whereas the Dutchman *Christiaan Huygens (1629-1695)* in 1690 introduced the concept of the *wave* character of light. The German physicist *Max Planck (1858-1947)* then proved that light must consist of tiniest particles, known as quanta[122] (see Part 3).

Since photons as "real particles" would have no chance of being transported through an "empty" space, their duality was *invented*. Up until today they are considered as being particle and wave simultaneously.

Although this is accepted physical knowledge and has already been awarded the Nobel Prize, I consider this notion to be wrong.

---

[121] Please understand light always as a synonym for all EMR.
[122] Quantum was originally an expression introduced by Max Planck as "quantum of action" which today usually means the smallest extent by which a "smallest" or "quantized" physical quantity, e.g. energy or the angular momentum, can be varied. The energy difference between two states is often absorbed (or contributed) by a "particle" known as a "quantum". The smallest "particle" of light, or in general of all electromagnetic radiation, is the photon.

Due to a creational process which is probably still happening, the smallest mass-containing physical particles are generated by means of photons. In my metaphor of a creational model they are the initial circles and correspond with the smallest finite points (see Part 2, Chapter 2.4). In the same way as a circle such as the first physical entity can clearly be determined with the aid of three informational points the first mass-containing particles are generated by photons. Their mass is *the result of the constant movement of the particles* which constitute it. They merge to form larger objects and ever more complex units of matter are slowly built up.

Exactly this, the creation of matter from practically pure energy, i.e. from "information in motion", again and again mistakenly called "creation from nothing"[123], was successfully proven by a number of experiments with the Stanford particle accelerator in California, USA, in 1998.

To do this a beam of light from a 1 trillion watt laser was directed on to an area of a billionth of a square centimetre for a period of a trillionth of a second. This laser beam was brought to collide with an electron beam of the particle accelerator. As a result of this cataclysmic impact "nuclear particles" were generated in a kind of chain reaction.

In this act of creation of matter by information, which we describe as energy because it is quantized and moves incredibly fast, lies in my opinion the real meaning of *Albert Einstein's, (1879-1955)*, famous formula: $E = m \cdot c^2$!

Not in this well-known version but rather in its inversion lies the true key to the evolution of our physical world. It is of course: $m = E : c^2$!

This means: by means of an immense amount of energy, i.e. moving information, matter is generated – i.e. smallest traces of mass.

According to this all matter is a complex form of energy and simultaneously of (spiritual) information.

Under the influence of gravitation they tend to "agglutinate" and to form large conglomerates. All finite physical points exert gravitational forces, i.e. information complexes "attract one another". Gravitation is an effect of space like light and thus dependent on the mass and, therefore, also on the total energy (information content) of the finite starting point. The gravitation of an object is, on the one hand, directly proportional to the square of its total energy, should there be two objects then it is directly proportional to the product of both masses (total energy). On the other hand it is indirectly proportional to the square of the distance between the object and the starting point.

---

[123] Oriental wisdom is often quoted in an attempt to prove by means of an incorrectly interpreted comparison: "nothing" as the translation of "not-being" is, according to Lao Tzu, (*approx. 604 B.C.) by no means really nothing but more the intangible, invisible counterpart to the physical existence. He calls the latter, therefore, "being" and the former "not-being".

Yet again it is the ordinal numbers which are solely responsible for this. Of course, they also control gravitation as an effect of space by means of their squares or the squares of their reciprocal values (see Part 3).

The conglomerates of matter, which are formed due to gravitation, are themselves transmitters of information, i.e. they "emit" light or reflect it when a beam of light is directed at them. In this way the visible universe with all its galaxies, stars and planets is composed and we can perceive it with our senses. All visible matter is arranged in a typical structure. It is comparable to a huge three-dimensional sponge which can be identified in every single section of random size (see illustration by Martin). The galaxies correspond with the many small beams of this sponge and the compactions between them (here: every light spot).

Viewed from any direction and from any randomly chosen point in the universe (which is in fact infinite) it all looks rather homogeneous and uniform.

All matter is obviously distributed very homogeneously. This is also known as being isotropic [124] (see Part 3).

The electromagnetic radiation (EMR or, simply, light) causes a uniform temperature everywhere in the universe which is known as microwave-background radiation (BGR) and can be measured.

It has a universally constant value of almost exactly 2.73 K and shows only very slight fluctuations (see Chapters 3.2 and 3.3). In contrast to the assumptions of most cosmologists, I believe that the BGR has always been constant at exactly this magnitude. Its value obviously varies slightly around an ideal number which is also the inevitable result of my geometrical creation model (see Chapter 2.4).

This also easily explains the slight fluctuations of the measured values which are evidently necessary. As little as we can describe the circumference or the area of a circle rationally, i.e. with a finite number value, although it is optically finite, as little can we describe a spiritual ideal in the physical world in exact values. The same applies to the velocity of light and all the other nature constants (see Chapter 2.12). It follows that the BGR is not the early result of the cooling down after an incredibly hot Big Bang.

Besides, if that were the case it must have had a much higher temperature earlier on (some billions of years ago).

---

[124] Isotropy, Greek "isos" = identical, and "tropos" = direction: distributed identically in all directions without preference. Isotropy is even more stringent than homogeneity.

An information space is generated around every ever so small mass, comparable to the smallest *finite* point in my creation model (see Chapter 2.4). This information space is four-dimensional and it is constructed by two perpendicularly intersecting infinite planes. It is completely plane, flat or Euclidian[125]. This is supported by all recent observations made by means of the latest technologies such as satellite pictures. It can be described mathematically with an x^2y^2 geometry. This idea goes back to the German chemist and natural scientist *Peter Plichta (*1939)*. With the aid of my little creation model which I already designed years ago and which I introduced again in Chapter 2.4, starting from a first finite point, this model is supported and completed in an even simpler, and now very plausible and impressive way. With this space model which is based solely on spiritual information – and numbers or geometries are that if we consider them to be real – space becomes as continuous as time. From a physical point of view this continuity, which we perceive in our daily lives, would not exist – neither for time nor for space.

And something else: since the really four-dimensional space becomes secondarily something spiritual again, due to the infinite ordinal numbers by which it is structured, it is itself infinite. This corresponds with the latest assumptions of some renowned cosmologists.

The entire world develops according to two interconnected and mutually interacting construction plans, namely the SCP and the MCP.

The spiritual construction plan (SCP) controls life in matter from the earliest possible point in time. It also instigates very early on the formation of neuronal structures which are then further improved in such a way that they are enabled to take up interaction with the spiritual potential. Interactions are carried out with the known information particles.

The neuronal structures prove themselves remarkably constant throughout the entire history of evolution with regard to their ever higher and simultaneously downward compatible complexity.

Thus they become another important interface for the spirit on the path to itself – after having achieved the highest possible perfection in the highest possible multiplicity.

The mathematical construction plan (MCP), which includes geometrical forms and ordinal numbers, controls the formal construction of all matter be it animate or inanimate. It is responsible for the "physical scaffolding". The *Pythagoreans* and later mainly the Greek philosophers, *Plato (427-347 B.C.)* and *Plotin (205-270 A.D.)*, already assumed that some simple geometrical basic forms and the ordinal numbers must exist in reality and must be elements of a

---

[125] Named after the Greek mathematician Euclid (approx. 300 B.C.)

defined plan. The Austrian *Karl Popper (1902-1994)* also supported this idea. In contrast to the ancient philosophers, however, he claimed that numbers were initially an invention of humans and only *thereafter* assumed a real existence.

The MCP is the first to swing into action and it keeps controlling the development and differentiation of the entire world in eternity.

It is light which transmits, manifests and represents the primarily purely spiritual quality of a continuous subjectively perceived time within the information space which is generated and which we know as the universe. Time is a dimension of the spirit and, therefore, of real continuity. Time is subjective, i.e. it is perceived.

In physical space there is no continuity at all and hence no time either. It is solely simulated by the movement of the quanta. Quanta are, however, discontinuous[126]. These movements are controlled by the number structure of space. Thus quanta acquire continuity. Since numbers are part of the spiritual foundation of the entire world, continuity of time is implemented in the physical universe solely by the spirit.

Any movement in physical space can be traced back to the movement of smallest particles or quanta and is discontinuous.

Controlled with the aid of numbers they become continuous. Without the "connecting" spirit the physical world could not exist, since it would have no continuity.

What we call periods which imitate the reality of real vibrations consist in reality merely of the frequency of quanta in motion. This frequency determines the distance between subsequent quanta and we speak of wavelength. The wavelength does not, however, result from light being a wave but rather because photons are transported by the waves of spiritual space. In the last instance, the quanta themselves are pure information. Their "internal physical connection", i.e. the period or the vibration – let us call it the wave – is thus produced solely by the cosmic information or number space.

It is generated around every smallest finite particle and possesses two completely different (polar and symmetrical) parts or qualities.

That, which we usually call the *one* physical space, our universe, is in fact divided into two parts, inner and outer space. Outer space is four-dimensional infinite space which is generated around every finite point. The finite starting point itself becomes an interface. Within every finite and thus three-dimensional body there is an inner space. Both are structured by numbers (see Chapter 2.4).

---

[126] Discontinuous = the opposite of continuous: interrupted, discrete.

With the aid of gigantic amounts of moving light quanta, i.e. purely spiritual information units, and their mutual bombardment and conglomeration, ever more complex mass-containing particles up to complete atoms are slowly generated. Matter is born. My metaphor renders this development understandable, since three immaterial, spiritual pieces of information determine clearly the first finite point, i.e. the physical smallest circle (see Chapter 2.4).

"The exploration of the universe demonstrated to me that the existence of matter is a miracle which can only be explained by supernatural causes!", so the words of the well-known American cosmologist at the Carnegie observatories *Allan Sandage (*1926)* in 2004.

The smallest and first atom is hydrogen. It is the basis for all other atoms which are generated in accordance with the underlying mathematical laws. The infinite physical space, which is automatically generated around every single finite and thus physical point, always results, due to the infinite number structure, in an infinite (basically informative) space. These processes of physical creation on a spiritual basis take place incessantly. Therefore, it may be better to speak of an incessant creation. A Big Bang as the first cause has probably never taken place. Creation is a "quiet" process. This also corresponds harmonically with the biblical story of a creation being achieved within "six days", which should be understood in a *symbolic* but not at all verbatim sense.

From the pluripotent spiritual field (PSF) quantized light is generated as single information units and thus as an interface between the spiritual and the physical world. This enables physical space to become "visible" which requires, of course, that it can be observed. Photons are aspects of both parts of this world. This is the reason why our classical physical laws of space seem not to be applicable to light. And it is also the reason why quantum physics seems to entail a number of apparent paradoxes (see Part 3). Viewed from a physical point of view time and light are quanta systems which follow mathematical laws.

We humans, however, are also interactive partners between the PSF and the physical world and we perceive quanta systems in accordance with the *spiritual* field. We *perceive* light as being a wave of its *own* and time as being its *own* continuum.

In reality all light quanta are transported according to the laws of a (spiritual) information space, the number space.

The wave theory, first developed by *Christiaan Huygens (1629-1695)* and much later by the French physicist *Louis-Victor de Broglie (1892-1987)*, therefore, only *seems* to be correct. The light *wave* only appears to us as such due to the real existence of the number space.

In the meantime the cognition of quantum physics that, for example, light is wave and particle simultaneously seems to have been supported by experiments, however, physicists have as yet been unable to explain it in a plausible way.

The verification of this is of course carried out by means of physical devices which are controlled by the same laws as those they are supposed to measure.

Thus all these experiments support *my* model as well, since I always attempt to include all observations and research results, it is only my *interpretation* which differs from those of modern physicists. Einstein himself always refuted the idea of the classical particle-wave dualism. In Part 3 of this book I already explained why I believe he was right.

His doubts were contradicted at the time by the Danish physicist *Niels Bohr (1885-1962)*, whose atom model you probably know. Bohr once said: "If Einstein were to send me a radio-telegram informing me that he has finally proved the particle nature of light, that telegram could only reach me because light consists of waves." We experience the continuity of light every day, but the reason for this lies elsewhere.

Light is of dual nature, but it must be understood in a completely different way: it is the dualism of its spiritual and physical aspects. Light is the quantized information of a continuous spiritual field (PSF). These information units generate matter and they add simultaneously a spiritual aspect. Light is thus an interface between spirit and matter.

Energy is moving information, information is spirit. Therefore, matter is a kind of an expression of spirit.

Light (and this means any kind of electromagnetic radiation EMR, of course) is pure information. These units of information hurtle through space with different frequencies and a constant speed – the upper limit of which is controlled by the actual spatial expansion. The further light moves away from its source the weaker it becomes solely due to the number laws of space, i.e. due to Isaac Newton's reciprocal square distance law which applies to all effects in space (see Part 3).

The information or the light quanta follow *only passively* the constant expansion of space which forms around every finite physical point because as "1" or "1^2" they are multiplied by every ordinal number. Only we humans render it into an *active* velocity of photons.

The number space alone determines the decisive parameters. In addition to the constant of space expansion, which limits the velocity of light, the so-called prime number ray presumably determines the frequency of light with an exponentially decreasing number of prime numbers towards infinity, and is thus responsible for the redshift of light (see Chapters 3.5 and 3.6).

In order to explain the redshift, it is no longer necessary that the universe, visible to us with all its galaxies, expands with increasing velocity postulated hitherto. For this reason the Big Bang is also no longer an essential precondition for the creation of the cosmos.

Time as a spiritual dimension is continuous and, when viewed solely from the spiritual perspective, is already relative since it is subjective. Time is what we perceive – and that is something spiritual.

In the physical world the actual subjectivity of time becomes an objective reality, since time here is dependent on the velocity of an object (see Part 3).

Time only makes sense when it can be perceived by a consciousness, whereas a physical space makes sense even without a perceiving consciousness.

Therefore time as a purely physical value can indeed be something discontinuous – space in the spiritual sense on the other hand is primarily a purely conditional space, as we know it from our dreams.

The spiritual conditional space is, in contrast to our dream world, the *joint* conditional space of the entire spiritual field (PSF) and thus it is equally valid for everybody and everything (see above). This does not exclude further individual conditional spaces.

Time without consciousness is worthless and is, therefore, unnecessary.

A physical space is, in contrast, initially without relevance for the spiritual field. This changes when – at some time or other – differentiated spiritual beings begin to "populate" the spiritual field. Alone the experience of a physical space gives a reason for their existence with and within such a spiritual space. The physical space is the basis of all physical existence and is, therefore, absolutely essential even when the existence of consciousness is ignored.

From this point of view space, as we understand it, is primarily a physical value, even if it possesses itself a spiritual character, purely because it is structured by numbers. With a physical space concept, the experience of its existence, is transferred to the spiritual world and manifested there only due to its own development. The initially purely spiritual space is thereby also in the spiritual respect spatially differentiated and structured. This does not mean that the "spiritual space" now becomes a real new space in a physical respect but rather that it exists with and within it. In addition to the physical space, which is open for both parts of the world, a space remains in the spiritual area, which is a subjective value transmitted into the imagination as happens in a dream, but in this case it affects the entire PSF.

Such a transmission is only possible when a basic imagination of space already exists. For this purpose the physical space must in fact have existed for whoever is imagining it.

All forms of life, which is surely to be found in abundance in many places in the universe, is purely anatomical and, therefore, from a physical point of view, also discontinuous. It follows that all senses are structured in the same way and that they perceive all the discontinuous processes in this world as a sensual experience. However, unconsciously at first but at some time or other consciously, their brains interpret the events in a completely new and different way. Everything is now perceived as being continuous although there are no parallels for this at all in the physical world. The spirit and our consciousness as the higher differentiated aspect of the spirit take care of this.

"Time and space" are as equally symmetrical inversions of each other as are "spiritual and physical world". Time has its own four dimensions and is, in my opinion, by no mans merely the fourth dimension of a mixed space-time continuum, as physicists have assumed since Einstein. Time in the spiritual field (PSF) is in principle not timeless as many philosophical or esoteric notions continue to claim. It is only timeless as long as it is not perceived subjectively. It is only timeless without the existence of BEING. Together with BEING time emerges from a timeless eternity. It is the real dimensionality of the spiritual world, in the same way as space is in the material world.

For us it is impossible to recognise the beginning of our physical universe, i.e. it is simply impossible to make a statement about it.

From our perspective it seems probable that everything started at some time or other. Nevertheless this happened not with a Big Bang but due to a comparatively "silent" first creation of finite particles based on pure information. This creational process has continued ever since and is still continually proceeding. There is also no limit at the end of the physical universe.

The spiritual field (PSF) on which it is based is inevitably eternal, since this is the first principle of its temporal four-dimensionality. The physical space of our universe, which emerges from here, is also eternal and infinite, this also being due to its mathematical basis. Infinity (eternity) is the last principle of its own real spatial four-dimensionality within this space.

All matter which has ever been generated and which ever will be generated in future is and will always be constructed indirectly by means of light as the source of information, according to strict mathematical rules and will behave from then on without exception in accordance with the mathematical construction plan (MCP) on which everything is based.

From a purely statistical point of view, i.e. considering a sufficiently large number of single events and, in addition, a sufficiently long period of time, there is no such thing as a real coincidence with respect to inanimate matter (see Chapter 2.16).

Long-term developments are insofar teleological deterministic – this means predetermined by the aim, because ultimately they follow the all-determining underlying plans. The great French philosopher, theologian and anthropologist *Pierre Teilhard de Chardin (1881-1955)* also assumed this.

Nevertheless, coincidental events occur at random on every level of single events and decisions. On the one hand coincidental events are of immense importance because they bestow real progress to a world which has not yet reached sufficiently high spiritual levels. On the other hand important processes and advantageous developmental directions could be retarded if coincidental events alone prevail – and the processes which are based on coincidence need an enormous amount of time. By no means do accidental mutations lead directly to mature improvements which may then achieve acceptance in the fierce battle for existence.

On the contrary, many developments need numerous generations before they provide an evolutionary advantage. Nevertheless, they occur because early on nature developed effective mechanisms to keep coincidences at bay (see Part 4). Here is a fitting comparison: In the human gestation period the fertilized egg cell develops in accordance with certain biochemical plans determined by its genome, i.e. its physical genotype, into an embryo. It passes through several stages and finally grows into a foetus which is born after an average of 273 days. This is such a teleological development determined by the long-term aim to give birth to a baby.

Various interfering and damaging influences may have a detrimental effect on the child's development during pregnancy. These include smoking, alcohol or drugs, incidental accidents of the mother, or even infections such as German measles.

Although the embryo will proceed to grow according to its genomes, all these partly undetermined, indeterminate coincidences might damage the embryo massively or even kill it. In contrast to the further development of an embryo where the end result, the baby, is determined within rather narrow limits, I believe that – with regard to cosmic development – the scope of the "emergent constant new development" (Karl Popper) is considerably larger. This must orientate itself to the prevailing environmental conditions and requirements.

Over and above the mathematical construction plan (MCP), the pluripotent spiritual field (PSF) also possesses the spiritual construction plan (SCP).
This contains all the information required for basic forms of life and the "thriving" towards a constant spiritual progress as well as spiritual, emotional, moral-ethical and aesthetic ideals.
Concepts such as love, justice, beauty and aesthetics are thus in principle really existing. Their opposites such as hate or envy inevitably arise from there.
In the course of time life develops wherever possible by means of, but not from, inanimate matter. *Carsten Bresch*[127], for example, the former full professor of Medical Microbiology at Cologne University, is in principle of the same opinion. In a discussion about life in the cosmos he said: *"Wherever life is generated on a suitable planet a biological evolution will take place which will inevitably (unless a catastrophe occurs) enter into an intellectual phase."* The SCP therefore becomes responsible for the generation of life.
In my well-founded convictions the *"inevitable intellectual phase"* cited by C. Bresch can only be something immaterially spiritual. It follows that this spirit itself must also be able to influence evolution and to control to an increasing extent the conditions and the mechanisms of evolution. Thus, increasingly, the spirit determines the parallel but significantly accelerated development of all essential, ever more complex organic "aggregates" and "devices" with which such interactions can be accomplished in a more and more efficient and differentiated manner.
First the basic organic substances essential for all forms of life (amino acids and protein building blocks) are generated.
This happens and has been confirmed by experiments carried out by Stanley Miller and many of his followers (see Part 4) and it is still largely accidental and undetermined as to where and when they are generated within this physical universe which is to such a large extent self-generating, i.e. emergent.
In a way these incidents are predetermined because they inevitably occur wherever possible due to their being controlled by the SCP and by the organization of the MCP. Amino acids and nucleic acids have been generated and are still being generated continuously wherever conditions permit, in the past, present and future. Therefore, it is beyond all question, in my opinion, that higher developed and intelligent life does indeed exist in a multitude of places in the cosmos.
The objection is often brought forward that the creation of intelligent life such as that of humans, or even higher species, would probably be impossible

---

[127] Professor Dr. Carsten Bresch, "Evolution zum Menschen", in Peter R. Sahm et al., "Der Mensch im Kosmos", see List of References. Here my special thanks go to Prof. Dr.-Ing. Willi Hallmann, formerly at the Faculty 6 of the Institute of Aerospace Engineering at the University of Applied Sciences of Aachen, who is a friend of mine and who supported me with this reference.

because narrowly limited starting conditions would render it too unlikely. This objection is definitely completely out of place.

My view is supported by the chaos theory which shows that, statistically, coincidence only plays a secondary role in the long run. Every chaotic process always merges sooner or later into a higher and long-term stable order.

In the fourth part of this book I explained why the purely coincidental generation of various extremely complex organic molecules of building blocks, which must closely cooperate to keep a cell alive, is practically *not* explainable in a plausible way. This cooperation is, however, exactly what we see, i.e. if we think of the building blocks for the construction and maintenance metabolism some of which are very complex enzymes[128].

Both groups of molecules must have been there simultaneously right from the start – in the same way as the chicken and the egg must have appeared at the same time and not one after the other.

To a certain extent this is supported by *Plato* and his Theory of Ideas as well as by his student *Aristotle* and his Theory of Forms. The basic principles of MCP and SCP act jointly in the creation of ideas and forms which are necessary for the simultaneous generation of all the essential complex, basic building blocks of life, i.e. the long-chained molecules. As the renowned scientific magazine New Scientist put it so aptly: *"It is the information content, or software, of the living cell that is the real mystery, not the hardware components"*[129].

I believe that this is the decisive key for the comprehension of spirit and brain. It is not the hardware, the fixed organic structures – the devices of the body – which plays the decisive role, it is the software, the programmes – or the *spiritual* content. And we know too little of these contents because we are still only searching for biological or biochemical programmes. While doing this we tend to forget that completely different ones already exist. But it goes even further: in the end only their *meaning* is important. In the same way as we can attribute completely different meanings to lyrics and melodies so can programmes and their spiritual contents be interpreted differently. This is always something subjective, of course, and requires an evaluating and thus conscious spirit.

Even though the great ancient philosophers conceded a practically overall power to the spiritual principles in the background of the world development, I am of a different opinion. The development of the world does not happen *passively* due to predetermined conditions for everything, but it is rather "creative emergent", more like the grasping twines of ivy growing up a trellis.

---

[128] Enzyme, Greek: en = in, and zymos = sourdough; proteins, i.e. very complex, long-chained so-called macro-molecules, which facilitate, the construction and metabolism processes, make them easier and accelerate them.

[129] New Scientist, No. 2204, 18th September 1999: "Life force", page 28.

And this entwining is a very *active* process. The Austrian, *Karl Popper (1902-1994)*, who supported the idea of the emergence of free self-determination, assumed that the plans themselves are also generated during the development and only thereafter start to influence the further process. Evolution is thus a kind of emergence of plan and product. I, on the other hand, assume that the plans for the important basic conditions or parameters of any development are at the ready at all times. At the same time I refute the perception that, over and above these plans involving the basic processes for the evolution of all life and the directions it will take, the detailed ideas and plans for all later *finished* products are already contained here at the beginning – practically determining destiny. This is, however, the exact meaning of Plato's Theory of Ideas and his Theory of Pre-existence.

Everything generated within this four-dimensional information space, the physical space we perceive, is of a three-dimensional corporeality directed towards the inside. Viewed from the outside all objects are finite, i.e. limited. Nevertheless, within these limits, there is the internal infinity of mathematics which focuses on the area between the smallest BEING, the 1, and nothing, the zero (see Chapter 2.13).

An example: any country on this earth has a finite size, it has borders. We can circumscribe them and express the finite length in metres and kilometres. If we attempted, however, to mark these borders with a small ruler, if we wanted to check, how many such ever so small straight lines would be necessary in order to determine the borders exactly, i.e. accurate to the very last millimetre, we would need an infinite number of them due to the many curved lines which could only be measured by decreasing the lengths of straight lines. They would all line up to an infinite length and, in consequence, we would be forced to conclude that every country is infinitely large.

This example resembles the paradox of the Greek philosopher *Zenon of Elea (approx. 460 B.C.)*, in which, as Aristotle quoted, Achilles (theoretically) tried in vain to overtake a tortoise in a race. And it also resembles Olber's paradox which I explained in detail in chapter 2.2. The error in reasoning in both cases is that infinite amounts of finite objects cannot exist. Apparently infinite amounts of finite objects finally always come to an end.

The three-dimensionality of physical bodies is found in all cells as well as in large organic molecules and in the genome which consists of the macro-molecules DNA and RNA.[130]

Another and probably very important physical consequence of this three-dimensional corporeality has hardly ever been recognised by scientists. As

---

[130] Deoxyribonucleic and Ribonucleic acid; basic building blocks of the genome.

long as he worked scientifically the German physicist *Albert Popp (*1938)* dealt with light emitted by organic tissue (see Chapter 4.10). Popp was certainly right when he assume this to be an important key for understanding a number of necessary processes in every living being. Every large organic molecule (macro-molecule) and every cell is a three-dimensional body. They are all ideal resonance bodies which can absorb, store and amplify digital information which is transmitted physically and not in a biochemical way.

Every single cell is probably involved in an interactive exchange of information with various spiritual field structures in this world. It would thus be enabled to expand continuously its own initially unconscious state of information and, much later, when the neuronal complexity had progressed sufficiently, its own conscious standard of knowledge as well.

Due to telecommunication, radio and TV we all might suspect that any piece of information irrespective of its complexity can be digitalized at some time at least. Complex number packets containing 1 and 0 can be transmitted over immense distances without any cable connections and without quality loss. An important transport medium for such encoded information is laser light. In 1922 already the Russian physician *Alexander Gurwitsch (1874-1954)* discovered that onion cells emitted light and he termed this mitogenetic radiation. Fritz Popp was then able to prove by means of modern experimental methods that living cells emitted a rather weak laser light which was nevertheless very effective for the transport of data (see Chapter 4.10). Today we know that even water droplets can communicate with each other and that they can react to external influences as the renowned professor for aerospace engineering at *Stuttgart University, Bernd Kröplin (*1944),* was able to prove experimentally. This must happen in a physical manner. We just do not know how, maybe by means of light?

Radiation (EMR or light) is generated by the pluripotent spiritual field (PSF) on which everything is based. As digitally encoded information it can affect all three-dimensional resonance bodies and thus every macro-molecule and every living cell. Thus photons are the interface in the interaction between spirit and matter.

Within the scope defined by the spiritual plans MCP and SCP, this form of information transmission enables the purposeful creation of organic (but still inanimate) molecules at first and, aided by these, of animate cells later, the real basic building blocks of all life.

Certain "spiritual" parameters are defined by concrete light information. Insofar a certain kind of determinism exists. Beyond this a kind of thread for further growth is provided rather like a trellis up which ivy may grow. Otherwise, however, pure emergence and indeterminism prevails. The basic laws and ideas of a spiritual construction plan (SCP) will ensure that all life which may be generated at some time or place in our universe will always be constructed in accordance with the same principles. A variety of versatile single adjustments to the prevailing rigid situations and environmental conditions may be made within the predetermined parameters. I assume that higher and intelligent life exists in many places in our universe and that it is basically structured similar to terrestrial life. Creatures which resemble us humans will posses a similar neuro-anatomical structure. They will probably have two symmetrical eyes, two symmetrical arms and legs and, at least constitutionally, ten fingers and toes as, for example, horses possessing only one hoof on each leg although two times ten toes and fingers were planned but not developed, such phenotypic adjustments to specific situations can occur at random if they prove to be helpful.

On every single level in the evolution of life coincidence finds the doors wide open. Random mutations can also induce arbitrary new variations at any time which may survive selection and propagate because they prove to be especially advantageous (see Chapters 4.2 and 4.3).

Or they could be eliminated if they do not prove to be of advantage. This probably occurs quite often. In spite of all dynamics and big opportunities for the completely unexpected this does not change the picture that – from a statistical point of view – evolution follows an organized path and, in the long term, in a clearly defined direction. Finally, a creature with a high neuro-anatomical level of development, such as humans are on this earth, seems to be at least the preliminary aim of a development of life wherever it takes place[131]. It seems sensible to me to describe the evolutionary process as a *"teleological and yet emergent determined indeterminism"*. We can roughly compare the roles of MCP and SCP with the competence of a German Federal Chancellor to determine the direction of politics. The ministers of his cabinet are allowed to develop legislative proposals on their own and they may allow their undersecretaries of state within their department to act freely. The chancellor is not forced to accept what in *his* view is not sensible, impossible or what can obviously be considered to be an aberration and he is entitled to put paid to such initiatives in the appropriate committees. On the other hand, he is also entitled to set guidelines and to expect that the members of his cabinet in principle adhere to them and that they take care of the details.

---

[131] This is also known as the "anthropic principle", Greek: anthropos = human. The form which is not accepted by scientist is known as the "strictly anthropic principle", which means that evolution practically strives to develop humans. I cannot comprehend this, however. Humans are, in my opinion, only the final manifestation on our earth, which has emerged due to various conditions. In my opinion not their appearance is important but the existence of a complex equivalent to the human central nervous system. This is the real aim of the SCP.

The development of all life follows such guidelines.

Within the spacious but stringently marked framework life develops independently, self-organized and constantly creates something new, i.e. "creative emergent".

In the course of time the creatures of this world become more and more complex.

Step by step the communication system which is generated no longer functions primarily on the basis of biochemical processes. The ability of these creatures to participate interactively in the surrounding all-penetrating spiritual field, which is inherent in all kinds of life, grows all the time.

Due to the cooperation between the spiritual construction plan (SCP) and the slowly forming highly complex neuronal networks (neuro-anatomical structures) information units can be exchanged better and more effectively.

Hence the spiritual field becomes more and more "creature oriented" differentiated and structured. If the neuro-anatomical complexity is sufficiently high, a consciousness is finally developed followed by a strictly individual subjectivity, self-awareness which is coupled to a clear self-knowledge.

In this context differentiation of the initially infinite possibilities of a basic pluripotent spiritual field (PSF) means the continuous filing of data on to a formatted but empty computer hard disk.

Every brain enters into a liaison with its own specific, quasi password protected and initially undifferentiated "part" of the PSF[132] in a similar way as the Noble Prize winner *John Eccles* suggested. The higher the anatomical complexity of the brain in the species achieved in the course of the species-specific development, the more extensive is the capability to actively differentiate this "creature oriented" spiritual field.

All information units experienced and obtained by every creature in the course of its life, including, of course, all those information units which determine the appearance, the character and the personality of every living organism, are completely and permanently stored. A perfect copy is generated, which equals the original but which has no "solid" physical body. It is, therefore, self-evident that a living creature which is already self-aware during its physical lifetime will keep being aware of its individual personality after its physical death. As long as no – or only very little – self-awareness has been developed, because the species-specific anatomical complexity is insufficient, that part of the (PSF) which is already collectively differentiated cannot become self-aware.

---

[132] The word "part" should not be considered as being spatial but rather in the sense of "proportional" to the existing possibilities. It can also be seen as a virtual store room.

Based on the information gathered during a life on earth the self-aware being will then experience himself in almost the same way as he did within his physical body. This notion seems to be supported by the high number of reliably analysed near-death experiences. Based on my own research, I can confirm this myself. I gave extensive explanations in my previous book "Nobody Ever dies!" which I dedicated to this subject matter.

The brains of all creatures are thus interfaces between the physical and the spiritual world, the PSF.

Just imagine that the "effervescent diversity"[133] of the digitally encoded world-wide internet were to go through a technical revolution. Functioning without cables and without hardware it would then be a completely virtual information network. In principle, all information bits could then be received and processed everywhere with appropriate receivers.

Just imagine you are sitting in your lounge at home. It is a fact that today we are engulfed by immense volumes of data based on a variety of satellite TV and radio programmes. Without appropriate receivers, however, we could neither hear nor see any of this. We would simply not perceive this clutter of data and it might remain like that until we die. We would be absolutely correct to say that we know nothing at all about this. We would not even know that all these information bits exist.

The next step would be to buy a radio set and now, depending on its design and quality, we might enjoy some of the programmes. With a TV set and a satellite dish we can receive a variety of terrestrial programmes, regardless of where the receiver is placed or connected. But we are still only consumers. We experience the programmes passively.

If we apply this scheme to a time grid covering the evolutionary history of living creatures, it would cover the time until the first mammals appeared on the scene. But then we took delivery of a modern and technically highly developed computer with a large variety of software.

At the push of a button we would literally experience much more of what our "lounge" holds in store for us which we cannot perceive through our normal senses. With a modem or another cable-free device we can for the first time actively access the immense amount of data. We can consciously download information from the internet at random while our activities are limited solely by the configuration of the hardware and software available – apart from any financial restrictions, because storage capacity, receiver quality and speed are limiting factors and they are expensive.

With the adequate equipment we are enabled to participate actively, or better interactively, in a variety of projects and offers within an unlimited internet. In

---

[133] I use here the advertising slogan of my home town Aachen.

future we might influence the information offered in the internet in accordance with our own notions.

We can also carve out our own very personal recourses and territories and we can carry out activities, such as online-banking, with exclusive access whilst others are denied access to our personal data[134].

We might wish to write a book in the internet on any subject of our choice (e.g. diaries) and make it accessible to a small group of people we trust such as certain friends.

You can design your own "homepage" and make it available only to a limited number of people you have chosen, for example your customers. For this purpose you encode your data with secure passwords or by means of digitally encoded biometric data such as fingerprints, eye structures or language, etc. Many companies and public institutions have already installed their own intranet in the internet, a practically infinite area for their own use with their own network and to which only authorized persons have access.

The so-called network computers do not possess large storage components of their own but, by means of the "virtual field", they make a randomly large amount of storage capacity available as well as the entire range of software which may be needed (that this is not free of charge on earth is of secondary importance in this context).

These data storages become our own very personal reserves to which only we have access.

In a similar way, the technical inventions and developments of our modern time can be carried over to living beings. In the history of evolution this would roughly correspond to the period of time which elapsed between the appearance of the first mammals and the first humans.

It is only with telecommunication and electronic data processing that we have started to develop all *those* devices on earth which, and I am convinced of this, have already been present for ages in a much bigger and unimaginably more fantastic and world encompassing or cosmic dimension.

We are not *inventing* all these things anew, but rather we are *rediscovering* them for us and we are implementing them in accordance with the circumstances surrounding us on each level of development.

And we are all an important, central part! Clearly, we humans have meanwhile been equipped with an appropriate highly developed and sufficiently complex hardware. This hardware can and should participate in this world-encompassing, "divine" internet in an eternally interactive, conscious, self-aware and self-recognizing manner. In contrast to a modern "technical

---

[134] Apart from successful hackers; however, this problem could also be eliminated in future by means of appropriate encodings.

computer", we humans organize ourselves. Whereas a computer needs a human programmer for all activities, we humans are interactive "living computers" which organize and improve themselves but which are also and primarily a kind of transmitter and receiver (see Chapters 4.11 and 4.12). Consciousness and self-awareness, which are some of the specific and higher forms of the PSF differentiation, are generated as soon as the complexity of the brain reaches a sufficiently high level. Due to constant interaction the eternal, initially pluripotent spiritual field (PSF) is "imbued" with "life" in the course of unimaginably vast periods of time by means of the extremely diverse and numerous experiences which are gathered during every single lifetime of development. It is spiritually structured, differentiated and – in the course of time – it becomes self-aware and self-recognizing.

Highly developed and neuronal complex living beings – those with a differentiated personality at least, as far developed as that of humans on this earth – thereby achieve the capability of recognising themselves as independent and individually definable personalities within the PSF. In the same way as a droplet of water is an independent part and yet in the ocean a part of the whole, the differentiated spirit, i.e. the soul of every human being, is an independent part and yet, within the PSF an inseparable part of the whole. As long as the human being is physically alive he is like a grain of sand in a heap. Although a part of it, he remains being a clearly separated part of the whole. All individual personal characteristics, all memories and capabilities which we gather in the course of our physical terrestrial life, remain preserved and become an independent spiritual unity, complete in every detail, within the PSF as a whole.

The possibility of there being constant interaction between the brain and a part of the initially undifferentiated PSF, which is differentiated by this brain, is the crucial point. This facilitates a purposeful and increasingly accelerated evolution of species and individuals – later also of societies and cultures. In return very slowly purely accidental developments fade into the background. At some time or other, decisions consciously controlled by a free will come to the fore. This free will is limited solely by construction-plan related parameters, such as natural laws, MCP and SCP, and also by self-induced social and political standards.

As to the individual human maturity –the new evolution so to speak *within* one species and no longer only *between* single species – the "intranet" emerges within the PSF. It becomes, as a product of this development, finally differentiated at the end of an individual physical life. Religiously accentuated

this is the individual immaterial soul of every human being[135]. It includes all characteristics of the personality. Everything is completely preserved beyond physical death. The human being remains fully self-aware after death. His soul is now simultaneously part of an unimaginable whole because in contrast to the physical part of the world the spiritual is undividable. The soul is simultaneously its individual whole and a part of a greater whole.
The soul does not leave the body during the process of dying but rather the body drops away from the soul. The soul is the real life!
The lifelong interactions between the spiritual world and the individual spirit, which controls its brain, take place in principle in all living beings that possess an appropriate cerebrum. As long as a living being *cannot* become aware of itself in its physical life, its spirit cannot mature to a self-aware and self-recognizing soul. Therefore, the *animal* spirit, i.e. the animal soul, which is differentiated at the time of death, remains being an impersonal part of the PSF which is unable to recognise itself.

Differentiated self-awareness and the capability for self-recognition paired with a certain free will and a lifelong individual spiritual maturation are the most important differences between humans and animals. They indicate the special qualitative quantum leap. As an individual personality, which is also independent after physical death, and as its own master, the soul will continue differentiating and improving itself within the PSF. From a purely subjective point of view, a difference to terrestrial life will hardly be discernible at first. Just as little do we notice that all seemingly solid matter, not least our own body, is in reality nothing solid at all (see Chapter 2.1).
In the PSF are found all thinkable and – presently for us – unthinkable possibilities for an accelerated, individual development. According to our knowledge, based on our logic, this development is on a par with our eternal BEING. Since we have experienced physical space during our physical life the spiritual BEING will be perceived as being at least equivalent right from the beginning.
The temporal perception of eternity is purely subjective, in the same way as time is perceived purely subjectively in a dream.

The "morphogenetic fields" postulated by the English biologist *Rupert Sheldrake* correlate to my model (see Chapter 4.6). There seems to be an active cooperation between the growing spiritual field humans still living "here" and the individual human souls – i.e. the complex spiritual "in*tra*nets" of people who are already dead.

---

[135] This is my very own use of the word soul for a preliminary finally differentiated individual spirit.

Please do not imagine your spiritual in*tra*net as being something technically as cold as it may sound here. On the contrary, it contains *everything* which constitutes the essence of your being, including your characteristics, properties and earlier actions; in short, it represents you in a much better and more extensive way than you could ever imagine. Every single body cell in every moment of your life is stored in the PSF as your very own coherent information.

Usually a spiritual interchange between "heaven and earth" takes place completely unnoticed for us as partners who are embodied "here". However, it may not be so rare that this interaction contributes to the individual and also collective change of behaviour in us humans.

Our actions can be influenced by such unconscious spiritual interchanges but they are certainly not controlled by them. Sometimes we speak of an "inspiration", probably without realizing how apt this expression really is.

Our concept of a "guardian angel" can also be integrated without difficulty into this schema of a constant spiritual interchange with closely connected souls which are manifested in the spiritual world.

The longer phase of life still lies in front of the individual human spirit upon its becoming a soul – i.e. after the physical death. As an individual (!) soul it starts out on its path towards its very own further and higher spiritual development. This is primarily to its own benefit, of course. Simultaneously, however, it becomes an indispensable part of the development of the spiritual whole.

With this notion the necessity for fulfilling the karmic law of mainly Asiatic religions by continuous "carnal" reincarnation no longer exists. Every human being will inevitably experience justice since justice as a spiritual and absolute experience must in fact exist in reality. Justice is in principle not just an invention and convention of humans. As such it would be completely meaningless since it would only be relative.

Even those who misused their own lives, and possibly also those of others, in the most hideous way will, in addition to self-punishing justice, experience mercy at some time or other, because this is also an absolute spiritual expression and must, therefore, really exist. If it were a purely human invention it would be without real meaning.

I have no doubt at all that the karmic law does indeed exist. However, it must not necessarily be fulfilled in a new physical life (see my book "Nobody Ever Dies!"). Furthermore, the perception of a carnal reincarnation contradicts the notion of the evolution of life and spirit. Life strives directly to become more spiritual.

In this direction evolution develops consistently and without detours an ever more complex nervous system until the human cerebrum has been achieved.
Passive information receivers turn into active and interactive creatures with a free will, self-awareness and self-recognition.
The spiritual side is unlimited and can infinitely develop further. All this is also found in the universe, the infinite and eternal information space.

5.2) Final Remarks

Our world is very diverse. Unilaterally philosophical or religious approaches are, therefore, misleading. Most great thinkers in history have probably been simultaneously right *and* wrong in their perceptions.
On the one hand our world has its determinist sides, as *Blaise Pascal (1623-1662)* and *Pierre Laplace (1749-1827)* already assumed. At the same time it has also been planned as being something indeterminist and unpredictable as *Karl Poppers (1902-1994)* maintained.
The basic principle of our world is surely teleological, i.e. target-oriented and purposeful as *Pierre Teilhard de Chardin (1881-1955)* claimed. At the same time it is also largely emergent, i.e. creatively and inventively generating something new, as *Karl Popper* and *John Eccles (1903-1997)* emphasized.
Early on, I myself already described our world as being "teleological and yet emergent, determinist and yet indeterminist" – just an amazingly multi-facetted world.
On the one hand it possesses vast materialistic aspects, as *René Descartes (1596-1650)* already claimed when he compared the world to a gigantic clockwork. On the other hand, the world is not materialistic at all since matter in the real sense of materialistic notion does not even exist. Just think back to the basic building block of all elements in the entire universe, the hydrogen. In a comparatively gigantic distance one tiny electron orbits around an atomic nucleus which is hardly any bigger and which consists of one proton. Between these two there is an absolute void (see Chapter 2.1).
Our world is certainly *not* panpsychistic as *Gottfried Wilhelm Leibniz (1646-1716)* and *Baruch de Spinoza (1632-1677)* believed, because "matter" generated from the PSF with the aid of MCP and SCP by means of EMR (according to Einstein "frozen energy") possesses no "smallest psychic units" at first, i.e. no monads, as Leibniz calls them.[136] Inanimate matter has no "soul"!

---

[136] PGF = pluripotent spiritual field; MBP = mathematical construction plan; GBP = spiritual construction plan; EMS = electromagnetic radiation or simplified "light" (see Chapter 1).

On the other hand any smallest finite BEING, i.e. any kind of inanimate matter provides the information to exist. This spiritual trace in every ever so small existence is eternally preserved. Thus Leibniz's and de Spinoza's perceptions can be easily integrated.

Our world is not pantheistic either, which means approximately "God is in everything" – an idea which goes back to de Spinoza. I believe that we must consider God with regard to the entire world and not merely, as is generally done, with regard to its physical side; it would then follow that God is transcendent and not contained in it.

My mathematical metaphor suggests this. "-1" and "+1" are rational realities (and are not invented by man); "i" on the other hand is irrational (but must exist as well, see Chapter 2.10). They are both derived from "i". In my opinion God is not part of the spiritual part of the world either, i.e. he is not immanent there.

Organic matter is generated everywhere and as soon as is possible in accordance to its construction plan which determines its target and purpose. It is capable of adopting the spiritual principle of life. With the expression "life" I describe any capability of complex organic structures to interact with the PSF. Like a radio station, which transmits programmes as long as it is complete and no transistor is missing, it constantly gathers information bits, those which contribute to its construction and function and later to its instinct and behaviour. All these attributes are implemented parallel to those provided by the biochemical genome. In the same way the living being transmits information bits back to the PSF thereby feeding its experiences and learned knowledge subconsciously and automatically into a pool which over a long period of time remains exclusively collective and species specific.

Such data then become available to their own species – and also to the entire evolution – for its emergent design process which is, due to mutations, naturally based on pure coincidences.

The capability of living beings to interact with the PSF is increasingly perfected by the development of extremely complex neuro-anatomical structures; this progresses at all times in a consequential and target-oriented manner. The end of this process is marked by a quantum leap whereby individuality, consciousness, self-awareness, self-recognition and free will within the scope of determined circumstances are developed. This leap has been taken by humans. Interactions with the infinite spiritual internet are now personalized and intensified in an accelerated form. An initially undifferentiated, immature area of the PSF – this should not be considered in a spatial sense – is increasingly differentiated in humans in the course of their physical lives. This applies on the one hand to their independent individual whole, and on the other also to their part of the inseparable real whole. In this way an independent, self-aware individual personality is generated. This personality remains developable even after its physical death but must then be understood as a purely spiritual but still individual personality.

The spiritual differentiation or maturation process also includes the initially "unconscious" use of already existing, ideal spiritual patterns for contents, emotions and properties of the PSF. Furthermore, it supports the development of an appropriate individuality and, finally, towards a perfection within a – by then –indestructible individual personality which finally is able to interact with its own spiritual background, to discover its various contents and properties and also to become self-aware. The personality is thereby enabled to order and to evaluate real interconnections, and to utilize the results consciously and for its own benefit and for that of all members of the society as well.

Since evolution no longer takes place between various species, and then for the entire collective species, but now rather within one and the same species mankind between single humans, ever wider gaps develop within these societies. This is similar to learning from a computer today, which is connected cable-free to the internet. Technology, science and the entirety of cultural developments are today inseparably connected with the utilization of this technology. However, where there is light, there is also shadow; everything inevitably has two sides. Not only good things are generated, but unfortunately also menacing ones. Therefore, the world must learn to domesticate the bad and, if possible, to turn it into something good in the long run.

The SCP is the basis for the target-oriented plan to build up an ever bigger general and also specific neuronal complexity.

Our world is not idealistic, even if it is based on certain ideas or forms (e.g. numbers, MCP). Most certainly a spiritual idea for everything does not exist right at the start, as *Plato (427-347 B.C.)* assumed, or a form as his student *Aristotle (384-33 B.C.)* later believed. There is an objective reality as *Ayn Rand*[137] *(1905-1982)* calls it. But there is no master blueprint for everything which, in the end, is completely developed, matured and finally differentiated.

However, spiritual ideas for certain basic principles must always have existed in the same way as our genes possess ideas in the biochemical sense for many things which remain in existence even if the physical feature based on it looks completely different later. Often these ideas become the basis or the connecting link for a completely different design. For example humans still

---

[137] Her real name is: Alissa Rosenbaum. Born in Russia, anti-communist, philosopher.

carry the disposition for developing gills although they will never have to live in water. They develop further, however, to become part of the face, mouth, neck, throat and ears.

From a purely materialistic point of view our world is also certainly emergent, as *Karl Popper* calls it, i.e. self-creating. However, it cannot leave its mathematical parameters (MCP).
Insofar the development of the world probably differs, for example, from the development of a human embryo which is not as emergent as the world, because emergence also involves creativity.
If we compare, however, the life of a human being from fertilization to death (and not only until birth) with the development of our world we will detect many correlations. The reason for this is that the course of life after birth proves to be in principle similarly emergent for a human being as it is for the world.
And this similarity is all the more pronounced the further advanced the human being is in his personal evolution. Maybe this is the reason why the difference between the development of a human being between fertilization and death and beyond and the development of the whole world is not all that significant.
It is possible that the world in many places and recurrently goes through a similar period when determination is stronger and creative emergence is diminished which might correspond approximately with the development of the human embryo. Such a period lasts always exactly until life enters the physical stage for the first time and starts to develop further, slowly at first and accelerating later. On our earth this has reached the level of humans today. Here *Pierre Teilhard de Chardin* is right again when he says that the world is "a God in emergence".
A monistic perception, according to which everything is made of one and the same substance, is neither completely right nor completely wrong. The origin of everything in this world is certainly spiritual, but of a different nature than that belonging to the spiritual world. My metaphor clearly defines this again (see Chapter 2.10). The "-1" as the symbol for the spiritual is derived from "i". Both are certainly of spiritual nature, although "i" remains irrational, whereas "-1" remains rational. The "i" being a metaphor for "God's spirit" must be different from the first reality, the spiritual world, which was created by it. And even if the physical world is generated by the spiritual one, in the same way as "+1" is derived from "-1", it is again a transformation. This renders any strict monistic perception obsolete. In contrast, dualism seems to be correct insofar as physical bodies are indeed generated and an independent spiritual

level exists which interacts with the bodies. However, should not this matter be attributed to the spirit again if it is generated from it through transformation? Insofar, at least our perceived world is a spiritual monistic one. You see, it all seems to be a question of definition.

Spirit, the origin of everything, is contained in all matter only in an abstract form, through numbers, coordinates or geometrical basic patterns. The spiritual information of its existence is engraved for ever in the PSF. Due to a creative emergent development, which is nonetheless determined in its basic principles, i.e. which is controlled, and strives towards physical structures being capable of interacting, i.e. it strives to create life, a mutual communication is built up between these structures and the infinite spiritual background.

Thereby the spiritual background becomes more and more structured and differentiated. The PSF itself matures. It is thus further developed to the highest possible perfection in a maximised multitude.

The human soul – by which I describe the spiritual structure at the time of the physical death – is a higher differentiation.

It is generated from a spiritually largely undifferentiated "substratum"[138] by means of fertilization and develops due to lifelong interactions aided by a physical but highly complex human brain.

In principle the same also happens in animals in a close interaction between the pluripotent spiritual field and every animal brain

The souls of humans, in contrast to those of animals, have meanwhile reached a completely new and much higher level of development. Due to the development of a differentiated consciousness and self-awareness and the capability for self-recognition – at least with regard to life on earth – only the human soul is able to recognise itself immediately after the physical death as a consciously acting part in the universal PSF. The additional spiritual possibilities available to it enable the soul to optimise itself further. This, however, also requires the perception of "real" space which is again a dimension of physical corporeality. This experience of space can only be acquired in the physical world. The spiritual and physical worlds are, therefore, mutually dependent.

Only the physical world provides a "real" spatiality and thus facilitates this experience which is essential for the further differentiation of the initially non-spatial condition in the spiritual world (PSF).

---

[138] Substratum is set in inverted commas since it is not to be seen as something physical.

It follows that death is not the absolute end for living beings who participate in the differentiation of the PSF – and this includes all those with highly developed complex neuronal structures.

Any even so rudimentary differentiation within the PSF exists forever. However, apart from humans no other living being on this earth today is able to recognise this for the lack of self-awareness and self-recognition. Due to a lack of consciousness, self-awareness and self-recognition the animal soul is finally differentiated as "individual soul", because it can only "be" but it cannot further progress to "grow". However, equally differentiated but as yet not self-aware sub-areas of the PSF will associate and will form a kind of collective information field on this level. It is the basis for the *subconscious* spiritual exchange with the brain of still living (animal) beings of the same species and on the same level of development. This is a passive exchange of information and thus rather unilateral (e.g. hypothesis of the morphogenetic fields according to *Sheldrake*, see Chapter 4.6).

This is the reason, by the way, why Sheldrake's fields are another indication that – at least as "a matter of routine" – reincarnation in its "classical" form, as a real return of the soul into a new body, cannot happen.

These "subconscious spiritual fields" mainly facilitate the implementation of improvements and simplifications for physically living creatures (animals) because of their largely unilateral passive interaction with the impersonally stored, really existing experiences of deceased animal generations. This might sensibly be termed as being a spiritual symbiosis. For a self-aware human being this interaction is personal and active.

The human spirit which develops and differentiates in a self-aware manner has the possibility of perfecting itself independently and actively within the PSF. To a certain extent it can even actively influence physically living beings. In most cases this happens directly by means of a subtle manipulation of the spirit of a physically living being.

In daydreams or during meditation many people can feel these influences. Certainly many ideas and problem solutions, which suddenly turn up *in* us, can be traced back to such influences. The term "inspiration"[139] would aptly describe this phenomenon.

The spirit, differentiated in the course of a human life, i.e. the human soul according to my definition, remains intact beyond physical death, of course. It stays where it already was while the human being was alive, as *Teilhard de Chardin* wrote. This means that not the soul changes after "death"; only the body, which helped to develop it, dies and perishes. It is the body which falls away from its further developed spirit, its soul.

---

[139] spirare: Latin = to breath, inspirare = to breath in or to blow into

It often happens that the separation from this body makes the soul become fully aware of its intrinsic, complete and absolutely integer existence for the very first time. This release can be compared to a "butterfly leaving its cocoon behind" as the Swiss physician Elisabeth Kübler-Ross (1926-2004) liked to phrase it.

The brain, as the initially necessary "differentiating hardware", is rather like an eggshell in which new life – being the human spirit in my analogy – is developed. Thus the brain is – again as a metaphor for the eggshell – a protective organ and simultaneously a shielding and – for some things indeed – an obstructive element. The brain is a reduction filter – it must be so because we are continuously bombarded with all kinds of information bits which we could not tolerate for one single day if we had to perceive them all consciously. The brain filters very nearly everything and discards it so that we are kept fit for our daily life in this physical world. There are some phenomena, situations and even some medical conditions where this filter does not work properly. Some affected people suddenly recognise things which remain hidden to others. For example there are autistic people who are hardly in contact with the external world and who are, therefore, not affected by many of its influences but who are able to quote prime number twins with 10, 12 or more positions[140], or who can play the piano expertly without showing any emotion.[141] Child prodigies probably belong into this category. Their brains "fail" as a reduction filter which in these cases has a beneficial effect. They all have one or the other direct and improved access to the information world of the PSF.

People with rare hereditary diseases also benefit from this, for example those with the Williams-Beuren-Syndrome (WBS). These people suffer some physical handicaps and although they have a rather reduced IQ they also have a peculiar mixture of particular spiritual strengths and weaknesses. For our purposes I would just like to mention one of their strengths especially. These patients are all, without exception, gifted with an amazing musical talent. One affected girl once said right to the point: "*I am thinking music*".

In a similar way as the autistic twins John und Michael described by the American neurologist and psychiatrist *Oliver Sacks (*1933)* seemed to have a direct contact to prime numbers, children with WBS seem to be imbued with a direct approach to melodies and rhythms, to music in general. For physiological reasons the reduction filter "brain" usually prevents us from gaining a deeper insight into the all-encompassing and all-penetrating information world of the PSF thereby helping us to master our "current" life

---

[140] O. Sacks, "The Man Who Mistook His Wife for a Hat", see List of References.
[141] Presently an exceptionally gifted autistic pianist who delights English audiences.

Our brain is thus more of a hindrance with respect to our gaining knowledge of the deep reality beyond our physical world, i.e. mainly of the world on the other side of our eggshell – and thus outside our brain. This perception finds a correlation in *Plato's* famous cave parable.

My unambiguous argument for a life after death results directly from my model. Humans do not survive their physical deaths in the sense of taking an impersonal, rather vague dive into an immense all-engulfing void. On the contrary death is for humans an important and individual level of development. It is simply the essential consequence of the teleological development of the world.
The human personality, which is self-aware and has already been differentiated in the course of life, remains unchanged, of course, and continuous to have all opportunity to further spiritual development. Yes, even more so: everyone *must* develop further and mature.
Every one of us is part of the further differentiation of an initially completely undifferentiated, pluripotent spiritual field (PSF).

The entire world is still constantly developing.
The creation is still in progress. A matured spirit, complete consciousness and self-awareness are the aim and objective. Everything is generated due to an incessant differentiation from a kind of spiritual "primordial soup". The necessary development aid (or catalyst) is the physical universe with all its bodies.

"Verily, verily, I say unto thee: Except a man is born again, he cannot see the kingdom of heaven"[142], and a little later: *"Verily, verily, I say unto thee: Except a men and women be born of water and of the Spirit he cannot enter into the Kingdom of God"*[143], this is what the Bible very aptly tells us.

It seems that the aim of this world is to create a finally differentiated world soul, perfected to the highest possible level and based on the highest possible amount of diversity. It may be that exactly this world soul is then a new God which would mean that the entire world is really an Emergent God. An Emergent God does not exclude other divinities, neither those in emergence nor those already in existence. Teilhard de Chardin clearly describes that which I call here the finally differentiated world soul as the Omega Point.

---

[142] Bible: New Testament; St. John, 03.03
[143] Bible: New Testament; St. John, 03.04

Every single human being, therefore, is to be considered as a very important component of this world. His existence is not threatened by his physical death, because his physical life is merely a transitional phase.

And, although every human being is only a small part of an immensely large whole, his uniqueness and great importance should not be disparaged.

A human being is not the manifestation of God, as *Baruch de Spinoza* believed. He is rather "God's Son"[144], in the sense of a divine "germ cell" and sits to "His right"[67] after the final differentiation of all viable matter. And when the famous German neo-Darwinist *Ernst Haeckel (1834-1919)* stated that the ontogenesis of humans, i.e. their individual development from a fertilized egg cell to their birth, is a kind of speeded-up phylogenesis, i.e. a presentation of their entire phylogenetic history from the very beginning of life on earth up to the emergence of humans as the temporary peak for this development, then maybe we can also say here: ontogenesis and phylogenesis are subordinate processes of a kind of *world* evolution and are simultaneously representations of its principles of development.

5.3) Excursion: Death is an Interface of Life

Humans are the first and only beings on earth which consciously experience their own "death" and the inevitable consequences of the total destruction of, at least, their bodies.

Therefore, humans suffer the worst of fates in contrast to animals which lead quite "carefree" lives.

Due to their being aware of their own "death" humans seem to be the only creatures which are condemned from the moment they are born. This may be the real meaning behind the concept of original sin as proclaimed by the Catholic Church. The christening frees a human being of this "sin" since he thereby confesses to the Christian faith and believes in the eternal life of his soul. This confession frees him of the burden he inherited when he became a human being. The original sin is not a sin in the real sense of the word but rather a burden or a load.

This should lead us to conclude that this is a religion which might also be considered as being the sum of intuitive experiences made by innumerable generations and which in principle has always been based on true knowledge. This does indeed support my conviction that basically all religions converge on the same truths. And much of this is already expressed in the contents of

---

[144] **Bibel:** New Testament, general Christian doctrine.

their doctrines. Unfortunately, however, the real quintessence is often mutilated by various influences and circumstances to the point of being unrecognizable.
If this is true, it would indicate the great importance especially of intuitive experiences. This would mean that scientists searching for knowledge should not lock out these experiences.
"We are not human beings who have spiritual experiences, but spiritual beings who have human experiences", this is how *Pierre Teilhard de Chardin* puts it. This emphasizes the necessity to put fundamental importance on intuition again because it is a form of spiritual experience.

Perhaps, if we were to reconsider basic religious principles it would make us correct and optimise our present more than often not unfortunate interpretations of actual observations.
This should, however, not result in a repeated reversal which would lead again to religious perceptions dominating natural science and other important sources of knowledge. No, that would result in a highly dangerous fundamentalism which is unfortunately still (or again?) at large.
Yet, it might just open some eyes in favour of a kind of "balance of power" with natural science. This could be a suitable basis for joining forces in the search for true knowledge without it being impeded by mutual discrimination. Each side would be taken seriously and could be compared to the other without breaking any taboos, and this not in the sense of competition but rather in the sense of complementing each other in a helpful way and for the benefit of their mutual progress.
"Oh, a king is the human being when he dreams – a beggar when he thinks."
This quotation from *Friedrich Hölderlin (1770-1843)* endorses the necessity of an intuitive search for knowledge.

Conclusion:
We know that matter is "frozen" energy *(Albert Einstein)*.
Energy is, as I pointed out here again, a kind of information in motion.
Physical structures are perishable; however, they continuously rearrange the energy contained in them. Energy never really disappears. Thence the information contained in it is preserved although its organization is altered. The evolution of all world events seems to be striving to develop ever more complex information structures. However, they are not the product of matter, but from the outset they are generated by information which is merely aided by matter.

Matter is the vehicle and the catalyst. It follows that such information complexes remain intact – and can develop further depending on their level of complexity – even long after the matter has changed. Therefore, death does not really exist.

"There is no escape from eternity!" (Rainer Maria Rilke, 1875-1926)

However, how does *Christian Morgenstern (1871-1914)* phrase it?
"A truth can only take effect when the recipient is ready for it!
It is not due to truth, therefore, that humans are still lacking so much wisdom!"

References

Alberts, B., „Molecular Biology of the Cell", Garland (1983)
Altea, R., „Sag Ihnen, daß ich lebe", Goldmann (1995)
D'Aquili, E.G., A.B. Newberg, "The Mystical Mind: Probing the Biology of Religious Experience", Augsburg Fortress Publishers (1999)
Araoz, D.L., "Selbsthypnose – Kreative Imagination in Beruf und Alltag", Econ (1992)
Ash, D., P. Hewitt, „Wissenschaft der Götter - Zur Physik des Übernatürlichen", (1991)
Asimov, I., J. Asimov, „Kosmos u. Materie – Wiss. an der Schwelle zum dritten Jahrtaus", (1995)
Auffermann, B., J. Orschiedt, "Die Neandertaler", Theiss, Stuttgart (2002)
Bache, Ch. M., „Lifecycles: Reincarnation and the Web of Life", Paragon House (1990)
Bagemihl, B., "Biological exuberance: animal homsex. and natural diversity", (1999)
Bambaren, S., "Der träumende Delphin", Piper (1999)
Barbour, J., "The End of Time", Oxford Univ. Press (2000)
Barnett, S.A., Instinkt und Intelligenz, Fischer (1972)
Barrow, J.D., J. Silk, „Die asymm. Schöpfung – Urspr. u. Ausdehnung d. Universums", (1986)
Barrow, J.D., "Ein Himmel voller Zahlen – Auf den Spuren mathematischer Wahrheit", Rowohlt (1999); Original: "Pi in the Sky", Oxf. Univ. Press (1992)
Bauby, J.D., "The diving-bell and the butterfly", Wheeler Pub. (1997)
Bell, J.S., „Speakable and Unspeakable in Quantum Mechanics", Cambridge Univ. Press (1987)
Berger, K., „Ist mit dem Tod alles aus?", Quell (1997)
Bindel, E., "Die geistigen Grundlagen der Zahlen", Verlag Freies Geistleben (1958, 98)
Bindel, E., "Die Zahlengrundlagen der Musik im Wandel der Zeiten", (1985)
Bischof, M., „Biophotonen-Das Licht in unseren Zellen", Zweitausendeins (1995)
Blackmore, S., "Die Macht der Meme", Spektrum d. Wiss. Dossier 2 (2002)
Block, A., "Du sollst nicht morden", A. Block Eigenverlag, Dortmund (1989)
Block, A., "Alle suchen Dich", A. Block Eigenverlag, Dortmund (1991)
Born, G.V.R., „Forschung macht frei-Freih. u. Grenz. der Wiss.", Festrede b. Grünenthal (1996)
Breuer, R., „Immer Ärger mit dem Urknall", rororo (1996)
Briggs, J., F.D. Peat, „Die Entdeckung des Chaos", Hanser (1990)
Brocher, T., „Stufen des Lebens", Kreuz, Stuttgart
Brüderlin, R., "Akustik für Musiker", bosse (1983)
Caldwell, R.R., M. Kamionkowski, "Der Nachhall d. Urknalls", Spektr. d. Wiss. Doss 2 (2002)
Capra, F., „The Turning Point", USA (1987)
Capra, F., „Uncommon Wisdom. Coversations with Remarkable People", USA (1987)
Cerminaria, G., „Many Mansions", W. Sloane Ass., New York (1950)
Clément, C., "Theos Reise – Roman über die Religionen der Welt", Hanser (1998)
Conze, E., "Buddhist Scriptures", Harmondsworth/Great Britain (1959)
Coward, H., „Life after death in the religions of the world", Orbis Books, N.Y. (1997)
Cox-Chapman, M., „The Case for Heaven", G.P. Putnam's Sons, NY (1995)
Cumont, F., "After Life in Roman Paganism", New Haven (1922)
Dacqué, E.: „Vermächtnis der Urzeit. Grundprobleme der Erdgeschichte". Aus dem Nachlaß hrsg. von M. Schröter (1948)
Dalei Lama, "Worte der Hinwendung", Herder (1993)
Dam, W.C. van, „Tote sterben nicht –- Erfahrungsberichte zwischen Leben und Tod", (1995)
Damasio, A.R., "Wie das Gehirn Geist erzeugt", Spektrum d. Wiss. Dossier 2 (2002)
Damman, E., „Erkenntnisse jenseits von Zeit und Raum -- Die Wende im naturwissenschaftlichen Denken", Knaur (1990)
Davidson, J., „Natural Creation & the Formative Mind", Element Books Ltd., UK (1991)
Davies, P., „God and the New Physics", J.M. Dent & Sons, London (1986)
Davies, P., „About Time. Einstein's Unfinished Revolution", Simon & Schuster, New York (1995)
Davis, P.J., R. Hersch, "Descartes' Dream - The World According to Mathematics", Penguin (London) 1986

Descartes, R., „Philosophische Schriften - in einem Band", Meiner (1996)
Diamond, J., "Why Is Sex Fun?" BasicBooks, N.Y.(1997)
Diederichs, E., „Laotse - Tao te king - Das Buch vom Sinn und Leben", Diederichs (1972)
Ditfurth, H. von, „Wir sind nicht nur von dieser Welt", dtv (1985)
Ditfurth, H. von, „Unbegreifliche Realität", Lingen (1987)
Ditfurth, H. von, „Innenansichten eines Artgenossen", Claassen (1989)
Ditfurth, H. von, „Kinder des Weltalls", Weltbild (1990)
Ditfurth, H. von, „Der Geist fiel nicht vom Himmel", Weltbild (1990)
Ditfurth, H. von, V. Arzt, „Dimensionen des Lebens - Reportagen aus der Naturwiss." (1990)
Diverse Autoren, "Forschung im 21. Jahrhundert", Spektrum der Wissenschaft Spezial (2000)
Diverse Autoren, "Gravitation – Urkraft des Kosmos", Sterne und Weltraum, Spezial 6 (2001)
Diverse Autoren, "Schöpfung ohne Ende – Die Geburt des Kosmos", Sterne und Weltraum, Spezial 2 (2002)
Diverse Autoren, "Die Evolution des Menschen", Spektrum der Wissenschaft, Dossier (2002)
Doucet, F.W., „Die Toten leben unter uns --- Forschungsobjekt Jenseits", Ariston (1987)
Dürr, H.-P., "Physik und Transzendenz", Scherz (1989)
Dürr, H.-P., W. Ch. Zimmerli, „Geist und Natur --- Über den Widerspruch zwischen naturwissenschaftlicher Erkenntnis und philosophischer Welterfahrung", Scherz (1991)
Durant, W., "The Story of Civilization", Simon & Schuster
Eady, B., „Embraced by the Light", Gold Leaf Press, CA/USA (1994)
Eccles, J.C., D.N. Robinson, "The Wonder of Being Human. Our Brain and Our Mind", The Free Press, New York (1984)
Eccles, J. C., „Creation of the Self", Routledge, London, New York (1989)
Eccles, J.C., „Gehirn und Seele. Erkenntnisse der Neurophysiologie", Piper (1991)
Eccles, J. C., „How the Self controls its Brain", Springer (1994)
Eddington, A, „Wissenschaft und Mystizismus", aus: „Das Weltbild der Physik und ein Versuch seiner philosophischen Deutung", F. Vieweg & Sohn (1935)
Einstein, A., L. Infeld, „Die Evolution der Physik", Weltbild (1991)
Endres, C.M., A. Schimmel, „Das Mysterium d. Zahl-Zahlensymb. im Kulturvergleich" (1995)
Elsaesser-Valarino, E., "On the Other Side of Life – Exploring the phenomenon of the near-death experience", Perseus books (1999)
Erben, H.K., „Die Entwicklung der Lebewesen", Piper (1988)
Ernst, H., „Die Weisheit des Körpers - Kräfte der Selbstheilung", Piper (1993)
Ewald, G., „Die Physik u. das Jenseits-Spurensuche zw. Philos. u. Naturwiss.", Pattloch (1998)
Federmann, R., H. Schreiber, „Botschaft aus dem Jenseits - Zeugnisse des Okkulten" (1992)
Ferris, T., „The Mind's Sky, Bantam Books, New York (1992)
Findlay, A., „Beweise für ein Leben nach dem Tod", Bauer (1983)
Fischer, E.P., "Grenzen des Wissens", Spektrum d. Wiss. Dossier 2 (2002)
Ford, A., „Unknown but Known. My Adventure into the Meditative Dimension", Harper & Row, New York (1968)
Ford, A., "The Life beyond Death", G.P. Putnam's Sons, N.Y. (1971)
Fox, M., R. Sheldrake, "The Physics of Angels. A Realm where Spirit and Science meet", (1996)
Franz, V, "Das Werden der Organismen", Jena (1924)
Genz, H., „Die Entdeckung des Nichts - Leere und Fülle im Universum", Hanser (1994)
Ghyka, M., "The Geometry of Art and Life", Dover/New York (1977)
Goldberg, Ph., „Die Kraft der Intuition", Scherz (1988)
Greene, B., "The Elegant Universe. Superstrings, HiddenDimensions, and the Quest for the Ultimate Theory", W.W. Norton&Co., N.Y. (2000)
Gribbin, J., „Jenseits der Zeit --- Experimente mit der vierten Dimension", Bettendorf (1994)
Gribbin, J., „In the Beginning. After COBE and before the Big Bang", Little, Brown and Company, Boston (1993)
Gribbin, J., M. Rees, „Cosmic Coincidences. Dark Matter, Mankind, and Anthropic Cosmology", Bantam Books, New York (1989)
Gribbin, J., "Schrödinger's Kitten and the Search for Reality", Weidenfeld & Nicholson, London (1995)

Guggenheim, B., J. Guggenheim, „Hello from Heaven", ADC Project, Longwood, FL/USA (1995)
Gurwitsch, A.G., „Über den Begriff des embryonlaen Feldes". Wilhelm Roux' Archiv für Entwicklungsmechanik der Organismen. Bd. 51 (1922)
Hallmann, W., W. Ley, "Handbuch Raumfahrttechnik", Hanser (1999)
Halpern, P., „Wurmlöcher im Kosmos - Modelle für Reisen durch Zeit und Raum", List (1994)
Haug, M., E.W. West, "The book of Arda Viraf", Bombay/London (1872)
Hawking, St.W., "A Brief History of Time: From the Big Bang to Black Holes", Bantam Books, New York (1988)
Hawking, St.W., "Is the End in Sight for Theoretical Physics? – An Inaugural Lecture", Press Syndicate of the Univ. of Cambridge, UK (1980)
Hayward, J.W., „Shifting Worlds, Changing Minds", Shambhala Publ. Inc., Boston, MA, (1987)
Hazen, R.M., "Der steinige Ursprung des Lebens", Spektrum d. Wiss. Dossier 2 (2002)
Heilige Schrift (Die Bibel): Die Heilige Schrift des Alten und Neuen Bundes, Herder (1965)
Heilige Schrift: die vierundzwanzig Bücher der Heiligen Schrift, übersetzt von L. Zunz, Goldschmidt (1995)
Heilige Schrift (Die Bibel): Elberfelder Bibel, revidierte Fassung, Brockhaus (1996)
Heimpel, H., Th. Heuss, B. Reiffenberg, „Die großen Deutschen", Ullstein (1983)
Hengge, P., „Es steht in der Bibel", Verlag Wissenschaft und Politik (1994)
Hensel, W., "Pflanzen in Aktion – Krümmen, Klappen, Schleudern", Spektrum (1993)
Herbig, J., „Im Anfang war das Wort", Hanser (1985)
Hermann, U., „Knaurs etymologisches Lexikon", Droemer Knaur (1983)
Hermann, U., et al., „Das deutsche Wörterbuch", Knaur (1985)
Herneck, F., „Einstein und sein Weltbild", Buchverlag Der Morgen (1976)
Høeg, P., "Fräulein Smillas Gespür für Schnee", Hanser (1996)
Högl, St., "Near-Death Experiences, Religions and the World Beyond. A Glance at the Other Side of Life and its Influence on Mankinds Religions", Magisterial-Treatise, University of Regensburg (1996)
Hoffmann, B., „Relativity and Its Roots", Scient. Amer. Books, NY (1983)
Hooper, J., D. Teresi, „The three pound universe", Macmillan Publishing Company, New York (1986)
Horneck, G., C. Baumstark-Khan, "Astrobiology, The Quest for the Conditions of Life", Springer (2001)
Hornung, E., „Geist der Pharaonenzeit", Artemis (1989)
Hornung, E., „Die Nachtfahrt d. Sonne - Eine altägypt. Beschreibung des Jenseits" (1991)
Huber, G., „Das Fortleben nach dem Tode", Origo (1996)
Ikeda, D., „Das Rätsel des Lebens - eine buddhistische Antwort", Herbig (1994)
Jakoby, B., "Auch Du lebst ewig – Die Ergebnisse der modernen Sterbeforschung" (2000)
Jürgenson, F., „Sprechfunk mit Verstorbenen - Prakt. Kontaktherstell. mit d. Jenseits" (1981)
Jung, C.G., „Briefe, Erster Band 1906-1945", Walter (1972)
Jung, C.G., A. Jaffé, „Erinnerungen, Träume, Gedanken von C.G. Jung", Walter (1976)
Junghanss, V., "Unterwegs zu den absoluten Dimensionen" BoD (2005)
Kahan, G., „Einsteins Relativitätstheorie --- zum leichten Verständnis für jedermann" (1987)
Kaku, M., „Hyperspace. A Scientific Odyssey Through Parallel Universes, Time Warps, And The Tenth Dimension", Oxford Univ. Press, N.Y. (1995)
Kaplan, R.W., „Der Ursprung des Lebens. Biogenetik. Ein Forschungsgebiet heutiger Naturwissenschaft", (1978)
Kaplan, R., E. Kaplan, "The Art of the Infinite: The Pleasure of Mathematics", Oxford Univ. Press, N.Y. (2003)
Kleesattel, W., "Überleben in Eis, Wüste und Tiefsee: wie Tiere Extreme meistern" (1999)
Klimkeit, H.J., "Der iran. Auferstehungsglaube. Tod u. Jenseits im Glauben der Völker" (1978)
Klivington, K.A., "The Science of Mind", MIT Press, Cambridge/USA (1989)
Knoblauch, H., "Berichte aus dem Jenseits. Mythos und Realität der Nahtod-Erfahrung" (1999)
Knoblauch, H., H.G. Soeffner, I. Schmied und B. Schnettler, "Todesnähe. Interdisziplinäre Zugänge zu einem außergewöhnlichen Phänomen", Universitätsverlag Konstanz 1999
Krisciunas, K., B. Yenne, „Atlas des Universums", Lechner (1992)

Kübler - Ross, E., „Über den Tod und das Leben danach", Silberschnur (1994)
Kübler - Ross, E., „Sterben lernen - Leben lernen --- Fragen und Antworten" (1995)
Kübler - Ross, E., „The Wheel of Life", Scribner, New York (1997)
Küng, H., „Ewiges Leben?", Piper (1982)
Küppers, B.-O., "Ordnung aus dem Chaos", Piper (1987)
Kunsch, K., St. Kunsch, "Der Mensch in Zahlen – Eine Datensammlung in Tabellen mit über 20.000 Einzelwerten", Spektrum (2000)
Laack, W. van, "Plädoyer für ein Leben nach dem Tod und eine etwas andere Sicht der Welt", Aachen (1999) und BoD-Libri, Hamburg (2000)
Laack, W. van, "Key to Eternity", (2000)
Laack, W. van, "A Better History of Our World, Vol. 1, The Universe, Vol. 2, Life, Vol. 3, Death" (2001-2003)
Laack, W. van, "Nobody Ever Dies!", Hamburg (2005)
Laack, W. van, "Nah-Todeserfahrungen – Vorhof zum Himmel oder bloß Hirngespinste?", die Drei, Z. f. Anthropos. in Wissensch.., Kunst u. soz. Leben, 12 (2004)
Laack, W. van, "Ohne Geist läuft wenig! – Teil 1, Kann aus Neuronen Bewusstsein entstehen?", die Drei, Z. f. Anthropos. in Wissensch.., Kunst u. soz. Leben, 2 (2005)
Laack, W. van, "Ohne Geist läuft wenig! - Teil 2, Zur Unfreiheit verdammt?", die Drei, Z. f. Anthropos. in Wissensch.., Kunst u. soz. Leben 3(2005)
Lashley, K.S., „Brain mechanism and Intelligence", Chicago Univ. Press (1929)
Lashley, K.S., „In Search of the Engram", Symposium Soc. Exp. Biol. 4 (1950)
Laudert-Ruhm, G., „Jesus von Nazareth, Das gesicherte Basiswissen", Kreuz (1996)
LeCron, L.M., "The complete guide to hypnosis", USA (1973)
Linke, D.B., "Die Freiheit und das Gehirn", C.H. Beck (2005)
Löbsack, Th., „Versuch und Irrtum --- Der Mensch: Fehlschlag der Natur", Bertelsmann (1974)
Löw, R., „Die neuen Gottesbeweise", Pattloch (1994)
Lomborg, B., "The Sceptical Enviromentalist", Cambridge Press (2001)
Lurija, A.R., „Einführung in die Neuropsychologie", rororo (1992)
Lüth, P., "Der Mensch ist kein Zufall", Deutsche Verlags-Anstalt (1983)
Mann, A.T., „The Elements of Reincarnation", Element Books, UK (1995)
Margenau, H., „The Miracle of Existence", Ox Bow, Woodbrisge CT (1984)
Matthiesen, E., „Das persönliche Überleben des Todes", de Gruyter (1987)
Meckelburg, E., „Hyperwelt -- Erfahrungen mit dem Jenseits", Langen-Müller (1995)
Meckelburg, E., "Wir alle sind unsterblich", Langen Müller (2000)
Méric, E., A. Ysabeau, „Seele ohne Grenzen: Übernatürliche Phänomene und der menschliche Körper als Indikator der Persönlichkeit", Gondrom (1997)
Mielke, Th.R.P., "Coelln – Stadt, Dom, Fluss", Schneekluth (2000)
Miller, S.L., H.C. Urey, „Organic compound synth. on the primitive earth", Science, 130 (1959)
Miller, S., „After Death. Mapping the Journey", Simon &Schuster, NY (1997)
Moewes, J., „Für 12 Mark 80 durch das Universum - über Zeit, Raum und Liebe" (1996)
Moody, R.A., „Life after Life", Mockingbird Books, USA (1975)
Moody, R.A., „Reflections on Life after Life", Bantam Books, NY (1977)
Moody, R.A., „The Light Beyond", Bantam Books, New York (1988)
Moody, R.A., P. Perry, „Reunions . Visionary Encounters with Departed Loved Ones", Villard Books, New York (1993)
Moody, R.A., P. Perry, „Coming Back. A Research Odyssey into the Meaning of Past Lives", Bantam Books, New York (1991)
Moosleitner, G.P., "Die unsterbliche Seele der Menschheit", Libri (2000)
Morgan, M., "Mutant Message Down Under", Harper Collins, N.Y. (1994)
Morse, M., „Closer to the Light", (1990)
Morgan, M., "Traumfänger", Goldmann (1998)
Morse, M, P. Perry, „Verwandelt vom Licht. Über die transformierende Wirkung von Nahtoderfahrungen", Knaur (1994)
Newberg, A., V. Rause, "Why God won't go away: Brain Science & Biology of Belief", (2001)

Nuland, Sh. B., „How we die", A. A. Knopf, New York (1993)
Oesterreich, K.T., „Der Okkultismus im modernen Weltbild", Dresden (1921)
Otto. M., "Worte wie Spuren – Weisheit der Indianer", Herder (1985)
Ozols, J.,. "Über die Jenseitsvorstellungen des vorgeschichtlichen Menschen". in: Tod und Jenseits im Glauben der Völker. Hg. Hans-Joachim Klimkeit. Harassowitz (1978)
Papst, W., „Der Götterbaum", Herbig (1994)
Passian, R., "Das Jenseits – reine Glaubenssache?", Weber-Verlag (2000)
Paulos, J.A., „Beyond Numeracy", A.A. Knopf, New York (1991)
Patch, H.R., "The Other World"
Penfield, W., „The mystery of the Mind", Princeton Univ. Press (1975)
Penfield, W., L. Roberts, „Speech and brain Mechanism", Princeton Univ. Press (1959)
Penrose, R., „Shadows of the Mind", Oxford Univ. Press, New York (1994)
Philberth, B., "Der Dreieine", Christiana-Verlag(CH) (1971)
Platon, Sämtliche Werke, Bd. 3: Phaidon, Politeia. Deutsch von F. Schleiermacher. Rowohlts Klassiker der Literatur und der Wissenschaft Nr.27, Rowohlt
Plichta, P., „Das Primzahlkreuz - Bd. 1: Im Labyrinth des Endlichen", Quadropol (1991)
Plichta, P., „Das Primzahlkreuz - Bd. 2: Das Unendliche", Quadropol (1991)
Plichta, P., „Gottes geheime Formel --- Die Entschlüsselung des Welträtsels und der Primzahlcode", Langen-Müller (1995)
Plichta, P., „Das Primzahlkrkeuz - Bd. 3: Die 4 Pole der Ewigkeit", Quadropol (1998)
Prawda, W., "Der Fall – Von Geist zu Materie und Mensch", BoD (2004)
Pribram, K., „Languages of the Brain", Englewood Cliffs (1971)
Prigogine, I., Vom Sein zum Werden", Piper (1982)
Prigogine, I., I. Stengers, „Dialog mit der Natur. Neue Wege naturwiss.Denkens", Piper (1993)
Popper, K.R., J.C. Eccles, „Das Ich und sein Gehirn", Piper (1982)
Popper, K.R., J.C. Eccles, „The Self and Its Brain – An Argument for Interactionism", Springer (1977)
Popper, K.R., „Alles Leben ist Problemlösen - Über Erkenntnis, Geschichte und Politik"(1994)
Pribram, K., „Languages of the Brain", Englewood Cliffs (1971)
Prigogine, I., I. Stengers, „Das Paradox der Zeit --- Zeit, Chaos und Quanten", Piper (1993)
Pschyrembel, W., „Klinisches Wörterbuch", de Gruyter (1977)
Quinn, H.R., M.S. Witherell, "Die Asymmetrie zwischen Materie und Antimaterie", Spektrum d. Wiss. Dossier 2 (2002)
Radhakrishnan, "The Principal Upanishads", London (1953)
Reeves, H., J. de Rosnay, Y. Coppens, D. Simonnet, "Die schönste Geschichte der Welt", Bastei-Lübbe (1998)
Reichholf, J.H., „Das Rätsel der Menschwerdung --- Die Entstehung des Menschen im Wechselspiel mit der Natur", DVA (1990)
Reitz, M., „Leben jenseits der Lichtjahre --- Die Wissenschaften auf der Suche nach außerirdischen Intelligenzen", Insel (1998)
Ricken, F., „Lexikon der Erkenntnistheorie und Metaphysik", C.H. Beck (1984)
Ring, K., „Heading Toward Omega", USA (1984)
Riordan, M., "The Shadows of Creation. Dark Matter and the Structure of the Universe", W.H. Freeman & Co., New York (1991)
Robert, R., "Chaostheorie und Schmetterlingseffekt", Spektrum d. Wiss. Dossier 2 (2002)
Roederer, J.G., "Physikalische und psychoakustische Grundlagen der Musik", Springer (1977)
Ruelle, D., „Zufall und Chaos", Springer (1993)
Rose, St.P.R., S. Harding, „Training increases ^{3}H fucose incorporation in chick brain only if followed by a memory storage", Neuroscience 12 (1984)
Rose, St.P.R., A. Csillag, „Passive avoidance training results in lasting changes in deoxyglucose metabloism in left hemisphere regions of chick brain", Behavioural and Neural Biology 44 (1985)
Ross, D., „The work of Aristotle; Select fragments. ", Clarendon Press, Oxford (1952)
Rüber, G., "Kleine gesammelte Geschichten aus Köln", Engelhorn-Verlag.
Ruppert, H.J., „Okkultismus --- Geisterwelt oder neuer Weltgeist ?", Edition Coprint (1990)
Ryzl, M., „Das große Handbuch der Parapsychologie", 3 Bde., Ariston (1978)

Ryzl, M., „Der Tod ist nicht das Ende --- Von der Unsterblichkeit geistiger Energie" (1981)
Sabom, M.B., „Erinnerungen an den Tod. Eine medizinische Untersuchung", Goldmann 11741
Sachs, R., "Perfect Endings. A Conscious Approach to Dying and Death", Healing Arts Press, Rochester (1998)
Sacks, O., „A leg to stand on", G. Duckworth, London (1984)
Sacks, O., "The Man Who Mistook His Wife For a Hat", Summit Books/ Simon & Schuster, New York (1985)
Sagan, C., A. Druyan, „Shadows of Forgotten Ancestors", Random House, New York (1992)
Sahm, P.R., G.P.J. Thiele, "Der Mensch im Kosmos", Verlag Facultas (1998)
Sahm, P.R., G.P.J. Thiele, "Der Mensch im Kosmos II", Shaker Verlag (2000)
Sandvoss, E.R., "Geschichte der Philosophie – Bd. 1 u. 2", dtv (1989)
Schäfer, H., „Brücke zwischen Diesseits und Jenseits --- Theorie und Praxis der Transkommunikation", Bauer (1989)
Schiebler, W., „Der Tod, die Brücke zu neuem Leben --- Beweise für ein persönliches Fortleben nach dem Tod. Der Bericht eines Physikers." Silberschnur (1991)
Schmid, G.B., "The six fundamental characteristics of chaos and their clinical relevance to psychiatry: A new hypothesis for the origin of psychosis. In: Orsucci, F., "The Complex of Matters of Mind", Vol. 6 (1998)
Schmid, G.B., "Is Distant Mentation in Livin Systems a Quantum teleportation Phenomenon? Kantonale Psychiatrische Klinik Rheinau (1999)
Schmid, G.B., "Tod durch Vorstellungskraft – Das Geheimnis psychogener Todesfälle" (2001)
Schmidt-Degenhard, M., Die oneiroide Erlebnisform: Zur Problemgeschichte und Psychopathologie des Erlebens fiktiver Wirklichkeiten" (1992)
Schmidt, H., "Das Märchen vom Urknall – oder Der Kosmos, ein unsterblicher Organismus", BoD Norderstedt (2004)
Schneider-Janessen, K., "Biochemische Persönlichkeitsforschung", Springer (1990)
Schröder, G.L., „Schöpfung und Urknall", Bertelsmann (1990)
Schröter-Kunhardt, M., "Das Jenseits in uns", Psychologie heute, Heft 6 (1993)
Schröter-Kunhardt, M., "Erfahrungen Sterbender während des klinischen Todes", in "Sterben und Tod in der Medizin", Wiss. Verlagsgesellschaft (1996)
Schröter-Kunhardt, M., "Nah-Todeserfahrungen aus psychiatrisch-neurologischer Sicht", In: "Todesnähe- Wissenschaftliche Zugänge zu außergewöhnlichen Phänomenen", Univ.-Verlag, Konstanz (1999)
Scholem, G.G., "Major Trends in Jewish Mysticism" , Schocken Books (1995)
Schroeder, G.L., „Genesis and the Big Bang", Bantam books, N.Y. (1990)
Schulte, G., "Neuromythen" Zweitausendeins (2000)
Seife, Ch., "Zero. The Biography of a Dangerous Idea", Viking, N.Y. (2000)
Schweitzer, A., "Kultur und Ethik", Beck (1981)
Seife, Ch., "Zwilling der Unendlichkeit", Goldmann (2002)
Sheldrake, R., „The Presence of the Past", UK (1988)
Sheldrake, R., „Das Gedächtnis. der Natur - Das Geheimnis der Entstehung der Formen in der Natur" (1992)
Sheldrake, R., "A New Science of Life", Park Street Press (1995)
Sheldrake, R., „Wunder und Geheimnis des Übersinnlichen --- Sieben Phänomene, die das Denken revolutionieren", Weltbild (1996)
Siegel, R.K., "The Psychology of Life after Death", in American Psychologist 35 (1980)
Singh, K., „The Mystery of Death", Delhi (1975)
Singh, S., "Fermats letzter Satz", dtv (2000)
Spirik, H.J., H.R. Loos, „Nachrichten aus dem Jenseits --- Erforschung paranormaler Tonbandstimmen", Ennsthaler (1996)
Spitzer, M., "Lernen – Gehirnforschung und die Schule des Lebens", Spektrum (2002)
Spitzer, M., "Selbstbestimmen", Spektrum-Verlag (2004)
Sprenger, W., „Der Tag, an dem mein Tod starb", Nie/Nie/Sagen (1995)
Steffen, P., "Eine Geometrie der Zeit", Stema-Verlag (1999), BoD LIBRI, Hamburg

Stelzner, M., "Die Weltformel der Unsterblichkeit", Verlag für außergew. Perspektiven (1996)
Stevenson, I., „Children who remember previous lives", USA (1989)
Stratenwerth, I., Th. Bock, „Stimmen hören -- Botschaften aus der inneren Welt", Kabel (1998)
Struck, P., „Netzwerk Schule", Hanser (1998)
Susskind, L., "Schwarze Löcher u. das Informationsparadoxon", Spektr. d. Wiss. Doss. 2(2002)
Tarassow, L., „Wie der Zufall will?", Spektrum (1998)
Tarter, J.C., C.F. Chyba, "Gibt es außerirdisches Leben?", Spektrum d. Wiss. Dossier 2 (2002)
Teilhard de Chardin, P., „Die Entstehung des Menschen", C.H. Beck (1981)
Teilhard de Chardin, P., „Der Mensch im Kosmos", C.H. Beck (1981)
Terhart, F., „Das Geheimnis der Eingeweihten --- Was spirituelle Persönlichkeiten uns erschließen", Ariston (1996)
Time-Life-Bücher, „Fernöstliche Weisheiten", Time-Life (1991)
Tipler, F.J., „The Physics of Immortality", Doubleday, New York (1994)
Toynbee, A., "Mankind and Mother Earth – A Narrative History of the World", Oxford Univ. Press, UK (1976)
Trefil, J., "The Dark Side of the Universe", C. Scribner's Sons, NY (1988)
Ulke, K.D., „Vorbilder im Denken", Gondrom (1998)
Wachholder, K., „Die Entwicklung der lebenden Natur und die Frage des Bestehens fortschreitender Vervollkommnung", In: Studium Generale, 2 (1949)
Wapnick, K., „A Course in Miracles", Roscoe, N.Y. (1983)
Weinberg, St., „The First Three Minutes. A Modern View of the Origin of the Universe", Basic Books Publ., New York (1977)
White, M., J. Gribbin, „Stephen Hawking – A Life in Science", Viking, London (1992)
Wiesendanger, H., „Wiedergeburt - Herausforderung für das westliche Denken", Fischer (1991)
Wilber, K., "The Spectrum of Consciousness", USA (1987)
Wilber, K., "Grace and Grit", Shambala Publ. Boston/USA (1991)
Wilder-Smith, A.E., „Die Naturwissenschaften kennen keine Evolution. Experimentelle und theoretische Einwände gegen die Evolutionstheorie" (1978)
Wolf, F.A., „The Body Quantum", Universe Seminars Inc. (1986)
Wolpert, L., The Triumph of the Embryo", Oxford Univ. Press (1991)
Woltersdorf, H.W., „Denn der Geist ist`s, der den Körper baut --- Die Irrlehren des wissenschaftlichen Materialismus", Langen-Müller (1991)
Zahrint, H., „Jesus aus Nazareth --- Ein Leben", Piper (1987)
Zahrint, H., „Das Leben Gottes - aus einer unendlichen Geschichte", Piper (1997)
Zaleski, C., "Otherworld Journeys. Accounts of Near-Death Experience in Medieval and Modern Times", Oxford Univ. Press (1987)
Zimmer, C., "Parasitus Rex", Umschau/Braus (2001)

Prof. Dr. med. Walter van Laack

English Books since 2000:

To Perceive The World With Logic
ISBN 978-3-936624-08-3, Softcover (SC), 340 p., (2007), 29,80 €

Nobody Ever Dies!
ISBN 978-3-936624-03-8, Softcover (SC), 272 p., (2005), 24,80 €

A Better History of Our World
Vol. 1, "The Universe"
ISBN 978-3-8311-1490-0, Softcover, 188 p. (2001), 15,80 €
Vol. 2, "Life"
ISBN 978-3-8311-2597-5, Softcover, 236 p. (2002), 17,80 €
Vol. 3, "Death"
ISBN 978-3-936624-01-4, Softcover, 276 p. (2003), 19,80 €

Key To Eternity
ISBN 978-3-8311-0344-7, Softcover, 256 p. (2000), 17,80 €

German Books since 1999:

Mit Logik die Welt begreifen
ISBN 978-3-936624-04-5, Softcover, 380 p., (2005) 29,80 €
ISBN, 978-3-936624-07-6, Hardcover, 380 p. (2005), 39,80 €

Wer stirbt, ist nicht tot!
ISBN 3-936624-00-7, Softcover, 312 p., (2003), 24,80 €
ISBN 978-3-936624-06-9, Hardcover, 312 p., 2. edit. (2005), 35,-- €

Eine bessere Geschichte unserer Welt
Band 1, "Das Universum"
ISBN 978-3-8311-0345-4, Softcover, 196 p. (2000), 15,80 €
Band 2, "Das Leben"
ISBN 97-3-8311-2114-4, Softcover, 248 p., (2001), 17,80 €
Band 3, "Der Tod"
ISBN 978-3-8311-3581-3, Softcover, 276 p., (2002), 19,80 €

Der Schlüssel zur Ewigkeit
ISBN 978-3-9805239-4-3, Hardcover, 288 p.,1. edit. (1999), 24,80 €
ISBN 978-3-89811-819-4, Softcover, 288 p., 2. edit. (2000), 17,80 €

Plädoyer für ein Leben nach dem Tod und eine etwas andere Sicht der Welt
ISBN 978-3-89811-818-7; Softcover, 448 p., 2. edit. (1999/2000), 22,90 €

My Books in the Internet: www.van-Laack.de   Email: webmaster@van-Laack.de
van Laack Book Publishers, D - 52072 Aachen (Gerrmany), Fax +49-(0)241-174269

www.ingramcontent.com/pod-product-compliance
Lightning Source LLC
Chambersburg PA
CBHW032128010526
44111CB00033B/169